15U 234

THE

NEW

YORK

CITY

BALLET

THE NEW YORK CITY BALLET

by Anatole Chujoy

NEW YORK: ALFRED A. KNOPF

1953

L. C. catalog card number: 52–6412

THIS IS A BORZOI BOOK,
PUBLISHED BY ALFRED A. KNOPF, INC.

FIRST EDITION

TO THE CITY OF NEW YORK

extolled and maligned, envied and disdained

whose people and administration

made possible the emergence and development

of a great cultural and artistic organization

that bears its name and does it proud

Acknowledgments

Of all the people to whom I am humbly grateful for encouragement and assistance in writing this book I am indebted to two above all others. They are Mr. Lincoln Kirstein, General Director of the New York City Ballet, and Miss P. W. Manchester, my associate in editing *Dance News*.

Mr. Kirstein submitted to unending questioning for a period of nearly one year and gave me frank and forthright answers to literally hundreds of questions, some of which must have been embarrassing to him. He opened his private correspondence files to me, let me read memoranda that had the character of personal diaries, permitted me to quote at will from his published works, and helped me in the acquisition and selection of pictures. Never was the hackneyed cliché more true: without his assistance this book could not have been written.

Miss Manchester relieved me from a hundred pressing chores during more than one year, making it possible for me to write the book. More important, perhaps, she kept on bolstering me in my weak moments when it seemed to me that I would be engulfed in a mass of detail and would never finish the work. She edited every draft of the typescript, fought a valiant battle with my erratic grammar, and gave me hundreds of hours of manual labor, typing and retyping chapter after chapter.

I am most grateful to Mr. George Balanchine, Mr. Morton Baum, Miss Jean Rosenthal, and Mr. Lew Christensen for giving me much vital information and authenticating some of the factual statements. My thanks go to Mr. John Martin of *The New York Times*, Mr. Walter Terry of the *New York Herald Tribune*, Miss Emily Coleman of *Newsweek*, Mr. Olin Downes of *The New York Times*, Miss Emily Genauer of the *New York Herald Tribune*, and Miss Ann Barzel of *Dance News* for permission to quote from their articles and reviews. Mr. Martin's blanket permission to quote was of inestimable help to me.

I am greatly indebted to Mr. George Platt-Lynes and Mr. Walter E. Owen for their generous contribution of the bulk of the photographs in this volume.

I acknowledge with thanks the permission of *The New York Times*, the *New York Herald Tribune*, and *Mademoiselle* to use material for which they hold the copyright.

Finally, I am deeply grateful to Mr. Herbert Weinstock, my editor at Alfred A. Knopf, Inc., for his suggestions and for his infinite care and warm interest in the preparation of this book for publication.

ANATOLE CHUJOY

Contents

I   *The Background: Kirstein, Balanchine, Dimitriew*   3

II   *1933–1935: The School of American Ballet*   23

III   *1935: The American Ballet*   34

IV   *1935–1936: The American Ballet at the Metropolitan*   60

V   *1936–1937: Ballet Caravan; The Stravinsky Festival*   75

VI   *1938: Ballet Caravan, Second Season*   90

VII   *1938–1939: End of a Phase*   98

VIII   *1938–1940:* Blast at Ballet; Billy the Kid; *The New York World's Fair*   107

IX   *1940–1941: The Tour of South America*   124

X   *1941–1946:* Dance Index; *The American Concert Ballet; Leon Barzin*   140

XI   *1946–1947: Ballet Society*   153

XII   *1947–1948: The New York City Center of Music and Drama*   174

XIII   *1948:* Orpheus; *The New York City Ballet*   194

XIV   *1948–1949: First Season; New Problems*   206

XV   *1949–1950:* Firebird; Age of Anxiety; Illuminations   220

XVI   *1950: A Season in London*   246

XVII   *1950–1951:* La Valse; *A Visit to Chicago;* The Cage   265

XVIII   *1951:* The Miraculous Mandarin; Tyl Ulenspiegel; Swan Lake; The Pied Piper   293

XIX   *1952 (1):* Bayou; Caracole; La Gloire; Picnic at Tintagel   322

XX   *1952 (2): A Season in Europe*   338

Appendix: Chronological Check List of Ballets   365

Index   *follows page*   382

Illustrations

(following pages 48 *and* 240*)*

(following page 48*)*

SERENADE *(photo George Platt-Lynes)*

ALMA MATER *(photo Gray O'Reilly)*

MOZARTIANA *(photo George Platt-Lynes)*

TRANSCENDENCE

DREAMS *(photo George Platt-Lynes)*

THE BAT *(photo Richard Tucker)*

ORPHEUS AND EURYDICE (Gluck) *(photos George Platt-Lynes)*

APOLLON MUSAGÈTE (Apollo)
(photos George Platt-Lynes and Fred Fehl)

CARD GAME *(photo George Platt-Lynes)*

BAISER DE LA FÉE *(photos Fred Fehl & Walter E. Owen)*

xi

PASTORELA   *(photo George Platt-Lynes)*

CONCERTO BAROCCO   *(photo George Platt-Lynes)*

TIME TABLE   *(photo George Platt-Lynes)*

PROMENADE   *(photo George Platt-Lynes)*

POCAHONTAS   *(photo George Platt-Lynes)*

YANKEE CLIPPER   *(photo George Platt-Lynes)*

SHOW PIECE   *(photo George Platt-Lynes)*

FILLING STATION   *(photo George Platt-Lynes)*

BILLY THE KID   *(photo George Platt-Lynes)*

CHARADE   *(photo Maurice Seymour)*

FOUR TEMPERAMENTS   *(photos George Platt-Lynes)*

RENARD   *(photo George Platt-Lynes)*

MINOTAUR

PUNCH AND THE CHILD   *(photo George Platt-Lynes)*

SYMPHONIE CONCERTANTE   *(photo Fred Fehl)*

THE TRIUMPH OF BACCHUS AND ARIADNE
                                    (photo George Platt-Lynes)

SYMPHONY IN C   *(photo George Platt-Lynes)*

ORPHEUS (Stravinsky)
                (photos Walter E. Owen & George Platt-Lynes)

MOTHER GOOSE SUITE   *(photo George Platt-Lynes)*

JINX   *(photo Fred Fehl)*

FIREBIRD   *(photo Walter E. Owen)*

BOURRÉE FANTASQUE   *(photo George Platt-Lynes)*

ONDINE   *(photo Fred Fehl)*

THE PRODIGAL SON
   (photos Fred Fehl, Walter E. Owen, & George Platt-Lynes)

(following page 240)

THE DUEL *(photos Fred Fehl)*

AGE OF ANXIETY *(photo George Platt-Lynes)*

ILLUMINATIONS *(photo George Platt-Lynes)*

LA VALSE *(photos Walter E. Owen)*

CAKEWALK *(photo Walter E. Owen)*

THE CAGE *(photos Walter E. Owen)*

THE MIRACULOUS MANDARIN *(photos Walter E. Owen & George Platt-Lynes)*

A LA FRANÇAIX *(photo Fred Fehl)*

TYL ULENSPIEGEL *(photos Walter E. Owen)*

SWAN LAKE *(photos Fred Fehl)*

LILAC GARDEN *(photo Walter E. Owen)*

BAYOU *(photo Fred Fehl)*

CARACOLE *(photo Fred Fehl)*

LA GLOIRE *(photo Fred Fehl)*

PICNIC AT TINTAGEL *(photo George Platt-Lynes)*

PICNIC AT TINTAGEL *(photo Fred Fehl)*

A THOUSAND TIMES NEIGH! *(photo Richard Tucker)*

Lincoln Kirstein *(photo George Platt-Lynes)*

George Balanchine *(photo George Platt-Lynes)*

Rehearsal in June 1934

Publicity Picture, 1937 *(photo Raymond Smith)*

Balanchine and Stravinsky at Orpheus Rehearsal, 1948 *(photo Gene Fenn)*

Vida Brown and George Balanchine in Costume *(Wide World photos)*

Some Choreographers and Principal Dancers, February 1952
(photo Ray Shorr. Reprinted from Mademoiselle;
copyright Street & Smith Publications, Inc., 1952)

THE

NEW

YORK

CITY

BALLET

————————————

The Background

Kirstein, Balanchine, Dimitriew

Obvious chronology and strictly verifiable fact would place the beginning of the organization we now know as the New York City Ballet in the late days of October 1933, when Lincoln Kirstein and his friend and Harvard classmate Edward M. M. Warburg brought George Balanchine and Vladimir Dimitriew from Europe to establish the School of American Ballet, the fountainhead of the New York City Ballet and the performing companies that preceded it.

A pragmatic historian, however, would go back to 1916 to find in Boston a tall, lanky boy of nine named Lincoln Kirstein being very angry with his parents. The famed Ballets Russes de Serge

3

Diaghilev had just come to Boston to play a few performances, and young Kirstein's parents would not permit him to attend any of them, not even the single matinee. It was not that they thought the performances something the young should not watch, but was just that a nine-year-old's wishes were not taken very seriously. For years, Kirstein admits, he harbored a deep-seated resentment for this denial, formulating revenges and retributions, the favorite being a plan to run away and become a dancer. He did not run away and become a dancer, but one is justified in thinking that the founding of the School of American Ballet and the companies that grew out of it, and his general devotion to ballet, may be a form of revenge and retribution for not being permitted to see the Diaghilev company in Boston.

However that may be, Kirstein does not remember when he did not want to be connected in some way with ballet.

To let Kirstein say it in his own words:

"It was not until 1924 that I actually saw the Diaghilev Ballet. It was in London. The first blaze of its great adventure was over. A small theatre housed the company, and it was by no means a good season. But I never knew that. It was exactly as if I had come home to that splendid country for which I knew I had been destined, but which up to that time I could not seem to find.

"Once, even, I was taken to tea with a minor dancer from the company. I was ashamed I had never noticed her on the stage before, and I looked in vain for her afterwards. But her stories about ballet were like true reports from Tartary.

"The ballet, as with so many others, became an obsession with me. I collected old programs and haunted theatrical photographers. My friends in college were frequently irritated at my constant parade of black and white memories, at my hopeless enthusiasm. It was impossible to describe or discuss the ballet with people who had never seen it, and yet, far more than the ordinary influences or attractions of Harvard, the ballet seemed my real education."

Kirstein watched the Diaghilev Ballet every season for six seasons. The more he watched the company, the greater was he stimulated for the future, although at no time during these seasons or for years afterward was he quite sure how his work would actually shape up, what aspect of what he had seen and learned could be adapted to American use, and how, if at all, it could be done. He realized very clearly that of all ballet to be seen at that time the Diaghilev company was the only manifestation of the art form which had artistic validity, that it did things that were important and needed to be done, that its performances and repertoire were motivated by something higher than box-office appeal. He admired Serge Diaghilev's artistic taste and skill in assembling dancers, choreographers, composers, painters, and poets who would work with him as a team and give the best that was in them.

And then Diaghilev died, in August 1929.

Quite by accident Kirstein attended the funeral of the great impresario. Here is how he describes it (in *The Hound and Horn*, Vol. III, No. 4, July–September, 1930):

"An American tourist was hunting the back alleys of Venice, one hot morning in the middle of last August, for a church in which Domenico Theotocopulos must have worshipped. He saw its tower from afar, on the edge of a small canal, and passing under an arch, found a barge of black and gold moored to the church steps. Beadles in cocked hats, holding brass rods, bore wreaths into the church and he followed into the cool noon dusk. When his eyes were accustomed to the gloom, he saw opposite him a great byzantine ikonostasis. The Baptism, the Last Supper, their gesso and gilding turned bronze, glowed above the bier, blanketed with heaped-up flowers. Suddenly he became aware of mourners, and the fact that this was, indeed, a funeral. Faces, somehow familiar, ignored him as he passed out into the sunlight, and leaving, heard the first words of the Greek Orthodox service for the dead. Not until three days later, reading the London *Times*, did he learn that he had unwittingly attended, in San Giorgio dei Greci, the obsequies of a great Russian."

The funeral apparently made a strong impression on Kirstein. Two years later, in his novel *Flesh Is Heir* (New York: Brewer Warren & Putnam), he again refers to it in great detail.

Kirstein was all of twenty-two then, and his connection with ballet was that of an enlightened dilettante with a desire to do something in it—but he still was not quite sure what. His perception of the ballet as an art form and of Diaghilev's place in it was much clearer than that of his seniors who had actually worked with Diaghilev. Even then he saw the potentialities of George Balanchine as the man who was destined to continue the tradition of the modern ballet despite the death of Diaghilev. In the article "The Diaghilev Period," from which the above passage was quoted, Kirstein wrote:

"The ballet disintegrated after Diaghilev's death and perhaps circumstances will not allow the full development of this brilliant choreographer [Balanchine], who must certainly have developed into one of the ablest of Diaghilev's designers, for not only was his energy and invention prodigious—but he well understood the dangers attendant on the unintelligent if entertaining implications of the 'clever' acrobatic Massine dance. . . . His dances had the spareness, the lack of decoration which is by no means a lack of refinement, the splendid capacity to display individual gestures against a background of unrhythmical massed gesture. . . . The ballet of Balanchine was more difficult to follow, perhaps, required more of an effort, in so much as the human eye accepts more readily easy variations, just as the human ear accustoms itself more readily to tones in transitions bounded by the more obvious tonal intervals. . . . The last period of the [Diaghilev] ballet was and must be considered a period of transition, not of decadence. Balanchine . . . was leading out of mere ingenuity into a revivified, purer, cleaner classicism."

But who was this George Balanchine of whom the twenty-two-year-old Kirstein held such a high opinion?

To give him his full Russian-Georgian Christian name, patronymic, and surname, Gheorghi Melitonovitch Balantchivadze was born in St. Petersburg, Russia, in 1904. His father, Meliton Balantchivadze, was a famous composer of Georgian music, often referred to as the Georgian Glinka for his work in collecting and popularizing Caucasian, especially Georgian, folk music. His mother stemmed from a military family, and young Gheorghi, being of excellent physique, was naturally proposed for the army. At a suggestion from one of the governors of the Imperial School of Ballet, Gheorghi, much against his wish, took the entrance examination and, with seven or eight other boys out of some one hundred and fifty applicants, was admitted to the School. That was in August 1914, the year and month of the beginning of World War I.

At first, hating the school, he ran away, only to be returned by an aunt. He was not very good in school and found it difficult to adjust himself to the discipline. Only a year later, when he began to participate with other little boys in performances at the Maryinsky Theater, did he begin to enjoy the school and his work.

Three years later, at the outbreak of the revolution of March 1917, the boy could not think of anything but dance. Times were hard and dangerous, food was scarce. All the niceties of a well-ordered and sheltered life under the direct patronage of the Tsar had disappeared. There was not even heat in the school; there was not enough to eat. Almost constant shooting went on everywhere in St. Petersburg, whose name by now had been changed to Petrograd. Then, in October

1917, came the Bolshevik Revolution. In the first flush of victory over the hated capitalistic regime the Bolsheviks closed the School as a bourgeois institution identified with the court and aristocracy.

In 1918, Anatole Lunacharsky, the first Commissar of Public Education, succeeded in getting Lenin to write an article about the necessity of preserving the arts of Russia as a national heritage, and the Ballet School reopened.

The tale of freezing classrooms, almost complete lack of food, and all other major and minor privations is too long to be told here. Suffice it to say that the three years during which Gheorghi had still to attend school left a mark on him that it took nearly twenty years to erase. Balantchivadze was graduated in 1921, at the age of seventeen.

At that time Russia, much as now, was completely isolated from the Western world. Moreover, nearly everyone who had done anything to advance the course of ballet in the early years of the century was "in Europe," mainly in Paris—among them Michel Fokine, Leonide Massine, Serge Diaghilev, Alexandre Benois, and Leon Bakst, all those who had created the Diaghilev ballet, as well as most of the dancers who had either remained in the West since the beginning of the war or had found a way to flee their country.

Actually there was only one man in Russia who thought at all about the necessity or desirability of doing something new in ballet. He was Kassian Goleizovsky, a soloist of the Moscow Bolshoi Theater. Brought up outside the influence of Fokine, he went about composing his strange ballets on stages other than that of the Bolshoi Theater, on sufferance, as it were, from the Soviet government and with little appreciation from his small band of spectators. In 1921 he went to Petrograd to give a performance at the former Hall of Nobles. The program consisted of his own compositions to Debussy, Scriabin, Ravel, Medtner, and Richard Strauss. The dancers appeared almost naked, and the performance created a scandal.

Young Balantchivadze was much impressed. He found in Goleizovsky a kindred soul, for he too was experimenting with "new" ballet, specifically with "erotic" ballet, which in those days was synonymous with modern ballet. Performances of Balantchivadze's ballets had been given on the stage of the School theater and had so shocked the authorities of the School that he was nearly expelled and the other participants were given a stiff dressing-down.

In 1923, two years after his graduation, Balantchivadze, with the help of a friend named Vladimir Dimitriew, a singer of the Theater of Musical Drama and later of the Maryinsky Opera, began his Evenings of the Young Ballet with a company of about fifteen young dancers from the Maryinsky. There were only two of these evenings, both given in the assembly hall of the Petrograd duma, the equivalent of our city council. The first program, perhaps a little presumptuously, demonstrated the evolution of ballet from Marius Petipa through Michel Fokine to Gheorghi Balantchivadze. The young people, mainly dancers and students of the various schools of higher learning, received the offering with enthusiasm; the older generation, among them a good number of dancers, found it wanting. The teachers of the School told their pupils and young dancers who had participated in the performances that they would have to choose between the Maryinsky Theater and Balantchivadze. This really meant that they had no choice, and the group was disbanded.

Nevertheless, some months later Balantchivadze succeeded in arranging a second Evening of the Young Ballet. This time the composition was a visualization of the famous poem "The Twelve" by Alexander Blok, with the poet's lines spoken by a rhythmic chorus, who also mimed the action. Once again Balantchivadze drew the disapproval of the theater authorities, and the performance was never repeated. But Balantchivadze became well known in Petrograd and began to be asked to stage dances for artists' clubs, benefit performances, and groups of dancers who went touring to supplement their meager earnings.

Meanwhile life was getting tougher and tougher in Petrograd and throughout the Soviet Union. Persecution for real and imaginary political crimes, nightly arrests and executions without process of law, purges, unlimited sway by the dreaded Tcheka (the secret political police), denunciations by neighbors and members of one's family—all the horrors of a police state in formation, coupled with a lack even of the most primitive necessities, including bread and salt (horse meat, in general and open consumption since 1918, had by now become an unobtainable luxury)—drove thousands of people to all kinds of subterfuges to find a way out of Russia. Only a few could succeed, but everyone who possibly could try, did, though the risk was immense: failure meant, at best, exile to Siberia, with execution as the general rule.

In January 1924 Lenin died. With his death came the struggle for power among his chief lieutenants and, at the end, the uneasy victory of Stalin and his clique. All who were not closely associated with Stalin came under immediate suspicion, and with them their friends, acquaintances, subordinates, subordinates of subordinates, and so down in ever-widening circles that engulfed literally millions of people innocent from any point of view.

A very literal, not literary, *Sturm und Drang* ensued. It looked as if everyone in the professions, in the arts, in commerce, everyone who was not a member of the Stalinist faction of the Communist party, especially in the western part of Russia, wanted to get out of the country. Only a few thousands succeeded in stealing across the border; still fewer risked the dangers of applying for a passport under some pretext and getting out legitimately. It took a brave, shrewd man to talk the suspicious Soviet government into issuing a foreign passport. Vladimir Dimitriew was such a man.

Dimitriew assembled a group of young dancers of the Maryinsky Theater, including his friend Gheorghi Balantchivadze, Alexandra Danilova (until recently *prima ballerina* of the Ballet Russe de Monte Carlo), Tamara Gevergeieva (now well known in the United States as the dramatic actress Tamara Geva), Nicholas Efimoff (now a *premier danseur* at the Paris Opéra), and two other people who have since returned to Russia. The little troupe assumed the name Soviet State Dancers; Balantchivadze choreographed a repertoire for them, and Dimitriew set out on the Sisyphean task of selling the authorities the idea of issuing foreign passports to the members of the group so that they could go into Germany and France to propagandize Soviet ballet.

In view of our understanding of the meaning of the expression "iron curtain," it seems even more unbelievable than it had seemed in 1924 that Dimitriew succeeded. But succeed he did, and the little band left Leningrad (the capital was thus renamed soon after the death of Lenin) aboard a small German steamship bound for Stettin, a port in East Prussia, on the Baltic Sea.

An inspection of documents on board ship by a zealous officer of the Tcheka nearly ruined the scheme five minutes before sailing time, but the gods were with the dancers. Even then they sat jittery and worried until the steamer passed Kronstadt, the Russian fortress and naval base in the Gulf of Finland which guards the approaches to Leningrad. Only when Kronstadt, with its impressive guns pointing westward, was left behind did the group relax. It was Danilova who trembled longer than the others. The daughter of a colonel of the Imperial Army, she was trying to figure out the range of the Kronstadt cannons: after all, they could shoot at the steamer, couldn't they?

That Balantchivadze, Dimitriew, and the dancers do not remember much about the voyage across the Baltic is not owing to lapse of memory. As soon as the ship cleared Kronstadt and duly saluted the fortress, the supper gong sounded and everybody went down to the dining-room. The view of the laid tables and large baskets of rolls and bread, flanked by long, deep dishes of butter, was enough to make them realize that they were out of Russia. They had not seen anything like this for six years; in fact, some of them could hardly remember having seen anything like it at any time. Rolls, real rolls, and bread, white, fresh, and soft—with no admixture of straw— and apparently without restriction. They ate so much bread that evening that they could hardly eat anything else, but they did eat everything that was served them. They could not sleep that night, their stomachs being too full.

Next morning everybody got up early, long before the other passengers, and went directly into the dining-room. They sat down at a table, ate all the bread and rolls set up for the passengers, and then moved to another table and repeated the procedure. By the time the stewards began to serve breakfast the bread and butter of three tables were gone. The dancers were ashamed of this table-hopping, but they also were very hungry.

The steamer docked in Stettin some sixty hours after it left Leningrad. All the expatriates remember, or ever did, of the trip was food—good, heavy German food, lots of it.

The arrival in Stettin brought new problems. Here they were in outlandish and decrepit street-clothes, most of them hand-me-downs from friends and relatives, others bought secondhand in the Leningrad version of a flea market, with their other belongings tied up in brown paper, and only the homemade costumes in wicker baskets. All of them spoke some French (French was a required subject in the Ballet School), but none spoke a word of German. And here they were in Germany with only the vaguest idea of what they wanted to do, without an arranged tour or a prospect of one. Their tickets carried them to Berlin, but it was summer and Berlin was empty, its theaters closed.

The dancers settled in a cheap hotel. Dimitriew went out scouting, ran into some other Russians (there was quite a colony of Russian refugees in Berlin at that time), and by ingenuity and complicated manipulations that would do honor to a first-rate diplomat succeeded in arranging a tour through summer resorts along the Rhine. The tour paid for itself. The dancers even managed to buy some clothes and began to look like "Europeans."

In early autumn they moved to Paris. The Diaghilev Ballet was having its annual season at the Théâtre des Champs-Élysées. Dimitriew succeeded in obtaining an audition with Serge Diaghilev, and Alexandra Danilova, Tamara Gevergeieva, Gheorghi Balantchivadze, and Nicholas Efimoff were accepted into the company. It may have been just a coincidence, of course, that Diaghilev was having one of his all-too-frequent misunderstandings with his principal choreographer (Bronislava Nijinska in this case) and was gratified that one of the Soviet State Dancers, Balantchivadze, was a choreographer. However that may have been, Balantchivadze found himself in a new troupe and also with a new name. The first thing Diaghilev did was to change the difficult Balantchivadze to Balanchine. A month or so later, when the company was performing in London at the Savoy Theatre, Nijinska left the troupe and George Balanchine, at the age of twenty, three years out of school, became ballet master of a company that was making history in the Western world.

Balanchine did not have an easy time of it. Most of the

dancers in the company, especially the older generation, resented the fact that he had replaced Bronislava Nijinska, the sister of the great Vaslav, and a gifted choreographer and dancer in her own right. It was difficult for him, a young man without a name so far as the dancers were concerned, to command the respect and obedience without which no ballet master can successfully create and work. On the other hand, Balanchine was not impressed with the standard of the dancers in the company. He realized the artistic wealth of the atmosphere that surrounded it—especially the great composers and painters who worked with Diaghilev and his choreographers —but when he found that many of the soloists of the famed company could not dance nearly so well as the members of the *corps de ballet* of the Maryinsky Theater, which he had left only a few months before, he was disillusioned. Balanchine sensed immediately that the Diaghilev Ballet was past its artistic prime and had been in decline for several years.

In his four years as ballet master of the Diaghilev company Balanchine choreographed ten ballets: *Barabau* (Rieti, 1925), *La Pastorale* (Auric, 1925), *Jack in the Box* (Satie, 1926), *The Triumph of Neptune* (Lord Berners, 1926), *The Nightingale* (Stravinsky, 1926), *La Chatte* (Sauguet, 1927), *Apollon Musagète* (Stravinsky, 1928), *The Gods Go a-Begging* (Handel, 1928), *The Prodigal Son* (Prokofiev, 1929), and *Le Bal* (Rieti, 1929). He also mounted the ballets for the opera seasons at Monte Carlo.

After Diaghilev died and his company dispersed, Balanchine went to Copenhagen as ballet master of the Royal Opera House. Later he staged some operettas, notably for the Théâtre Mogador in Paris, and several revues. It was at this point that he discovered in the Paris school of Olga Preobrajenska, a former outstanding ballerina of the Imperial Theater, Irina Baronova and Tamara Toumanova, the future "baby ballerinas" of the thirties. He gave them their first professional engagements and later took them into the Ballets Russes de Monte Carlo.

When René Blum and Col. W. de Basil set about organizing the Ballets Russes de Monte Carlo, Balanchine was the first choreographer invited to join the company. He staged *La Concurrence* (Auric), *Cotillon* (Chabrier) and *Le Bourgeois-Gentilhomme* (Richard Strauss), all in 1932. But the atmosphere of elaborate intrigue and constant machinations created by Col. de Basil and his lieutenants was thicker than Balanchine could stand, and he left after one season.

As a sort of declaration of independence from the Diaghilev inheritance—which the Ballets Russes de Monte Carlo vociferously claimed for itself, in defiance of its publicized intentions—Balanchine with Dimitriew and Boris Kochno, an associate of Diaghilev, founded in Paris Les Ballets 1933.

It was a simple matter to declare one's artistic independence on paper, and almost as simple to found a ballet company, also on paper. It was another matter to make the company function. For this one needed talent, of which there was an abundance; administrative ability, of which there was some; and, most important, money, of which there was none. Fortunately some of Diaghilev's backers had not gone over to the Ballets Russes de Monte Carlo, and among them was a gentleman with vision, Mr. Edward James, an Englishman married to the Viennese dancer Tilly Losch. He placed himself at the head of a group that assumed the financial risk of the new organization.

Les Ballets 1933 had Balanchine as choreographer, Tamara Toumanova and Tilly Losch as ballerinas, and an array of composers and designers never surpassed even by the Diaghilev company in its heyday. Among them were André Derain, Henri Sauguet, Darius Milhaud, Pavel Tchelitchew, Charles Koechlin, Christian Bérard, Berthold Brecht, Kurt Weill, Emilio Terry, and Caspar Neher. The repertoire included *Errante, Songes, Mozartiana, Les Sept Péchés Capitaux, Les Fastes,* and *Les Valses.*

In the words of Kirstein (*Blast at Ballet,* New York, 1938):

"Their dozen or so evenings of ballet in London and Paris in the summer of 1933 were in reality the swansong of the Diaghilev period. Here was the real artistic discovery, real theatrical invention, true collaboration on Diaghilev's own ground, even without him. It could not have been greatly different even had he been alive to supervise the scene, for every new talent of the day, with the possible exception of Salvador Dali and the surrealists (who had refused on ideological grounds to be included) was somehow involved. Significant and novel ideas in music, dance, poetry and social-comment were presented. Nothing as powerful, influential or original as this has happened in the world of theatrical dancing since that time. If the responsibility for the success of Les Ballets 1933 was due to any one person, it was their choreographer, George Balanchine."

This, then, was the George Balanchine with whose work young Kirstein was so much impressed when he wrote about the Diaghilev period in *Hound and Horn* in 1930.

Kirstein was much less impressed with the Ballets Russes de Monte Carlo despite the on- and off-stage glamour attendant upon it. Here was dancing, some of it very good, in a repertoire much of which consisted of the standard works of the early Diaghilev period with some new ballets by Leonide Massine and Balanchine, and with the collaboration of talented composers and designers, but with a distressing lack of artistic direction. It was clear to Kirstein, as it was indeed to most discriminating students of ballet, that Col. de Basil's shrewd and calculating catering to the more opulent Parisian balletomanes was no substitute for Diaghilev's enlightened artistic leadership. The general public did not concur in this opinion: Col. de Basil's Ballets Russes de Monte Carlo was to hold sway for nearly six years as "the" ballet company.

Meanwhile Kirstein was invited by Romola Nijinska to help her collect and organize the material for the biography of the great dancer which she had undertaken to write. The work entailed careful research in documents about the St. Petersburg Imperial Maryinsky Theater and the Ballet School attached to it, from which came Nijinsky and all the other great Russian dancers of the Diaghilev period. The research and documentation made it clear to Kirstein that if America were ever to have great ballet, or even just a good ballet company of its own, it must first of all have a school where the future dancers could be trained. Not just a dance school, like most of the other schools of that period in America, but an institution modeled after the Imperial School in St. Petersburg, which would fire the imagination of the pupils, bring them into the tradition of classic ballet, give them a true classic dance education. Some good ballet schools were in existence in America at that time, specifically in New York, Chicago, San Francisco, and Los Angeles, but none of them had aimed quite so high.

He often discussed this matter with Madame Nijinska, and she mentioned on several occasions that she herself might do something in this direction. But it was all vague, and the possibility of her establishing a school in the United States seemed very remote. In addition, with Diaghilev dead and his company disbanded, the time did not seem auspicious for any undertaking in the ballet field. The prospect for the future was less than encouraging. Did not nearly everybody say that ballet had died with Diaghilev and could never be resurrected?

In the United States, Kirstein was at that time editing *Hound and Horn*. It was a magazine of a general literary nature, and he could devote only limited space to articles on dance. The other editors also had something to say about the contents of the magazine, and their interests were more catholic.

He had also been working in the field of fine arts with Edward M. M. Warburg, his old Harvard colleague, who was then teaching at Bryn Mawr.

Says Kirstein: "More to quiet me than for any other reason, Warburg, since he had heard my ballet legends for years, invited me to lecture on dance to his students. And in spite of being twenty-five and over six feet tall, I even committed the folly of taking ballet lessons myself from Michel Fokine, which embarrassed me far more than him, but at least I learned a great deal of invaluable critical material from this historic personality."

Some years later, when the American Ballet company was a functioning organization, Fokine once said to me: "How can Kirstein be a director of a ballet company? He took some ballet lessons from me, and he can't get his feet off the floor."

To my gentle remonstration that Diaghilev had never taken a ballet lesson in his life and that Kirstein had no intention of dancing, the great choreographer did not reply.

All these activities of Kirstein, however absorbing they may have been at the time, seemed only in the nature of preparation for something else.

In June 1933 he again went to Europe. This time he had something definite in mind. Eighteen years later he said: "I had already more than a hint of what I wanted to do. I felt that I was about to put all the pieces together in my puzzle, pieces I had been unconsciously collecting for the previous ten years. Moreover I had preliminary, if not very definite, assurances from interested friends."

Balanchine, who had organized his Les Ballets 1933 a few months before, was in the midst of his final rehearsals, and

Virgil Thomson, then living in Paris, took Kirstein to the Théâtre des Champs-Élysées to watch some of them. Kirstein attended all the Paris performances and later went to London to see the performances there.

"I cannot pretend," Kirstein says, "that watching the Paris and London seasons of Les Ballets 1933 was an unheralded revelation to me, nor that I immediately took them to my private and personal Golden Age of Ballet. Nor had I discovered everything new and wonderful in Les Ballets 1933. What I did find was much of a healthy, creative direction, which after the four-year interregnum since Diaghilev's death seemed more satisfactory than novelty."

In all the time that Kirstein spent in Europe he never developed a desire to live abroad, to become an expatriate or an artistic refugee. He began early to translate into American terms the artistic experiments being tried out in Europe, the creative work that, admittedly or not, was for the most part already affected by American ideas in music, books, architecture, or clothing. When he saw Les Ballets 1933 he realized that it was a point of contact and a place to start.

One has to know the extent of Kirstein's reserve not to be surprised that in all his years of watching Balanchine's work and admiring his creative genius he had never made an attempt to meet the choreographer. Romola Nijinska finally introduced them backstage in London's Savoy Theatre, where the company was dancing. Balanchine looked distraught and tired. Roman Jasinsky, his principal dancer, had just hurt his leg, and Balanchine himself had to take the very difficult male role in *Errante*.

Kirstein realized that there was no use talking to Balanchine at the time, and indeed he had little to say but express his admiration for the master's work.

"The next time I saw Balanchine," Kirstein relates, "was

in the parlor of my small hotel, dusty with propriety and full of provincial English beauties who had come up to London to be presented at Court.

"As Balanchine came into the room, three girls in white full court dresses, with three nodding plumes in their hair, followed him and sat down at the next table for their tea. They had returned from the court photographers, but it seemed as if they had stepped out of *Cotillon*, his own touching ballet.

"I asked Balanchine if he would like to come to America to found a school and a ballet company. I was not, at the time, decisive as to how this could be arranged. I could not afford to be.

"He replied that something like that had always been his hope, but at the present he had a good offer to become ballet master of the Royal Opera House, Copenhagen, where he had already served, and also the Paris Opéra wished to have him. But he readily admitted that America was far more tempting.

"He had no reason to believe that I offered any real security, for I mentioned no contract, but he said he would speak to his friend Vladimir Dimitriew and would let me know.

"After he left, the three provincial young ladies were still at their tea. I could not discover whether they were the three muses of Apollo or the three fates. My mind jumped forward in time and I saw the completed school achieved and functioning, and even more, a great stage swarming with dancers the school had trained, situated somewhere in America. It was exasperating and exhausting to think concretely of ways and means to make the mirage a miraculous reality."

Meanwhile, the London season of Les Ballets 1933, and indeed the company itself, had come to an end, and after three or four other meetings with Kirstein, Balanchine and Dimitriew went off to rest in the south of France, leaving

Kirstein with the vague address of a château and not much hope that he would ever see the two again.

Nevertheless, he immediately cabled Edward Warburg about his negotiations with Balanchine and Dimitriew, asking for a guarantee of funds which would make possible the signing of a contract.

Again in the words of Kirstein: "Edward Warburg permitted himself to be idealistically involved in my highly irresponsible negotiations, and finally he made it possible for me to guarantee enough capital to permit Balanchine and Dimitriew to give up definite work in Europe for indefinite possibilities in a country they did not know, assured only by a young man they had seen less than half-a-dozen times in their lives."

After writing to Balanchine and Dimitriew about Warburg's promise, Kirstein left for New York. A short while later Warburg cabled the necessary funds to Balanchine, and the two friends settled down to an anxious wait for word of the sailing date of Balanchine and Dimitriew. In Kirstein's plan, Balanchine was to head the faculty of the projected school and later be director of the company, and Dimitriew was to be director of the school.

Two weeks passed, and then three, without a line from Balanchine or Dimitriew. Neither Kirstein nor Warburg could imagine what had happened. The awful thought that Balanchine had changed his mind suggested itself to Kirstein several times. But then, he would reason with himself and with Warburg, even if Balanchine had changed his mind he certainly owed them an explanation and the return of the cabled money. At the end of the three weeks Warburg asked the bank that had transferred the money to put in a tracer, something he should have done two weeks before. The bank replied a few days later that the money was still in the Paris bank through which it had been sent, and that Balanchine had not called to collect it. As was later discovered, the address of the château in the south of France which Balanchine had left with Kirstein in London was not correct; Kirstein's letters and cables never reached Balanchine. Not hearing anything for three weeks, Balanchine decided that Kirstein had changed his mind or could not get the money, and accepted the position in Copenhagen. When Kirstein's letters and cables and, finally, the money reached Balanchine, he succeeded somehow in getting a release from the Royal Opera House in Copenhagen and sailed with Dimitriew in the *Olympic*.

The *Olympic* was due to dock in New York on Tuesday morning, October 18, 1933. Kirstein and Warburg went down to meet the ship. After all the passengers had been discharged, and Balanchine and Dimitriew were not among them, the two friends realized that something was wrong. They couldn't have *not* sailed! Or could they?

Frantic inquiries brought the intelligence that the immigration authorities were about to send Balanchine and Dimitriew to Ellis Island, where a bond would have to be posted before they would be permitted to land. Kirstein and Warburg succeeded in obtaining permission to board the ship and talk to the immigration officers. The magic of Warburg's name and a few telephone calls made it possible for Warburg to sign a guarantee that the bond would be posted later in the day, and Balanchine and Dimitriew were finally permitted to set foot on United States soil.

II

1933-1935

The School of American Ballet

Few schools in America were started with more complete plans or with quite so many apparently unsurmountable obstacles as was the School of American Ballet.

Complete as the plans were, they were drawn up by sincere and well-intentioned young men who had never had any experience in running a school, and who were (let us face it) somewhat snobbish. Kirstein and Warburg, only recently out of Harvard, had an idea that the School should be located in a small town, away from hubbub of New York and the "contaminating" false glitter of Broadway.

On Sunday, October 23, 1933, five days after the arrival of Balanchine and Dimitriew, John

Martin, then the only full-time dance critic in the United States, devoted his column in *The New York Times* to the School. Here, in part, is what he wrote:

"In spite of all the skeptics who said it could never be done, the actual preliminaries in the establishment of an American ballet are now under the auspices of the Morgan Memorial Museum in Hartford. The organizers of the project are A. Everett Austin, director of the museum; Lincoln Kirstein, one of the editors of 'Hound and Horn' and perhaps our most energetic 'balletomane' [Kirstein must have loved this appellation]; James Soby; and E. M. M. Warburg.

"They have engaged George Balanchine to head the enterprise and have wisely refrained from talking about it until it was ready to begin work. . . .

"It is planned to give three years to the development of dancers before any productions are made, although in the meantime there will be informal performances and exhibitions in the school and elsewhere. Only American dancers will be admitted to the courses and every effort will be made to develop a distinctly American organization. . . .

"There are two questions that will perhaps arise at once with regard to such a plan. The first is: Why import a Russian ballet master to found an American ballet? And the second is: Why Hartford? Both questions have perfectly reasonable answers.

"As to the matter of an American ballet, there have always been divided opinions. One is to the effect that the American dance must come exclusively out of American soil, finding its technique in its own necessities. Another is that the ballet is an art form which has been developed through hundreds of years, and if it is given a foothold in America it will be enriched by new impulses, just as it was when it was transplanted into Russia. There is really no conflict here, except in so far as either school attempts to exclude the other from the field. They are, as a matter of fact, quite different in scope and can dwell side by side in perfect amity.

"If, however, a ballet stemming from the classic tradition is to be established here, it is essential that it have as its director some one who has had practical experience. Since there has never been an American ballet of this sort, it is obvious that a director must be found elsewhere.

"The reason for choosing Hartford as the centre of activities is simply that the Morgan Memorial there placed at the service of the enterprise not only its enthusiasm but also its admirable facilities. These include excellent class rooms and a completely equipped auditorium, all new and ready for occupancy.

"It is by no means to be a local organization, however, but a national one situated in Hartford. Its location away from New York has certain things to recommend it in addition to the hospitality of the Morgan Memorial. One is its lack of competition with the regular commercial schools and the other the lessening of the temptation to burst prematurely into performances. . . ."

John Martin's article summed up very well the plans and hopes of Kirstein and Warburg and brought into focus two problems that were to cause the organizers a good deal of trouble: the "Americanism" of the projected School and company (about which more later) and the advisability of setting up the School away from New York.

As Martin indicated, the primary reasons for establishing the School in Hartford were the sponsorship of the Morgan Memorial—which not only gave the School prestige, but also shared the burden of supporting it—and the desire of the organizers to keep American ballet artistically pure and the School sheltered from the questionable influences of the Broadway theater. The sponsorship of the Museum, with its attendant prestige and financial assistance, was a very important consideration. The desire to keep away from the theater, good or bad, was unrealistic. A professional ballet school can no more be sheltered from the theater and succeed than can an art school be kept away from art galleries. The strength and achievements of the Russian Imperial School of Ballet, for half a century without peer, lay not only in the system of teaching, great instructors, and the lavish support of a rich Court, but also in the close connection with the theater, the participation of young pupils (beginning with their second year in school) in ballet performances, and the general, all-pervading atmosphere of professionalism and theatricality. Kirstein was to realize this twelve or thirteen years later and make excellent use of it, but in 1933 the idea was to run the ballet school as great universities are run, away from big cities and worldly influences.

The consideration of competition was attributable to the idealistic tendencies of Kirstein and Warburg. Any practical man could have pointed out to them that the School would offer much less competition to the dozen or so professional and semiprofessional ballet schools in New York, who drew their enrollment from all over the nation, than to the four or five ballet-plus-tap-plus-acrobatic schools in Hartford, which depended for their existence entirely upon a local student body.

Kirstein and Warburg realized this truth in a much shorter time than anyone might have expected.

As soon as the formation of the School of American Ballet was announced in the newspapers and mothers began to apply for admission for their children, Hartford teachers raised the cry of unfair competition "from outsiders." Letters in local newspapers, resolutions of teachers' organizations, visits to the mayor—a dozen wheels were set in motion to prevent the opening of the School in Hartford. Those protesting saw only competition in the School, and they were willing to fight to

drive it out. Whether they could have succeeded by themselves is a moot question.

But unbeknown to them and unsuspected, they found
powerful allies in Balanchine and Dimitriew just a few days
after the newcomers had arrived in Hartford.

Brought up and educated in St. Petersburg, and accustomed to working in the world's capitals creating ballets for
renowned ballet companies with famous dancers, Balanchine
could not see himself settling in a provincial American town
for an indefinite time, teaching small children the rudiments
of ballet and hoping that advanced students and professional
dancers would trek to him in search of his instruction and the
ideal ballet company. Dimitriew, similarly a product of a big
city, had imagined that he was going to America to direct a
ballet school more or less of the scope of the Imperial School
in St. Petersburg; he was equally averse to the carefully laid
plans of the American dilettantes. With a lack of subtlety
which came as a shock to Kirstein, they announced that they
would not remain in Hartford and would return to Europe as
soon as transportation could be arranged. No constructive
proposition, no alternative, no compromise, no conditions, not
even an ultimatum—just a categorical statement, a revolt.

To Kirstein this was the end of the world, certainly the
end of all his plans and dreams about American ballet.

A few days later, back in New York, Balanchine was
taken ill: a direct and recurring manifestation of the effects of
privation in post-revolutionary Russia. He was ordered to
bed for several weeks, and his departure from the United
States was delayed.

Balanchine's illness gave Kirstein and Warburg time to
try to find a way out of the critical situation. Long discussions
and consultations brought the problem into relief and indicated the only possible solution: to give up Hartford and the

sponsorship of the Museum, the idea of and premise for keeping the School out of New York. The protest of the Hartford teachers played an important part in this decision.

The new plan was laid before Dimitriew and the recovering Balanchine, and they agreed to stay on with the School.

After weeks of search, a classroom was found in New York, on the fourth floor of an old building at Madison Avenue and 59th Street, in a studio that had once belonged to Isadora Duncan. The School of American Ballet was opened on New Year's Day, 1934. Classes began next day with about twenty-five of the thirty pupils who had appeared for the first entrance audition. Dorothie Littlefield, a young dancer from Philadelphia, later ballerina of the Philadelphia Ballet company, and currently a well-known choreographer of ice shows, took over the teaching of the junior grade, and Balanchine and Pierre Vladimiroff began teaching the seniors and professional students.

Vladimiroff, Vaslav Nijinsky's successor as *premier danseur* of the Maryinsky Theater, and the last partner of Anna Pavlova, had not come to New York with Balanchine and Dimitriew. He arrived about the same time with a small troupe organized and headed by Serge Lifar, with Lucille Lamballe as ballerina. Not very happy in his surroundings, he readily accepted an invitation to join the faculty of the School.

Dimitriew became Director of the School, the first time such a title was used in connection with a ballet school in America. Eugenie Ouroussow, a Russian princess by birth who had immigrated a few years earlier, was appointed Secretary. Well-educated, gracious, and charming, she was also efficient and businesslike despite her princely upbringing, and a born diplomat. She managed to run the School unhampered by internal and external crises, steering a straight course, as it were, in all kinds of balleto-political weather. Miss Ouroussow is still running the School, now as Assistant Director, and still managing to steer clear of occasional snags.

The purpose of the School, as outlined in its first announcement, was "to develop trained American dancers who will continually provide material for a permanent company, which will create the combined ballets of the best American painters, musicians, poets, and eventually choreographers." The curriculum of the School was based on that of the Russian Imperial School, modified by the demands and possibilities of American life. The system of teaching was strictly Russian, as distinguished from the Italian, or Cecchetti, and French systems. In addition to classes in ballet and its ramifications, there were lectures by Kirstein and Warburg and make-up lessons by Dimitriew.

As John Martin noted in his article quoted earlier in this chapter, a certain amount of criticism was directed at the School from the very beginning for assuming an American name and yet staffing itself mostly with Russian teachers and adhering to a Russian system of teaching. The criticism came mainly from other ballet teachers, some of them Russians, who could understand neither the goal toward which Kirstein and Warburg were directing their efforts nor the way they elected to reach that goal.

The School soon outgrew the studio in which it began, and new classrooms were added. It is still located in the same building where it began eighteen years ago, but it now occupies the entire fourth floor and could use additional accommodations, were they to be found.

Work on building a producing company began soon after the School opened. Balanchine found that in the advanced class he had a group of students with whom he could work. Several of these were professional dancers with a few years of stage experience; others were students on the professional level. Rehearsals began early in February. After five months the School of American Ballet was ready to present three ballets, all new to the United States: *Serenade*, to Tchaikowsky's Serenade for Strings in C Major, an entirely new work; *Mozartiana*, to Tchaikowsky's Suite No. 4, a revival from Les Ballets 1933; and *Dreams* (née *Songes*), to a commissioned score by George Antheil (replacing the original music by Darius Milhaud, used in the Les Ballets 1933 production of this work).

The performance, semiprivate, by invitation only, was scheduled for June 9 at Woodland, the estate of Felix Warburg (father of Edward Warburg), near White Plains, New York.

Ariadna Mikeshina and Nicholas Kopeikine, two concert pianists, were to play for the performance. The company spent two days at Woodland rehearsing the program on an especially built outdoor platform.

As often happens in New York, the June of 1934 was a rainy month. On the 9th it rained intermittently all day, but began clearing a bit toward evening. Indeed, when *Mozartiana* went on, everybody concerned had high hopes that the weather had relented and that the performance would be achieved. However, more rain fell toward the end of *Mozartiana*, and though this ballet was finished, the other two could not be danced.

There was not an unbroken heart in the whole company that evening.

The performance was postponed until the following evening, and the guests promised to return. Some of them did. The rain let up just enough to permit the dancers to give the performance.

Said Kirstein: "A more agonizing and inauspicious occasion could scarcely have been planned by the Devil himself."

The School continued to function until the end of June and then recessed for a summer vacation. This was novel, because no New York dance school, with the exception of the Metropolitan Opera ballet school, had ever closed for a summer vacation.

It reopened early in September, and Balanchine began rehearsals almost immediately after the opening. The plans were to work for a New York season sometime in the spring and to give a few semipublic performances before the New York season. As rehearsals progressed Balanchine and Kirstein decided that the company should be ready for an out-of-town showing before Christmas. A performance was consequently scheduled at the Avery Memorial Theater in Hartford, Connecticut, the same Hartford where the first major disaster had threatened to end the School of American Ballet before it ever began.

The performance at Woodland had been announced as of the School of American Ballet; i.e., a show by students of the School. The announcement of the Hartford performances reflected a new and stronger confidence on the part of the direction of the School, and a growth in stature of the performing unit itself. The program of the Avery Memorial Theater read "The Producing Company of the School of American Ballet, George Balanchine, Maître de Ballet, presents . . ." The company was still an activity of the School, and not a separate organization—but it had acquired an identity, however unpretentious.

The Hartford season was modest. It only lasted three days, December 6, 7, and 8. The repertoire included four ballets: *Mozartiana* and *Serenade*, which had been given in Woodland in June; *Transcendence*, to music by Franz Liszt arranged by George Antheil; and *Alma Mater*, to music by Kay Swift, in costumes by the cartoonist John Held Jr. The last-

named was the only ballet on an American theme: in it
Edward Warburg, a Harvard man, was poking fun at Yale
and Princeton students.

The audience was glamorous, well-wishing, most con-
scious of the importance of the occasion, and enthusiastic.
The season was a distinct success not only *per se*, but also as an
augury of the future of the American Ballet, perhaps of ballet
in America. It must be said, however, that the audience, especially on the opening night, was not a typical, average, or
even representative American audience. There were more
New Yorkers and Bostonians at the Avery Memorial Theater
those nights than there were Hartforders. Painters, musicians,
writers; friends of Balanchine, Kirstein, and Warburg; sophisticated and well-heeled balletomanes—all went to Hartford to see the birth of the American Ballet and enjoyed it
and understood everything that Balanchine offered them.
They were conversant with new trends in ballet, music, poetry,
drama, and painting, and they took Balanchine's work in
their stride.

Not so the local spectators. So far as they were concerned
the company presented only one ballet they could understand and enjoy: *Alma Mater*. Here was something with a
definite plot, familiar, and a merry romp to boot. It was
almost like the Sunday comics. One could laugh and applaud
and have a good time. The other ballets were above their
heads, especially *Mozartiana* and *Transcendence*, and they accepted the proceedings at their face value without worrying
about the history-making aspects of the occasion. What was
Hecuba to them?

"The Producing Company of the School of American
Ballet" lived through its baptism of fire without major casual-
ties, and scored an impressive artistic victory. The founders
and directors could relax and be happy for the first time
since Lincoln Kirstein had had that memorable interview

with George Balanchine in the lobby of a small London hotel. A New York season, which everyone wanted and of which everyone was scared, was set for sometime in March, depending on the availability of a theater.

Before the New York season the company gave another, last-minute, shakedown performance at the Godhart Hall of Bryn Mawr College, near Philadelphia, on February 7, 1935. The program included *Serenade*, *Alma Mater*, and *Transcendence*. Although Warburg had been at one time an instructor at Bryn Mawr, and Kirstein had lectured there on dance, and the students and instructors could therefore be suspected of having a warm feeling toward the company, sight unseen, it can be fairly said that the company had a distinguished success entirely on its own merits. The college audience experienced no difficulty in accepting the company's ballets, enjoying them very much indeed.

III

1935

The American Ballet

The ballet picture in New York, and indeed in the United States, in 1935 was radically different from what it is now or has been in the past ten or twelve years.

There had been little ballet in America during the fifty years preceding the debut of the American Ballet in New York. In 1885–7 the American Opera Company, directed by Theodore Thomas, presented ballets as well as operas during its brief existence, among them Delibes's *Coppélia* and *Sylvia*, with Maria Giuri as ballerina. Luigi Albertieri, a disciple and foster-son of Enrico Cecchetti, offered a few ballet performances at the turn of the century with the *corps* of the Chicago Opera and the Metropolitan Opera. The Danish dancer, Adeline Genée, made her debut in New York in 1908 in a musical comedy called *The Soul Kiss,* and later danced as guest artist at the Metropolitan Opera House.

Two years later, on February 28, 1910, Anna Pavlova and Mikhail Mordkin, supported by the *corps* of the Metropolitan, created a sensation at the Metropolitan Opera House in a performance of *Coppélia.* The performance began after the regular opera performance, about midnight, and lasted until nearly two in the morning. Gertrude Hoffman presented "unauthorized" versions of Michel Fokine's *Scheherazade, Cleopatra,* and *Les Sylphides* some two years later in New York and on tour. The Diaghilev company played one season in America in 1916. The following year Adolph Bolm, then in Chicago, organized a small group, Ballet Intime. In 1918 Bolm staged at the Metropolitan Opera House the Fokine-Diaghilev version of *Le Coq d'Or,* with Rosina Galli, *première danseuse* of the opera house and wife of its director Gatti-Casazza, in the role of the Queen of Shemakhan. The following year he mounted *Petrouchka* at the same theater. There were sporadic attempts at ballet productions by the Neighborhood Playhouse and the League of Composers.

Michel Fokine settled in New York in the early 1920's and opened a school. In the autumn of 1922 he assembled a group of "the most talented of his graduate pupils" and gave performances at the Strand (now Warner) Theater in New York. In 1923 Anatole Bourman, a former dancer of the Maryinsky Theater and the Diaghilev Ballet, became ballet master at the Strand Theater, which installed a permanent ballet troupe. Some years later (1929–31) Leonide Massine headed a ballet unit at the Roxy Theater. When Radio City Music Hall opened in December 1932, it had a separate *corps de ballet,* as well as a group of "precision dancers," the

Rockettes. Maria Gambarelli, Harriet Hoctor, Patricia Bowman, Albertina Vitak, and Florence Rogge were garnering fame in musical shows and the "presentations" of the huge motion-picture palaces.

And that was how it stood until the winter of 1933, when impresario Sol Hurok brought over from Europe what was then called the René Blum and Col. de Basil Ballets Russes de Monte Carlo, and thus saved the company from imminent bankruptcy and America from its balletic doldrums. The company played a two-week season in New York at the St. James Theater and then went on a three-month tour. It returned to New York in the autumn of 1934 and again played two weeks at the St. James. Ballets Russes de Monte Carlo was a young and enthusiastic company. It danced well and had brought a repertoire that was varied, colorful, easy to follow, and simple to understand. It was, in short, an "artistic leg show," as a Broadway columnist termed it, entertainment pure and simple, a wonderful escape in the troubled times of the great depression. In addition, the company had famous names connected with it, was rich in real or assumed glamour and—also real or assumed—tradition, a perfect source of publicity and what Hollywood calls exploitation. No mean showman, Hurok knew how to present the company and how to extract from it the last ounce of promotion material. Pictures and articles in newspapers and magazines, radio interviews, window displays in all of the important Fifth Avenue shops, merchandise "tie-ups," everything that could in any way help to promote the ballet was brought into play—and succeeded.

The American Ballet had little of all this and, apparently, cared less. From the point of view of Kirstein and his associates, promotion of the imported company would have reeked of commercialism, and they would not have any of it. New York would have to accept the American Ballet for what it was, a young, serious, artistic endeavor that had something to say and was going to say it without the chromium-plated trappings that rightly belonged to the circus, not to ballet.

Then as now, this point of view on publicity was open to dispute. A ballet company is a theatrical enterprise that in the best of circumstances depends for its existence on a paying public, the lowly, perhaps, but all-important cash customer. To survive, it has to do everything in its power to attract the public; everything, that is, within the limits of good taste. Serge Diaghilev, an organizational genius and a man of impeccable taste, was also a master in matters of publicity. His publicity may not have been so obvious or, perhaps, so flamboyant as that of the Ballets Russes de Monte Carlo, but then he lived in a different time and on a different continent. Basically, however, his publicity methods and means did not differ materially from the ones exercised on behalf of the Ballets Russes in America.

But the founders of the young company would not have anything like it.

They did several things, however, to put the company on a more professional footing. First of all, the company's name was changed from The Producing Company of the School of American Ballet to The American Ballet, and the company ceased to be an activity of the School of American Ballet, becoming a separate corporate unit. This was necessary not only for the sake of a proper title for the company but also to separate the financial structures of the School and the company. Warburg became director of the American Ballet, Balanchine its *maître de ballet*. Not a man to be interested in titles, Kirstein became secretary.

The second important step was to engage a professional manager. The choice fell on the Musical Art Management Corporation, headed by Alexander Merovitch, a man who enjoyed an excellent reputation in American and European musical circles. He had brought out of Russia Vladimir Horowitz, Nathan Milstein, and Gregor Piatigorsky, was managing Feodor Chaliapin and Igor Stravinsky, among others, and had been at one time vice president of the Arthur Judson office. Merovitch took a sincere interest in the arrangements and in the company itself, and contributed to its success. Oliver M. Saylor, who had to his credit the publicity for the Moscow Art Theater, the *Chauve-Souris*, and similar attractions, was appointed press representative.

The New York season was announced for one week, March 1 through 7, at the Adelphi Theater, and was later extended through March 15.

The program included *Errante* (to Schubert's "Wanderer" Fantasy for Piano, orchestrated by Charles Koechlin, in costumes by Pavel Tchelitchew), *Mozartiana* (to Tchaikovsky's Fourth Suite, in scenery and costumes by Christian Bérard), *Alma Mater* (to music by Kay Swift, orchestrated by Morton Gould, in costumes by John Held, Jr.), *Transcendence* (to music by Franz Liszt, arranged and orchestrated by George Antheil, in costumes by Franklin Watkins and décor by Gaston Longchamp), *Serenade* (to Tchaikowsky's Serenade for Strings, in C Major, orchestrated by George Antheil, in costumes by Jean Lurçat), *Reminiscence* (to music by Benjamin Godard, arranged and orchestrated by Henry Brand, in costumes and décor by Sergei Soudeikine), and *Dreams* (to George Antheil's music, in costumes and scenery by André Derain).

The dancers were Gisella Caccialanza, a god-daughter of Enrico Cecchetti, who danced under the name of Sylvia Giselle because she was skeptical about people's ability to pronounce or spell her surname, Leda Anchutina, Ruthanna Boris, Annia Breyman, Elena De Rivas, Audrey Guerard,

Rabana Hasburgh, Holly Howard, Hortense Karklin, Albia
Kavan, Helen Leitch, Annabelle Lyon, Frances Mann,
Hannah Moore, Kathryn Mullowny, Yvonne Patterson,
Elise Reiman, Daphne Vane, Heidi Vosseler, Douglas Coudy,
William Dollar, Arthur Frederix, Charles Laskey, Joseph
Levinoff, Eugene Loring, Jack Potteiger, and Jack Quinn.
Sandor Harmati was the conductor.

All dancers were technically students of the School of
American Ballet, though none of them was (or could be)
actually a product of the School, which had been in existence
only for about eighteen months. Some of them had been on
the stage for quite a while, and others were beginners.

The American Ballet company had two guest artists,
Tamara Geva (whom the reader will remember as Tamara
Gevergeieva, one of the dancers who succeeded in leaving
Russia with Balanchine and Dimitriew) and Paul Haakon, an
engaging young technician—a pupil and protégé of Michel
Fokine—who showed tremendous promise.

A swank, sophisticated, befurred, and bejeweled audience, which would have been a credit to an opening of the
Metropolitan Opera or the Horse Show, filled the eight hundred and ninety-four seats in the orchestra and boxes. The
arts, letters, capital, business, and society were represented in
quality and quantity. The combined names of Balanchine,
Kirstein, Warburg, and Tchelitchew and their entourage
worked their magic spell, and Oliver Saylor did an excellent
job with dignified press publicity. The five hundred and forty
seats in the mezzanine and balcony were filled by the modest
representatives of Greenwich Village, the Art Students
League, and practically every dancer, student, and teacher
in New York. It was a grand audience: warm, receptive,
knowing, appreciative, and well-wishing. Ovation after
ovation followed the presentation of the four ballets on open-

ing night: *Serenade, Alma Mater, Errante,* and *Reminiscence.* Tamara Geva, Paul Haakon, and William Dollar came in for the largest share of the applause.

The opening was a great success.

To one spectator who not only enjoyed every moment of the performance, but who also suffered the agonies of the opening night with every dancer in the company, one thing appeared certain the moment the curtain came down on the third ballet, *Errante:* the American Ballet, Balanchine, Kirstein, and Warburg were years ahead of their time.

Here was ballet, real ballet, exciting ballet, but ballet for which there was not a ready public, but only a few hundred individuals who could not possibly support it even if they went to every performance.

Kirstein had been steeped in ballet for years. He had watched it, studied it, eaten it, and slept it until he knew it to the smallest, most esoteric aspect of choreography, music, décor, and story, so intimately that he had unavoidably lost the perspective of ballet as a theatrical performance, as a show for which people bought tickets, which they came to see expecting something they could understand. Balanchine, on his part, had been used to staging ballets for the sophisticated audiences of Paris and London, who had gained, or at least intimated that they had gained, understanding and appreciation of ballet under the tutelage of Diaghilev and his entourage. The rarefied, and quite often artificial atmosphere, in which the modern European composers, painters, and poets lived was Balanchine's own atmosphere. He flourished and reveled in it; he found in it stimulus and inspiration. And, consciously or not, he composed for his colleagues, for their taste, for their mentality, for their knowledge and experience.

The American Ballet was ahead of its time and just a little snobbish. Most of the members of the New York audience that went to see the American Ballet (not the opening-night audience) were from entirely different surroundings. To them this atmosphere was alien; they were unsophisticated, their tastes were simple; they could not understand, much less enjoy, the subtleties of Balanchine, Tchelitchew, Kirstein, and almost everyone else connected with the American Ballet.

Certainly they came to see the American Ballet, but the ballet they liked most was that which Hartford had liked before them: *Alma Mater*. Here was something that was fun, that could make them forget for some twenty-five minutes the continuing depression, WPA projects, Hitler's occupation of the Saar Territory, the rejection of the Versailles Treaty, persecution of Jews and Roman Catholics in Germany, and all the rest.

The press reception of the opening night was what is generally called mixed.

The *Sun*'s report on March 2 was typical of those written by nonspecialists, mostly music critics. Here is a paragraph from it:

"The American Ballet, which hopes to establish itself here on a basis similar to that of the Russian Ballet in Moscow, opened its season last evening at the Adelphi Theater. A brilliant audience showed every evidence of delight in a performance which had variety, vivacity, fancy, humor and several disclosures of promising talent to recommend it. As ballet it was sometimes more lively than finished, but as a show it ought to catch the town. The members of the company are young, the girls are good to see and the men are accomplished in comedy as well as in agility. The choreography by George Balanchine is laudable. There was a good orchestra under Sandor Harmati and some striking costumes designed by John Held Jr."

Note, please, that of the four designers represented in the first program, Jean Lurçat, John Held, Jr., Tchelitchew, and Soudeikine, the *Sun* mentioned only Held, a cartoonist who used to add to his signature the phrase "who never took a lesson in his life." Obviously this review was not ballet criticism, just a friendly report on the "disclosures" of the evening, the sort of report that has always been, and is today, more than welcome to directors and impresarios, Lincoln Kirstein excepted.

John Martin of the *Times* took a different view. He wrote a real review, three quarters of a column of it, but it was not a friendly review and it contained some notable examples of damning with faint praise. This review is an important document because, with two or three other articles written by the same critic at that time, it influenced the development of ballet in America for a few years.

Here is what John Martin wrote in *The New York Times* of March 2, 1935:

"It is not surprising that in making any report on the New York debut of the new American Ballet last night at the Adelphi Theatre, it should be necessary to temper the wind somewhat to the shorn lamb. The surprising thing is that not nearly so much tempering is called for as might reasonably have been expected. With the exception of one very bad ballet, for which the dancers can be held in no wise responsible, the evening was a most encouraging success.

"The question which inevitably arises at the outset is just how American it is, and the answer just as inevitably follows that it is not very much so. At this period of its development, with a Russian ballet master, a Russian teacher, and for the most part European musicians and designers to work with, it would be miraculous if it exhibited any strikingly native characteristics. Yet beneath this imported surface, there shines through the unmistakably American quality of free and forthright physical movement, and on this the future of the organization must inevitably be built. As yet there is

not much unity in the ensemble and there are perfectly
natural evidences of immaturity to be seen here and there.
On the whole, however, the technical foundation of the group
is excellent, and its youthfulness and verve are completely
disarming.

"Only one individual stands out from the group as a
potential artist of high rank and this is William Dollar, who
has everything in his favor. If he is not heard from in a big
way before many seasons have passed it will be a distinct
surprise. Several of the other principal dancers have excellent
qualifications, but not many of them have as yet developed
as personalities.

"Of the four ballets on the opening program, all of them
created by George Balanchine, two are worthy of serious consideration as dance works, while the others fall into other
categories. 'Errante,' for example, falls naturally into the
same class of cosmic nonsense as the Monte Carlo Ballet's
'Les Présages,' which up to now has held the record for
choreographic silliness. To the music of Schubert's 'Wanderer'
Fantasy, Tamara Geva suffers prodigiously in a really stun-
ning décor by Paul Tchelitchev. With all due respect to a
platinum and diamond audience that cheered it to the echo,
this is exactly the sort of thing the American Ballet must not
do if it is to assume the place in the dance world to which it is
entitled.

" 'Alma Mater' is a thoroughly amusing little burlesque
of college life as it is lived in the minds of the fiction writers.
It is relatively unimportant, not because it fails in any degree
to do what it sets out to do, but only because it is really a
revue sketch rather than a ballet. Charles Laskey is extremely
amusing in it as the stupid football hero.

" 'Serenade' to music of Tchaikovsky, opens the evening.
It is a serviceable rather than an inspired piece of work. No

doubt Mr. Balanchine had his problems in devising choreography for an inexperienced company, but whatever the reasons, 'Serenade' lacks spontaneity to a great extent.

"The real delight of the evening is the closing number, 'Reminiscence,' to music by Godard. Here Mr. Balanchine has taken actual dances from his memories of the Russian ballet and adapted them to his own uses. Here the real abilities of the company get their first showing, and it is a decidedly impressive showing. Though the brilliant Paul Haakon is the guest star in this number, he by no means overshadows his colleagues. Especially impressive are little Leyda Anchutina and Mr. Dollar, though all the dancers give good accounts of themselves. On the basis of such technical discipline as is here evidenced fine things can certainly be expected in the not too distant future. The only thing that such a thoroughly promising and attractive young group needs to guard against at the moment is too attentive an ear for applause."

One has little reason to doubt the sincerity of a critic of the stature and integrity of John Martin. He is accepted as the dean of American dance critics by his colleagues, not because he is a year older than the next in age, but for far more important reasons. Yet his preference for *Reminiscence*, at best a simple divertissement of classic dances without particular brilliance or élan, over *Serenade*, a true classic masterpiece that is still one of the greatest Balanchine has ever composed, or the exciting *Errante*, is difficult to accept at face value.

John Martin's review of the second program, printed on March 6, was just as critical and just as patronizing as his first review, and must have irritated the direction of the American Ballet no end. The second bill included *Dreams, Transcendence, Alma Mater,* and *Reminiscence.*

It seemed to Martin that *Dreams* was "scarcely worth the

labor that has been spent on it, for it is trivial in subject matter and utterly unsuited in style to the young dancers who make up the company." *Transcendence* fared little better: "Though totally obscure, [it] is of far greater interest. . . . It has the quality of phantasmagoria and some of its incidents are of distinct power, but whether because of the straining for choreographic novelty or because again of its complete unsuitability to the talents of the company, it remains largely incomprehensible. Throughout the performance there was manifest a sense of strain. A young and inexperienced company is being pushed beyond its limits of accomplishment, and thereby the future of a promising enterprise is being seriously jeopardized."

In connection with Martin's appraisal of *Transcendence* it is interesting to see what Kirstein's reaction to this ballet had been.

"I personally liked *Transcendence* best. This ballet had a strange history: to music by Liszt, with remarkable painting by Franklin Watkins of Philadelphia, it independently anticipated Frederick Ashton's *Apparitions*, Nijinska's *Well-Beloved* (*Bien-Aimée*) and Massine's *Symphonie Fantastique*, all ballets on the same theme, all produced within a year and a half of each other, by choreographers working independent of one another. As a ballet based on the life of the virtuoso Nicolò Paganini, with overtones from *The Golden Bough*, it was a perfect example of Balanchine's framing an individual artist of exceptional and very personalized gifts [William Dollar]."

The last sentence in Martin's review seemed as obscure to the direction of the company and to some of his readers as *Transcendence* had seemed to Martin. Was he complaining that the dancers were being worked too hard physically, given *enchaînements* that were technically "beyond the limits of accomplishment"? Or did he think that the esthetic of the ballet was beyond the young company's comprehension? Would he

have preferred the company doing a sort of simplified ballet,
something light and easy? And how could two weeks of even
the most difficult dancing seriously jeopardize "the future of a
promising enterprise"?

No one asked Martin for an explanation, and he himself
never chose to elaborate. But his article on Sunday, March 10,
offered a clear statement of his attitude toward the American
Ballet and American ballet in general. Eloquent and brilliantly written, the article is well worth reproducing here *in
toto:*

"The American Ballet, which is scheduled to close its
first season at the Adelphi Theatre tonight (unless another
extension is decided upon after these lines are written), has
had a success which it would do well to meditate over seriously for the next few weeks. On the result of such meditation,
one ventures to believe, depends the entire future of the enterprise, and that is a future too bright with potentialities to be
forfeited lightly. The problem resolves itself into one fundamental decision: is the organization to attempt the fulfillment
of its original policy of developing an American ballet, or is it
to follow the direction of its present season and go on being
merely 'Les Ballets Americains'?

"The latter is certainly the better decision from the
standpoint of opportunism. There is a large audience for the
chic and outré. It is an audience which shifts its bravos from
fashionable fad to fashionable fad, but its dollars are good
while they last and its applause is deafening for the same
period of time. There is also another type of audience which
is useful. It consists largely of expatriate Europeans, mostly
Russians, who are honestly homesick for the kind of dancing
they used to know at home. In addition, count those who are
subject to indiscriminate rapture over anything in the nature
of 'toe dancing' and those who froth easily at the mouth at the
thought of the modern dance. By a combination of all these

elements (and they have been present and in good voice at the Adelphi) something impressive can no doubt be done in the direction of show business.

"It is not, however, in this direction that an American ballet is to be found, nor was it to be so pursued, according to the announced policy of the present organization at its inception.

"It was the original plan to nurture during its period of growth a group of dancers, trained in the fundamentals of the classic ballet, in the belief that a form of dance born in Italy, developed in France, broadened in Russia, would, when subjected to the environment influences of America, again be transformed with a new vitality. There was no suggestion that American dancers were to be fitted into Continental molds, but that a fundamental technique developed abroad should find new molds of American making.

"Now it is unreasonable to expect that in the short space of a year or so any great results could be obtained in this direction. It was a century and a half before the introduction of the French ballet into Russia gave birth to the Russian ballet. Nevertheless, it seems not only fair but wise to look for symptoms at the earliest possible moment. Of the six ballets which constituted the present season, all created by George Balanchine, only one gave signs of being useful in building toward the ultimate goal. This was 'Reminiscence,' an aggregation of divertissements in the classic manner, adapted somewhat from dances in the repertoire of the Russian Imperial Ballet and its school. It is not calculated to cause any sort of sensation, but it is exactly the sort of thing that one would expect to find in the repertoire of what is at present actually an apprentice group with guest stars.

"For the other ballets it seems a colossal waste of time and energy to train dancers in the strict routine of the classic dance. 'Dreams,' 'Errante,' 'Serenade' and 'Transcendence' all belong to another style. They are evidences of the decadence of the classic tradition as it is found in certain European environments, examples of what some one has aptly called 'Riviera esthetics.'

"While every region is entitled to whatever decadences it pleases, there is nothing to be gained by our importing them. If we are to build an American ballet from fundamental bases, let us be sure that the bases are fundamental. We can be counted upon to develop our own decadences. 'Alma Mater,' the college ballet, is to be excepted from this classification, but it departs so slightly from the type of dancing that has been done for years in revues that it is of little consequence and leads nowhere.

"For the essential training of the young company, there is nothing but praise. Their technique is clean and simple and has the dignity and purity of the classic style at its best. There is nothing overly pretty about it, no flopping hands or marshmallow softness. It is not always perfect in practice, for the dancers are young and inexperienced in the discipline of a ballet organization. There are many evidences of coltishness that only time will remove. But, on the whole, it is a good group of hard-working youngsters, far too good indeed to be forced, like square pegs into round holes, into choreography that does not and never will belong to them.

"With all due respect to George Balanchine, the great need of the company is American direction. If this sounds like flag-waving, put it down to the basic idea of the organization and either accept or discount it at that point."

Martin was less than fair in his accusation of opportunism and his relegation of the company to "show business," and he probably knew it at the time. He was incorrect in saying that there was a large audience for the *chic* and *outré*, and was completely wrong in stating that the expatriate Russians liked the American Ballet because they were "honestly homesick for

SERENADE
(New York City Ballet version, 1949):
Melissa Hayden, Frank Hobi,
Maria Tallchief (partly hidden)

ALMA MATER: *front row—*
Hannah Moore, Ruthanna Boris,
Jack Potteiger, Arthur Frederix,
Gisella Caccialanza,
Charles Laskey, Helen Leitch,
Frances Mann, Joseph Levinoff,
Leyda Anchutina

MOZARTIANA:
facing camera—Frances Mann,
Helen Leitch, Leyda Anchutina;
back to camera—Hannah Moore,
Gisella Caccialanza, Holly
Howard

TRANSCENDENCE:
center—*William Dollar,*
Elise Reiman

THE BAT:
Annabelle Lyon,
Charles Laskey,
Leyda Anchutina

DREAMS:
Heidi Vosseler,
Charles Laskey

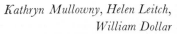

William Dollar, Daphne Vane, Lew Christensen

ORPHEUS AND EURYDICE (Gluck)

Kathryn Mullowny, Helen Leitch,
William Dollar

William Dollar,
Lew Christensen

Diana Adams, Tanaquil LeClercq, André Eglevsky, Maria Tallchief

APOLLON MUSAGÈTE (APOLLO)

Diana Adams, Maria Tallchief, Tanaquil LeClercq, André Eglevsky

CARD GAME:
Jillana,
Patricia Wilde,
Doris Breckenridge,
Janet Reed,
Todd Bolender

BAISER DE LA FÉE:
standing left center—
Tanaquil LeClercq;
right center—
Nicholas Magallanes

BAISER DE LA FÉE:
Nicholas Magallanes,
Tanaquil LeClercq

PASTORELA: *Nicholas Magallanes, Charles Dickson, Gisella Caccialanza, José Martinez, Lew Christensen*

CONCERTO BAROCCO:
William Dollar, Marie Jeanne, Mary Jane Shea

TIME TABLE:
Gisella Caccialanza, Lew Christensen, Beatrice Tompkins, Mary Jane Shea

POCAHONTAS:
*standing—Ruthanna Boris,
Lew Christensen,
Charles Laskey;
sitting—Hannah Moore,
Frances Mann,
Albia Kavan,
Ruby Asquith*

PROMENADE:
*Eugene Loring,
Ruby Asquith,
Rabana Hasburgh,
Albia Kavan*

SHOW PIECE:
*Fred Danieli,
Marie Jeanne*

YANKEE CLIPPER: *front—Fred Danieli, Eugene Loring,
Michael Kidd; back—Lew Christensen, Harold Christensen*

FILLING STATION:
Todd Bolender, Douglas Coudy,
Fred Danieli, Marie Jeanne

BILLY THE KIDD: *front row center—Erick Hawkins, Eugene Loring, Lew Christensen, Michael Kidd*

CHARADE:
Harold Christensen,
Lew Christensen,
Gisella Caccialanza,
Ruby Asquith

FOUR TEMPERAMENTS: *(above) Maria Tallchief, Nicholas Magallanes*

*Maria
Tallchief*

RENARD:
The Rooster—
Lew Christensen;
The Ram—John Taras;
The Fox—Todd Bolende
The Cat—Fred Danieli

MINOTAUR:
Francisco Moncion
and group

PUNCH & THE CHILD:
Beatrice Tompkins,
Herbert Bliss

SYMPHONIE CONCERTANTE: *front row—Tanaquil LeClercq, Todd Bolender, Diana Adams*

THE TRIUMPH OF BACCHUS AND ARIADNE:
Nicholas Magallanes, Tanaquil LeClercq

SYMPHONY IN C:
Maria Tallchief, Nicholas Magallanes

Herbert Bliss as Apollo

ORPHEUS (Stravinsky)

Maria Tallchief as Eurydice

MOTHER GOOSE SUITE: *front row—Barbara Bocher, Dick Beard, Tomi Wortham;
back row—Peggy Karlson, Margaret Walker*

JINX: *center—Todd Bolender, Janet Reed; on floor—Herbert Bliss;
recognizable in background—Beatrice Tompkins, Barbara Walczak*

FIREBIRD: *Francisco Moncion, Maria Tallchief*

BOURRÉE FANTASQUE: *Tanaquil LeClercq, Jerome Robbins*

ONDINE: *Francisco Moncion, Tanaquil LeClercq, Yvonne Mounsey*

center—Yvonne Mounsey, Hugh Laing

THE PRODIGAL SON

Yvonne Mounsey, Francisco Moncion   *Hugh Laing*

the kind of dancing they used to know at home." What the expatriate Russians (and even non-Russians) knew at home was so completely different from what the American Ballet danced that they never did recognize the American Ballet for a ballet company as they knew that term. To them the American Ballet was modernistic, anticlassic, untraditional. They believed that if the American Ballet were permitted to continue (they never said who could stop it), it would ruin ballet forever.

But Martin did bring up, by inference at least, the question of what was and what would be American ballet. He did not make any specific suggestions beyond saying that the company needed "American direction" and the rather vague admonition that American ballet "should find new molds of American making."

Some nine years before Martin's article, Ted Shawn wrote a book called *The American Ballet* (New York: Henry Holt and Co.; 1926) in which he came out with a rather pat formula for American ballet: "American born and trained dancers, dancing to music by American composers, with scenery and costumes designed by American artists, and under the direction and management of American business men of great vision."

Martin did not go quite so far as Shawn in his formula for American ballet, but the hint was there just the same.

The question of what is American ballet is still a lively topic of discussion. Is it, as Ted Shawn would have it, ballet staged by American choreographers to music by American composers in settings designed by American painters and danced by American dancers? And if so, who is and who is not an American in this conception? Or is that ballet American which reflects the spirit and life of America in the manner of creation, in the style of dancing, in the freedom from conventions, in the mixture of races and creeds, countries of origin, language of forefathers, and all the other characteristics that made this country great?

The question has not yet been answered properly, at least not in so many words, but we are well toward the establishment of a style in ballet which cannot be called anything but American. And when this style has crystallized we shall know without explanations what American ballet is. Even now, however, we realize (and this at a time of understandably intense nationalism) that art is neither the property of a nation nor the result of patriotism. This was not clear to some people in 1935.

After the season at the Adelphi Theater, Kirstein, Balanchine, and Warburg took stock. On the one hand they had had a very successful season, the first New York season of an American ballet company. The audience liked the company, liked most if not all of the repertoire. The dancers had proved their mettle beyond the most optimistic expectations. They had been nervous at the beginning, of course; they were tired at the end, quite naturally. How many of them had ever before danced every day for two weeks? The direction of the company knew that the ballets in its repertoire were not any more decadent than the times themselves. They realized, if others did not, that the ballet had to reflect the state of the world. Unlike the Ballets Russes de Monte Carlo, the American Ballet did not engage in escapism, and if *Transcendence* and *Errante*, for example, were disturbing and "obscure," so was the world. The depression had not yet run its course, across the Atlantic Hitler was rampant—everybody was "dancing on the edge of a volcano." The American Ballet was in step with the times.

On the other hand, there was John Martin, whose epithets "Les Ballets Americains" and "Riviera esthetics" stuck, or seemed to Kirstein to stick. It was small wonder that

Kirstein thought that the world, his ballet world, was coming
to an end. That is what he thought at every crisis in the
existence of the company before and after the Adelphi season;
he still thinks it before the opening of every season of the New
York City Ballet. But the sensation was newer in 1935, and
Kirstein younger.

After a short rest the company went back to the School
of American Ballet, which by then had added to its faculty
Muriel Stuart, an Englishwoman who had been an outstanding dancer in the Pavlova company; Anatole Vilzak, a
premier danseur of the Maryinsky Theater, the Diaghilev company, and several other organizations; and Erick Hawkins, a
senior student of the School, who had been given the title of
assistant instructor.

By mid-July the company was back in rehearsal for the
few performances that Merovitch had booked for it at the
Lewisohn Stadium in New York and at the Robin Hood Dell
in Philadelphia, the two big outdoor stadia in the East.

The New York performance was scheduled for August 5,
a Monday night, and the program included *Serenade, Alma
Mater,* and *Reminiscence.* Jupiter Pluvius, whom Kirstein had
considered a personal enemy of his and of the American
Ballet since June 9, 1934, lived up to his name: it rained
Monday night, and when the performance, as was the custom,
was postponed until "the first clear night," it rained on
Tuesday and Wednesday. It cleared up in New York on
Thursday, August 8, but on that day the company had to go
to Philadelphia to dance at the Robin Hood Dell, so it rained
in Philadelphia. It rained again Friday night. Finally on
Saturday, August 10, the night was clear and the American
Ballet gave so successful a performance that the company was
held over for another night. On Monday night, August 12,
the American Ballet gave its much-postponed performance at

the Lewisohn Stadium. Again the company was very successful and was invited to give another performance one week
later—which was achieved without undue trouble.

After the first Stadium performance, when the company
had just begun rehearsals for an ambitious tour booked by
Merovitch to begin in the middle of October, Edward Johnson, the newly appointed general manager of the Metropolitan
Opera House, invited the American Ballet to become the
resident company of the Metropolitan Opera; i.e., to create
the opera ballets and present its own repertoire.

In Kirstein's own words:

"The invitation was so unsuspect, the opportunity seemingly so wonderful, there was scarcely a thought of refusal."

Contracts were signed, and there was general rejoicing
in the company, among balletomanes, and in parts of the
press. Parts of the press, because John Martin took a dim
view of the new appointment and spared neither vitriol nor
space to make his view public. Here is what he wrote in *The
New York Times* on Sunday, August 18:

"The announcement that George Balanchine is to be the
new ballet master of the Metropolitan Opera comes not altogether as a surprise. It was reported as a possibility in these
columns last March, when the American ballet of which Mr.
Balanchine is maître de ballet was concluding its first season
at the Adelphi Theatre.

"The engagement gives rise to a number of conflicting
opinions. It is deeply to be regretted that once again American
artists have been passed by for a high artistic post for which at
least half a dozen of them are eminently fitted. This, too, in an
organization which has gone on record as favoring the use of
native talent wherever available. Apparently the old tradition
has not yet been eradicated that we are a crude pioneer people
and must import our culture from the European fountainhead. Perhaps more in the dance than in the other arts this

type of thinking prevails, and if we do not guard ourselves we will begin to accept what seems to be a growing theory hereabouts that Pavlova and Nijinsky invented the art.

"In the case of Mr. Balanchine, however, we happen to be in luck, for he is a gifted artist beyond the shadow of a doubt, and not merely the latest Russian to arrive. That he will grace his new position goes without saying. He is unusually inventive in his choreography, and all his work is stamped with the highly personal mark of a creative individual. After the shocking state of the dance in the opera house in recent years, he will be doubly welcome. Of the American Ballet company which he is to take with him to his new berth, it is not possible to be so confident. Looking at the young dancers in their performances at the Stadium last week, it was difficult to picture them as representatives of what has sometimes been termed the world's leading lyric theatre. They are still an apprentice group rather than a company of artists.

"From the practical side, the combination is obviously an advantageous one. The American Ballet is financially well backed, its school is well equipped and staffed, and no doubt a considerable burden can thus be taken off the shoulders of the opera guarantors. In the matter of ballet performances it will make possible that rarest of novelties, a new work now and then in the opera house, and will give the company of dancers, on its parts, a less intensive and hectic producing period as well as greatly heightened prestige and a subscription audience.

"There is, however, a fairly gloomy aspect to the situation, from the standpoint of the American Ballet project. Its original plans were laid in a very definite direction, namely, the creation of a type of theatrical dance that should develop the full flavor of American life and culture, starting with the technical tradition of the academic ballet as nothing more than a framework. That such an undertaking would require years of hard work and experimentation, as well as a substantial subsidy and inexhaustible patience, was clearly recognized in all the advance planning of the organization. But in practice things took a different turn almost from the start.

"Mr. Balanchine, for all his talent, came to the artistic directorship of an institution pledged to the development of American possibilities with no experience whatever of these possibilities on either side of the footlights. Whether it was at his instigation that productions were got under way too early in the life of the group the records do not reveal, but certainly it would be easy to understand if it was. It was also easy to understand that, with his brief background in a new country, he should have directed his compositions not to the new, potential audience that required development, along with the whole scheme of the enterprise, but rather to the type of audience he already knew in Europe. This was the audience of social position and wealth, to whom, as a rule, the ballet, when it is anything more than a diversion, is a collector's item. With the throwing of the whole organization into the very lap of this audience, which so largely dominates the opera house, any hope of recovering the original purpose of the enterprise appears to have been extinguished.

"It was the privilege of the present writer to listen on one or two occasions to Lincoln Kirstein's enthusiastic exposition of his plans for the American Ballet in its pre-organizational days. Now that he is no longer a director of the producing company but confines himself entirely to the operation of the school, perhaps he will take in friendly part a whole-hearted suggestion. It is that he charge his whole experience to date to profit and loss, congratulate himself on having helped to get better dancing into the opera house, shake hands cordially with Mr. Balanchine, and get to work starting an American ballet."

What an ogre John Martin seemed to the ballet world that summer!

Lincoln Kirstein would not have been Lincoln Kirstein if he had not answered John Martin. On Sunday, August 25, the *Times* printed the following Letter to the Editor:

"Without imposing on your space for what may seem a personal matter, I nevertheless wish to correct certain errors of fact your John Martin made Aug. 18 in his Sunday column on the Dance. In recalling a conversation with me before the American Ballet was organized, he now regrets I am no longer a director of that organization. The American Ballet Company and the School of American Ballet have the same four directors: George Balanchine, Vladimir Dimitriew, E. M. M. Warburg and myself. Mr. Warburg is executive director of a producing company, whose maître de ballet is Mr. Balanchine. Mr. Dimitriew is the head of the school, and I aid him.

"Mr. Martin permits himself what he euphemistically calls 'friendly' suggestion, that I charge my whole experience in the American Ballet to profit and loss, shake hands with Mr. Balanchine, and get to work starting an American ballet.

"Mr. Martin makes himself very free not alone with the private policy of the American Ballet, but in interpreting my personal position. He has already made himself an authority on the word 'American.' We differ with his chauvinistic construction of it. But his influence of antipathy to the form of ballet may have discouraged some young dancers from at least a trial at the technique, though this has obviated a necessity for sound training in many 'modern' interpreters.

"American ballet is not tap-dancing, though it may use it. It is not the Virginia reel, though country dances can be added to its context. Nor is it the hypnotized idiosyncrasies of a small group of concert-dancers who happen to have been born in America, and who draw their ideas from Central

Europe. Ballet in America is a form of dance expression no more indigenous than American violin or piano playing. Mr. Martin feels Russians are unsuitable to transmit this 400-year-old medium of Italian, French, German, Scandinavian and Slav origin and collaboration to fit the capacities of native Americans without corrupting them by foreign tricks. That is his opinion and he has a right to it. We should perhaps be grateful in these times of aggressive nationalism that he does not limit his definition of American to Anglo-Saxons alone.

"The American Ballet is interested in the development of ballet on the continent of America. That an enthusiasm for this kind of dance exists can be proved by the existence of the School of American Ballet, which has given instruction to over three hundred students in a year and a half, to a successful New York engagement of the ballet company composed entirely of artists trained by its teachers, and by its fourteen weeks of advance bookings outside of New York for 1935–1936.

"In one of the conversations to which Mr. Martin refers, I expressed to him the hope that the ballet would be in America a popular, widely loved institution, as in Russia today, not the property of the rich, as before the revolution. Mr. Martin infers that since the American Ballet is supervising the dances at the Metropolitan Opera House, its policy has sold out to the upper classes of the diamond horseshoe. On the contrary. Will Mr. Martin suggest a house which can support ballet that has a numerically larger audience, except possibly Radio City Music Hall?

"I am more than ever personally occupied with the creation of a national ballet. Mr. Warburg and myself, from no superficial attitude, believe a school founded on the finest Russian standards, is only temporarily an American necessity. This school exists. It has produced a dancing troupe. It will take time and real friendliness to achieve its best possibilities. We have all the time in the world, and our friends at the Lewisohn Stadium in New York and at Robin Hood Dell in Philadelphia triumphantly showed their belief in us during these last two weeks. Perhaps Mr. Martin, who has not always been slow to try to understand youthful American groups, will not grudge us the benefit of his reconsideration.

LINCOLN KIRSTEIN

New York, Aug. 20, 1935"

At the foot of the letter the *Times* printed the following rebuttal from John Martin:

"It is rather surprising to find Mr. Kirstein reading things into the article in question which were not there. In no place was there any expression of regret that he was not a director of the American Ballet's producing company, nor were there any liberties taken with the company's private affairs by stating that he was not. Neither on the programs of the company's season at the Adelphi Theatre last March nor on those of its recent performance at the Stadium is Mr. Kirstein's name mentioned as director. Indeed, in both cases it is distinctly stated that E. M. M. Warburg is the director.

As to chauvinism and the other subjects touched upon, they are largely matters of opinion, and Mr. Kirstein is fully entitled to his own views about them.

J. M."

A week later, on September 1, John Martin printed three letters addressed to the Dance Editor, not to the Editor of *The New York Times*, all in opposition to Kirstein and all from just readers of the *Times*, not from anyone in the dance field, ballet or modern. These letters ended the public issue, but the relations between Kirstein and Martin remained strained for four or five years.

The season at the Metropolitan Opera was still more than three months off, and the company, its morale bolstered by the contract, continued the rehearsals for the tour.

On September 28 the company gave a preview performance, as it were, at the Westchester County Center in White Plains, New York. The company had had no performances in a theater since March, and it was thought that a few rehearsals and an actual performance in a theater would help it to reorient itself. A new ballet, *Chopin Concerto*, by William Dollar, to the Piano Concerto in F Minor, was added to the repertoire.

The actual tour began on October 14 with a performance at the Greenwich (Connecticut) High School Auditorium. Trouping was such a new and exciting experience to the members of the young company that the tour appeared to them more a prolonged picnic than a theatrical tour. Chartered buses transported them and the orchestra from town to town and from hotel to theater and back, and everybody seemed to have a very good time. In the course of one week the company danced in Greenwich, Bridgeport, and New Haven, Connecticut; Princeton, New Jersey; and Harrisburg and Scranton, Pennsylvania.

The Scranton performance marked the unscheduled, unforeseen, and what seemed to the company the tragic, end of the tour.

What happened was that Alexander Merovitch, president of Musical Art Management Corporation, which had booked the tour, suffered a nervous collapse. His staff could find no way to meet the accrued expenses of the tour, and the salaries of the dancers and musicians could not be paid at the end of the week. The musicians, the only unionized members of the organization (ballet dancers were not unionized until much later), were, quite naturally, told by their union representatives to quit, and the tour came to an end.

Edward Warburg, who had remained in New York, was notified of the situation after the performance. Early next morning he arrived in Scranton and announced to the company that everyone would be paid in full, but that the tour was canceled.

A sad and disillusioned group of dancers returned to New York that evening. This had been their first taste of managerial trouble, and they did not quite know what to make of it. They knew that the cancellation of the tour was not their fault, nor the fault of the direction of the American Ballet, yet they felt a certain guilt for it. Also, they were a little ashamed. The story was told of one of the boys in the company who stayed on with friends in Manhattan for a whole month before joining his family in Brooklyn. He just could not tell them that the tour had collapsed.

Before the year 1935 came to an end, another important event took place: on November 15 G. P. Putnam's Sons brought out Lincoln Kirstein's book, *Dance,* subtitled *A Short History of Classic Theatrical Dancing.* Despite its modifying subtitle, the book's three hundred and sixty-nine pages presented an erudite and comprehensive history of dance from primitive times through the establishment of the School of American Ballet. It was, and still is, a major contribution to the literature on dance. There have been bigger and more lavishly illustrated volumes on dance, notably in the Russian language, but none has offered more substance or been more accurate, better organized, or based on so much exhaustive research. Even now, some seventeen years after its publication, it is still the finest book on the subject in any language.

IV

1935–1936

The American Ballet at the Metropolitan

Although the association between the American
Ballet and the Metropolitan Opera House, which
lasted from the autumn of 1935 to the spring of
1938, was never a happy one, Edward Johnson, the
Opera's general manager, must be given credit for
saving, unconsciously to be sure, the American
Ballet. The fiasco of the abortive tour made such a
deep impression upon the young and inexperienced
direction of the company that it would have given
up, or at least have postponed for a long time, the
idea of having an American ballet company. The
Metropolitan contract, however, offered a home
and work for the company, the possibility of appearing in its own repertoire in addition to opera ballets,

60

and, the directors felt, a workable if not ideal plan for its continuation.

Like many people before them and quite a few after them, they failed to understand the complicated mechanism of an opera house that is interested only in opera and considers the ballet a necessary but only tolerated adjunct to its basic activity.

If you speak to opera people, they have a high regard for opera ballet. But, they will point out, the dance in opera ballet should not be identified or compared with the dance in ballet. The dance in opera ballet is only an auxiliary instrument in the development of the stage action. Opera contains forms of vocal, instrumental, and dramatic arts. The dramatic part of the opera performance embraces several artistic forms, only one of which is dance. Consequently dance in opera must be fused with the general production.

This is the opinion of enlightened opera ballet choreographers, and it is correct in theory. In practice, however, the primary function of opera ballet seems to be to occupy the stage and fill in so many measures of music that the composer wrote to enable the singers to rest their voices between arias, or perhaps change costumes.

Only opera houses with a long tradition of separate ballet performances, such as the opera houses in St. Petersburg, Moscow, Paris, London, and Copenhagen, accept a ballet company as a more or less equal member of their organizations. In other houses, and among them the Metropolitan Opera House, the ballet is not more than a necessary evil. In these houses the management feels that it cannot provide the necessary stage, costume, and orchestra rehearsals for the ballet, and is reluctant to spend any funds for costumes and shoes, especially shoes.

Moreover, an opera company that engages a ballet troupe to dance the incidental ballet numbers in operas pre-

fers to have the ballet company under the direction of a ballet
master who knows the so-called opera tradition well, who can
rehearse his dancers in a rehearsal hall and then bring them
onto the stage at the final general rehearsal with the entire
company and not have them get into the way of the soloists
and chorus. This is a policy in line with the usual practice of
hiring singers who not only can sing their parts well but who
also "have the repertoire"; i.e., know their operas, entrances
and exits, stage business, and the location of set pieces and
props. Under this policy, and it is accepted in nearly all opera
houses, a singer can appear this season at the Metropolitan,
the next in La Scala, and the season after next at the Colón, or
sing as guest artist in all three of them in one season, without
ever needing a single costly rehearsal.

In addition, there are few, if any, opera directors who
would like to have a brilliant ballet in an opera. The role of the
ballet in opera is subservient to opera proper, and it should not
detract from the success of the singers by having a success of
its own.

There are optimists even now who think that this policy
can be changed, and that opera ballet can assume a more important place. They are only optimists, and opera history is
not with them, whatever temporary proof they may be able
to assemble. They tend, or perhaps wish, to forget the basic
truth that the place of ballet in opera is not set, as it may seem,
by the whim of the director or the taste of the lady responsible
for the collection of funds in support of the opera house, but
by the composers of the operas themselves. In the heyday of
Russian ballet at the Maryinsky Theater, the opera ballet
there was never above the mediocre, with the single exception
of that in *Prince Igor*, for which Fokine staged the dances, and
which subsequently became a great character ballet. Outstanding dancers in the Maryinsky used all kinds of subterfuges to avoid dancing in operas, and generally speaking it

took a performance of a patriotic opera like *A Life for the Tsar* or the attendance of the Tsar himself at an opera performance to have ballerinas or *premiers danseurs* appear in an opera.

Lincoln Kirstein and Edward Warburg could have been excused for not being familiar with these phenomena, but George Balanchine was brought up in the Maryinsky Theater, and Vladimir Dimitriew had himself been an opera singer. They should have known better. Yet they interpreted Johnson's request for "freshness, youth and novelty" from a balletic, not an operatic, point of view. Had they interpreted the director's request from his view, they would have had no reason to accept the Metropolitan contract. Balanchine, who had been too revolutionary for the revolutionary masters of the Maryinsky Theater in 1923, and who had succeeded in saying something new in 1933, would not settle down to be a run-of-the-mill opera ballet master in 1935.

The first appearance of the American Ballet in a separate ballet took place during the pre-Christmas week of 1935, when *Hansel and Gretel* was presented at the Metropolitan on a program with a short ballet. The ballet on this occasion was *Reminiscence*. Kathryn Mullowny, Leda Anchutina, Annabelle Lyon, Sylvia Giselle, Rabana Hasburgh, Elise Reiman, Holly Howard, Annia Breyman, Charles Laskey, William Dollar, and Anatole Vilzak danced the solo parts. Vilzak, who had earlier joined the School of American Ballet as instructor, was engaged as a dancer especially for the Metropolitan. His initial appearance was in the "Mazurka" with Rabana Hasburgh. *Reminiscence* was acclaimed by the audience and the delighted management. Here was something young, fresh, novel—and safe.

Balanchine's choreography for the opera ballets was also young, fresh, and novel, but not nearly so safe. The box-holders, various committees members, the management, and most of the press (i.e., the music critics) abhorred Balanchine's innovations intensely and said so loudly and repeatedly. The general audience liked some of the opera ballets very much, specifically those in *Carmen* and *Aïda*, and was quietly cool toward the others. Singers once in a while complained to the management that the ballet received too much applause and thus interfered with such of their numbers as followed it. The late Edward Ziegler, associate general manager of the Metropolitan, once told Balanchine that he would have to rework the finale of the ballet in *Aïda* because the ballet received so much applause that it stopped the show.

Before coming to the Metropolitan, Balanchine had created opera ballets successfully in London, Copenhagen, Monte Carlo, and Paris. What was wrong with his work at the Metropolitan?

In his *Blast at Ballet*, Kirstein tells something of Balanchine's approach to opera ballets and the preliminary work he did before staging them. For instance, Balanchine's acrobatic divertissement for the "Victory" dance in *Aïda* and the *danse du ventre* for the priestesses in the same opera were based on religious sculptures at Sakkarah and Beni-Hassan, and on La Fage's archeological engravings. For the Bacchanale in *Tannhäuser*, Balanchine studied Wagner's stage directions, read the composer's correspondence about this opera, and acquainted himself with Isadora Duncan's experience at the Bayreuth Festival. The Bacchanale was original and exciting; the dancers were alive. Yet both the *Tannhäuser* ballet and the first version of the *Aïda* ballet were failures. The management protested so much about *Aïda* that Balanchine restaged it three times, and finally put on the program: "Dances by George Balanchine, after Marius Petipa," which silenced the management. Some of the box-holders and the management protested about the dances in *Tannhäuser* after every performance. *Lakmé*, *Samson and Delilah*, and some of the other opera ballets were accepted with equally bad grace. Part of the audience and even some of the music critics liked most of the opera ballets, but they remained clearly in the minority. In two cases the management liked Balanchine's work: the divertissement in *Carmen* saved the opera after the Metropolitan's favorite Carmen lost her voice (this the management admitted, however reluctantly), and the market scene in *Faust* had an excellent press.

Said Kirstein of the *Faust* ballet: "I think Balanchine must have composed it in a deep sleep."

The American Ballet knew at the beginning of the season, right after the production of *Aïda*, that it would not remain long at the Metropolitan. The management was openly dissatisfied with Balanchine. But Balanchine, too, had reason to complain. The management refused the extra orchestra rehearsals that would have made it possible for the American Ballet to present its own repertoire, ostensibly one of the main purposes for which the American Ballet had been invited to join the Metropolitan, and certainly the main reason why the American Ballet had accepted the invitation. The explanation for the refusal was lack of funds.

Balanchine and Kirstein found a compromise: they presented ballets to music the orchestra knew, and hence did not have to have extra rehearsals. There were two of them: *The Bat*, to the overture of Johann Strauss's *Die Fledermaus*, choreographed by Balanchine in a touchingly nostalgic mood set off by a gay Viennese waltz and an infectious can-can, the latter danced by a plumed "pony-ballet" ensemble; and William Dollar's choreographic debut, *Chopin Concerto*, to the Piano Concerto in F Minor, a white ballet in the romantic mood.

Neither the Balanchine nor the Kirstein of that period was or wanted to be (or perhaps knew how to be) diplomatic, politic, or even calm. Kirstein was to write in 1938: "My zeal exceeded a crusader's. I had not yet learned the first rule of diplomacy: *Surtout point de zèle.*"

Balanchine, on his part, in speaking to newspaper reporters, said exactly what was on his mind. He told one of them in an interview that New York music critics knew nothing about dancing and not much more about music, as they were continually proving in their reviews. He may have been right, and his words made excellent copy, but they also led to an aggravation of the delicate relations between the American Ballet and the Metropolitan and, naturally, the music critics.

While this was going on, a new field of activity opened up for Balanchine. A well-known Broadway producer, the late Dwight Deere Wiman, invited him to stage the dances in a new musical, *On Your Toes*, which was to star the famous actor-dancer Ray Bolger and the onetime guest artist of the American Ballet, Tamara Geva.

This invitation marked the beginning of a career for Balanchine which bought him new fame and a means of earning a livelihood outside the ballet. It also established a new era in musical-comedy dancing.

With a few exceptions, the dance in American musicals had been done to a rigid formula: one or more "specialty dancers" (they could be tap dancers, acrobatic dancers, or "toe" dancers), who did their routines, generally arranged by themselves or by someone who had no direct connection with the show, and fitted to the music, and a "line" of chorus dancers who could tap or just dance, but who mainly kicked high and in rhythm with the music.

Balanchine discarded the formula. He selected a *corps* that could really dance and set for it not routines, but dances that had a meaning and stemmed from the plot of the show. They were not interpolated dances, which could be cut out if necessary, but part of the action. For the principals he set at least two dances that advanced the action, helped to tell the story of the play. One of these, for Geva and Demetrius Villan, was a hilarious parody of *Scheherazade;* the other was the never-to-be-forgotten "Slaughter on Tenth Avenue," for Geva and Bolger, which became a classic of ballet in musical comedy.

When *On Your Toes* was about to open in Boston, Wiman showed a proof of the house program to Balanchine to see whether he was satisfied with his credit line, which read: "Dance director George Balanchine."

Balanchine told Wiman that the line should read "Choreography by George Balanchine," as he had created ballets for the show rather than just directing numbers. Wiman was afraid that the public would not understand the meaning of the word, but agreed when Balanchine pointed out that the audience might be interested in the unfamiliar word, and that anyway it was high time audiences learned the word and began to understand the difference between choreography and dance direction. It was in this manner that the words "choreography by" made their first appearance in a program of an American musical comedy.

When *On Your Toes* opened at the Imperial Theater, New York, on April 11, it won the acclaim of public and press alike. It established a precedent for a number of most successful "spring" musicals by the same producers, and dislodged, probably forever, the formula of specialties-plus-high-kicks from Broadway shows. The wholehearted co-operation of the producer, the absence of backstage intrigue and constant complaints, the sympathetic attitude of the entire cast, created a wonderful release for Balanchine.

Meanwhile, just across the street from the Imperial Theater, the regular 1935-6 season of the Metropolitan Opera was drawing to a close, and the opera management, much to

the surprise of the direction of the ballet, was not telling them
that the American Ballet would be at liberty come autumn.
Far from firing the ballet company, Johnson agreed to let
Balanchine stage an opera, Gluck's *Orpheus and Eurydice*, during the spring season.

The spring season was an innovation introduced by Edward Johnson. It was held after the "official," or glamorous,
opera season with the idea of popularizing opera by attracting
the people who could not afford to pay the high prices for
tickets during the regular season. Ticket prices for the spring
season were at 25 cents to $3, and seats were made available to
the general public without a preferential subscription plan.

It is still not clear how the Metropolitan management
risked making the daring decision to let Balanchine stage an
opera. Did Johnson actually wish to experiment within the
sacrosanct premises of the Metropolitan and bring the audiences something "young, fresh and novel"? Did he decide,
perchance, to give Balanchine, Kirstein, *et al.*, the proverbial
"enough rope"? Or was he influenced in his decision by Edward Warburg's offer to assume half of the cost of the production? It was probably a combination of all these elements, or
perhaps an entirely different motive. Whatever it was, Johnson agreed to permit Balanchine to stage *Orpheus* in a novel
way: with the singers in the orchestra pit and the dancers on
the stage.

In Kirstein's words: "We were, naturally, all eager to put
into immediate action all our theatrical ideas we had developed from Diaghilev's days to our tenure at the Metropolitan, concerning the proper contemporary presentation of
lyric drama. These ideas were in essence revolutionary, and
hence, unsuitable for the Metropolitan. The Metropolitan is
scarcely the place for experiment, even in an 'experimental'
spring season. We knew that at the time, but there was little
enough to lose and everything to gain by going ahead.

"After considerable study and discussion of the legend of Orpheus and Eurydice, we decided to present what was most living for our epoch in the Orphic myth. We saw it as the eternal domestic tragedy of an artist and his wife, with Love himself a male angelic embodiment, with real feather wings and real muscles for flying, not a girl androgyne, which was the tradition of the Paris Opéra. Balanchine had also suggested that the singer who sang the role of Orpheus while Lew Christensen danced should not have a woman's voice, in the Franco-Italian tradition of the *castrati*, but instead be a tenor. This replacement had long since been achieved in Russian theaters. Instead, the Metropolitan permitted the dancer to be a male (which Paris still refuses), but insisted his voice should remain female.

"We saw Hell as a concentration camp with flying military slave drivers lashing forced labor; the Elysian Fields as an ether drama, a desiccated bone-dry limbo of suspended animation, and Paradise as the eternity we know from a Planetarium arrayed on the astronomical patterns of contemporary celestial science.

"The movement was danced and mimed in some of Balanchine's most accomplished erotic patterns, touching and electric encounters, and noble plastic groups. In his love-knots and amorous garlands, Attic vase-drawings, and not polite dancing-school scarf-dances, had really come to life. Pavel Tchelitchew's scenery and costumes, which in tonality and atmosphere recalled Masaccio, Piero della Francesca, and our everyday work-clothes, clad pseudo-Elysian mysteries equal in dignity and grandeur to Gluck's superb score."

Pavel Tchelitchew's participation in the early stages of the development of the America Ballet was much more active and fruitful than shows on the surface. The few sets and costumes that he designed for the company were only outward manifestations of his work with the ballet. Of much greater importance was his intangible but direct influence on Balanchine and Kirstein in their approach to ballet as a whole, especially during the first, tentative, and direction-searching steps.

A great painter and scenic designer, an artist of genius and impeccable taste, he did much to help formulate the artistic credo the company holds to this day. He was also instrumental in breaking down the isolation of Kirstein and Balanchine during the early years of the company. It was Tchelitchew more than any other single person who created a semblance of entourage for the ballet without which no artistic organization can long endure.

Orpheus and Eurydice was the second work he did for the American Ballet. The first was *Errante*, which had been originally designed for Les Ballets 1933 and was later somewhat altered for the American Ballet.

The *première* of *Orpheus and Eurydice* took place on May 22, on a bill with *Cavalleria Rusticana*. *Orpheus* was the nearest to what the French call a *succès de scandale*, so dear to the heart of Diaghilev, whom it allowed to stand up in his box and shout in a high and penetrating voice that rose above the din of the current *scandale: "Mesdames et Messieurs, laisser achever le spectacle, s'il vous plaît!"*

But New York is not Paris.

The audience did not stand up and shout and hiss. Beyond a few titters during the performance, it behaved quietly. It did not like *Orpheus*, and that was all there was to it. The *scandale* came later in the offices of the Metropolitan Opera Association and on the pages of the New York newspapers, especially the *Times*.

Olin Downes, music critic of *The New York Times*, wrote in the May 23 issue of that paper: "It [the choreography] is absurd as interpretation of the opera. It is ugly and futile, impudent and meddlesome, wholly ineffective in performance.

There is no genuine relation whatever between the style of the pantomime and the style of the opera.

"There is far-fetched and ridiculous manoeuvring on the stage. Were it not inevitable that Mr. Balanchine and his confreres had made some study of Gluck's score it would be hard to believe that they had ever looked at it seriously. They have evolved an arbitrary and vaguely symbolic choreography which in no true sense represents either score or libretto. They had an opportunity to show what modern and profoundly considered choreographic interpretation of a master work could be. They have misused this opportunity in a way which is patently unjust to the opera.

"The scenic setting is equally absurd. There is no good reason to discuss it in detail, but it is to be added that there is hardly any excuse, even in the name of original experiment, for this mannered, uninventive and incongruous fabrication being presented on the Metropolitan stage.

"The writer is perfectly aware that certain sophisticates and dilettantes of the operatic stage will claim the contrary, and accuse him, as they do those who disagree with them, of blindness, antagonism, prejudice and all the rest of it. If there were not such deep thinkers among us the ballet seen last night would not have reached the stage. It is, however, simple fact that this production, so far as the stage and the choreography are concerned, is plain bad—bad and dull, bad and unconducive to any appreciation of the real nature of Gluck's opera. It is therefore a kind of pretentious dilettantism that is superfluous. . . ."

In trying to explain the failure of *Orpheus* in *Blast at Ballet*, Kirstein had many a bitter word to say about the audience, the management, and the critics. Most of what he said was true: some of it applied to some of the people involved, some to others. But because he made his accusations general rather than specific, his arguments were just as unfair and just as

invalid as what the critics and the management and the public
said about *Orpheus*.

Here is an example: "The critics loathed it because it
made them think. Rather, it didn't quite make them, because
most of them were incapable of the function. However, the
act of thought was indicated, and they punished us for their
incapacity to face it."

Had Kirstein written about *Orpheus* in 1936 or in 1952, he
would not have said this. But in 1938 he was, as we shall see,
angry enough, embittered enough, and unreasonable enough
to say that and more.

Actually, the reasons for the failure of *Orpheus* were much
simpler and a good deal less sinister. An analysis will indicate
two of them:

Balanchine, Kirstein, and Tchelitchew were ahead of
their time, much more so, in fact, than they had been the year
before when choosing the repertoire for the first New York
performances of the American Ballet. *Orpheus* was not only a
revolution in ballet and ballet décor, but also a revolution in
the entire conception of the lyric theater, the most conservative branch of the stage, and New York was simply not ready
for it either in experience or in taste. This, of course, is not to
say that they should not have done it. Whether the Metropolitan, its audience, and the music critics will admit it or
not, *Orpheus* effectively paved the way for many of the experiments and reforms the Metropolitan or the New York City
Opera have had in the past sixteen years. But the American
Ballet should have been prepared for the failure of *Orpheus*,
and should have taken it in better grace.

The other reason for the failure was the very fact that
Orpheus had been done at the Metropolitan during an opera
season. The point here is that the opera audience is basically
anti-balletic; and this applies to the box-holders and sub-

scribers as well as to the frequenters of the upper regions of the
Metropolitan or the standees. The majority of them at best is
not interested in ballet and knows nothing about it, at worst
considers ballet on the same level as acrobatics and ice-skat-
ing. One has only to attend performances of opera and of
ballet to see that as a group the two audiences are entirely
different in temperament, artistic inclination, and general
interest. Certainly, there are people interested in both art
forms, but these are in such a small minority that they cannot
be considered here. This is the reason why ballets given at the
Metropolitan on programs with short operas never receive
any kind of response from the audience, except at children's
matinees, when the young and uninhibited spectators accept
ballet at its face value and enjoy it immensely. This is the reason, incidentally, why the directors of the Metropolitan do not
realize the attraction ballet has for non-opera audiences and
cannot understand why some people talk about the advisability of having separate ballet evenings at the Metropolitan.
They never see any other ballet except that which is danced as
part of the opera or given on a bill with the opera, for the
opera audience.

And this was the reason why *Orpheus* failed as it did. So
far as the opera audience was concerned, *Orpheus* was not an
opera. There were no pudgy tenors, no overweight sopranos,
no one came forward on the apron for the high C, nary a
mezzo looked at the conductor for a cue, no one flailed his
arms or walked around as if on stilts. It was not opera at all.
Yet they had come to hear an opera. How could they have
been expected to accept *Orpheus?* The American Ballet should
have remembered that there have been few real changes in
opera production since Monteverdi, and that they were not
the ones to bring about a change.

Fortunately for those who saw and appreciated *Orpheus*,

the American Ballet disregarded this truth. Otherwise *Orpheus* might never have been produced, and could never have precipitated the latter-day *Orpheus* to Stravinsky's music, in décor by Noguchi, which Balanchine choreographed for the New York City Ballet some thirteen years later, and which has become one of the greatest ballets of our time.

V

1936–1937

Ballet Caravan; The Stravinsky Festival

The failure of *Orpheus* affected Lincoln Kirstein more than anyone else in the American Ballet. The dancers had done their job rather well and, as is usual, they felt no responsibility for the artistic conception of the work, the basis of its unacceptability to public and press. Balanchine and Tchelitchew, the experienced professionals, took the lack of success in their stride; they had wanted to say something new in the lyric theater and had said it, and if the public and the press were unwilling or unable to appreciate their effort, that was too bad for the public and the press. Edward Warburg, the co-sponsor of *Orpheus*, felt that his investment was worth while; he had made it possible for Balanchine and Tchelitchew to stir up the muddy waters that engulfed the Metropolitan, and it was of little importance to him whether or not the Metropolitan and the public liked the results. But Kirstein, the passionate, uncompromising, inexperienced dilettante turned director of a ballet company, could not take it calmly. He had participated more closely than Warburg in the preparations for *Orpheus* and in the actual day-by-day work of putting it on the stage, and consequently accepted a greater responsibility for its failure, without realizing, just then, the magnificence of the failure. Once again he was certain that the world, his world, had come to an end.

This time the certainty was not based on such simple things as Balanchine's refusal to settle in a provincial city, an early summer rain canceling a performance of a group of students of the School of American Ballet, or the sudden illness of a manager forcing the collapse of a tour. This time the reasons were more serious, more fundamental.

The original plan of Kirstein and Warburg had been to open the School of American Ballet and not start a company until the student body of the School was sufficiently advanced to furnish the dancers. In the estimate of Kirstein, three to five years would be necessary for this process, and then the company would have to make a modest start before it began performances open to the general public, especially in a house like the Metropolitan. This plan was upset by Balanchine, who began rehearsals almost immediately after the opening of the School, when he saw that the School attracted enough professional dancers and advanced students to make performances feasible. The result was that the American Ballet gave its first New York season in March 1935, just eighteen months after the School opened. And now, a little more than a year after the initial season, and less than two and one-half years after the School opened, it had completed its first season in the Metropolitan with the greatest failure any ballet company had ever had in New York. Was this a mere coincidence, or was there a cause-and-effect relation here?

And further, Kirstein's original idea had been to import Balanchine and build around him an American ballet company. A cosmopolitan with a broad outlook and a highly developed taste, whose education and appreciation of art were not the result of mere textbooks and visits to picture galleries and museums, Kirstein felt sure that ballet, developed over three centuries in Europe, could be transplanted to American soil without losing its accumulation of historic, esthetic, and technical fine points, and then be adapted to American conditions, taste, and usage, and not have to start *ab ovo* from a narrowly local aspect and a primitive conception of national art. Was his original idea basically wrong? Was John Martin right when he sarcastically dubbed the American Ballet "Ballet Americain," accused it of being founded on Riviera esthetics, and later suggested that Kirstein shake hands with Balanchine and begin building a true American ballet? Were Martin and the others who sided with him right? Perhaps the formula for a real, successful American ballet did lie in the nationality of the choreographers, dancers, composers, and painters. Perhaps a true American ballet should be built in the extreme way suggested by Ted Shawn.

Kirstein was not sure. The American ballet that he had helped to build on his own plans was apparently not working out. True, the Metropolitan management renewed the contract with the American Ballet for the 1936–7 season. But it was also true that the American Ballet was at the Metropolitan on sufferance, and, anyway, it had not achieved what Kirstein had hoped for it. And another consideration: how were the dancers to exist between opera seasons? The Metropolitan season then ran some six months. How would the dancers eat the other six months?

What was he to do?

He had the alternatives of withdrawing from active participation in ballet, reverting to his status of writer and observer, or of starting a new enterprise, this time based not on his ideas of 1933, but on what he thought he had learned since then, through actual experience. He chose the second alternative.

Early in June 1936, Kirstein organized a small troupe of dancers from the American Ballet and advanced students from the School and gave them the name Ballet Caravan. The dancers included Ruby Asquith, Ruthanna Boris, Gisella Caccialanza, Rabana Hasburgh, Alibia Kavan, Annabelle Lyon, Hannah Moore, Harold and Lew Christensen, Erick Hawkins, Charles Laskey, and Eugene Loring. The young American dancers were to dance in ballets created by young American choreographers: Lew Christensen, Douglas Coudy, William Dollar, and Eugene Loring.

Frances Hawkins, a puritanical, clear-headed, and efficient young woman who had been connected with the Pond Lecture Bureau and had managed tours of Martha Graham and Harold Kreutzberg, was engaged as manager.

Kirstein plunged into work with, if possible, an even greater abandon than he had displayed at the American Ballet. He helped choose the repertoire, wrote scenarios for ballets, discussed costumes with designers and choreographers, attended rehearsals, seemed to be in three places at once. It was to be his show from the beginning.

He realized that he had a small company and could not compete (nor did he want to) with the Ballet Russe de Monte Carlo or even the American Ballet. Pageantry, full stages of dancers, sumptuous décor, orchestras, everything connected with a big ballet company, was out of the question.

"We needed," he said later, "something that would seem familiar to our hoped-for audiences, something with which they could feel at home, and yet something in which our specifically American-styled dancers could be shown to their best advantage. The familiarity of our subject matter must never duplicate the familiarity of the Russian formula. The American classic style should never be dulled by a veneer of Russian glamour."

The repertoire of the first season of the Ballet Caravan was only partly American: it had one ballet on an American theme, *Pocahontas*, to Elliott Carter, Jr.'s music. The other ballets had a strong European tinge, though they were entirely in music or subject matter free from any Russian influence, which Kirstein apparently wanted to avoid.

Lew Christensen staged two ballets: *Encounter*, to Mozart's "Haffner" Serenade, in costumes by Forrest Thayr, Jr.; and *Pocahontas*, a ballet-pantomime, based on a scenario by Kirstein, to music by Elliott Carter, Jr., in costumes by Karl Free after the drawings of John White. William Dollar choreographed *Promenade*, to Maurice Ravel's *Valses nobles et sentimentales*, in costumes after designs entitled *Merveilleuses et Incroyables* by the French painter Horace Vernet. Douglas Coudy mounted *Folk Dance*, a character divertissement, to music selected from Emmanuel Chabrier's compositions. Eugene Loring arranged *Harlequin for President*, a ballet-pantomime in the style of the *commedia dell'arte*, based on a scenario by Kirstein, to music from the sonatas of Domenico Scarlatti, arranged by Ariadna Mikeshina, in costumes by Keith Martin.

Only Dollar had had any choreographic experience—his *Chopin Concerto* was in the repertoire of the American Ballet. For the other three choreographers these were their maiden efforts.

The ballets were prepared in six weeks, a record of a sort, especially considering that the choreographers did not really know how to work with a company and the dancers themselves had only limited experience. Frances Hawkins had succeeded

in booking twenty-five performances at summer sessions of
New England colleges, in New York, and in a few other cities.
The initial performance was set for July 17 at Bennington College, Bennington, Vermont, then the center of modern dance
in the East, and consequently as anti-balletic a place as one
could find.

The ideological and esthetic differences between the
modern dance and the ballet were more pronounced then than
they are now. Modern dancers, and especially choreographers
and theorists, were actually belligerent toward the ballet, as
perhaps they had good reason to be, and they did not care
whether they showed it. So the debut at Bennington involved,
or seemed to involve, a certain risk. Kirstein and the dancers
did not quite know what sort of risk, and everyone concerned
was nervous, expecting a hostile reception as a matter of principle.

Said Kirstein: "The debut was a nightmare, although the
Bennington audience was a great deal more patient, tolerant
and interested than many people for whom we would dance
when we became better known."

But what *première* has not been a "nightmare" for Kirstein?

Actually the *première* went fairly smoothly and, considering the anti-balletic feeling of the spectators, the Ballet
Caravan had a good if not overwhelming success. Other performances followed the pattern established in Bennington: no
great receptions but interested acceptance and a certain
tolerance toward a domestic product. While the company
toured, Frances Hawkins succeeded in getting additional
bookings, so that when the tour ended in December the company had chalked up thirty-eight performances, which paid
all the touring expenses. An interesting highlight of the tour
was the reaction of the manager of a chain of motion-picture
theaters in New England. Feeling the competition of the nu-

merous summer playhouses in his territory, he signed the
company to appear on the stages of his theaters in lieu of the
usual films. The spectators gave the company cordial receptions.

Toward the end of the season, on October 31 and November 1, the Ballet Caravan appeared in the Kaufmann Auditorium of the Young Men's Hebrew Association (the so-called
"92nd Street Y") in New York, which, much like Bennington
College, was a stronghold of the modern dance. The company
played in competition, as it were, to the Ballet Russe de
Monte Carlo, which was having its season at the Metropolitan
Opera House. The Caravan performances did not empty out
the Metropolitan, but on the other hand, they did not suffer
much from the Russian opposition, except that they had few
"real" balletomanes in the audience. But Kirstein did not
want them, anyway.

The first tour of the Ballet Caravan came to an end in
early December, and Kirstein summarized it thus:

"The first season was not of much interest except to the
dancers and myself. It was more of a hard vacation than work,
a feeling-out for our future."

My personal memory of this first season recalls a certain
a-theatricality, an over-all dryness and coldness. There was
creditable, even slick, dancing; most of the ballets, though
rather tenuous and tentative, had craftsmanship, if not real
talent, about them; but that was all. There was no *élan*, no
humor (except a not very successful attempt at *commedia
dell'arte* in Loring's *Harlequin for President*), no warmth. Everybody seemed to be trying hard, too hard, to give a performance. But there was little of a performance in what they did,
which was rather an exhibition that could not fire, enchant,
or even seriously interest. To put it simply: it was no ballet.
One was glad at the success of the youngsters, but that was as
far as one went.

After the tour, the dancers who had been with the American Ballet the previous season rejoined it for rehearsals for the Metropolitan Opera season, which was scheduled to begin December 21. The Caravan was laid off until the spring.

The personnel of the American Ballet for the 1937–8 season was officially listed as follows:

Artistic director, choreographer, and maître de ballet, George Balanchine; assistant to Balanchine, William Dollar; *premier danseur*, Anatole Vilzak; company manager, Douglas Coudy. Premiers: Leda Anchutina, Kathryn Mullowny, William Dollar—classic; Ruthanna Boris—character; Daphne Vane, Charles Laskey—modern. Soloists: Gisella Caccialanza, Rabana Hasburgh, Holly Howard, Annabelle Lyon, Elise Reiman, Lew Christensen—classic; Kyra Blank, Madeline Leweck, Monna Montez, Joseph Levinoff—character; Heidi Vosseler—modern. Ensemble: Ruby Asquith, Jane Burkhalter, Ann Campbell. Hortense Kahrklin, Albia Kavan, Marjorie Matlin, Hannah Moore, Lillian Moore, Yvonne Patterson, Felicia Perlman, Micheline Petolas, Vera Volkenau, Hilda Wagner, Harold Christensen, Douglas Coudy, Iolas Coutsoudis, Erick Hawkins, Joseph Lane, Eugene Loring, Serge Temoff, George Volodine. After the season opened, the company engaged the Mexican-born Spanish dancer Maclovia Ruiz for performances in *Carmen* and *Lakmé*.

The distinction between premiers and soloists in classic ballet and those in modern ballet was never clear to anyone and was never explained. The difference between classic dancers and character dancers was also very slight, as was the difference between soloists and ensemble. But that was how the personnel was announced.

The first ballet of the season was *The Bat*, given on the afternoon of December 24 on a bill with *Hansel and Gretel*, as custom dictated. Of the new operas announced two required the services of the American Ballet: *Caponsacchi* (Richard

Hageman) and *Il Matrimonio Segreto* (Domenico Cimarosa).
Revivals included *Samson et Dalila*, *Le Coq d'Or*, and *La
Gioconda*.

The second season opened and proceeded rather placidly.
The Opera did not change its attitude toward the ballet
company, nor the ballet company its attitude toward the
Opera management, but there were no upheavals.

The only pyrotechnical, and one must add refreshing,
interlude in which anyone from the American Ballet was involved concerned Lincoln Kirstein and took place outside the
Metropolitan. It actually had no relation to the story of the
American Ballet, and is recorded here only because it helps
to explain the personality of Kirstein, without whom there is
no story of the American Ballet.

At that time New York had a Dance Project, a part of
the Theater Project, a division of the Work Projects Administration. Hallie Flanagan was the head of the Theater Project,
with offices in Washington. Don Oscar Becque was Supervisor
and Managing Producer of the Dance Project in New York.
The Dance Project, which made it possible for some two
hundred dancers to eat and to do a little work in their field,
was a hotbed of politics and intrigue. Most of the dancers on
the Project were modern dancers, and Helen Tamiris, one of
the choreographers on the Project, had much to say about the
whole Project—and did.

Don Oscar Becque resigned his post at the beginning of
December, and Hallie Flanagan was faced with the necessity
of appointing a new supervisor. She appealed to Kirstein.
Kirstein talked it over with several of his friends, and though
nearly all of them advised him not to go near the Project, he
decided to accept the position on a volunteer basis. He made
it clear that he would assume no administrative duties, but
would confine himself to co-ordinating the activities of the
several choreographers on the Project, among them Doris

Humphrey, Charles Weidman, Tamiris, Gluck-Sandor, Becque, and Arthur Mahoney. His plan was to produce a huge spectacle in which all choreographers and their groups would participate. The pageantlike spectacle was given a working title, *The History of American Dance*.

Cynics gave Kirstein one month on the Project. They pointed out that he was a "ballet man" whereas five of the six choreographers on the Project were modern dancers, and that their basic difference in approach doomed *a priori* the new supervisor's plan.

The cynics were wrong: Kirstein lasted just one day. He took his job on January 2, 1937, met once with the choreographers under his supervision, and resigned in the evening.

The official reason for his resignation was that the choreographers of the Project could not accept his plan because they wanted to see theatrical productions of the works they had been rehearsing for a long time and therefore refused to release their dancers for Kirstein's spectacle. Actually, the choreographic staff accused Kirstein of being actively anti-modern-dance and just did not want to work with him. Kirstein realized that he could do nothing under such circumstances.

At the only meeting he had with the choreographers he outlined in detail the plan for the production of *The History of American Dance*, and in the course of it turned to Tamiris, saying: "And you, Miss Tamiris, will dance Isadora Duncan."

To which Tamiris replied: "And who, Mr. Kirstein, will dance Tamiris?"

And that was the end of Lincoln Kirstein's twelve-hour tenure of the post of Supervisor of the New York Dance Project (WPA).

Meanwhile the American Ballet was beginning its preparations for a Stravinsky Festival in the spring—three Balanchine ballets to Stravinsky's music. Two of the ballets would

be taken from the Stravinsky repertoire; the third was commissioned by Warburg from Stravinsky especially for these
performances. Mindful of the failure of *Orpheus* the year before,
the Metropolitan did not wish to participate in the sponsorship of the performances. More than that, it would not present
them during the spring season. The American Ballet would
have to go alone on the plan.

The ballets selected for the performances were *Apollon
Musagète*, *Le Baiser de la Fée*, and *Card Party*. *Apollon Musagète*,
which had been commissioned by Mrs. Elizabeth Sprague
Coolidge in 1927, and which was originally performed at the
Library of Congress, Washington, D. C., in April 1928, with
choreography by Adolph Bolm, had had its *première* in the
Diaghilev company at the Théâtre Sarah Bernhardt, Paris, on
June 12, 1928, with choreography by Balanchine and with
Serge Lifar as Apollo and Alexandra Danilova (alternating
with Alice Nikitina), Lubov Tchernitcheva, and Felia Dubrovska as the Three Muses. *Le Baiser de la Fée*, originally commissioned by Ida Rubinstein for presentation at the Paris
Opéra in 1928, had initially had choreography by Bronislava Nijinska, who subsequently (1933) redid it at the Teatro
Colón, Buenos Aires, and later had had choreography by
Frederick Ashton (1935) for the Sadler's Wells company in
London. *The Card Party* (*Jeu de Cartes*) was the new ballet commissioned by Warburg.

Kirstein was against the Balanchine-Stravinsky performances from the very first. He felt that Stravinsky was universally recognized as a great dance-musician, that he had received his due from all Europe, and that he would never lack
a chance to produce his own ballets. He also thought that all
three ballets chosen were, each in a different way, retardative.
He found an ally in Vladimir Dimitriew.

Dimitriew was opposed to the Stravinsky performances
for a different reason. He was afraid of another failure, and

failures of the American Ballet had unpleasant financial repercussions on the School of American Ballet, of which he was a partner as well as director. He could not explain to every mother that a failure could be as important in the development of the company as a success (he was not convinced of it himself). Generally, he was not in accord with the principles upon which the company was run.

But Balanchine and Warburg decided to have the performances anyway, and Kirstein, his objection made known, did all that he could to assist them.

To begin with they induced Igor Stravinsky, then living in Paris, to come to New York to conduct the performances; then they rented the Metropolitan Opera House for the evenings of April 27 and 28, 1937, for what was to be called a Stravinsky Festival, and engaged seventy members of the New York Philharmonic-Symphony Orchestra to play for the performances. The Concert Management Arthur Judson (a division of Columbia Concerts Corporation) was charged with the managerial details of running the two performances.

Stewart Chaney was commissioned to design the scenery and costumes for *Apollon Musagète;* Irene Sharaff those for *The Card Party*, and Alice Halicka those for *Le Baiser de la Fée.*

The roles were distributed as follows:

in *Apollon Musagète:* Apollo, Lew Christensen; Calliope, Daphne Vane; Polyhymnia, Holly Howard; Terpsichore, Elise Reiman;

in *The Card Party:* Joker, William Dollar; Kings, Lew Christensen, Joseph Lane, Douglas Coudy, Erick Hawkins; Queens, Annabelle Lyon, Leda Anchutina, Ariel Lang (who had changed her name from Helen Leitch), Hortense Kahrklin; Jacks, Charles Laskey, Joseph Levinoff, Eugene Loring, Serge Temoff;

in *Le Baiser de la Fée:* Fairy, Kathryn Mullowny; Bride, Gisella Caccialanza; Friend, Leda Anchutina; Bridegroom,

William Dollar; Mother, Annabelle Lyon; Shadow, Rabana Hasburgh.

Stravinsky arrived in New York in March, and not only took a lively interest in the production of the ballets, but gave interviews to the press, posed for publicity pictures, and tried to do everything he could to help the American Ballet in its ambitious project. He attended most of the rehearsals, especially those of *The Card Party*. It was a new ballet, and in addition he, as an inveterate poker-player, thought that he could be of "technical" assistance to Balanchine, who knew little about card games.

Writing in *Stravinsky in the Theatre*, Kirstein says: "The creation of Jeu de Cartes was a complete collaboration (with Balanchine). Stravinsky would appear punctually at rehearsals and stay for six hours. In the evenings he would take the pianist home with him and work further on the tempi. He always came meticulously apparelled in suede shoes, marvelous checked suits, beautiful ties—the small but perfect dandy, an elegant Parisian version of London tailoring. During successive run-throughs of the ballet he would slap his knee like a metronome for the dancers, then suddenly interrupt everything, rise and, gesticulating rapidly to emphasize his points, suggest a change. This was never offered tentatively but with the considered authority of complete information.

"Thus at the end of the first deal, where Balanchine had worked out a display of the dancers in a fan-like pattern to simulate cards held in the hand, Stravinsky decided there was too great a prodigality of choreographic invention. Instead of so much variety in the pictures he suggested a repetition of the most effective groupings. . . .

"Before his arrival we had been attracted by the idea of using a set of medieval playing cards and adapting them in all their subtle color and odd fancy to the stage. Forty costumes and the complete scenery were designed before he arrived in

America. Upon seeing the sketches Stravinsky insisted they would place the work in a definite period and evoke a decorative quality not present in his music. He called for the banal colors of a deck of ordinary cards, forms and details as to be immediately recognizable. Stravinsky's precise delimitation gave Irene Sharaff, the designer, a new orientation, and strangely enough a new freedom for clarity and originality."

Probably no other ballet performance in New York was ever more carefully rehearsed or given a more loving presentation than the Stravinsky Festival. It had a brilliant reception by the public and a very good press.

The quality of the performances did not seem to suffer from the interruptions in the rehearsals, which became necessary when the American Ballet went on the spring tour with the Metropolitan Opera in March. Balanchine, too, had to interrupt rehearsals while he choreographed the dances in the Dwight Deere Wiman production of the musical *Babes in Arms*, which went into rehearsal on February 19 and opened in New York on April 14 at the Shubert Theater.

In his *Blast at Ballet*, written a little more than a year after the Stravinsky Festival, Kirstein underestimated both the success of the Festival and its results.

"The congratulations," he said, "were colossal, Stravinsky beamed, and the result was completely zero, although it did prove the American Ballet Company was a splendid technical organism. For me, however, it was a triumph in a vacuum. . . . The only tangible result of the Stravinsky Festival seemed to be that the American Ballet did return to the Metropolitan in the fall of 1937 for its third and final year."

Here Kirstein's usual perspicacity and broad horizon failed him. Still embittered by the failure of *Orpheus* and the general attitude of the Metropolitan's management toward the American Ballet, he did not see that the Stravinsky Fes-

tival, presented to a ballet public (as opposed to an opera
public) who could and did appreciate it, was a portent of the
role the American Ballet was to play in ballet in America and,
later, in Europe. Here were the first independent performances of the American Ballet since its rather tentative debut
in March 1935, two years before, performances that showed
the growth and early maturity of the company, its ability to
perform choreographically and musically the most complicated works, and a sincere and serious acceptance by the
public.

Kirstein is not being blamed here for his failure to realize
the significance of the Stravinsky Festival at the time. Such
blame at this time could be justifiably charged to my hind-
sight. It should be recorded, however, that Kirstein's faith in
the American Ballet and, at least inferentially, in Balanchine
was not so deep as it had been in 1933 and 1935. In fact,
Kirstein was probably more depressed about the American
Ballet in the fall of 1938, when his *Blast at Ballet* was published,
than he had been in the spring of 1937.

The jubilation of the American Ballet at the success of
the Stravinsky Festival was increased by the realization that
despite the considerable cost of the performances the company had almost broken even, a rare achievement in ballet.
Warburg was not particularly worried about losing money on
the venture. When the performances were over he effectively
wiped out all possibility of breaking even by giving a sizable
bonus to every dancer in the company.

VI

1938

Ballet Caravan: Second Season

Soon after the Stravinsky Festival, twenty-five dancers of the American Ballet, headed by Balanchine, left for Hollywood to appear in the *Goldwyn Follies* of 1938, a "colossal" song-and-dance film. Samuel Goldwyn, impressed with Balanchine's work in *On Your Toes* (not, one could guess, with *Orpheus*), had invited the choreographer to stage the dances in his *Follies*. Balanchine was flattered by the invitation, but insisted that the dancers be recruited from the American Ballet. Goldwyn agreed to Balanchine's demand, and after preliminary screen tests in New York the dancers were selected. Vera Zorina, then a star of the London production of *On Your Toes*, and before that a soloist in the Ballet

90

Russe de Monte Carlo, was imported from England as the ballerina. William Dollar was given the leading male role. The ensemble included Leda Anchutina, Gisella Caccialanza, Holly Howard, Hortense Kahrklin, Helen Leitch (Ariel Lang), Madeleine Leweck, Annabelle Lyon, Marjorie Matlin, Hannah Moore, Lillian Moore, Kathryn Mullowny, Yvonne Patterson, Micheline Petolas, Elise Reiman, Maclovia Ruiz, Daphne Vane, Heidi Vosseler, Hilda Wagner, Joseph Lane, Charles Laskey, Joseph Levinoff, Jack Potteiger, Jack Quinn, Serge Temoff, and George Volodine.

The dancers spent a very pleasant five months in Hollywood, had a good time, and earned some money. Balanchine staged a spectacular "water-lily" ballet, in which Zorina came out of a real pool bone-dry, and a very amusing parody on *Romeo and Juliet*, much of which remained on the cutting-room floor. Balanchine's choreography was a radical innovation for Hollywood, which up to then had doggedly stuck to the safe routines staged by local dance-directors and tap dancers.

Kirstein did not go Hollywood. In early May he resigned from the board of directors of the American Ballet to devote himself entirely to Ballet Caravan and the School. Warburg and Balanchine, at the same time, resigned from the board of directors of the School. It was an amicable division of responsibility and of interest.

In February Kirstein had begun preparations for the second season of the Ballet Caravan. Frances Hawkins began booking the young company at the same time. Together they planned to have a troupe of eighteen dancers and a repertoire of eight ballets.

By March, Kirstein had still other plans. He wanted to rent a Broadway theater for five or six consecutive Sundays, beginning December 5, and organize a dance season in New York. The Ballet Caravan would present at least four performances, Martha Graham and her group another four. One evening or more would be given over to a new composition by Graham on an American theme which would be danced by members of her group and the Caravan ensemble. Other performances would feature tap dancer Paul Draper, supported by the Caravan ensemble, in Bach's Double Violin Concerto (which music Balanchine used later for his *Concerto Barocco*), choreographed by Balanchine. Balanchine would also stage Stravinsky's *L'Histoire d'un soldat* for the Caravan, and Eric Satie's *Parade* for Harald Kreutzberg, who would be a guest artist. Composer Louis Horst (then accompanist and musical director of the Martha Graham group) would stage a set of pre-classic dances for a combined group of Graham girls and Caravan boys. It was also hoped that Frederick Ashton would come from London to choreograph one or two ballets for the Caravan.

As if that were not enough, Kirstein also planned to present a number of chamber operas, among them Henry Brant's and Cecil Helmy's *Miss O'Grady*, Aaron Copland's *The Second Hurricane*, and Darius Milhaud's "Minute" operas.

A fifteen-piece orchestra, directed by a young American conductor was to play for the entire season.

This ambitious plan did not materialize at the time. Kirstein in 1937, like Balanchine in 1935, was ahead of his time. But the plan contained the germ and the *modus operandi* upon which Ballet Society was to be built nearly a decade later. It also contained a clear indication that Kirstein's preoccupation with Americana, sincere as it had been, was of an episodic nature. This is the more interesting because Ballet Caravan itself was never just an episode in Kirstein's struggle to build an American ballet, whatever its name.

According to Kirstein, Ballet Caravan was in microcosm a permanent laboratory for classic dancing by, with, and for

Americans, which served as a fountainhead for further development of ballet in America and, as later events will show, in Europe as well.

In 1938 we find Kirstein writing in *Blast at Ballet:*

"The American classic style should never be dulled by a veneer of Russian glamor. Just as there is always a literary diction like Tennyson's as opposed to lyric speech created from the vernacular of our own epoch, by poets like W. B. Yeats or A. E. Housman, so is there an opera-house post-Imperial ballet-ballet style in dancing as differentiated from that simple stage elegance which always distinguishes a true classic dancing-artist, whether he or she be Russian, Polish, Danish, French or American. . . .

"The style of the Russian dancers whom we are now privileged to see, echoes the faded aristocracy of the Imperial schools or its Parisian reflection. The style is not a simple affectation. It is an accurate reflection, and for thirty years has framed the most intense and vital lyric theatre we have had.

"The American style will not imitate the Russian, but instead be its equivalent for our time and place. Our legitimate reflection of a Democracy is of necessity not distant, but immediately intimate. There is pride in both styles, the awareness of the human body in all of its super-human released essential energy. . . . American style springs or should spring from our own training and environment. . . . Ours is also the style bred from basket-ball courts, track and swimming meets and junior proms."

Of the four ballets produced for the second season of the Ballet Caravan three were on American themes.

Yankee Clipper, subtitled *A Ballet-Voyage* in one act, was choreographed by Eugene Loring to music by Paul Bowles, in costumes by Charles Rain. It told the story of a farmer boy who goes to sea, visits many strange countries, and returns to his Quaker girl, only to find that he cannot remain at home and be happy.

Show Piece, A Ballet-Workout in one act, was choreographed by Erick Hawkins to music by Robert McBride, in costumes by Keith Martin. It was a divertissement designed to give the soloists of the troupe an opportunity to do complicated and effective dancing.

Filling Station, A Ballet-Document in one act, was staged by Lew Christensen to music by Virgil Thomson, in costumes and décor by Paul Cadmus. It was the most ambitious work of the season, and as the title implied dealt with events that did or could happen in a roadside filling station.

The one non-American work on the program was Douglas Coudy's *Folk Dance*, a suite of character dances to Emmanuel Chabrier's pieces, in costumes by Charles Rain, which had been planned for, but not done, the previous season.

Yankee Clipper, Show Piece, and *Folk Dance* were planned for the summer season, *Filling Station* for some time in autumn or winter.

Rehearsals began early in May for an opening in July. As the Caravan was scheduled to continue touring past the beginning of the Metropolitan season, the dancers could not combine work in the Caravan and the American Ballet. Consequently Ruby Asquith, Ruthanna Boris, Albia Kavan, Harold and Lew Christensen, Douglas Coudy, Erick Hawkins, and Eugene Loring left the American Ballet to stay with the Caravan, and one dancer, Rabana Hasburgh, remained with the Caravan until November and then returned to the American Ballet.

The company now included the following dancers: Marie Jeanne Pelus, Rabana Hasburgh, Ruthanna Boris (soloists); Ruby Asquith, Jane Doering, Mary Heater, Albia Kavan,

Lorna London, Marjorie Munson, Helen Stuart, Dorothy
Tucker, Audrey White (ensemble); and the men: Harold
Christensen, Lew Christensen, Douglas Coudy, Fred Danieli,
Erick Hawkins, Eugene Loring. Lew Christensen was named
ballet master, Douglas Coudy company manager.

The season opened July 11, and on July 19 and 20 the
company danced at the Robin Hood Dell in Philadelphia, accompanied by a symphony orchestra for the first time in its
career. The tour on the whole was very successful.

Ann Barzel, reviewing the Robin Hood Dell performances in *Dance Magazine* (September 1937) wrote: "There is
much to commend about the Ballet Caravan, but outstanding
is the general good taste that pervades the entire enterprise.
There is always evidence of Lincoln Kirstein's intelligent
guiding hand. The girls in the company are lovely, the boys
well-built, the choreography clever, the music good and the
costumes artistic; but what predominates is the dance. Never
have I seen such finished work. Not only is it perfect, but it is
imbued with qualities that make even the lowly and elemen-
tary glissade a thing of beauty, while the flashier pas of the
ballet vocabulary literally sparkle. . . . All the dither about
personality and the American artist is further dispelled with
the emergence of Marie Jeanne Pelus, one of the young
dancers with the Ballet Caravan. Hers is a strangely compell-
ing presence which, added to her superb technical equipment
makes her an exciting performer to watch."

The summer season ended in mid-August. After a short
vacation, the company began rehearsals for its fall season,
which opened November 1 in Boston. Washington and New
York were also on the itinerary; the Caravan was beginning to
come out of its barnstorming era. On December 12 it appeared in New York on the program called "An Evening of
Ballet," an event in the ambitious Dance International festival and exposition held at Rockefeller Center. The com-

pany danced in the huge Center Theatre and presented
Erick Hawkins's *Show Piece*, not the best choice for the occasion. It was a rather dull and uninspiring divertissement that
meant nothing to the people who had never seen the Caravan
before. On December 27 and on January 2, 1938, the company appeared in the series of the Young Men's Hebrew Association and Students' Dance Recitals, respectively.

January 6, 1938, was a very important date in the history
of the Ballet Caravan: the *première* of Lew Christensen's *Filling
Station* at the Avery Memorial in Hartford, Connecticut,
jointly sponsored by the Wadsworth Atheneum and an organization bearing the fascinating name of Friends and Enemies of Modern Music. *Show Piece* and *Yankee Clipper* were also
on this program.

At the time Lincoln Kirstein attached great importance
to *Filling Station*. Here, he thought, was an indigenous modern
fairy tale, the American answer, as it were, to *Sleeping Beauty*
and *Swan Lake*. Mac, the filling-station attendant, was the
modern American Prince Charming, the rich girl our Princess
Aurora, the gangster the Evil Genius or the Fairy Carabosse
(take your choice), and so on. He never said it in so many
words, but one got the distinct impression that Kirstein hoped
that the comic-strip-like *Filling Station* would replace for American spectators the fairy-tale ballets of other companies.

For its period in American ballet *Filling Station* was an
excellent work. But it could not alter the daydreams that
Sleeping Beauty induced in the spectators or dry up the enchantment of *Swan Lake*, ragged as these ballets may have been even
then.

Here is what I wrote about *Filling Station* in *Dance Magazine* (March 1938): " 'Filling Station' is a concentrated reflection of a day in a typical American filling station complete
with its neon signs, rest rooms, maps, radio sets, and the people
one is apt to meet there. Lew Christensen brought them to-

gether in a balletic tragi-comedy composed with adroit skill and remarkable economy and terseness. Not a single character is superfluous, nor is one missing. And it must have been so tempting and easy to clutter up the stage with an ensemble of more attendants, more truck drivers, more cops, more anybody. Without losing for a moment his close connection with ballet tradition, Lew Christensen fits the separate dances to the characters and uses acrobatic and ballroom dances that deviate from the conventional enchaînements, yet remain within the realm of ballet."

As at the opening of the American Ballet in the same town three years before, a good half of the auditorium was filled with New Yorkers. *Filling Station* was a great success.

Some six weeks later, on February 18, Ballet Caravan made its first New York appearance accompanied by an orchestra. The occasion was the Festival of American Music, sponsored by the WPA Federal Music Project at the Federal Music Theater. The Greenwich Orchestra under Edgar Schenkman played the scores of *Show Piece*, *Yankee Clipper*, and *Filling Station*. The Orchestra did for the Ballet Caravan what no Kirstein, no choreographer could do until then: it revealed the inherent richness of the balletic material in the Caravan productions; it proved the company an artistic self-sustaining young American ballet troupe, independent of great masters of choreography, music, or design.

The theater was sold out to the last seat. There were flowers, ovations, and all the other trimmings of ballet success. Thus the Caravan finished its winter season in a blaze of glory. Even Lincoln Kirstein was satisfied, though he did not permit himself the pleasure of unqualified enjoyment of the success. He said to me at the end of the evening: "Yes, but when will the Caravan have another chance of dancing with an orchestra?"

VII

1938–1939

End of a Phase

The American Ballet finished its Hollywood task by the end of September. It was back in New York and ready for rehearsals in mid-October. Fears that some of the dancers would be lured by Hollywood's fame and money and not return to New York proved groundless. With the exception of two girls who had married, the troupe returned intact.

The roster of dancers for the season 1937–8 included Leda Anchutina and Annabelle Lyon (ballerinas); Gisella Caccialanza, Rabana Hasburgh, Holly Howard, Kathryn Mullowny, Elise Reiman, Kyra Blank, Hortense Kahrklin, Madeline Leweck, Heidi Vosseler (soloists); May Block, Hermione Hawkinson, Lillian Kalin, Anne Lazarewitch, Jane

Moon, Hannah Moore, Lillian Moore, Yvonne Patterson, Micheline Petolas, Lillian Rilley, Eugenia Stepkowska, Adelaide Varicchio, Vera Volkenau, Hilda Wagner (ensemble). The male soloists were William Dollar, André Eglevsky, and Charles Laskey. Paul Godkin, Joseph Levinoff, Serge Temoff, Arthur Frederix, Basil Galakhoff, Joseph Lane, and George Volodin were in the male ensemble. William Dollar was designated as assistant ballet master. Lillian Moore was in charge of the ensemble.

The company was in a happy state when it was about to begin its third season with the Metropolitan. Its spring Stravinsky Festival performances had been a distinct success; its Hollywood sojourn had left little to be desired; it even had an informal promise from Samuel Goldwyn of another film the following summer.

And then came a shock: Edward M. M. Warburg, cofounder with Lincoln Kirstein of the School of American Ballet and the American Ballet company, and director of the company since its inception, resigned in early November.

A schoolmate of Kirstein's at Harvard, Warburg was brought into the ballet field by Kirstein. Kirstein had persuaded Warburg to help him financially when he was planning to bring Balanchine and Dimitriew to the United States and to organize the School of American Ballet. Warburg generously contributed the necessary funds for the venture and stayed with the School and later with the company. While Kirstein and his family subsidized the School, it was Warburg's money that made possible the existence of the company.

Although Warburg was glad to play his part in the establishment and development of ballet in America, his interest in it was never so deep as Kirstein's. In the late summer of 1937 Warburg's father, Felix Warburg, died and left a considerable fund for philanthropic purposes. In his will he requested that Edward undertake the management of the fund.

Edward Warburg told me at the time: "People don't seem to realize that the administration of a large philanthropic estate requires a great deal of thought and time. The fact that money is being spent rather than earned is only a detail. The necessity of careful management is still there. It is a full-time job, and just because I am not getting paid for it there is no excuse to neglect it."

When he resigned a few months later from the American Ballet, Warburg issued a statement which read in part:

"The success of the American Ballet in Hollywood, its growth and reputation resulting from two years' work at the Metropolitan Opera House (climaxed last season by the Stravinsky performances) has placed this organization in a secure and permanent position. This, I feel, warrants my decision to relinquish the reins of administration to the guiding spirit and artistic director, Mr. George Balanchine.

"I came to this conclusion several months ago. The recent sudden death of my father served to intensify my need of more freedom wherever possible in order to devote more time and energy to other communal fields of endeavor. . . .

"During these years it has been simply my task, through proper avenues, to make it possible for Mr. Balanchine to demonstrate our joint convictions. . . . In yielding the directorship of the ballet to Mr. Balanchine, I am confident that the company can now continue without such assistance as I was able to render. . . . Therefore, I now leave this post most regretfully, but with complete confidence in the brilliance of the future of the American Ballet."

If Warburg's statement reads somewhat like a manifesto of an abdicating monarch, that was its effect on the minuscule empire that was the American Ballet. Much like a modern monarch, Warburg was a symbol of unity, a nonpolitical head of the organization, whose presence tended to minimize any attempt at internal and external intrigue, of which few ballet companies are entirely free. That he—and here the similarity with a modern monarch ends—spent his own money on the American Ballet was another, and most significant, factor in keeping the management of the company on an even keel.

When Warburg resigned he deeded all the physical properties and rights of the American Ballet to George Balanchine, and Balanchine became the sole owner of the corporation. With characteristic modesty Warburg did not make a public announcement of this fact.

The company began its third Metropolitan season placidly enough, and outwardly there was little to indicate the impending crisis in the American Ballet, this time a real one.

Balanchine, never a good businessman or a businessman of any sort, found himself out of his depth in discharging the administrative duties laid upon him by Warburg's resignation. Kirstein was absorbed in Ballet Caravan and would not hear of rejoining the American Ballet. So Balanchine turned to his old friend, Vladimir Dimitriew, director of the School of American Ballet.

Dimitriew did rather well as the director of the School, which was flourishing. Enrollment had been at a peak since the very beginning; new classrooms had been added to accommodate additional classes. If the School still had a deficit, that was only because it paid high salaries to its director and faculty members. This condition did not disturb Kirstein and his family, who contributed large amounts to the maintenance of the School. They had not planned on having the School make a profit. Dimitriew's success in running the School was the more remarkable considering that he had never had any experience in running an institution like it and that he actually had no personal interest in ballet; as a matter of fact, he disliked it. His wife, Kyra Blank, was a member of the American Ballet, and that was his only connection with the company. The ideals and principles upon which the American Ballet was established, its hopes and aspirations, were entirely foreign to him. He could not, or did not wish to, understand or appreciate them. He was perfectly content to run the School, which paid him an excellent stipend, and in which he owned stock. Moreover, he suffered constant apprehension that public performances by the American Ballet might somehow damage the reputation of the School and be reflected adversely in its enrollment and income.

But he had been associated with Balanchine in Les Ballets 1933, and Balanchine felt that he might be helpful in running the American Ballet.

At the suggestion of Dimitriew, Balanchine invited to New York Jacques Lidji, a French lawyer of Bulgarian extraction, an attorney, a friend and confidant of Col. W. de Basil, and an associate of his in the Ballet Russe de Monte Carlo. Lidji was everything a member of the board of the American Ballet should not have been. He was at home in the ballet machinations and intrigue of which Col. de Basil was a past master, and was fresh from Australia where he had been one of the two directors of the so-called second Ballet Russe de Monte Carlo, an adventure that was the ultimate in managerial shenanigans in a field where managerial shenanigans were often a fine art.

Lidji arrived in New York in December, at a time, incidentally, when Leonide Massine was about to leave Col. de Basil to join still another Ballet Russe de Monte Carlo, organized sometime before by René Blum in Monte Carlo. This tragi-comical period in the history of Ballet Russe de Monte Carlo need not concern us here. It is only mentioned because New York was never more surcharged with ballet intrigue than at that time.

Lidji was even less interested in the hopes and ideals of the American Ballet than was Dimitriew. If Dimitriew had no plans for the future of the American Ballet and cared less, Lidji approached the American Ballet with the idea of converting it into another Ballet Russe de Monte Carlo, or de New York, or de Coney Island—it made little difference to him. Meanwhile he could have meetings, conferences, and negotiations, issue statements, make elaborate plans, and, yes, threaten someone with legal action. Lidji was really accomplished in threatening to sue people and in actually going to court. Until a year or so ago there were still cases pending in New York courts begun by Lidji on behalf of Col. de Basil. Now, with Lidji and Col. de Basil both dead, the cases will probably never be called.

The whole winter and spring passed in conferences and negotiations. Every month, nearly every week, there was a new plan, a new idea. At one time it was almost certain that S. Hurok would sign the American Ballet for a tour of ten or twelve weeks (Hurok had actually announced the American Ballet on his list of touring attractions, but nothing ever came of that); at another time it was said that the American Ballet would tour on its own accord; at a third— One cannot list all the wonderful schemes, there were so many of them. None of them materialized, none of them could have. This was clear at the time to everyone not directly connected with the American Ballet, and probably to those connected with it, though of course they gave no sign of it. The basic reason that the company could not develop a workable plan was, of course, the lack of funds. No one spoke about this, at least not openly. Balanchine, the actual owner of the company, had no money to invest, nor had Dimitriew. To Lidji it seemed incomprehensible, even grotesque, that the director of a ballet company should invest more than a nominal sum in his own company.

Meanwhile, Balanchine was working with the company at the Metropolitan under deteriorating conditions. The management was apparently little impressed with the success of the Stravinsky Festival performances the spring before, and was unwilling to let the American Ballet have its own performances during the opera season, except for an occasional ballet on a bill with a short opera or during a Sunday "concert." It denied the company a minimum of stage and orchestra rehearsals. It even went so far as to question the necessity of shoes for the dancers. Balanchine, who found little satisfaction in staging only opera ballets, became rather testy in his relations with the management. It is easy to understand how the uncooperativeness of the Metropolitan and the constant dickerings over a dozen pairs of shoes obscured the one advantage the American Ballet enjoyed at the opera house: a weekly salary for the dancers over a period of about six months each year, and with it a modicum of security that guaranteed the existence of the company, if nothing else.

The time was approaching for Edward Johnson, general manager of the Metropolitan, to make his decision about a contract with the American Ballet for the 1938–9 season. Apparently he was more occupied with the signing of singers and conductors than with the American Ballet, and the expected announcement from him was late in reaching Balanchine. Dimitriew, much more than Balanchine, was growing impatient, and suggested to Balanchine that he should force the issue. Other friends of Balanchine advised patience, but Dimitriew's suggestion prevailed, and Balanchine went to see Johnson. The result of the visit was a letter from Johnson to Balanchine, dated March 19, 1938, which read in part: "Confirming our talk of today, I regret to tell you that it has been decided that the contract of the American Ballet at the Metropolitan Opera will not be renewed for the season 1938–39."

There are people in both the opera and ballet fields in

New York who are still convinced that, despite the dissatisfaction of the Metropolitan with the American Ballet at the
time, the contract would have been renewed had Balanchine
not forced the issue. Balanchine, it must be said, disagrees with
this opinion.

He was understandably incensed by Johnson's letter. On
April 12, some three weeks after the receipt of the letter, he
called a press conference at which he made some provocative
and not very diplomatic statements about the Metropolitan,
its management, patrons, and so on. He said: "I tried to adapt
myself to the Metropolitan, but of no use. The tradition of
ballet at the Metropolitan is bad ballet. That is why I cannot stay."

This was true, but the statement was mistimed. In answer to the statement Johnson, as could have been expected,
released to the press a copy of his March 19 letter to Balanchine, which had the effect of saying: "Balanchine cannot
quit. He was fired three weeks ago."

There was little talk and still less action in the American
Ballet during the summer. Balanchine had taken on several of
the company's dancers for the musicals he was choreographing. Late in June the School closed for the summer, as had
been its custom. As a novelty it opened a six-week summer
course in Bermuda for those of its students who wanted to
combine a vacation with study.

When Dimitriew returned to New York, he found Balanchine at work on a plan that would have had the dancers of
the American Ballet give Sunday performances while working
weekdays in a musical, *Carousel*, composed by Vernon Duke,
and to be produced by John Krimsky. The musical was
planned for December. By December the musical was postponed until February 1939, but Balanchine had a new plan.
Dwight Deere Wiman and his associate J. H. Del Bondio, for
whom Balanchine had choreographed several musicals, ex-

pressed a willingness to sponsor a New York season of the American Ballet in March. Marie Jeanne (of Ballet Caravan) and Annabelle Lyon were mentioned as ballerinas. Vera Zorina (whom Balanchine had married on Christmas eve 1938), Betty Bruce, Paul Draper, and Paul Haakon would be guest artists. Balanchine, Dimitriew, and Lidji were still listed as directors of the company. Despite the utter naïveté of the plan, the company, which for some reason was now called the Balanchine Ballet, actually began rehearsals on January 30 for an opening in New York on March 19.

A few weeks later the plan underwent another change: the company would open, in Chicago rather than New York, around the middle of April instead of March 19, and Sunday performances in New York would follow a two-week season in Chicago. Another few weeks brought another change in plans: the opening of the Balanchine Ballet would be deferred from the spring to the autumn; the company would have a pre-New York tour and then open a New York season under the sponsorship of "a prominent charitable institution."

This plan was permitted quietly to evaporate, and the first phase of the American Ballet came to an end. During this phase the American Ballet lost a little more than one hundred thousand dollars, most of it contributed by Edward Warburg.

VIII

1938–1940

"Blast at Ballet"; "Billy the Kid"; The New York World's Fair

To keep the narrative straight we must now turn back a year to Ballet Caravan, which had enjoyed its first taste of dancing with a full orchestra in New York. The date was February 18, 1938, the culmination of the company's winter season.

The dancers could take only a short holiday after the season because Frances Hawkins had booked a short Southern tour to begin April 16 in Charlotte, North Carolina. It was a pleasant if unremarkable tour. Its only outstanding feature for the dancers was a two-day appearance in Havana, Cuba, May 5 and 6, the company's first performances on foreign soil. The dancers enjoyed the vacationlike tour, and Kirstein was glad that they escaped the unpleasant turmoil attendant on the American Ballet's separation from the Metropolitan.

The company was strengthened with additional dancers, and the roster now included: Ruby Asquith, Anne Campbell, Mary Heater, Marie Jeanne, Albia Kavan, Lorna London, Marjorie Moore, Todd Bolender, Lew and Harold Christensen, Douglas Coudy, Fred Danieli, Erick Hawkins, and Eugene Loring. Gisella Caccialanza, Kathryn Mullowny, and William Dollar of the American Ballet joined the company as guest artists.

The season ended May 13 at State Teachers College, Glassboro, New Jersey, and the dancers scattered for the summer: a few of them going with the School of American Ballet to Bermuda, most of them going home.

For the first time since the organization of the Caravan, Lincoln Kirstein had time to take stock of the company's achievements and to write a book he felt should be written. He was satisfied with the Caravan's progress, but only just satisfied. The company was doing exactly what he wanted it to do, the way he wanted it done, but something was missing. The missing thing was the excitement that usually surrounded a ballet company. Kirstein had his own choreographers, his own composers, and his own painters, but somehow these talented, on occasion brilliant, young people could not create an artistic atmosphere to compare with that created by a combination like Balanchine, Stravinsky, and Tchelitchew, for example. He would not admit it to himself, and certainly not to others, but he had already begun to sense that what he was doing was more a crusade to wrest ballet in America from infidel foreign troupes, choreographers, and such, than it was a movement in ballet, which he had hoped it would be. The tours of the Caravan were proof that ballet by and for Americans was viable, in a limited way. But was it good ballet because it was by and for Americans? This he had to prove, not

only to audiences but to himself as well. And he tried very
hard to prove it. It was obviously not a generally acceptable
commodity, and it mostly appealed to two categories of spectators: those who did not come within the pale of the big
ballet companies; i.e., in small towns these companies did not
visit, and those in the bigger cities, who had a stronger than
usual interest in ballet as a whole. Others, the vast majority,
remained outside. The dancers sensed the limitations of the
Caravan earlier than Kirstein and voiced it more openly if not
so eloquently as Kirstein was subsequently to do.

The book that Kirstein wrote that summer was *Blast at
Ballet*, subtitled *A Corrective for the American Audience*. Its title
page carried a stock mail-order illustration of the American
eagle holding a shield decorated with the stars and stripes.
It was as patriotic as the Fourth of July advertisement of a
provincial grocery-store.

Blast at Ballet was an excellently written, straightforward,
angry, libelous and, in many instances, grossly unfair pamph-
let. The art of pamphleteering, and pamphlets themselves as
a medium of expression for men with a grievance or a case,
receded into obscurity with the growth and development of
the daily newspaper and, especially, the monthly review,
which provided opportunities for the airing of controversial
issues in politics, religion, and the arts. But Kirstein had to
resort to this outmoded medium of expression because he had
both a grievance and a case and what he had to say was so
explosive and frankly libelous that he knew that no periodical,
however openminded and daring, would print his material.
Hence he wrote *Blast at Ballet*.

Part One of *Blast at Ballet* was entitled "Our Back-Drop"
and contained a concise but comprehensive review of modern
ballet from the Diaghilev days to the spring of 1938. Part Two
was entitled "The Great Conspiracy" and denounced managers of ballet companies, patrons of ballet, and newspaper

critics, who, Kirstein thought, formed a "sinister alliance" to the detriment of ballet in America. Kirstein's description of the conspiratorial activities of managers and impresarios was inaccurate and clearly showed that he knew of their activities only from hearsay. His description and analysis of ballet patrons and social balletomanes was true and devastating. In writing about critics he mentioned nearly every writer on dance in America and England, but most of his criticism was directed towards John Martin of *The New York Times*, especially for his "prejudice against theatrical values in dancing."

Despite the many accusations and unpleasant things Kirstein said about Martin, his was an honest, even chivalrous attack.

"By his energy and interest in dancing," wrote Kirstein, "he has almost single-handed created a place for the dance critic in New York, and hence, in America. His job has not been easy, for on the one hand he has been assailed by the ballet managers for his contempt of ballet as a theatrical form, and on the other, by a large section of young dancers in this form who fear his influential opposition to the future of their art. He is incorruptible, and this is no idle homage, for in the last two years I knew very well at least one powerful ballet manager and one ballet patron have done their best to have him displaced from the position he has done so much to dignify. . . . My disagreement with Mr. Martin is the sincerest form of flattery because there is hardly any other name in the American field which represents the expression of a conviction based on preference rather than on second-hand reading."

Further, Kirstein analyzed Martin's anti-balletic attitude as expressed, among other ways, in the critic's condemnation of important developments in ballet, in his praise of ballets that, in Kirstein's opinion, had a retarding effect on the development of ballet (Fokine's *Coq d'Or*, for example), and in his consistent defense "of the ephemeral amateur, the lay dancer, the grand spawn of experimental 'Modernists.' "

It was true, of course, that at the time Martin was going through a period of "anti-theatricality" so far as the dance was concerned; and this attitude of his applied equally toward ballet and the modern dance, which was then just beginning to acquire the forms and appurtenances of a theatrical, as opposed to a "concert," art form. It was also true that Martin was much less favorably disposed toward ballet as an art form than he is now.

In the anger of writing *Blast at Ballet*, Kirstein did not realize that Martin was actually an ally of his. In his crusade against the "enemies" of American ballet, Kirstein was much more violently anti-balletic than Martin ever had been. Kirstein's opposition was directed, not toward all ballet, but toward the imported product, specifically the Ballet Russe de Monte Carlo, which then toured the length and breadth of the country. Martin, like nearly everyone else, accepted Ballet Russe de Monte Carlo as representing ballet in general, and when he denounced ballet as an art form actually meant the art form that manifested itself in the Ballet Russe. Moreover, if Martin, as was his right, expressed a definite preference for the modern dance, Kirstein, as was his right, exhibited a definite dislike and contempt for the modern dance. Both men have changed considerably since 1938.

Part Three of *Blast at Ballet* was entitled "Program and Manifesto," in which Kirstein attempted to outline a plan for an organized audience and an alliance of American ballet companies. His rather vague plan did not much differ from the existing plan for organized audiences, except that the existing plans were drawn up for musical attractions with dance companies playing a minor part, while his plan encompassed only dance attractions.

"I propose," wrote Kirstein, "that the American ballet companies pool their resources and set up their own independent management office, which will be entirely occupied with furthering their particular interests, by building a national circuit and stimulating a national audience."

There was a twofold fallacy in Kirstein's reasoning. He sincerely supposed that there existed a conspiracy against native ballet on the part of the booking managements, and he assumed that native ballet was, *ipso facto*, good ballet. Neither of these theses had a strong basis in fact.

If booking managements were in any conspiracy at all, they were in a conspiracy to make money, the principal reason for their being in business. It was perhaps difficult for Kirstein to understand how anyone could deal with ballet in any way and not have the good of ballet as his first consideration. A booking management is in effect a sales organization whose business is to sell a commodity to as many people as possible. The more salable (not necessarily the better) the commodity, the less effort to sell it, the greater the turnover, the more substantial the profit. If booking managers at that time preferred to sell imported ballet rather than native, that was because the foreign troupes had greater names, a more popular repertoire, an aura of exoticism, and attendant glamour (true or imagined). Local managers and the majority of spectators were more impressed with Tamara Toumanova, the "Black Pearl of the Russian Ballet," who was born in a freightcar while her parents were escaping from the Soviet regime, than with, say, Jane Doering, a wonderful dancer, who was born in unspectacular Philadelphia, had a normal childhood, worked hard in school and in ballet classes, and developed an admirable style that only true connoisseurs could admire.

Similarly, spectators and local managers, Kirstein's lofty ideals notwithstanding, found more enjoyment in sloppy productions of *Aurora's Wedding*, *Swan Lake*, and *Le Beau Danube* than in meticulous ones of *Filling Station*, *Yankee Clipper*, and *Harlequin for President*.

It was not, as Kirstein imagined it to be, a sinister boycott of native troupes that made booking managers prefer imported foreign companies; it was a simple matter of dollars and cents. From the point of view of the booking managers, American ballet companies were not yet salable in the open market.

Kirstein had been very critical of booking managers and critics, but had not used the same strictness in writing about the existing American ballet troupes. Had he applied the same demands to ballet troupes as to managers and writers, he would have had to remain aloof from them, because none of the companies he wrote about could have been placed in the same artistic category as the Ballet Caravan or the American Ballet before it. It was obvious that none of the other American companies would respond to Kirstein's plea for an alliance. They knew their station, if Kirstein alleged that he did not.

Blast at Ballet had to be written, and the American dance world was the richer for its having been written, but it did not achieve any of the results Kirstein had hoped for. It created quite a stir in the professional field, but, as Kirstein foresaw, the people whom he had attacked accepted it with "a conspiracy of silence." Although at least one manager discussed with his lawyers the possibility and advisability of a libel suit against Kirstein, no action was taken. Kirstein called *Blast at Ballet* both an "irritant" and a "corrective." It did irritate a number of people, as Kirstein had wanted; its corrective features had their strongest effects on the author himself: he got a load off his chest and slowly began to be more realistic in his approach to the managerial aspects of a ballet company.

When *Blast at Ballet* was coming off the press, the Ballet Caravan began preparations for its longest tour, booked by

Frances Hawkins in association with Paul H. Stoes. The tour
was to last four months and take the company to the West
Coast. Three important dancers joined the Caravan at rehearsal time, Beatrice Tompkins, Jean Vallon, and Milton
Forest (better known now as Michael Kidd). The principal
addition to the repertoire was *Billy the Kid*, to commissioned
music by Aaron Copland, book by Lincoln Kirstein, in costumes by Jared French, with choreography by Eugene Loring,
whose *Yankee Clipper* was one of the mainstays of the repertoire.

Like Lew Christensen's *Filling Station* before it, *Billy the
Kid* was a fine example of true Diaghilevian collaboration,
with Kirstein directing the efforts of the choreographer, composer, and costume-designer toward one goal: the homogeneity of the ballet as a whole.

The story of the ballet concerned the desperado, William
Bonney, who at the age of twelve killed his first man to avenge
the accidental killing of his mother, a ladylike pioneer. Before
he reached twenty-one, he had shot a man for each year of
his life. He continued killing people until he was finally am-
bushed in the home of his Mexican sweetheart by Pat Garrett,
his former friend turned sheriff.

On the canvas of this simple story which reminded one of
a Western movie (Billy the Kid did emerge as a gory Western
some ten years later), Kirstein embroidered a saga of the
opening of the Western frontier and the bringing to it of a
modicum of civilization through the establishment of law and
order, a collective necessity for people who were to live in
peace in a new place. Billy's career itself was no more than a
fragmentary, perhaps symbolic, incident in this saga.

To say that Kirstein wrote the scenario for *Billy the Kid*
is to tell only part of the story. For actually he had done
enough research and accumulated enough material to write
an exhaustive volume on the subject. All this material he
placed at the disposal of Loring, who studied the material as

carefully as had Kirstein. Copland and French made their own investigations.

The result was the first great all-American ballet. Even now, some fifteen years after *Billy the Kid* was first produced, there are few ballets on American themes to equal it. Parenthetically it may be noted here that Loring, who has produced a number of ballets since, has never again risen to the lofty choreographic heights of *Billy the Kid*. In fact, the ballets he staged after it have long since been forgotten, while *Billy the Kid* remains an American classic.

The autumn 1938 tour of the Ballet Caravan opened October 12 in Detroit. The *première* of *Billy the Kid* took place on October 16 in the Civic Theater, Chicago. It was an instantaneous success.

Wrote Ann Barzel in *Dance* (December 1938): "Billy the Kid . . . marks a milestone in American ballet. . . . Loring's choreography is marked by inventiveness and imagination. He assumes the audience too has imagination, and yet his work is never obscure. Loring's inventiveness is shown in the movements devised, whether it be to illustrate riding a horse or pushing west. His details are excellent. . . ."

Spectators nearly everywhere accepted *Billy the Kid* as the great American ballet it was. *Nearly* everywhere, because certain localities showed opposition to the ballet. Kirstein, who went on tour with the Caravan, kept a diary, and some of the entries are illuminating, not only with regard to the taste of the American provincial spectators and local managers, but also with regard to Kirstein's own observations. Here are a few excerpts from it:

"Milwaukee. This is Eugene Loring's home town. I had wanted to do his two ballets, Yankee Clipper and Billy the Kid here. But the sponsors refused to permit Billy; they said it was not a fit subject for ballet. I increasingly realize that what most American sponsoring committees think they want is a moderate-sized Russian ballet. If it's American it isn't ballet. After the performance, our success was indicated by the fact that we were requested to perform Billy the Kid next year. . . .

"Visalia [California]. The performance was a Sunday matinee and due to the presence of the clergy and the competition with their services, we were not allowed to do either Filling Station or Billy the Kid.

"Dallas. As soon as I got to the hotel I found Mr. John William Rogers, an excellent theatrical critic and playwright, waiting to interview me. Mr. Rogers had perhaps justifiably been nettled by my continual insistence on 100% Americanism in the ballet. I tried to show him that my program was not one of nationalist prejudice or blind chauvinism, but merely a personal attitude I was attempting to demonstrate in the work of my own company. . . . I had very much wanted to present Billy the Kid in Dallas, but due to the two recent big state celebrations in the vicinity, the sponsors felt they had had enough of Wild West pageantry. However, the next night at Denton, the Dallas newspapers sent over their critics to cover it and indeed many of the previous audience came again.

"San Angelo [Texas]. All the ranchers were particularly pleased with Billy the Kid. I had fears that they might have considered it pretentious of us, easterners, to show them bronco-busting and gunplay, but as a matter of fact they were quite pleased that we thought the Wild West a fitting subject for the classic dance.

"Toronto [Canada]. A very official audience with the Lieutenant Governor-General, etc. We felt the Canadians would have preferred some white tarlatans and Russian music. Everyone was as polite and as cold as the weather.

"New York. The tour was a remarkable adventure for me. I learned not only that New York is not America, but that Americans genuinely love good dancing if they are allowed to see it. I realized that we were best received in places where they either had seen no dancing at all or had seen everything. In those places, for example, where they had seen a little and where, as one manager told me, 'we want to be transplanted into realms of fairyland,' the reaction was occasionally cold and frequently negative. Maybe we should have done a ballet with swans and Viennese waltzes. But I still doubt it. It only takes a little more time for all of America to recognize and love the quality of indigenous dancing to which it has given birth."

The Caravan finished its tour in the early spring of 1939, but was not laid off until June because it had an opportunity to appear in New York in May as part of the then newly organized and short-lived American Lyric Theatre, headed by Lee Pattison, pianist and one-time director of the Metropolitan Spring Season. The aim of the American Lyric Theatre, as the name implied, was the encouragement of American musical, dramatic, and choreographic arts. Its season had been originally planned for April, but was later postponed until May. The season opened May 18 at the Martin Beck Theater and ran through May 31. On May 18, 19, and 20 the company danced Lew Christensen's *Filling Station* as a curtain-raiser for Douglas Moore's opera *The Devil and Daniel Webster*. On May 24 and 31 it had its own performances, dancing for the first time in New York *Billy the Kid*, William Dollar's *Air and Variations* (to fifteen of Bach's "Goldberg" Variations), and Christensen's *Pocahontas*. The ballets were danced to the accompaniment of an orchestra under the direction of Fritz Kitzinger, a former conductor of the Berlin Staatsoper. *Billy the Kid* made a deep impression on the spectators and press.

The company was laid off for the summer. It reassembled on September 10 for rehearsals for a ten-week tour that began on October 10 and took it as far as Los Angeles. On December 26, 28, 30, and 31 it appeared in New York as part of the

Holiday Dance Festival organized by Frances Hawkins at the
St. James Theater. The Festival also included performances
by Martha Graham and her group and the Korean dancer
Sai Shoki.

Two new ballets were added to the repertoire: Eugene
Loring's *City Portrait*, to a scenario by Kirstein, score by Henry
Brant, in costumes by Forrest Thayr, Jr.; and Lew Christen-
sen's *Charade, or The Debutante*, also to a scenario by Kirstein,
to a selection of American melodies arranged by Trude
Rittmann, the company's pianist, in costumes by Alvin Colt.

Both ballets were disappointing.

Loring's creative ability had seemingly spent itself on
Billy the Kid. He substituted for it a certain obscuration that
never could have a place in ballet, the most outward of
theatrical arts. *City Portrait* appeared to me a sort of city
edition of *Billy the Kid*, without the spark of genius illuminating
that ballet. Reviewing *City Portrait* for *Dance Magazine*, I wrote:
"Modernism, documentism, or Loringism, it [*City Portrait*]
takes Loring farther and farther away from the ballet, from
dance, in general, and the direction into which he is headed
is not apparent, perhaps not even indicated."

For one reason or another, Loring did not have as much
of Kirstein's collaboration on *City Portrait* as he had had on
Billy the Kid, and the results showed it.

Christensen's *Charade* was not more than an adequate ensemble piece designed to show off the technical prowess of the
dancers in the amusing setting of an early twentieth-century
domestic comedy. It had some excellent dancing and a comic
situation or two, and that was all.

Clearly Ballet Caravan, only three and one-half years
old, was showing signs of artistic exhaustion. Not that the
company was not dancing well (actually it was dancing better
than ever) or that Kirstein had lost his zeal and determination.
Somehow the company, despite its tours and public accept-

ance, was not getting anywhere. After three and one-half years Ballet Caravan was still, so to speak, a chamber ballet, playing mostly in out-of-the-way places and not acquiring the public following or artistic entourage that Kirstein, if no one else in the organization, wanted and needed. Ballet Caravan was small potatoes and Kirstein by education, outlook, inclination, and custom, was not a man to be satisfied with that. He never admitted it then, and probably would not now, but he was getting just a little bored with keeping the company for the two avowed reasons: offering ballet by and for Americans and furnishing employment and a medium of expression for young American dancers, choreographers, musicians, and painters. Moreover, during those three and one-half years he had been growing artistically, developing his taste, acquiring ever-broader horizons, while the people who worked with him remained where they had been when they joined him. Kirstein never was and is not now a patient man. He very seldom took the trouble to make allowances for other people's unpreparedness and failings. He could not accept honest mediocrity and a willingness to work as a substitute for talent. Ballet Caravan, as a conglomeration of human beings, was not fulfilling Kirstein's expectations, was not reaching the level he had set for it arbitrarily and by a criterion of his own, a criterion that could not be and should not have been applied to it.

Ballet Caravan was going through an internal artistic crisis, but Kirstein that winter had also reached an external crisis.

Lucia Chase, until then a devout disciple of Mikhail Mordkin and ballerina of the Mordkin Ballet, which she had generously supported, decided that the time was ripe to expand the Mordkin Ballet into a big and glamorous organization, the Ballet Theatre. Richard Pleasant, thitherto manager of the Mordkin school, was named director, and there was set in motion a plan of operation more elaborate than ballet in

America had ever seen before or was to see again. Nearly every choreographer then in America was invited to stage ballets for the new company, among them Michel Fokine, Bronislava Nijinska, Adolph Bolm, Mikhail Mordkin, Agnes de Mille, Eugene Loring, Anton Dolin, and José Fernández. At the suggestion of Agnes de Mille, Pleasant brought over from England Antony Tudor and Andrée Howard as choreographers and Hugh Laing as a dancer.

Nearly everyone was invited—except George Balanchine, who was then in New York choreographing one smash-hit musical comedy after another, but not staging any ballets. Why Balanchine was not invited to stage a work for Ballet Theatre remains a mystery to this day.

Kirstein was obviously hurt by Ballet Theatre's neglect of Balanchine. Only to a lesser extent was he displeased by Ballet Theatre's disregard of what he had advocated the year before in his *Blast at Ballet*. Here was being organized a big, rich American ballet company, something Kirstein had always wished and hoped for America, yet its artistic approach was exactly that of the Ballet Russe, not the one he had advocated so passionately and eloquently all these years. Was he wrong, by any chance?

In the situation there was nothing that Kirstein could do; there was not even anything he could say which would not be construed as motivated by fear of competition or, worse, by a sour-grapes complex. So he did not do or say anything, but he knew well that he and Ballet Caravan had reached an external critical situation and that the time of Ballet Caravan was coming to an end.

Everyone closely watching the structure of Ballet Theatre knew that the company had no solid artistic or business foundation. It was no surprise, except to the company's management and the dance critics on the New York dailies, that after the much publicized three-week season at the Center Theatre from January 11 to February 3, 1940, Ballet Theatre had to suspend operations temporarily and lay off the troupe. This was no comfort to Kirstein.

Soon after Ballet Theatre closed, there were some negotiations between its management and Kirstein about uniting Ballet Theatre with Ballet Caravan, but nothing came of them. Ballet Theatre's idea was to absorb Ballet Caravan into its framework, and Kirstein was understandably against that.

The low ebb of Kirstein's enthusiasm toward ballet in general at this point did not prevent him from making an important and lasting contribution to it: early in the year he donated his extensive private collection of books on dance to the Museum of Modern Art in New York. On March 4 the Museum opened its Dance Archives, with Paul David Magriel as curator. Probably the richest collection anywhere, and certainly the finest of its kind in America, the Dance Archives attracted researchers, writers, choreographers, and dancers and, as such collections do, provided facilities for study and enjoyment. Unfortunately, like many of Kirstein's unselfish undertakings, the Dance Archives brought him more grief than satisfaction. A few years after the establishment of the Dance Archives, the Museum of Modern Art was confronted with a lack of space and decided to transfer part of Kirstein's collection, that part which predated 1900, to the Harvard University Library.

Kirstein complained to me: "If I want to consult one of my own books I have to go to Boston to do it. What a situation."

Ballet Caravan would have gone out of existence quietly in the spring of 1940, as the American Ballet had the year before, had it not been for the *deus ex machina* appearance of the Ford Motor Company in the unlikely role of ballet impresario.

In those disquieting months before World War II, a group of optimists had organized the New York World's Fair on Flushing Meadows. The Ford Motor Company built a very imposing pavilion, complete with a very modern and comfortable theater seating about five hundred. For the second summer of the Fair the Ford Motor Company wanted to present something special in its theater, and finally decided on a ballet company.

The industrial designer Walter Dorwin Teague approached Kirstein with his idea about having a ballet company dance a sketch that would illustrate the fate of old Dobbin being displaced by the automobile. The ballet would be part of the program, which would also include a motion picture illustrating the work of the Ford Motor Company and a fashion show to exhibit the latest in clothes as well as automobiles.

Kirstein readily agreed.

The ballet, conceived by Teague, was entitled *A Thousand Times Neigh!* Edward Mabley wrote the story and lyrics, Tom Bennett composed the music, William Dollar designed the choreography, and Lincoln Kirstein assumed general direction.

Perhaps not the greatest ballet composition in the world, *A Thousand Times Neigh!* was imaginative, amusing, and in excellent taste. No one will know whether it sold Ford cars, but it did furnish six months of pleasant employment to forty-two dancers. The ballet, which ran eighteen minutes, went on twelve times a day, on the hour. It required two full groups of dancers, companies A and B, as they were called, each of which danced six times a day. Every dancer, according to union requirements, had one day off each week, and there were so-called "swing dancers" to replace those who were resting or indisposed.

The following dancers constituted the two companies: Leda Anchutina, Mary Colbath, Peggy D'Arcy, Jean Davidson, Vera Bobitcheff, Betty Gilmore, Babs Heath, Jeanne

Isaacs, Marie Jeanne, Margit de Kova, Peggy Noonan, Maria Quarequio, Pearl Schwarz, Mary Jane Shea, Barbara Stuart, Charlotte Sumner, Hilda Wagner, Anne Wiener, Virginia Wilcox, Anna Deere Wiman, Billie Wynn, Robert Armstrong, Todd Bolender, Douglas Coudy, Fred Danieli, Vladimir Dokoudovsky, William Dollar, John Duane, John Paul Dunphy, William Garrett, Kari Karnakoski, Alexis Kosloff, Nicholas Magallanes, Jay Martinez, Robert McVoy, Rem Olmstead, Newcomb Rice, John Schindehette, Serge Temoff, Nicholas Vasilieff, Ray Williams, and Robert Wolff.

Without exception they were all good dancers. Most of them came from the Ballet Caravan and the professional class of the School of American Ballet; others came from Ballet Theatre and Broadway musicals. For several of the dancers this was their first professional engagement and proved an excellent training-ground, though no other company could provide quite the same nearly ideal working conditions.

But the summer soon came to an end, and with it the World's Fair and the Ballet Caravan.

IX

1940–1941

The Tour of South America

Although Lincoln Kirstein had long since outgrown
the stage where every dress rehearsal seemed a
disaster and every dancer's sprained ankle a ca-
lamity, the bright spring and summer of 1940
looked very dark to him.

He knew very well, if others did not, that the
Ballet Caravan had come to its end, that the com-
pany at the Ford Pavilion at the New York World's
Fair was the Caravan in name only.

Of all Kirstein's activities only the School of
American Ballet was doing well, but even there
things were not as Kirstein would have wanted
them to be. The faculty now included George Balanchine, Kyra Blank (Mrs. Dimitriew), Lew Chris-

124

tensen, Ludmila Shollar, Muriel Stuart, and Anatole Vilzak. Vladimir Dimitriew was director. Balanchine taught so seldom that his name was carried on the faculty list more for prestige than anything else. Pierre Vladimiroff resigned in April 1937 as a result of a dispute with Dimitriew and left for Europe. In the spring of 1940 Ludmila Shollar was notified that her contract with the School would not be renewed, whereupon her husband, Anatole Vilzak, also left the School.

Meanwhile, it was becoming obvious to Kirstein that he could no longer work with Dimitriew. They had not been seeing eye to eye since 1935, but Kirstein, who had never had any experience in running a school and did not want to tie himself down to active directorship of it, let Dimitriew have his way in most cases. By the spring of 1940 he had had his fill. After a series of conferences in which representatives of his family were involved, Kirstein agreed to purchase the stock Dimitriew owned in the School. Dimitriew resigned in June 1940. Kirstein became director of the School. With Ballet Caravan inactive except for the performances at the Fair, Kirstein decided to devote himself to a reform of the School.

By autumn Kirstein had persuaded Balanchine to take a more active part in the School. A little later Pierre Vladimiroff, who had returned from Europe at the beginning of the war and was teaching privately in New York, rejoined the faculty. At the start of the school year Kirstein announced a faculty consisting of Balanchine, Vladimiroff, Stuart, Blank (who remained on the faculty despite her husband's resignation), William Dollar, and José Fernández (for Spanish dance). At the same time he did something he had always wanted to do: he incorporated the School as a nonprofit educational institution under the Board of Regents of the State of New York.

Kirstein was listed officially as President and Director of the School. Eugenie Ouroussow became Executive Secretary.

Outlining the basic purpose of the School, Kirstein stated: "The School of American Ballet tries to give, as broadly as possible, a complete practical education to those who wish to make their living by dancing. . . . Its fundamental purpose is to provide students of this continent with a training equivalent to that offered professional dancers by the great state-endowed Russian academies of the nineteenth and twentieth centuries. . . ."

When the School opened in early September, Kirstein announced a competition for three scholarships. The competition attracted about one hundred and thirty entrants. The level of the contestants was so high that Kirstein decided to grant five scholarships instead of three. One of the winners was a long-legged wisp of a girl named Tanaquil LeClercq.

Kirstein was going full blast, doing all the things he had wanted to do but had been unable to do because of Dimitriew's opposition. It is to Kirstein's credit that since that time, and to this writing, there have been no upheavals in the School. Several instructors have been added to the faculty during this period, among them Mme Felia Dubrovska (in private life Mrs. Pierre Vladimiroff), formerly a soloist in the Maryinsky Theater and later a ballerina in the Diaghilev company, who joined in the autumn of 1949; Elise Reiman of the American Ballet; Yurek Lazowski (for character dancing); and Janet Collins (for modern dance).

Kirstein was very busy that summer of 1940, but not very happy. Ballet Caravan, to which he had devoted so much time, energy, talent—and, yes, money (during the four years of existence of the Caravan, Kirstein had spent approximately one hundred thousand dollars of his own funds to support it)—was out of the running, and this weighed heavily on him, so heavily, indeed, that he had developed an animosity and suspicion toward everybody and everything in ballet.

This was the more strange because by then he knew exactly the reasons for the failure of the Caravan.

In a brilliant and (even for Kirstein) uncommonly frank article that appeared in the September issue of *Theatre Arts*, entitled "Ballet: Record and Augury," he related what had been wrong with the Caravan and himself. Here, in excerpts, is what he said; it could not be improved by a paraphrase:

"In 1934 ballet by American dancers, choreographers and designers seemed to be on the verge of a bumptious but healthy future. The years of groundwork . . . seemed finally to have provided the necessary mulching to force our native product. The present writer has been so involved with this particular phase that the ordinary discount must be allowed for personal failure. Nevertheless, he is sufficiently far from it and cynical about it to be as generally trustworthy as anyone else. . . .

"The times were almost ripe for an American Ballet; its initial success [in 1935] guaranteed a continuation. Why did it disappear? There was a confusion of personal, financial and administrative ailings which added up to the facts. A single choreographer, however talented, is not enough, even for a small company; no mere choreographer, however brilliant, can be the executive head of a permanent troupe. . . .

"I was depressed by the continual subservience of its sprouting American choreographers to European imaginative standards, and in my impatience tried to shortcut the unforgiving slow spiral of growth. . . . Combining a certain forgivable chauvinism with an amateur taste, and just a little too much or too little money, knowing all the questions, I thought I had all the answers.

"Our small company, the American Ballet Caravan, sprung phoenix-like from the original American Ballet, was to have been a model of efficiency, on a small scale the pattern for a big company. The director (myself) would delegate congenial American subjects to American choreographers, whose ballets would be executed by American dancers in backgrounds and to music by American painters and musicians. I was so absorbed in the details that I overlooked any doubts as to the quality of the collaboration. While I could not have soberly believed it, I behaved as if to be native was to be enough. No Nazi could have been more zealous. I was alone, a theatrical amateur with a little professional experience. I had some good young dancers, and there was more than a trace of freshness and even of talent about the proceedings. As the effort of a school it was admirable. As a commercial competitor of the large international traveling companies it was hopeless. And I could not afford to wait before plunging our small efforts into this competition. The Caravan went to Cuba, Canada and twice from New York to the Pacific coast and back.

"At the end, even before the money gave out, I knew what was wrong, and even the dancers themselves scarcely believed in the venture. To be sure, there were a handful whose creative future was involved, boys who will be choreographers in spite of my luck or the impossibility of getting a chance in the big Russian troupes. They had had the chance to see their dances on stages all over the country. But the general run of my company had a much more surgical eye than I had. They were more professional. They knew our company had only its self-constructed repertory, without the prestige of a Spectre or Sylphides. And to be just, one must admit that in their dancing-school they had been taught their idiom via Spectre, Sylphides and Lac des Cygnes. In the Caravan there were no ballerina roles for them, no numbers already tested by public familiarity, no parts at all except through continual experiment with stray hybrids, classic ballet infused with Martha Graham movement or with Broadway revue. They knew the taste of the American public better than I did in my naïve, reckless and expensively hopeful testing. The experiments which didn't even partly succeed I carefully analyzed, to forgive all the mistakes involved. But the audience did not. I heard our toe-shoes squeak over all the music our two excellent pianists could muster. I realized that twenty on a stage is half a crowd. The audience had seen the Russian Ballet and had paid no more for it than for us. There was no question about the money's worth.

"And yet there was no other way to do it at that time, even if one would never do it again. It was an education of a sort for all of us, audience, dancers, directors. We saw our country, which heretofore had been a vague rumor, and we saw our own strength. Our quality was thin and tentative, rather than poor and mean.

"When I said I had either too much or too little money, I meant merely this: too much, because it was enough on which to be independent, to permit no interference however sage, no advice however considered; too little, because it was never enough to have a proper orchestra, advance man, stage manager, sufficient troupe, or commercial exploitation. It was a bare minimum on which one could occasionally count for an illusion of theatrical brilliance. It was a minimum commercial risk and brought a minimum return. I doubt if a similar venture could be done otherwise or even again, bucking as we did the combined resources of the concert booking monopolies."

There is no other theatrical person so active or so passive that he would so frankly and openly admit his mistakes as Kirstein did. Mistakes there were. And the greatest of them—and, when one comes down to fundamentals, the only one—was the lack of theatricality in the whole undertaking. The Caravan's (read Kirstein's) revolt against the existing ballet had two directions: against the tradition and subject matter and the utilization of the individual talents of the artists responsible for the creation of the repertoire, and against the *modus operandi* of the commercial ballet companies. The first was intellectual rather than artistic in its goal, the second personal rather than businesslike in attempts to achieve the goal. Both tended to take the ballet away from the theater, its natural habitat. It became a hybrid that satisfied neither the dancers (and later, Kirstein) nor the public.

But it would be wrong to think that the Caravan slipped out of existence without leaving its imprint on ballet in America. As a matter of record, its influence on ballet in America was much stronger than that of the American Ballet and of any other company save the present New York City Ballet. The influence was, and still is, twofold.

First, the Caravan demonstrated to directors of ballet companies and the public that one does not have to be Russian or French, or foreign in general, to be an excellent dancer or a talented choreographer. It exploded the myth about the *âme slave* being a prime necessity for ballet by demonstrating that Americans could be excellent dancers.

Even before the war effectively stopped the influx of foreign dancers, Americans were beginning to find places in the so-called Russian companies and to make names for themselves. The novelty of having American dancers in "Russian" ballet companies was still so fresh in 1937–8 that the French and emigrée Russian girls called the American girls foreigners. The acceptance of American dancers by the big companies may not sound of great importance now, but fifteen or sixteen years ago it played an important part in the American dance world.

One must not forget that up to 1935 or 1936, the late Col. de Basil used to accept Americans only as students or apprentices who worked without salaries and often had to pay their own transportation. There were also several cases of American dancers actually having to pay the director of a ballet company for the privilege of working in it. It seems incredible now, when American dancers make up ninety per cent of the three big ballet companies in the United States and are represented in nearly every European ballet company with the possible exception of the two Sadler's Wells troupes in London and the ballet of the Opéra in Paris. Fifteen years of hard work and dedication have had much to do with this accomplishment, but its beginning lay in the work of the American Ballet and, especially, the Ballet Caravan, for they not only set the example, but also established the discipline and the style of the dance; in effect, they created what can now be called the American tradition in the ballet dance.

Second, the American Ballet, and after it the Ballet Caravan, brought forth the idea that there actually could be such a thing as an American ballet company, an idea that had few followers. There had been attempts at organizing American ballet troupes before 1935, all of them abortive. For better or worse, the American Ballet existed three full years, the Ballet Caravan four. If they ceased when they did it was not because they failed as organic matter dies because it is not viable. Rather, they ran their course, fulfilled their function, ended their experiments so that other companies could begin where they finished and proceed on a new course without repeating the mistakes they had made and paid for.

It may be denied all around, and particularly by those who were concerned with the organization of Ballet Theatre in 1939–40, but the stimulus for the formation of Ballet Theatre stemmed directly from the American Ballet and the Ballet Caravan. That Ballet Theatre did not pursue the artistic principles of the American Ballet or the Ballet Caravan and did not profit by the obvious mistakes made by those two companies need not be discussed here.

Another direct influence of the Ballet Caravan was the

establishment of more than a score of semiprofessional and nonprofessional ballet groups with regional and local spheres of activities in cities and towns of the United States and Canada. Few people outside the localities involved know about them, but there are and were troupes, large and small, well or badly run, in New York, New Jersey, Pennsylvania, the District of Columbia, Virginia, Massachusetts, Georgia, Illinois, Michigan, Missouri, Kansas, Minnesota, Oregon, California, Washington, Florida, Quebec, Ontario, Manitoba, and British Columbia, to name only those which come to my mind from personal knowledge. All these troupes patterned themselves after the Caravan, were stimulated into existence because Lincoln Kirstein took a group of sixteen dancers to tour New England in the summer of 1936.

Some of the performances of these troupes maintain a fairly high artistic standard, others are on little more than the dance school annual "recital" level, but all of the troupes and their leaders are honest, sincere, and hard-working. All of them contribute more than their share to create and sustain the general interest in ballet. All of them furnish ballet companies in America with the most important part of the audience: the knowing and appreciative ballet-goer, as opposed to the superficial, autograph-seeking balletomane.

Moreover, not a few of these groups furnish talented, intelligent, and disciplined dancers for the professional ballet-companies. The *corps* of any American ballet-company lists a number of dancers who had their first experience in local or regional troupes, and in the New York City Ballet alone there are at least two exquisite artists, Janet Reed and Melissa Hayden, who began their careers in local ballet-groups.

All this is quite apart from the significance of the local groups as outlets for advanced ballet-students who have a deep interest and sincere devotion to ballet, but who cannot or do not wish to pursue a professional career in ballet. In this

respect, some of the local groups are comparable to many of
our well-known provincial symphony orchestras, staffed with
a combination of professional and nonprofessional musicians.

Ballet Caravan ceased to exist with the closing of the
New York World's Fair in September 1940. This was the end
of its activities under the Caravan name, but it had another
fling in the summer of 1941 under the resuscitated name of
The American Ballet.

Nelson A. Rockefeller, a friend of Kirstein and a co-
worker on behalf of the Museum of Modern Art, had been
appointed by President Roosevelt to head a new agency bearing the long and cumbersome name: United States Office for
Coordination of Commercial and Cultural Relations between
the American Republics. The agency was under the jurisdiction of the State Department. Early in 1941 Mr. Rockefeller decided that Latin America should be given an opportunity to see something of United States art, something
that would show our southern neighbors that our art as well
as our industry was exportable, something that would, at the
same time, transcend the language barrier between the United
States and the Spanish- and Portuguese-speaking countries.
His choice quite naturally fell on a ballet company, and just
as naturally on a company headed by his old friend Lincoln
Kirstein. Kirstein's direction, he reasoned, would assure a
high artistic level in the repertoire and its execution.

In a friendly, very loose, and rather unbusinesslike arrangement Mr. Rockefeller guaranteed that his office would
pay the minimum expenses of the company for a six-month
tour of Latin America and underwrite any deficit the company might incur on the tour. Production costs would have to
be borne by the American Ballet; i.e., by Kirstein.

Kirstein readily accepted the arrangement and set to
work organizing a company. His first thought was to get
George Balanchine to become artistic director and choreo-

graph several new ballets for the company, thus bringing him back to ballet from Hollywood and Broadway. Balanchine accepted Kirstein's invitation.

Departure for South America was scheduled for early June; rehearsals began in March.

Balanchine staged two new ballets: *Ballet Imperial*, to Tchaikovsky's Second Piano Concerto, in scenery and costumes by Mstislav Dobujinsky; and *Concerto Barocco*, to Bach's Double Violin Concerto, in costumes and décor by Eugene Berman. Both of these ballets, one may add parenthetically, are still being performed by several ballet companies here and abroad. He also revived *The Bat, Errante, Serenade,* and *Apollo*.

Other new ballets included Antony Tudor's *Time Table* to Aaron Copland's *Music for the Theater* (1925), in costumes and décor by James Morcom; the Lew Christensen-José Fernández *Pastorela* (which was billed as an opera-ballet because it had some singing in it), to a score by Paul Bowles, in costumes by Alvin Colt; and William Dollar's *Juke Box* (which was called in Spanish *Tertulia de Swing*), to music by Alec Wilder, its décor and costumes by Tom Lee.

Besides these, the repertoire listed three ballets from the Ballet Caravan repertoire: Loring's *Billy the Kid* and Christensen's *Filling Station* and *Charade*.

The repertoire was rather uneven and at least one of the ballets (*Juke Box*) pretty bad, while another (*Pastorela*), based on Mexican folklore, was calculated to please the patriotic sense of Latin American spectators. (Did not the Ballet Russe do the same thing for the same reason with such "American" ballets as *Union Pacific, Ghost Town,* and *Saratoga?*) It did, however, offer a chronological account of Balanchine's work from *Errante* (1933) to *Ballet Imperial* and *Concerto Barocco* (1941), and a cross-section of the work of American choreographers from *Filling Station* to *Juke Box*.

Auditions for the new troupe brought out some very good

dancers, among them Todd Bolender, Gisella Caccialanza, Lew Christensen, Mary Colbath, Douglas Coudy, Fred Danieli, Margit de Kova, Charles Dickson, William Dollar, John Dunphy, Betty Gilmore, William Garrett, June Graham, Babs Heath, Georgia Hiden, Marie Jeanne, Hortense Kahrklin, Helen Kramer, John Kriza, Lorna London, Nicholas Magallanes, José Martínez, Marjorie Moore, David Nillo, Peggy Noonan, Yvonne Patterson, Maria Quarequio, Newcomb Rice, Mary Jane Shea, Zachary Solov, Olga Suarez, John Taras, Beatrice Tompkins, Adelaide Varricchio, Hilda Wagner, and Billie Wynn. Lew Christensen was ballet master, Douglas Coudy stage manager. All told there were thirty-six dancing members, quite a large company for that time.

Some of the dancers came from the Ballet Caravan, some from the American Ballet, some from the World's Fair show, others from Ballet Theatre, the Philadelphia Ballet, and the Metropolitan Opera Ballet. It is interesting to note that a few of the dancers in this last venture of the American Ballet are still with the New York City Ballet.

By the time the company was ready to leave for South America it also included eleven nondancing members, among them Lincoln Kirstein, director general (who traveled with Mrs. Kirstein, the former Fidelma Cadmus, whom Kirstein had married in April); George Balanchine, artistic director; Emanuel Balaban, musical director and conductor; James Graham Luján, assistant to the director general; Doris R. Levine, executive secretary; Trude Rittmann, Simon Sadoff, and James Doyle, pianists; Robert Avray, technical director; Eudokia Mironowa, wardrobe mistress; and Michael Rainer Horwitz, booking manager.

On May 27, 29, and 30 the American Ballet gave a series of performances for invited audiences at New York's Hunter College Playhouse. There was a threefold reason for the performances. First, they were in the nature of break-in shows, or full-stage dress rehearsals, for the company, which until then had rehearsed only in studios; second, Kirstein wanted to show Mr. Rockefeller and his associates what their office was getting for the money it was spending; and last, it was felt that the people one way or another connected with the company and the School should see what the company had been doing during the preceding few months.

Kirstein had at that time developed an animosity and suspicion toward everyone in the dance world not directly connected with the American Ballet or the School. A little incident that occurred the day after the first performance serves as an excellent illustration.

I was then on the staff of *Dance Magazine*. A few days before the performances at Hunter College, the New York dance critics, except myself, received press tickets to cover the shows. I could not account for the omission, and instead of calling the office of the American Ballet accepted the invitation of Walter Terry, critic of the *New York Herald Tribune*, to attend the first performance as his guest.

Early the following morning Kirstein telephoned me: "I did not invite you to come to last night's performance because I didn't want you there. I consider it uncouth on your part to sneak in on someone else's ticket. If you show up tomorrow night I'll see to it that you are not admitted."

And bang went the receiver.

What with Kirstein's absence from New York and his subsequent military service, it took several years to clear up this misunderstanding. It seems that someone, known to both Kirstein and myself, said something (it is still not clear what specifically, because Kirstein does not remember it) about me which Kirstein did not take the trouble to verify, and the onesided feud was on.

This sounds unimportant and even comical now, but I was deeply hurt at the time. The fact that a zealous editor, without my knowledge, later published an account of it in *Dance Magazine* further aggravated the incident.

The performances were given with an orchestra conducted by Fritz Mahler. Most of the ballets were well received by the knowing spectators, and the company sailed in high spirits on June 6 in the *Santa Rosa*. The season opened June 26 at the Teatro Municipal in Rio de Janeiro. During the tour the company danced in São Paulo and Santos, Brazil; Montevideo, Uruguay; Buenos Aires and Rosario, Argentina; Santiago, Chile; La Paz, Bolivia; Lima, Peru; Guayaquil, Ecuador; Bogotá, Colombia; and Caracas, Venezuela.

Despite the excellence of the dancing personnel and the well-rehearsed repertoire, the American Ballet had only a moderate success in South America. There were reasons for this.

The summer before, the Ballet Russe de Monte Carlo had toured South America in full force. It was headed by four ballerinas of international fame: Alexandra Danilova, Alicia Markova, Irina Baronova, and Mia Slavenska. Leonide Massine, Igor Youskevitch, André Eglevsky, Frederic Franklin, and George Zoritch were in the male contingent. The repertoire included all the company's popular and spectacular ballets. The company spelled glamour, entertainment, and just a little intrigue. Dark-eyed *caballeros* constantly hung around backstage and at the stage door. The girls were nightly showered with flowers and more costly gifts. There were rumors, probably false, about duels between impetuous young men for the privilege of having supper with a little soloist. Several young men traveled with the company from city to city and country to country. (One of them even came back with the company to the United States.) Two or three proposed marriage to some of the girls. There were receptions and parties everywhere the company went. In short, all bells were ringing full peal.

Nothing of the sort happened or could happen to the American Ballet. It had excellent dancers, but nary a ballerina of any fame. The girls were nice, fun-loving, well-mannered American kids, but not more exciting or intriguing than Brazilian or Argentine kids of their age would be to Brazilian or Argentine young men. Most of them were youngsters with healthy appetites and tastes that inclined toward ice cream sodas rather than champagne; besides, night clubs robbed one of one's sleep and rehearsals were early in the morning.

The ballets were good but not exciting. The South Americans, like the North Americans before them, had never heard of the ballets the company presented, and they all somehow smacked of high art rather than entertainment. No *Swan Lake*, no *Scheherazade*, no *Beau Danube*, no *Gaité Parisienne*. Some of the ballets seemed downright educational: who in South America was interested in Mexican folklore on the ballet stage (*Pastorela*)? Others treated of "*automobilismo*" (*Filling Station*), the conquest of the West (*Billy the Kid*), and applied jazz (*Juke Box*). This was not what the South Americans wanted.

It was not that the American Ballet was neglected or unfeted. It did have its entourage: embassy and consular attachés, bright young men and women from the higher schools of learning, young artists, musicians, and writers, editors of literary reviews, heads of museums—the intellectual cream of the various nations. But it was not the entourage to create a successful ballet season, to surround it with the glamour a ballet company needs to succeed, especially in South America, where each city has one or two important families around whom all artistic (or perhaps pseudo-artistic) and theatrical activity revolves.

In short, the American Ballet had all the intellectual support and good will it could have wished for, but little of the social and popular acceptance it needed to be really successful. Like the first American Ballet and Ballet Caravan after it, the new American Ballet was still an *avant-garde* organization, unable to attract the two strata of society it needed most: the upper crust for glitter and excitement, the middle class to fill the theaters.

The financial arrangements that Kirstein had made with Mr. Rockefeller were not working out so smoothly as had been anticipated. The American Ballet was having a deficit in nearly every city it played, and the Coordinator's office was not supplying so promptly as promised the funds necessary to make up the deficits. Kirstein, in fact, was forced to hurry to the United States to get money so that the company would not be stranded.

Despite all this, the company had a very good time in South America. The people who attended the performances liked the ballets very much, and the dancers had their share of enthusiastic receptions. The American Ballet had on the whole an excellent press, perhaps a little too serious and learned in its praise, which had the effect of keeping away the entertainment-seekers; i.e., the majority of the theater-going public.

The tour, which had been scheduled to run six months, did not last quite that long. Complicated transportation problems could not be solved in actual practice so simply as on paper when the schedules were being drawn up; theaters supposed to be available on specific dates were still occupied when the dates rolled around; flying conditions over the Andes were not always what they were expected to be.

As a result the company returned to the United States in October instead of December as had been planned. On arrival in New York the American Ballet was formally disbanded.

X

1941–1946

"Dance Index"; The American Concert Ballet; Leon Barzin

The American Ballet (to use these words as a generic term) has always been a movement in American ballet rather than just a performing company. The future historian will refer to it as a school in ballet, not a school of ballet, in the sense that we now speak of the Flemish School in painting, for instance.

For not only did the American Ballet seek and, as we shall see, eventually find a new and unique style in the ballet dance, but it also spread activities beyond classroom study and performances. The American Ballet was a school and a company (under different names), but it also participated in ramifications of ballet which are not so glamorous

140

as a ballet company itself and do not attract nearly so much attention, but which are just as necessary for the continuation and progress of this art form.

Lincoln Kirstein's contribution of his rich collection of books and memorabilia on dance to the Museum of Modern Art as a nucleus for its Dance Archives in 1940 has already been mentioned. The Archives, the first in this country, both chronologically and in importance, is perhaps equaled only by the Archives Internationales de la Danse in Paris, which, incidentally, ceased to exist as a separate institution in January 1952, and was transferred by its founder, Rolf de Maré, to the museum of the Opéra.

Also mentioned here were some of the articles Kirstein wrote over the years in the general and theatrical press, as well as his books, *Dance* (1935) and *Blast at Ballet* (1938). In 1939 Kirstein wrote another book, *Ballet Alphabet* (*A Primer for Laymen*), a small dictionary encompassing the history, esthetics, and technique of ballet, excellently illustrated by Paul Cadmus. In February 1952 the publishers of the present volume issued *The Classic Ballet* (*Basic Technique and Terminology*), for which Kirstein wrote a chapter, "Historical Development," which in effect is a lucid history of ballet. Muriel Stuart, still a member of the faculty of the School of American Ballet, supplied the descriptive text, George Balanchine wrote a preface, and Carlus Dyer did the clear and exciting illustrations. *The Classic Ballet* is now the standard textbook on ballet technique, superseding, as it were, that of the great Russian teacher, Agrippina Vaganova, *Fundamentals of the Classic Dance*, which I translated into English, and which had been in general use in the United States and Great Britain since 1946.

In December 1936 the H. W. Wilson Company brought out Paul Magriel's *A Bibliography of Dancing*, a comprehensive list of titles of books and articles on dance and related subjects. The compiler had been an associate of Kirstein since the opening of the School of American Ballet, and was closely identified with the formation and running of the Ballet Caravan. He was the first curator of the Dance Archives of the Museum of Modern Art. A trained, careful, and erudite researcher, and later the author of books on dance, Magriel did magnificent work in an almost virgin field. The basic *Bibliography* and the annual *Cumulated Supplements*, which were issued through 1940, are standard and very valuable reference books. They are now entirely out of print and, regrettably, not being continued.

The Dance Archives, Kirstein's books and articles, and Magriel's *Bibliography* were as much organic activities of the American Ballet as were the school and the companies themselves—less glamorous, perhaps, and less talked about, but always directed toward the same objective, the creation, development, clarification, and articulation of American ballet.

It was no surprise then, when the American Ballet company was disbanded in October 1941, following its South American tour, that Kirstein would not be satisfied with simply biding his time until he could assemble a new company. Had he been just another director of a ballet company who wanted to score a financial success with his undertaking, he would have proceeded immediately to organize a ballet company with the most popular repertoire possible. For the Second World War was bringing a new prosperity to the United States, and ballet companies, along with other theatrical entertainments, were doing unprecedented business. Defense work brought employment to new millions of people; workers and farmers who had been doing menial jobs for small pay found themselves almost overnight on a new earning level. They were beginning to get the feel of folding money and, not used to it or quite knowing how to make the best of it, were looking for ways to spend it. The theater, or amusement if you wish, was one such way, and a new audience

began to flock to the theater, to live shows in particular. There
were many in this new audience who had never before seen
a live show. Managers all over the United States reported that
people were asking why spoken plays and musical shows
needed intermissions. One manager of a ballet company told
me that in town after town spectators would come out during
intermissions to inquire whether there would be any singing
in the next act.

Kirstein was not the man to do the thing that would be
normal for a commercial entrepreneur. He decided not to
organize a new company or tour the existing one for the
duration of the war. Instead, he embarked on a publishing
venture, which, like all the activities of the American Ballet,
was vital, sincere, erudite, and in the best of taste, but also,
like some of them, cerebral and occasionally personal.

The new venture was a magazine called *Dance Index*.
Listed as official publishers and copyright owners were Dance
Index, Ballet Caravan, Inc. Now, eleven years after Volume
I, Number I, was published in January 1942, and four years
since its last issue (Volume VII, Numbers 7 and 8) was published in the early spring of 1949, one can truthfully say that
no more lastingly significant dance magazine has ever been
published.

The first editors of *Dance Index* were Lincoln Kirstein,
Paul Magriel, and Baird Hastings. They were subsequently
drafted into the army one by one, and *Dance Index* was to
change editors several times during its six years of existence.

The first issue of *Dance Index* was a monograph by John
Martin, entitled "Isadora Duncan and Basic Dance." It also
carried a "Dance Almanac," a list of dance performances and
exhibitions relative to dance for the month of February. A
Foreword by the editors set forth the reasons for the publication of *Dance Index* and some of its aspirations. Here are
excerpts from it:

"It takes some justification to start anything new, now. We have the example of England before us in many things, even newsprint priorities. A year from now it may be undesirable or impossible even to think of manufacturing anything as apparently useless as a sober review concerned with one rather specific branch of theatre, and that lyric and unrealistic.

"Naturally, it is exhilarating, too. What we do must be more than useful, better than good. At the present moment there is no place in America where articles as exhaustive as those to be published here are available. At a modest guess, there must be a thousand people all over the country, willing to pay a quarter a month to read them. These articles will be concerned with the visual arts, music, human gesture and behavior, traditions of morals and habits. Certainly they can be as interesting as far fatter and more frequent journals devoted to clothes and cosmetics.

"Like other arts, dancing has survived every disaster the Western world has known. It seems to exist instinctively in response to some blind necessity, which in an almost preposterous sense, ignores all the frightening facts of human survival. We even recall the names of ballets along with famous battles.

"The prospectus for Dance Index went out before Pearl Harbor. But the returns to it came in afterwards. We were surprised at the warmth of its reception and how pleased so many people were at its promise and plans. There were a number of men in service who expressed a lively interest, and this, if nothing else, convinced us to persevere. We shall issue at least the twelve numbers. A year is a long time. No history of dancing in the United States exists, and by next December, due to material which Dance Index will have called into being, it will be possible to embark on such a history."

The editors' modest guess that "there must be a thousand

people all over the country willing to pay a quarter a month"
to read *Dance Index* was exactly right. *Dance Index* did have a
thousand readers, but no more. And these thousand readers,
paying a quarter a month, could not possibly support *Dance
Index*. A very simple calculation should have shown Kirstein
at the outset that a thousand quarters is only two hundred and
fifty dollars a month—just about one fourth of what it cost
to produce an issue. And this was the only income *Dance
Index* had. The publishers—i.e., Kirstein—did not wish to
accept advertising, and did not place the magazine on the
newsstands. Beyond sending out the initial prospectus they
made no effort to gain additional subscribers. This was and
still is a pity. *Dance Index* should have had a much wider
circulation, and could have had it, almost for the asking.
Kirstein's estimate of a possible thousand readers for *Dance
Index* was much below the potential figure. I have had considerable experience in publishing dance periodicals, and I
can safely say that there are, and were in 1942, at least five
thousand people in the United States who would be willing to
spend two dollars and fifty cents a year for a subscription to a
magazine of the caliber of *Dance Index*. But these five thousand
either did not know about *Dance Index* at all or heard about it
only vaguely.

As it stood, *Dance Index* was losing money from the very
beginning to the very end. True to Kirstein's oft-expressed
remark, he was again "in business to lose money." In the
seven years of publishing *Dance Index*, he contributed to it
about fifty thousand dollars. It was a financial loss, yes; but
it was a most important, constructive contribution to the
history of dance in America and all over the world. The few
hundred full sets of *Dance Index* still in existence are probably
the most valuable source material we have ever had in the
United States.

Most of the issues of *Dance Index* were monographs, written by one author on one subject; a few contained several articles by different writers on one subject; two or three had several articles by one author on a variety of subjects. It is not easy to say which issues were more important than others. In my own opinion the following issues (in chronological order) deserve special consideration: the already mentioned first issue, "Isadora Duncan and Basic Dance," by John Martin; "The Dance in Shaker Ritual," by E. D. Andrews (April 1942); "The Denishawn Era," by Baird Hastings (June 1942); "Augusta Maywood," by Marian Hannah Winter (January–February 1943); "Mary Ann Lee, First American Giselle," by Lillian Moore (May 1943); "The Romantic Ballet in London: 1821–1858," by George Chaffee (September–December 1943); "European Dance Teachers in the United States," by Ann Barzel (April–May–June 1944); "Notes on Choreography," by George Balanchine (February–March 1945); "George Washington Smith," by Lillian Moore (June–July–August 1945); "Jules Perrot," by Yury Slonimsky, translated by Anatole Chujoy (December 1945); "The Stage and Ballet Designs of Eugene Berman," by Allison Delarue (January 1946); "Birth of the Waltz," by Paul Nettl (September 1946); "Juba and American Minstrelsy," by Marian Hannah Winter (February 1947); "The Ballet d'Action Before Noverre," by Artur Michel (March 1947); "Marius Petipa," by Yury Slonimsky, translated by Anatole Chujoy (May–June 1947); "Strawinsky in the Theatre," a symposium prepared by Minna Lederman (Vol. VI, Nos. 10, 11, 12, 1947, published in the spring of 1948)—the crowning glory of *Dance Index;* and "Dance in Bali," by Colin McPhee (Vol. VII, Nos. 7 and 8, 1948, published in early 1949), the last issue of the magazine. One might note in passing that Lincoln Kirstein wrote only one issue during the entire existence of *Dance Index*—the penultimate, entitled "Elie Nadelman: Sculptor of the Dance."

By the end of its first year of publication two of the three original editors of *Dance Index*, Baird Hastings and Paul Magriel, had been drafted into the army. The December 1942 masthead listed them as Founders. The editors were now Kirstein and Donald Windham, a young writer and playwright with an interest in dance and in need of a job. In the editorial comment that preceded the text the editors thanked John Martin, dance critic of *The New York Times*, "for anonymously running Dance Index when two editors were called to the army while the third [Kirstein] was half a year in South America." Kirstein had gone to South America on behalf of the State Department and the Coordinator's Office to do research on painting in Latin America and had later written a book on the history of it. He also wrote a book entitled *The Latin-American Collection at the Museum of Modern Art* (1943).

The March 1943 issue carried another change on the masthead. Kirstein's name was moved from the listing of Editors to that of Founders, and Donald Windham remained as sole editor.

Kirstein joined the army on February 19, 1943, and served in it for thirty-two months, until October 1945. He was shipped to Europe as a member of the Corps of Engineers, served as a dispatch rider, but later, after the invasion, was attached with the modest rank of Private First Class to the Monuments, Fine Arts and Archives office, under the direction of the American Commission for the Protection and Salvage of Artistic and Historic Monuments in War Areas. His work in tracing and recovering works of art stolen by the Nazi leaders and the eventual return of these works to churches, museums, galleries, and private owners earned him a citation in the Report of the Commission to the President of the United States in 1946 and a medal from the Netherlands Government. In this action incidentally, he discovered some hitherto unknown works of art, specifically, a series of mid-sixteenth-century wall paintings in the damaged church of Mont-Saint-Martin (Meurthe-et-Moselle), France.

Donald Windham carried on alone through the November 1945 issue. The December 1945 masthead omitted the listing of Founders, and Kirstein's and Windham's names appeared as editors. With the January 1946 issue Marian Eames joined the magazine as managing editor. By March 1946 Paul Magriel had rejoined the magazine as editor; with the April–May issue Baird Hastings's name was back on the masthead, only to disappear again after the August issue of that year. Donald Windham withdrew after the April 1947, issue, Paul Magriel after the July issue of that year. Lincoln Kirstein and Marian Eames carried on until the last.

Dance Index ceased publication for a very simple reason: Kirstein did not have enough money to support both the magazine and Ballet Society, which he launched in 1946, soon after his return from the war, and Ballet Society was more important to him than *Dance Index*.

During the war years the School of American Ballet (which incidentally added to its faculty in 1941 Anatole Oboukhoff, a former *premier danseur* of the Maryinsky Theater) and *Dance Index* were the principal activities of the American Ballet. This does not mean, however, that Balanchine, who now headed the school in fact as well as in name, and the dancers of the American Ballet were inactive.

In the fall and winter of 1942 Balanchine staged the opera ballets for the New Opera Company's productions in New York, among them *Rosalinda* (*Die Fledermaus*), which ran for more than one year. During that season the American Ballet danced his *Ballet Imperial*, sharing a bill with an opera.

On April 9, 1943, more than one hundred students of the School of American Ballet participated in Bach's St. Matthew Passion, produced by Balanchine and Leopold

Stokowsky at the Metropolitan Opera House, and conducted
by Stokowsky. The Passion was staged in the form of a pageant, closely following the text used by the composer, depicting the various scenes as they unfold in the composition.
There was no dance in the strict sense of the word, but only
mass, group, and individual movements kept within the limits
of the exalted theme. The figure of Christ was never visible
on the stage, but was symbolized by a ray of light which was
kept moving on the stage as the text demanded.

In the fall of 1943, Balanchine staged the dances in the
New Opera Company production of Léhar's *The Merry
Widow*, in which a number of dancers from the American
Ballet were employed.

On November 14, a new offshoot of the American Ballet
made a bid for public interest. It was the American Concert
Ballet, organized by Mary Jane Shea, William Dollar, Todd
Bolender, and Douglas Coudy. The group included the dan-
cers Georgia Hiden, Jeanne Jones, Lillian Lanese, Zoya
Leporsky, Yvonne Patterson, Carlyle Ramey, Adelaide Var-
ricchio, Jane Ward, Patricia White (now better known as
Patricia Wilde), Edward Bigelow, Aaron Girard, Francisco
Moncion, and Stanley Zompakos. Simon Sadoff and Angelo
Cafarelli were the pianists. At its initial performance, at the
Kaufmann Auditorium of the Young Men's Hebrew Asso-
ciation (the so-called Ninety-Second Street Y), the group
presented Bolender's *Mother Goose Suite*, to Ravel's music;
Shea's *Sailor Bar 1943*, set to Arthur Honegger's Concertino
for Two Pianos; Dollar's *Five Boons of Life*, based on Mark
Twain's fable, to music by Ernst von Dohnányi; and Balan-
chine's *Concerto Barocco*, originally produced for the South
American tour of the American Ballet in 1941.

The American Concert Ballet was very obviously an
interim organization and gave only a few performances in and
around New York. Its importance lay in the fact that the

young choreographers and most of the dancers were em-
ployed in Broadway musicals: their work in the American
Concert Ballet was a spare-time activity. Characteristically,
most of the dancers were members of one or another of the
companies stemming from the American Ballet and the Ballet
Caravan; several of them are now in the New York City
Ballet. Two of the works presented, *Concerto Barocco* and
Mother Goose Suite, are now in the repertoire of the New York
City Ballet.

In the early summer of 1944 Balanchine went to Hollywood to stage the dances in the operetta *Song of Norway*, based
on the life of Edvard Grieg, with music culled from Grieg's
works. Producer Edwin Lester gave Balanchine a free hand in
selecting the music for his ballets, as well as in staging, then a
rare occurrence on the musical-comedy stage. The company
of the Ballet Russe de Monte Carlo, including Alexandra
Danilova and Frederic Franklin, was engaged as a unit as the
dancing personnel of the operetta, and Balanchine had a field
day. He staged all the singing ensembles (for the first time in
years the chorus actually moved around) and what was probably the finest example of musical-comedy ballet. He even
took the liberty of finishing the operetta with a long and complicated ballet set to Grieg's Piano Concerto, an unprecedented final number for an operetta. *Song of Norway* opened in
New York on August 21 at the Imperial Theater and was a
smash hit.

Balanchine's work with the Ballet Russe de Monte
Carlo brought him into a close association with the company
which was to last several years and, in effect, to save the company from ruin. The repertoire and personnel of the company
had deteriorated since Leonide Massine had left in 1942 to join
Ballet Theatre. Balanchine brought new life to it with his new
ballets: *Danses Concertantes*, to Igor Stravinsky's music, in décor
and costumes by Eugene Berman, and *Le Bourgeois-Gentilhomme*,

to music by Richard Strauss, also in décor and costumes by
Berman. In addition, the training and rehearsals under Balanchine, and his very presence in the company, were a stimulus
for all dancers.

When the Ballet Russe de Monte Carlo opened its season at the New York City Center on September 10, it was, in
effect, a new company. Obviously the company could not
dance its own season and appear in *Song of Norway* simultane-
ously, so a new troupe was engaged for *Song of Norway* and
many of the American Ballet and Ballet Caravan dancers
found long and gainful employment in the operetta. Some of
the American Ballet dancers were also engaged by the Ballet
Russe, among them Mary Ellen Moylan, who had danced
Ballet Imperial in New York and also appeared in the New
Opera Company's productions, and Nicholas Magallanes.

Between 1944 and 1946 Balanchine choreographed for
Ballet Russe de Monte Carlo, *Ballet Imperial* (a revival) with
Mary Ellen Moylan and Maria Tallchief; *Mozartiana* and
Concerto Barocco (both revivals); *Raymonda* to Alexander Glaz-
unoff's music, in collaboration with Alexandra Danilova, with
scenery and costumes by Alexandre Benois; and *Night Shadow*,
to music by Vittorio Rieti, based on melodies by Vincenzo
Bellini, in scenery and costumes by Dorothea Tanning. Also in
1944, Balanchine staged for Ballet Theatre *Waltz Academy*, to
Rieti's music, in décor by Oliver Smith and costumes by Alvin
Colt.

In October 1945, Lincoln Kirstein received his discharge
from the army. It did not take him long to return to ballet.
Legend has it that he went from the separation center direct to
the School of American Ballet, but this cannot be verified.

On November 5 some eighty-five dancers and students of
the School of American Ballet appeared in a joint performance with the orchestra of the National Orchestral Association
at Carnegie Hall in a program entitled "Adventure in Ballet."

For this performance Balanchine choreographed ballets to Mozart's Symphonie Concertante in E-flat major, and Stravinsky's Elegie (for viola) and *Circus Polka;* and Todd Bolender staged dances to two movements of Tchaikovsky's Suite No. 2, op. 53 ("Valse" and "Danse Baroque"). It was a successful, semi-educational event that had excellent publicity value for the School, but might have passed without much notice or carried little consequence were it not that the performance brought together Balanchine, Kirstein, and Leon Barzin (founder and director of the National Orchestral Association and conductor of its orchestra). Barzin, a sensitive and open-minded musician who subsequently (1946) received the Alice M. Ditson Award for outstanding contribution to American musical education, proved to be a kindred spirit. In the few weeks of work with Balanchine and Kirstein he understood what they wanted to do in ballet and did not hesitate to agree to a co-operation in any undertaking they might want to launch. This was something they had been hoping for since the days of the American Ballet: a conductor and an orchestra interested in experimenting, worried not so much about the number of performances they could play as about the quality of the performances they could give.

Here was an alliance that might make it possible for them to build a permanent organization.

XI

1946–1947

Ballet Society

To those who have not watched at close range the
activities of Lincoln Kirstein and George Balanchine, their work often seems illusory, arbitrary,
even accidental. Actually, this is not so. Some or
many of their undertakings may have been, and
still are, impractical from a business point of view
—they themselves have never denied that—but
artistically their work has been, and is now, sound
and well planned. One reason for the seemingly
accidental quality of their activities is that both
Balanchine and Kirstein talk very freely about their
plans long before they are ready for fruition. In the
interim between the planning and the execution the
original plans undergo changes of which they do not

153

tell anyone simply because they are not asked. When a scheme finally takes shape, it is quite naturally somewhat different in detail from what it had been at its first stage, and the impression often is created that they do not do what they plan to do and do things that had not been planned. In actuality, the change in their plans is an indication of the careful preparation attendant on the development of a project. The difference between the basic plan and the ultimate result is generally no greater than the difference between an architect's first rendering of a well-designed home and the finished building, with all the water pipes in and the landscaping done.

When Ballet Society was founded in 1946, it looked like a spontaneous and rather tentative organization with not much of a plan behind it. In fact, however, the plans for Ballet Society, so far as Kirstein and Balanchine were concerned, had had their origin back in 1937, nine years before Ballet Society came into being. Kirstein outlined the plan for it in fair detail to me in March of that year (see Chapter vi) and the final organization of Ballet Society differed from that plan only in degree, not in substance.

Rumors about the organization of Ballet Society began to circulate in the spring of 1946. By mid-September Balanchine and Kirstein had assembled a company and begun rehearsals. In early October, Ballet Society sent out a well-laid-out twelve-page announcement, with a beautifully designed cover by Corrado Cagli, which has since become a collector's item.

"Ballet in America," said the introduction, obviously written by Kirstein, "has so developed over the last ten years that it is now acceptable as a major form of popular art and entertainment. Not only have we created first-rate touring companies, but Americans have demonstrated an inexhaustible power to create classic dancers who perform with a brilliance rivalling the most distinguished foreign artists. Since ballet in the United States is relatively new, our interest has been primarily in the revival of productions already famous, or the creation of works based on national themes. Now, with the close of a second world war, broader directions are possible and desirable."

Kirstein apparently thought that he had to justify the *démarche* from a basic folklore repertoire of the Ballet Caravan to one of the international scope of Ballet Society. Actually he did not have to do so because the homespun repertoire of Ballet Caravan had satisfied few people in the audience and still fewer in the company. Eugene Loring's *Billy the Kid*, Agnes de Mille's *Rodeo*, and Jerome Robbins's *Fancy Free* furnished all the folklore ballet Americans wanted to see.

Incorporated as a nonprofit membership organization "for the encouragement of the lyric theatre by the production of new works," Ballet Society promised "to present a completely new repertory, consisting of ballets, ballet-opera and other lyric forms. Each will have the planned collaboration of independent easel-painters, progressive choreographers and musicians, employing the full use of avant-garde ideas, methods and materials. The first season will perforce be modest. There will be no touring nor attempt at a continuous run. Each work presented is designed for the particular stage upon which it will first be seen.

"Emphasis will be on expert musical and dance direction to insure an essential elegance and freshness, rather than on famous stars or the residual prestige of the standard ballet repertory.

"In offering to its members certain books, records, films and articles the Ballet Society will provide a background for appreciation and continued enjoyment. It is hoped that the programs will have a lasting value. From their inception, preservation for further repetition is planned together with constantly added new ballets."

George Balanchine was mentioned in the outline as

artistic director, Leon Barzin as musical director, Lew Christensen as ballet master, Lincoln Kirstein (characteristically) as secretary. Paul Magriel was designated as editor of books and records and Jean Rosenthal as technical supervisor.

Some of the statements in the announcement were taken with a grain of salt by most of the recipients. How could anyone, for instance, accept at face value a declaration that "each work presented is designed for the particular stage upon which it will first be seen"? Most people knew, if Balanchine and Kirstein did not, that to find any theater in New York for a single performance was a difficult assignment, to find one that would have a "particular stage" for a definite ballet was entirely out of the question. The promise that the "emphasis will be on musical and dance direction rather than on famous stars" evoked a knowing smile. If a company does not have "famous stars" it must emphasize some other aspects of the ballet.

The six-point program of Ballet Society listed:

PRESENTATION of new theatre-pieces, including ballet, ballet-opera, and chamber-opera, either commissioned by the Ballet Society or unfamiliar to the American public, as well as individual concert-dancers.

CO-OPERATION with other educational and cultural institutions, to enable the production of performances, exhibitions and publications, difficult or impossible to accomplish alone.

PUBLICATION of books, prints and articles that award to the dance a consistent and serious attention long enjoyed by painting, sculpture, architecture, and music.

PRODUCTION and circulation of documentary dance-films recording contemporary activity in ballet companies, individual dancers, and national dances, as well as experimental films using dance as a main element.

PUBLICATION of record albums of music in the performances of the Ballet Society, with photographic documentation and full program notes.

AWARDS of fellowships enabling talented young dancers and choreographers to work by themselves or with groups of dancers to develop technically and professionally.

The organization offered two classes of membership: Associate and Participating. Associate Membership privileges, costing fifty dollars a year, provided for full participation in the over-all program, including: two seats for all stage productions and special events (lectures, film showings, *etc.*); all books, including the *Ballet Society Year Book*, and record albums to be published during the season; subscription to *Dance Index;* invitations to dress rehearsals and demonstrations of dance technique. Participating Members, who paid fifteen dollars a year, were offered one ticket for all stage productions; subscription to *Dance Index;* and the *Ballet Society Year Book*. In addition, all members were to receive the *Ballet Society Bulletin*, a two-to-four page publication appearing four times a year at irregular intervals.

Some eight hundred people responded to the initial announcement.

Quite obviously the program promised much more than the Ballet Society could afford to give its subscribers and more than anyone could ever dream of receiving. It was a minor miracle that the membership, during the first season, 1946–7, received everything the organization had promised with the exception of the phonograph records.

It received three books, all monographs on famous dancers, edited by Paul Magriel: *Vaslav Nijinsky, Isadora Duncan, Anna*

Pavlova; the *Year Book of Ballet Society;* subscriptions to *Dance Index* and the *Bulletin;* and the specified allotment of tickets for performances and special events.

To the dismay of skeptics and professional ballet people who pooh-poohed the idea of subscription performances as impracticable, no tickets were sold for individual performances, as the announcement had warned. A step that caused many a raised eyebrow was the elimination of the press list. Publications that wanted to cover the performances—and these included most of the New York dailies, the weekly newsmagazines, the professional dance press, and many monthlies —had to subscribe for their critics, an unprecedented occurrence, at least for New York.

Five programs were given during the first season: on November 20, 1946, and February 18 (and 20), March 13 (repeated the next evening), March 26, and May 18, 1947.

The official roster of dancers for the first season of the Ballet Society, as given in the *Year Book*, included seventy-nine names. Among these were several guest artists and many apprentice dancers, students of the School who participated in only two or three productions. The full-fledged professional dancers in the company—i.e., members of the dancers' union (The American Guild of Musical Artists)—were Virginia Barnes, Edward Bigelow, Hubert Bland, Todd Bolender, Gisella Caccialanza, Lew Christensen, Fred Danieli, William Dollar, Paul Godkin, Georgia Hiden, Brooks Jackson, José Martínez, Francisco Moncion, Mary Ellen Moylan, Betty Nichols, Jean Reeves, Elise Reiman, Walter Stane, John Taras, Beatrice Tompkins, and Adelaide Varricchio. The apprentices had special working-permits from the Union. Quite a few of these are familiar names now: Jacques d'Amboise, Joan Djurop, Dorothy Dushok, Ruth Gilbert, Gerard Leavitt, Tanaquil LeClercq, Pat McBride, Job Sanders, Irma Sandré, Ruth Sobotka, Barbara Walczak, Jenny Workman.

The first performance of the new organization, on November 20, was given in the auditorium of the Central High School of Needle Trades, as unlikely and unsuitable a place to present ballet as one can find in New York. A huge, barn-like hall, cold and uninviting, it is as impersonal as a railroad station, with just about as much intimacy. It is decorated with huge murals of the "tuppence-colored" variety, style, taste, and workmanship, reflecting the artistic standards of the Board of Education. It has hard, uncomfortable chairs and a stage devoid of any facilities: its claim to be called a stage is its elevation above the floor and a curtain separating it from the audience. There being no orchestra pit, the fifty-odd musicians of the National Orchestral Association sat on the floor level in plain view of the spectators, the doublebasses and harps very effectively obstructing part of the makeshift stage. The conductor, Leon Barzin, stood on a small elevated platform, blocking the stage from still another angle. The whole thing looked hopelessly amateurish, provincial, and depressing.

If Kirstein was serious at all when he said in the announcement that "each work presented is designed for the particular stage upon which it will first be seen," what would the works presented here look like?

The first curtain was just about half an hour late, during which time the audience could hear hammering and excited voices behind the curtain and a great deal of tuning and practicing of extra-difficult passages by the orchestra. The evening was getting to be as uninspiring and untheatrical as one could imagine.

And then the curtain went up.

The long wait, the uncomfortable seats, all the impedimenta of the auditorium and stage were immediately forgotten, for there was magic on the stage: *The Spellbound Child* (*L'Enfant et les sortilèges*) by Maurice Ravel.

Billed as a lyric fantasy in two parts, this opera for children with a text by Colette (in a free English translation by Jane Barzin and Lincoln Kirstein) was staged by Balanchine in the same manner he had used for Gluck's *Orpheus* in 1936: the singers sitting with the musicians, the dancers acting out the story on stage. Only one member of the cast both sang and acted, twelve-year-old Joseph Connoly, who took the principal role of The Child. Aline Bernstein supplied the inventive fairy-tale-like décor and costumes, and Jean Rosenthal, for the first time in ballet, showed what can be done on a stage even with the most primitive switchboard and lighting equipment. There were forty-three dancers on the stage. How they ever got on or, having got on, did not spill into the audience, will remain Balanchine's secret. The singing ensemble had nineteen soloists and a chorus of twenty-four, all members of the National Music League.

It was an enchanting show, sensitive, whimsical, imaginative—true lyric theater. It succeeded in transporting the audience from the cold November night into a realm of fantasy ostensibly designed for children, but actually meant for adults.

Captivating though *The Spellbound Child* was, it was only a curtain-raiser as far as the ballet-minded majority of the audience was concerned. Kirstein and Balanchine may have been sincerely concerned with the broader aspects of the lyric theater: Ballet Society's subscribers were mainly interested in ballet, and for them the main event was Balanchine's new ballet *The Four Temperaments*, choreographed to a score by Paul Hindemith (Theme and Four Variations for string orchestra and piano), in scenery and costumes by Kurt Seligmann.

The score of *The Four Temperaments* had been commissioned by Balanchine and Kirstein in 1940 for the Latin-American tour of the American Ballet in the summer of 1941. It was then proposed to call the ballet *The Cave of Sleep*, and

Pavel Tchelitchew was commissioned to do the décor and costumes. The ballet was not mounted at that time because of the dissatisfaction of the composer with Tchelitchew's sketches. He felt that the visual presentation offered him, however beautiful, was overwhelming and contained ideas extraneous to his original program. (Tchelitchew's sketches are now in the Department of Theatre Arts of the Museum of Modern Art).

New décor was commissioned from Seligmann in the spring of 1946. (It might be noted parenthetically that Seligmann's scenery and costumes were discarded in 1952 in favor of a plain background and simple classic costumes, and that the ballet thereby gained considerably.)

Here is the line-up of the world *première* of what turned out to be one of the most exciting Balanchine ballets: Theme: Beatrice Tompkins and José Martínez; Elise Reiman and Lew Christensen; Gisella Caccialanza and Francisco Moncion. Melancholic Variation: William Dollar, with Georgia Hiden and Rita Karlin, and ensemble. Sanguinic Variation: Mary Ellen Moylan and Fred Danieli, and ensemble. Phlegmatic: Todd Bolender and ensemble. Choleric: Tanaquil LeClercq, William Dollar, Todd Bolender, and ensemble. Nicholas Kopeikine, remembered from the first steps of the School of American Ballet, was the solo pianist.

Edwin Denby, reviewing the performance for *Dance News*, had this to say in part:

"The ballet holds one spellbound by the constant surprise of its dance development; by the denseness and power of the dance images which the figures on stage create from moment to moment. . . . Neither sequences nor figures looks familiar. The grandiose force of these crowded large motions seems to correspond in its accents to the dense tensions of the score's counterpoint, and the unexpected continuity (as the phrases evolve) to the score's smooth melodic surfacing. . . . No choreography was ever more serious,

more vigorous, more wide in scope or penetrating in imagination. And none could be more consistently elegant in
its bearing. . . . The décor and costumes were disappointing.

"The new Ballet Society . . . will do a great deal for
ballet in this country if they can maintain the standards of this
performance. But a ballet like Balanchine's The Four Temperaments is an event one cannot often expect. . . ."

The spectators loved every minute of *The Four Temperaments*. They even accepted Seligmann's cumbersome backdrops with painted fabrics that seemed to weigh tons yet
floated in the air, and the overornate and uncomfortable-to-
dance-in costumes, which detracted from the choreography.
Choreographically only the finale of the ballet was weak.
Somehow Balanchine could not find himself there.

Ballet Society's debut was an overwhelming success.

There were requests for a repeat performance for nonsubscribers, but Kirstein and Balanchine held steadfastly to
the original intent of performing only for the membership of
Ballet Society. As a result there was a new spurt of subscriptions: the plan caught on.

The second program of Ballet Society was given at the
Hunter College Playhouse, a much more suitable auditorium
for ballet than the Central High School of Needle Trades, but
with a stage as small and as ill-equipped. Due to the increased
membership and the small seating capacity of the theater, the
second program was given two performances, on January 13
and 14. Earlier subscribers attended the first performance,
newcomers the second.

For this program Kirstein introduced an innovation: in
addition to three ballets the program presented the modern
dancer Iris Mabry in two works, and a suite of Javanese Court
and Popular Dances by a group headed by Ratna Mohini to
music arranged and transcribed from original sources by Colin

McPhee. The innovation did not go well with the predominantly ballet-minded audience. They were frankly bored with the overlong Javanese suite and they could not have understood or cared less about Iris Mabry. Mabry had appeared earlier in the season with the same program in a performance of her own, and those who wanted to see her had already done so. This is not to say, of course, that Mabry is not a fascinating dancer. She is very gifted, entirely original, and most exciting, but she did not fit into a ballet program. The equally incongruous presence of the Javanese group can probably be attributed to the victory of friendship over management. Colin McPhee, who arranged the music, was a friend of Kirstein. (McPhee subsequently wrote a monograph, "Dance in Bali," for the last issue of *Dance Index*.) Ratna Mohini, the principal Javanese dancer, was the wife of the French photographer Henri Cartier-Bresson, another friend of Kirstein. (Incidentally, in 1947 Kirstein wrote an appreciation of Cartier-Bresson's work in a book entitled *The Photographs of Henri Cartier-Bresson*, published by the Museum of Modern Art, which was a masterpiece of critical analysis.) Thus friendship, perhaps coupled with a diminishing but still lingering a-theatricality in Kirstein, led to the presentation of this mixed program.

The three ballets on the program were:

Lew Christensen's *Pastorela*, to music by Paul Bowles, based on the Mexican Christmas-play *Los Pastores*, with a libretto by José Martínez, in scenery and costumes by Alvin Colt. The work was originally commissioned by Kirstein in 1940 for the Latin-American tour of the American Ballet in the summer of 1941, and this was its first North American performance.

Renard (*The Fox*), a ballet-burlesque for singers and dancers, composed by Igor Stravinsky in 1916. It had choreography by Balanchine, scenery and costumes by Esteban

Francés, and an English text by Harvey Officer. *Renard* was first presented at the Paris Opéra in 1922 by the Diaghilev company, with choreography by Bronislava Nijinska.

Divertimento, a new ballet by Balanchine to a score by Alexei Haieff, presented without scenery, in practice tunics and tights.

Of the three ballets only *Divertimento* was important, exciting and, frankly, worth doing. It presented Balanchine and his dancers at their best. It had wonderful form and line, and was done with true classic simplicity. Also it gave a chance to a group of male dancers to do more than just support the girls or dance character parts. One still remembers the ovation for *Divertimento*, and it is still a favorite ballet in the repertoire of the New York City Ballet. Mary Ellen Moylan, Elise Reiman, Gisella Gaccialanza, Beatrice Tompkins, Tanaquil LeClercq, Francisco Moncion, Lew Christensen, Todd Bolender, Fred Danieli, and John Taras were the dancers.

Pastorela was a pleasant folk-piece with many characters and little important dancing. Not unlike a film travelogue, it filled a relaxing twenty minutes or so and did not mean much one way or another. What one remembers chiefly about it is the wonderful lighting by Jean Rosenthal, which gave space and form to the colorful décor and costumes by Alvin Colt. Emanuel Balaban, who had toured with the American Ballet in Latin America, was guest conductor for the piece.

Renard was overwhimsical, overdressed, and overproduced, a long and rather pointless joke. May Mr. Stravinsky forgive a nonmusician for saying it, but neither his music nor his story was worthy of the effort Balanchine and the dancers expended on it. To boot, it was as dated as the fashions of the period would appear now.

The result of the second program, then, was approximately that of the first: one excellent new ballet by Balanchine.

Between the first and the second programs, Ballet Society

presented an interim program that brought it more fame in a wider circle (and incidentally some money) than anything it had done before or was to do after until it became the New York City Ballet. The interim program presented two lyric pieces, one a tragedy, the other a farce, by Gian-Carlo Menotti: *The Medium* and *The Telephone*. It opened on February 18 at the Heckscher Theater on upper Fifth Avenue and ran for three days.

The Medium was originally commissioned by the Alice M. Ditson Fund of Columbia University, and was first performed on May 8, 1946. *The Telephone* was commissioned by Kirstein for Ballet Society.

Menotti was born in Italy in 1911. He came to the United States in 1928 and entered the Curtis Institute, Philadelphia, where he subsequently became a teacher of composition. His first opera, *Amelia Goes to the Ball*, was premièred at the Curtis Institute in 1937 and later performed at the New Amsterdam Theater in New York. In 1938 it was given by the Metropolitan Opera Company. He wrote, among other compositions, *The Old Maid and the Thief*, a radio opera commissioned by the National Broadcasting Company. This was performed on radio in 1939, and was later given many stage performances. In 1942 he composed a tragic opera, *The Island God*, for the Metropolitan. Marquis George de Cuevas commissioned Menotti to write a ballet, *Sebastian*, for Ballet International in 1944. Later he wrote the opera *The Consul*, and in 1951 he composed the first opera specifically written for television, *Amahl and the Night Visitors*, which was premièred on Christmas Eve, 1951, and subsequently repeated several times on NBC-TV. The New York City Opera company performed it on the stage during its 1952 spring season.

Ballet Society's production of *The Medium* was staged under the supervision of the composer, in scenery and costumes by Horace Armistead, a Yorkshireman who came to the United States in 1925 and worked in Boston with the Fine Arts Theatre and the Civic Repertory. *The Medium* was his first work in New York and evoked a great deal of enthusiastic comment. The entire design for *The Medium* was painted in black and white on a single piece of net; the paint was loaded with opaque pigment to reflect whatever color was desired to heighten a particular scene. The scenery combined intense realism with extreme fantasy in a fusion of observation and imagination not often seen in the United States. Kirstein would not admit it, but according to his colleagues in Ballet Society he had much to do with originating the idea for the set.

Much of the effect of the scenery must be credited to Jean Rosenthal's elaborate and inventive lighting. Jean Rosenthal, whose work has been mentioned here before, proved more than just an important asset to Ballet Society. It was a stroke of genius on the part of Kirstein to acquire her close collaboration with the organization. All through the existence of Ballet Society and now, in the New York City Ballet, this shy and unobtrusive magician of the incandescent lamp has brought saving illumination to many a drab setting and colorless costume or to an entirely bare stage.

Jean Rosenthal was educated at Smith College and heads the Theater Production Service. She has superintended a great number of Broadway productions and she did much for the general effectiveness of the early works of Orson Welles at the Mercury Theater. Her connection with ballet dates back to 1941, when she supervised the technical production of the Latin American repertoire.

These, then, were the artists who contributed their genius to the success of *The Medium* and *The Telephone*. The performing artists included the singers Marie Powers and Evelyn Keller and the dancer, Leo Coleman, a student of the Katherine Dunham School of the Dance, who made his first professional appearance as Toby, the Mute, in *The Medium.*

It was a stormy February in New York, but the performances were sold out every night. The costume designer, Edith
Lutyens, who had made many of Ballet Society's costumes,
was one of the many who came the first and second nights.
She was so enthralled with *The Medium* that she came back
the final night, during the winter's worst blizzard, and brought
with her the young producer Efrem Zimbalist, Jr., who, she
thought, should present *The Medium* and *The Telephone* on
Broadway. Zimbalist was as excited by *The Medium* as Edith
Lutyens had been, and agreed on the spot for himself and for
his partner, Chandler Cowles, to produce the show.

The Broadway production opened May 2 at the Ethel
Barrymore Theater with the same cast and in the same setting
used by Ballet Society. It was an immediate success, and ran
two hundred and fifteen performances, a distinguished record
for a "highbrow" show. Ballet Society received a royalty for
the production and use of the scenery and costumes, a most
welcome and much-needed addition to its modest fund.

The rest of the story of *The Medium* and *The Telephone,*
their United States tour, London and other European engagements, film version, phonograph recording, *etc.,* is common
knowledge and need not be detailed here.

For the third regular program of Ballet Society, scheduled
for March 26, Balanchine was supposed to choreograph a
new ballet, *The Minotaur,* to music by Elliott Carter, in décor
and costumes by the Spanish painter and sculptor Joan
Junyer. The previous October, Balanchine had received a
flattering invitation from the Paris Opéra to stage several
works for its resident ballet company in the spring of 1947.
He had hoped to have enough time to produce *The Minotaur*
before leaving for Paris, but his plans did not work out quite
as he wanted, and he could not prepare the ballet before his
sailing on February 26.

Not wishing to postpone the work, Kirstein and Balanchine asked John Taras to choreograph the ballet. Taras was
a graduate of the School of American Ballet and had danced
with the Ballet Caravan, the Philadelphia Ballet, and Ballet
Theatre. He had made a successful debut as a choreographer
with the mounting of *Graziana* (to music by Mozart in costumes by Alvin Colt) for Ballet Theatre in September 1945.
In October 1946 he staged *Camille* (to music by Schubert-
Rieti, in décor and costumes by Cecil Beaton) for Alicia
Markova and Anton Dolin, when they danced with the
Original Ballet Russe.

The other two ballets on the third program were *Zodiac*,
choreographed by Todd Bolender to music by Rudi Revil, in
scenery and costumes by Esteban Francés; and *Highland Fling*,
a romantic ballet in three scenes, choreographed by William
Dollar to a score by Stanley Bate, in scenery and costumes by
David Ffolkes.

This program, again given at the Central High School
for Needle Trades, was, in a way, the most significant of those
thus far presented; it gave three young American choreographers a chance to experiment, offering them an outlet for
their inspiration, their talent, and their mistakes. It also
afforded an insight into the future of choreography in America, assuring that our generation would eventually take its
place with other generations in the ability to produce gifted
choreographers (that *rara avis* in any generation, in any
country). At the same time it pointed up the necessity for a
more definite artistic direction and strict supervision from
those who would shape the destinies of ballet in America. The
fact that the program was artistically only moderately successful heightened rather than diminished its significance.

All three choreographers represented on the program,
John Taras, Todd Bolender, and William Dollar, had done
better work for other companies, had exhibited clearer think-

ing and truer genius on other occasions. Taras's *Graziana*, staged in the simplest of costumes and without scenery, was an infinitely finer choreographic composition than his over-elaborate *Minotaur*. Bolender's *Comedia Balletica*, staged for Ballet Russe de Monte Carlo, was far superior to his *Zodiac*. Dollar's *Constantia*, for Ballet International, was a superb choreographic invention, while his *Highland Fling* was only a lukewarm exhibition of balleto-Scottish steps within a scenario that was not clearly developed.

The basic defect of the three ballets was the same: the choreographers, and with them the dancers, were over-whelmed by their collaborators. In *The Minotaur* and *Zodiac* one could not see the dancing for the décor and costumes. In *Highland Fling* there was too much music for what Dollar wanted to, or could, say with his choreography. In all three works the principle that in ballet the final summation must be in terms of dance seemed to have been forgotten by all concerned.

It is quite simple to say that it is the duty of a director of a ballet company, experimental or otherwise, to exercise strict supervision over the collaborating artists and see to it that all three—i.e., choreographer, composer, and painter—are matched as evenly as possible. It is another thing to do the actual matching. Where is the choreographer who will agree *a priori* that a certain stage designer is strong enough to swallow up his choreographic invention, or that a great composer's score will render his dances a superfluous illustra-tion, or perhaps a boring interference with the music? What choreographer, especially what young choreographer, will openly admit that he is not a genius? And, for that matter, where are the composers and painters willing to admit that a ballet, any ballet, stands and falls on the work of the choreographer alone, and that it is his work, and not that of the designer or musician, that justifies the existence of the work, that makes ballet an art form, sufficient in itself and quite apart from painting and music? The millennium is not here yet.

The net result of the third program was many-faceted, if not very spectacular. Three young American choreographers received an opportunity to work under as near-ideal conditions as one can create in ballet outside the few state-subsidized opera houses of Europe. Three young American composers heard their works produced with loving care and played by a first-rate orchestra. One English and two Spanish painters were given full rein to create décor and costumes without interference from the producer. One of them, Joan Junyer, was given the first chance to try out his own ideas on an architectural approach to the design of scenery, in which the dancers now and then formed part of the scenery and the scenery, on the other hand, participated in the choreography. A young dancer, still officially a student of the School and not a full-fledged member of the Union, Tanaquil LeClercq, appeared for the first time in an important role (Ariadne in *The Minotaur*), and was immediately recognized by the audience and critics as a dancer of great promise and hope.

The fourth program of the first season had been scheduled for May 14, again at the Central High School of Needle Trades, but was shifted to the Ziegfeld Theater and was given on May 18. This was the first time that Kirstein had consented to a performance at a professional theater, what is called on Broadway a "legitimate house." There were misgivings about this change because some people, and Kirstein with them, felt that the shift might, physically at least, take Ballet Society out of its experimental sphere and place it on a professional basis, a step for which Ballet Society was not yet ready.

Although three new ballets had been previously announced for the fourth program, only two were given: *The*

Seasons, a contemporary ballet in one act, choreographed by the modern dancer Merce Cunningham, to music by John Cage, in scenery and costumes by Isamu Noguchi; and *Blackface*, a dramatic ballet in one act, choreographed by Lew Christensen, to music by Carter Harman, in scenery and costumes by Robert Drew. The third ballet, *Blue Bell, or The Favorite*, a ballet in three scenes with choreography by William Dollar, to music by John Colman, in scenery and costumes by Dorothea Tanning, did not materialize.

The Seasons brought together Merce Cunningham, a former soloist of the Martha Graham company, who had recently left the company for a career as a solo dancer, and was considered in the *avant garde* of the modern dance; John Cage, a prolific young composer who was specializing in percussion music and had created quite a stir in extreme modern music circles with his compositions for the "prepared" piano (the conventional instrument equipped with various mutes of rubber, wood, and plastic), and whose score for *The Seasons* was his first work for a large orchestra; and Isamu Noguchi, the son of a Japanese father and an American mother, a leading American sculptor who specialized in modern techniques in handling stone and metals, and who had done a number of settings for Martha Graham.

It was a well-matched team and the result of its work was an impressive production, controversial rather than exciting. It proved, if proof was needed and if it was the province of Ballet Society to furnish that proof, that ballet dancers could work with a choreographer whose artistic roots and technical training were in the modern dance. *The Seasons* was probably the most extreme work in terms of experiment offered during Ballet Society's first season. As in the case of the appearance of Iris Mabry on an earlier program, the ballet-minded subscribers remained very cool toward the experiment, and there were many rumbles about the direction Ballet Society was taking. If Kirstein had made his peace with the modern dance some years before, the subscribers to Ballet Society were not quite so broadminded, artistically tolerant, or liberal. Most of the subscribers came to Ballet Society from the audience of the big touring ballet companies, and they were a conservative lot; a work like *The Seasons* went against their grain.

Lew Christensen's *Blackface* made little impression. It was a rather static choreographic interpretation of a minstrel show, with a scenario that got lost in the repetitive solo and ensemble numbers. Young Robert Drew's scenery, designed as a formal minstrel-show in the proscenium of a nineteenth-century theater was rather conventional and not theatrical enough. Carter Harman's music fitted well into the show: it was as uninspired as the choreography and the décor. On the whole, *Blackface* would have been more in place on a program of the Ballet Caravan than of Ballet Society. Its effect in the scheme of Ballet Society was rather retardative.

A repeat performance of *The Minotaur*, with some changes in the cast, completed this last program of the season.

Kirstein summed up pretty accurately the achievements of Ballet Society's first season in the *Year Book*. He said, among other things:

"The productions offered by Ballet Society in its first year combined unfamiliar works by eminent composers with new works by musicians, choreographers, painters and dancers who are embarking on their careers.

"The performances of these works were a fusion of professional standards and amateur taste (the word amateur understood in its original mean of careful selection, a cultivated taste, but an absence of the timeworn formulæ of production intended to guarantee safely commercial success).

"Not in the last fifteen years have so many first performances been offered by a single sponsoring unit in this country. The programs, however, were presented not for their newness alone, but rather because performing them offered the three-fold experience in education. Collaborating musicians, chore-ographers and painters learned how to work with each other in unsuspected ways; dancers could develop themselves through the performance of the results; while the audience accustomed itself to unfamiliar aspects of the youthful spec-tacle."

Other, less spectacular, achievements of Ballet Society during its first season included the publication of three books and *Dance Index*, already mentioned here; the commissioning of several reels of 16 mm. films photographed by Ann Barzel of a performance of *Billy the Kid* in 1937, early tours of the Ballet Caravan, and the first performances in the United States of several Balanchine ballets; the preparation of a program of dance films by Arthur Rosenheimer, Jr., of the Film Library of the Museum of Modern Art, for the Associate Membership of Ballet Society; and the granting of a Fellow-ship to Tanaquil LeClercq, a junior member of the company, for further study at the School of American Ballet.

Summa summarum, the first season of Ballet Society was a most auspicious beginning, an impressive record of achieve-ment, and an optimistic augury of things to come.

XII

1947–1948

The New York City Center
of Music and Drama

George Balanchine sailed for France on February
26 in the *America*, to be guest choreographer at the
Paris Opéra through July. He was to stage several
ballets, give some company classes, and re-establish
discipline, which had been lacking since Lifar's
temporary suspension as choreographer and ballet
master as a result of charges of collaboration
with the Nazis during the German occupation
of Paris.

Balanchine found a competent if not brilliant
troupe, a few well-trained soloists who danced in a
rather indifferent style, and a guest ballerina—
Tamara Toumanova—who had been signed earlier
and had been in Paris since mid-February.

174

Soon after his arrival Balanchine and Toumanova were honored with a luncheon given by the Association of Dance Critics and the weekly theatrical publication *Opéra*, and attended by nearly all the outstanding Parisian writers, dancers, composers, and painters.

Most of the dancers worked willingly and with enthusiasm for Balanchine, but a small faction was hostile to the choreographer. The press and the public were also divided. Most of them hailed Balanchine's presence as a long-needed reform in the Opéra ballet; some felt that what the Opéra needed was a permanent choreographer rather than a foreign guest. In fact, a petition signed by several hundred people was addressed to the Minister of Fine Arts requesting the appointment of a permanent choreographer and ballet master. Lifar's name was not mentioned in the petition, but both the government and the administration of the Opéra knew perfectly well whom the petitioners had in mind.

Early in April Balanchine was joined by his wife, Maria Tallchief, who could not arrive sooner because she was then ranking soloist with the Ballet Russe de Monte Carlo and could not leave the company until the end of the season. (Balanchine had married Tallchief on August 16, 1946, having been divorced from Vera Zorina, his former wife, on January 17 of the same year. He had married Zorina on December 24, 1938.)

During his stay at the Opéra, Balanchine revived his ballets *Serenade*, *Baiser de la Fée*, and *Apollon Musagète*, and choreographed a new work, *Le Palais de Cristal*, to Bizet's Symphony in C. Maria Tallchief made her debut at the Opéra on May 21 in *Apollon Musagète* (Terpsichore) at a gala performance attended by the late King Gustav of Sweden, and also danced the Fairy in *Baiser de la Fée*.

Balanchine worked a near-miracle in the Opéra ballet, especially with the *corps*, which has never been famous for its accomplished technique, model discipline, or stage behavior. He succeeded in raising the artistic and technical standards of the company to heights it had not known for years. Even rabid xenophobes had to admit that the presence of Balanchine, Toumanova, and Tallchief did much to revitalize Parisian interest in ballet. The traditional Wednesday ballet evenings at the Opéra had not been so crowded in a long time. The post-opera July ballet season had an unprecedented success. So much so, in fact, that the directorate of the Opéra invited Balanchine to return the following season.

Most of the press had nothing but praise for Tallchief (for some reason they spelled her name Tall Chief and Parisians pronounced it Tahl-Sheff), Toumanova, and Balanchine, but there was also some sniping. When *Dance News* (of which I am editor) printed a favorable account of Balanchine's work at the Opéra by its Paris correspondent, the theatrical weekly *Spectateur* came out with a half-page article (July 22) entitled *"Sur Un Panegyrique de M. Balanchine et Mme. Toumanova,"* blasting *Dance News*, its correspondent, and its editor. Lincoln Kirstein wrote to me soon after the *Spectateur* article appeared:

"You have probably seen that you have really started something. French national pride has been stung to the quick. I should not be surprised if you hear from the State Department."

The State Department was not heard from, and there were no further repercussions. On the contrary, the famous French writer and critic Léandre Vaillat, reviewing Balanchine's last ballet for the Opéra, *Le Palais de Cristal*, in *Carrefour* (July 30), ended his article with this paragraph:

"The season of ballet at the Opéra is over. One feels a little like the spectator of a brilliant display of fireworks who returns silently home, at night, the eyes kissed by an inner vision through which pass emeralds, rubies and, above all, a black diamond. One asks oneself with a somewhat indiscreet curiosity: 'And now what?' "

Balanchine and Tallchief returned from Paris on August 14. A week later they flew to Los Angeles, Tallchief to rest in family surroundings, Balanchine to work with Stravinsky on the ballet *Orpheus*, which Ballet Society had commissioned in the autumn of 1946.

Balanchine had to return to New York right after Labor Day to stage Tchaikovsky's *Theme and Variations* (Suite No. 3, in G Major) for Ballet Theatre. Only after this ballet had opened on September 27 in Richmond, Virginia, could he turn his attention to the new season of Ballet Society, planned to open on November 12.

Kirstein had been hard at work all summer on the details of the second season. In July he engaged a general manager to take care of the business end of the organization, which was getting too complicated for him. The new general manager was actually an old-timer so far as Kirstein was concerned. She was Frances Hawkins, onetime manager of the Ballet Caravan and later connected with the Museum of Modern Art. Frances Hawkins was the right person for the job: she was sincerely interested in what Kirstein and his colleagues were doing, had enough experience and ability to run an organization like Ballet Society, and, what was most important, would not dream of sacrificing the artistic integrity or standing of the young company for the sake of business expediency or financial gain.

Her first step was to find a way to present all performances of Ballet Society in the same theater. She reasoned that Ballet Society should have a permanent home even if that home would only be occupied four times during the season. She realized that the perambulations of Ballet Society during the first season had detracted from its standing as a permanent organization and, what was more, presented difficulties in the construction of scenery, which had to be built in varying dimensions, depending on the theater where the company would dance a particular ballet. It also presented inconveniences for the choreographers and dancers, who seldom knew in advance what size a particular stage would be, how many exits it would have, or how much backstage space would be available.

After a long and tiring search, Frances Hawkins found such a theater—the City Center, or, to give it its full title, the New York City Center of Music and Drama. She talked to Morton Baum, Chairman of the Executive Committee of the City Center, its prime mover and chief of operations. He agreed to rent the then two-thousand-four-hundred-seat house for four performances at a flat fee of $500 per performance, and the theater problem for the season was solved.

The City Center is a unique undertaking, one of the very few blessings the depression brought to New York. The building originally belonged to a fraternal order, and was called the Mecca Temple. During the depression the lodge could not keep up the payment of city taxes on the building. By 1941 the indebtedness of the Mecca Temple reached such a sum that the City of New York had no alternative but to foreclose on the organization for tax liens.

Newbold Morris, President of the City Council in the administration of Fiorello H. LaGuardia, and Morton Baum, a councilman in the same administration, had an idea that the building, a white elephant from the point of view of real-estate interests at any time, and more so during a period of limited real-estate activities, could be put to a cultural use that would benefit the people of New York. They worked out a plan that would provide symphonic concerts, dramatic performances, and, subsequently, operatic performances and ballet at stipulated popular prices. These performances, they hoped, would eventually show enough profit to pay off the tax liens that Mecca Temple owed the city, and after that would pay its way, maintaining the building at no cost to the city and being prompt about taxes. Mayor LaGuardia made a study of the plan and gave Morris and Baum his blessing.

The two gentlemen rounded up the necessary board of directors and committees, and in the fall of 1943 incorporated the New York City Center of Music and Drama as a non-profit membership corporation under the State Board of Education. Newbold Morris became Chairman of the Board, Morton Baum Chairman of the Executive Committee.

At the beginning, the Mayor leased the building to the new corporation for a period of eleven months. Eleven months and not a full year because, according to the city laws, an eleven-month lease could be given the City Center without getting the approval of the City Council and the Board of Estimate. Both the Mayor and the new corporation were apprehensive, probably not without reason, that the Council and Board of Estimate might not be culture-minded and perspicacious enough to see the value of the project.

A number of individuals, several musical organizations, and some labor unions gave their support to the City Center, and it opened early in 1944. During its first year the City Center paid the city the equivalent of the taxes the city would have received from private owners, some $26,000. After another year of equally successful operation the City Center obtained a five-year lease—a result of bidding against other participants and of accepting the specifications imposed by the city for a limitation of the admission price (set at that time at a $2.40 top) and for a diversity of entertainment, which included opera, drama, and, later, ballet. Through the efforts of Newbold Morris $75,000 was raised as an operational fund.

Ballet made its first appearance at the City Center on

April 9, 1944, when Ballet Russe de Monte Carlo opened its three-week spring season there "By Special Invitation of Hon. F. H. LaGuardia, Mayor," as the company proudly announced, evoking a chorus of protest from private theater-owners and the press because Ballet Theatre opened the same evening at the Metropolitan Opera House, and the City Center opening was construed as unfair competition.

Between 1944 and 1948 the City Center played host to Ballet Russe de Monte Carlo and Ballet Theatre. Both companies carried their own financial responsibilities and generally occupied the theater on a percentage basis, usually ten per cent of the gross income.

To return to Ballet Society. One cannot overestimate the importance of Frances Hawkins's deal with Morton Baum, and Frances Hawkins deserves all credit for it. It was not that either she or Morton Baum realized in the fall of 1947 the consequences of the arrangement between Ballet Society and the City Center, but leasing the house created the conditions for the subsequent far-reaching co-operation.

Three other important events marked the preparation for the second season of Ballet Society: Maria Tallchief joined the company as ballerina; Herbert Bliss became a soloist; and Tanaquil LeClercq was elevated to the position of ranking soloist.

Press agents of various ballet companies have made much of Maria Tallchief's Indian descent. She is in fact half Indian, her father being a full-blooded Osage chief, and her Indian family name is Ki He Kah Stah Tsa, a useless bit of information recorded here only because it took some diligent research to uncover it; Tallchief herself did not know it.

She was born in 1925 in Fairfax, Oklahoma, was graduated from the Beverly Hills, California, High School, and studied ballet under Ernest Belcher, Bronislava Nijinska, and David Lichine, and later at the School of American Ballet.

She began her professional career in 1942 in the *corps* of Ballet Russe de Monte Carlo, and by 1946 had become the company's ranking soloist and its most exciting dancer. It was Balanchine who discovered Tallchief's inherent dance-qualities when she was a soloist in the Ballet Russe, and it was he who found a way to develop her talent. It is quite probable that Balanchine took a greater interest in Tallchief, his future wife, than he would have taken in another dancer, but it is also true that Tallchief was a more nearly perfect "Balanchine dancer" than anyone else in the Ballet Russe. She has a lithe, strong body, technique to spare, and the rare musicality so necessary in Balanchine's ballets. Her musicality is both innate and cultivated: she was a gifted pianist before she became a dancer. Balanchine knew long before the summer of 1947 that he had in Tallchief a ballerina for Ballet Society. If he needed additional proof he got it in Paris when she danced Terpsichore in *Apollo* and the Fairy in *Baiser de la Fée*.

Tanaquil LeClercq's elevation to soloist was perhaps an even more significant event for Ballet Society. Tallchief came to Ballet Society from the outside, already a soloist with an established reputation. LeClercq, however, was a product of the School of American Ballet; she had never danced in any company except Ballet Society. In short, she came from within. She was born in Paris in 1929 of a French father and an American mother, attended a Paris *lycée*, and later, when the family moved to New York, received her education at the King-Coit School. She won a scholarship competition at the School of American Ballet in 1941 and a Ballet Society Fellowship in 1946. Tall, lanky, and rather coltish in 1947, she possessed a good technique and a soft, fluid, what is often called romantic, line juxtaposed, in seeming paradox, with a tendency toward staccato movements. She also was very musical.

Herbert Bliss was born in Kansas City, Missouri, in 1923.

He received his initial ballet training at the Kansas City Conservatory of Music. In 1939 he went to New York to join the School of American Ballet. Before joining Ballet Society he had danced with the Ballet Russe de Monte Carlo (1943–4) and in the musicals, *Rosalinda* and *Song of Norway*, both staged by Balanchine. A soft, lyric dancer, he fitted well into most of Balanchine's ballets.

Rehearsals for the November 12 performance began in September. The program included a revised version of William Dollar's *Highland Fling;* a new ballet, *Punch and the Child*, by Fred Danieli; and *Symphonie Concertante*, to Mozart's Symphonie Concertante in E flat, choreographed by Balanchine, the same ballet that had been given on the Adventure in Ballet program at Carnegie Hall two years before.

With the business details of Ballet Society safely in the hands of Frances Hawkins, Kirstein found time to lecture in various parts of the country on ballet, on the lyric theater, and on Ballet Society. He was the principal speaker at the annual meeting of the American Society of Æsthetics in Baltimore, in September. In October he lectured at the Cleveland Museum of Art on "The Language of the Classic Ballet" and for the Theatre Group of Western Reserve University on problems of producing nonrealistic theater. He also had engagements at Harvard, the Boston Institute of Modern Art, the National Theatre Conference annual meeting in New York, and the Art Institute in Chicago. He was spreading the gospel.

The first performance of Ballet Society's second season proved many things. The company had noticeably improved during its estivation. There were several new and stronger dancers in the *corps;* there were more professional dancers than advanced students; the company had somehow crystallized: those who did not quite fit had left or had not been reengaged.

The auditorium and the stage of the City Center gave the company a professional quality that it had not had before, and one saw many new faces in the audience, a welcome sign of increase in the subscription rolls.

Dollar's *Highland Fling*, with Gisella Caccialanza as the Bride, Elise Reiman as the Sylphide, and Todd Bolender as the Groom, was presented in a shortened and revised version. It had not gained much by the change. The main defect of the ballet was that Dollar obviously did not believe in Sylphides, and without this belief he could not do a successful ballet in the romantic style.

Fred Danieli's first try at a long ballet, *Punch and the Child*, to music by Richard Arnell, in scenery and costumes by Horace Armistead, was very successful. He varied the age-old story by introducing a child who, attracted by the show, succeeds in getting into the Punch and Judy booth and participates in the performance. The Child associates the characters with the people who surround her in real life. Thus, her father becomes Punch, her mother Judy; a fishwife suggests the ugly Polly; the puppeteer becomes the Devil. Herbert Bliss, Beatrice Tompkins, Gisella Caccialanza, Charles Laskey (a returning alumnus of the American Ballet), Lew Christensen, and Edward Bigelow gave excellent performances in the principal roles, and little Judith Kursch, who played the Child, was adored by the audience.

Danieli, the choreographer, was a graduate of the School and a member of the Caravan. He had also danced with Ballet Theatre, served nearly four years in the army during the war, and appeared in the shows *This Is the Army* and *Call Me Mister*. *Punch and the Child* was a major choreographic achievement for him.

Horace Armistead's scenery, costumes, and masks had a delightful story-book quality tinged with scary realism. Richard Arnell's music was theatrical and interestingly composed, if not particularly brilliant. The young Britisher came to New York for the performance.

The outstanding event of the program was Balanchine's *Symphonie Concertante*. James Stewart Morcom designed for it a classic set, the magnificent arch for which was suggested by the famous French architect, Claude-Nicholas Ledoux. It was painted in golden hues, and offered a fine, dignified background for the dancers. The simple short tutus for the girls and the functional costume for the single man filled out the picture. (Kirstein had planned to use the Morcom set as a permanent frame for classic ballets to be staged by Balanchine, but soon gave up the idea.)

The ballet itself, with Tallchief, LeClercq, and Bolender in the principal roles, was another example of Balanchine's genius in choreographing plotless (often erroneously called abstract) ballets. Here was an aristocratic work of lucidity and simplicity, the marks of true greatness in ballet. The economy of movement, a hallmark of Balanchine's work, was carried out here to a degree where one had the feeling that a single change would upset the entire design of the ballet. The juxtaposition of the theatrically mature Tallchief (who suggested the viola solo) with the youthfully brittle and stage-wise-innocent LeClercq (the violin) was a happy idea. Bolender did not have much to dance for himself, but partnered both girls in excellent style and with assuring ease. The large and very young *corps* danced better than ever before.

Symphonie Concertante was a decided hit. It remains to this day a favorite work in the repertoire of the New York City Ballet.

A novelty of the program was the presentation of an orchestral work, Cantilena for Oboe and String Orchestra, by John Lesand, unaccompanied by dancing. This, according to Ballet Society's announcement, was in line with the tradition established by Diaghilev and Comte Étienne de Beaumont, who had presented "interesting" new music on some of their ballet programs. The Cantilena, sandwiched in between *Highland Fling* and *Punch and the Child*, fell on deaf ears: with the exception of the few musicians in the auditorium, the audience could not have been less interested. A ballet specta-tor at a ballet performance is uninterested in anything but ballet. Ballet is what he has come to the theater for, and ballet is what he wants to see; anything else, no matter how talented, is program-padding to him, and he is bored by it, if he does not actually resent the intrusion into his balletic mood. Kirstein, however, kept up the practice through two more programs before giving it up. It is worth noting here in pass-ing that for the second season Ballet Society acquired for the cover of its program booklet a new and handsome design by Carlus Dyer.

As part of its season's activities, Ballet Society presented on November 20 the American *première* of Jean Cocteau's film *La Belle et la Bête* (*Beauty and the Beast*) at the Auditorium of the Museum of Modern Art. With music by Georges Auric and décor by Christian Bérard, this fairy-tale film was almost a ballet in the late Diaghilev style. The cinematographic masterpiece was enthusiastically received by the audience and later enjoyed a successful run in New York's art movie houses.

On December 12, George Balanchine gave a demonstra-tion of the choreographer's creative work at the Auditorium of the Museum of Modern Art, with Tanaquil LeClercq and Herbert Bliss executing Balanchine's extemporaneous ar-rangements of dances. At the end of the delightful and in-structive demonstration, Kirstein announced that the second annual Ballet Society fellowship had been awarded to Bliss.

The second stage program of the season was an opera (or, as it was called officially, a lyric drama) in two acts, *Far Harbour*, with music by Baldwin Bergerson, text by William Archibald, in scenery and costumes by Horace Armistead.

William Archibald directed it. *Far Harbour* was given on January 22 and 23, 1948, at Hunter College Playhouse, not at the City Center.

Kirstein commissioned the production of *Far Harbour* on his own, not through Ballet Society, and he supervised the whole work in all its preliminary stages and up to actual rehearsals. He found the justification for the production of what amounted to a small-size opera in the earlier productions of *The Spellbound Child*, *The Medium*, *The Telephone*, and *Renard*, all of which had singing in them. To an outsider the connection was rather tenuous. It was true that the works mentioned were sung, but they were also danced (with the exception of *The Telephone*, which was only a curtain-raiser). Moreover, *The Spellbound Child* was staged by Balanchine as a ballet-pantomime, not as an opera; *Renard* was called a "ballet-burlesque"; and in *The Medium* the dancer's part was equal in importance to those of the singers. *Far Harbour*, whatever Kirstein chose to call it, was an opera.

Kirstein's program for *Far Harbour* read: "An aim of Ballet Society is creating a repertory of lyric drama suitable to the conditions of our own time. Lyric drama differs from the formal opera repertory insomuch as the music itself is felt to be only as important as the words, the choreographed action, the lighting and the visual production. The entire work is synchronized as a coherent whole without any single element emphasized at the expense of another, but rather, with each part contributing its intensification of the basic poetic and dramatic idea."

This was a rather intellectual explanation; it read much better than the reason for it looked on the stage. *Far Harbour* was not a success, for all the supervision and collaboration. It lacked the spark of genius which the collaborative effort did not produce.

Just before the company began to work on its third

program, two talented dancers, both alumni of the School of American Ballet, joined Ballet Society. They were Marie Jeanne and Nicholas Magallanes.

New York-born Marie Jeanne, or, to give her her full name, Marie Jeanne Pelus, began her career as all dancers hope but very few do—as a ballerina. She was only eighteen when she signed her first contract: ballerina with the Ballet Caravan (1937–9). She subsequently danced with that company at the New York World's Fair in the summer of 1940 and went on the Latin American tour with the American Ballet. For a short time she was guest artist with Ballet Russe de Monte Carlo (1940) and the Original Ballet Russe (1942). In 1944 she danced with the Ballet International. From 1945 to 1947 she was with Ballet Russe de Monte Carlo.

A very beautiful young lady, with a distinctly Gallic charm (both her parents are French), an extraordinary technique and grace, she was a "Balanchine dancer" at her very best. But her very qualities and the fact that she had never had to go through the mill of the *corps de ballet* and small solos played havoc with her career. She never seemed to be able to develop inner discipline, perseverance, and the propensity for hard work, without which there is no ballerina. The result was habitual boredom on her part with roles and companies, frequent changes of companies, and a growing disinterest in her profession. In early 1948, when she joined Ballet Society, these idiosyncrasies were only in the development stage.

Nicholas Magallanes was born in a small Mexican town whose name makes it the ideal birthplace for a dancer— Camargo, in the state of Chihuahua. He went to New York at an early age, attended high school and the School of American Ballet. He made his professional debut with the Ballet Caravan at the New York World's Fair and went with the American Ballet on its Latin American tour in 1941.

From 1943 to 1947 he danced with the Ballet Russe de Monte Carlo, working his way up from *corps de ballet* to first roles.

Magallanes possesses a considerable technique, has a very fluid, romantic style of movement, and is an excellent partner, probably among the top half-dozen. He is handsome and well built and has a very winning stage personality.

For its third program, on February 9, Ballet Society returned to the City Center, which it should not have left.

The program, an all-Balanchine evening, included only one new ballet, *The Triumph of Bacchus and Ariadne*, a ballet-cantata by Vittorio Rieti, in scenery and costumes by Corrado Cagli. It was the most ambitious work of Ballet Society up to that time. It employed some forty dancers and a choral ensemble of about forty singers as well as the full orchestra.

Styled after the triumphs of the Italian Renaissance, when the arts were being revived after the long hiatus of the Middle Ages, the ballet was based on a Florentine carnival song written by Lorenzo de' Medici. The ballet was a parade, as it were, of classic mythological legends staged for the enjoyment of the populace, which acted both as spectators and as a Greek chorus commenting on the various scenes and pointing up their significance and moral.

Balanchine succeeded here in creating a many-faceted spectacle of wide scope, ranging in its details from simple groupings and pantomime (the Spectators), through a lyric and tender *pas de deux* (Bacchus and Ariadne), a throbbing, theatricalized tarantella (Satyrs and Nymphs), broad *commedia dell'arte* (Silenus), *ballet d'action* (Midas), and a wild and exciting bacchanale—all projected through a prism of modern choreography. One remembers with particular pleasure Le-Clercq and Magallanes as Bacchus and Ariadne, Marie Jeanne and Bliss as the principal Nymph and Satyr, Charles Laskey as Silenus, and Francisco Moncion as Midas. But it was the company as a whole that was responsible for the success of this engrossing and adult ballet. The company displayed an *esprit de corps* that comes only as a result of long and continuous work together, when each dancer, without losing his personality, becomes a part of the whole and the company itself is transformed into a homogeneous unit.

Cagli's décor formed an imaginative setting for the ballet. His backdrop, a house with cut-out windows through which the chorus sang, gave style and coherence to the proceedings on the stage. His stylized costumes were effective and, with the exception of those for Bacchus and Ariadne, well designed.

Conductor Leon Barzin had his hands full, directing the orchestra, soloists, chorus, and ballet, but succeeded in getting a well-integrated performance—no mean task, indeed.

The other two ballets on the program were repeat performances of Hindemith's *The Four Temperaments* and Haieff's *Divertimento. Four Temperaments* had acquired a new and much more effective finale, and there were some minor changes in two or three other spots. Seligmann's scenery and costumes still dominated the ballet, as in the original production, and obscured some of the beauty inherent in it. In the Melancholic variation Herbert Bliss replaced William Dollar, who had left Ballet Society to become ballet master of Marquis Georges de Cuevas's Grand Ballet.

In *Divertimento*, Maria Tallchief replaced Mary Ellen Moylan, who had left Ballet Society to join Ballet Russe de Monte Carlo. The new ballerina gave a sparkling performance, strictly classic, as the ballet demanded, yet with a warmth that arose from an inner understanding of what she was doing. Also new in the cast of *Divertimento* were Magallanes, Bliss, and Dick Beard.

Nearly the entire membership of Ballet Society attended the performance and gave it a most enthusiastic reception.

The announcement of coming events in the February 9 program booklet mentioned that the program of the fourth performance, on March 22, would include *Beauty and the Beast*, a ballet in two acts by Balanchine to the music of Haieff, in costumes and scenery by Esteban Francés, and a repetition of Merce Cunningham's *The Seasons*. It did not quite work out that way. Ballet Society's *Bulletin* No. 8, published on March 15, said that *Beauty and the Beast*, the classic ballet in *three* parts, "has been postponed until next fall, due to serious production difficulties." The production difficulties were of the simplest kind: Ballet Society did not have and could not get enough money to do this elaborately planned ballet. The *Bulletin* went on to say that "Mr. Balanchine will revive the tradition of the full evening's spectacle of the Russian state theatres. Beauty and the Beast has a consecutive story ending with a transformation scene and divertissements in the line of The Sleeping Beauty. . . . Ballet Society will open the 1948–49 season with the world *première* of Beauty and the Beast."

This announcement was in a way typical of Ballet Society's overoptimistic attitude toward its production possibilities, which more than once resulted in announcements of productions that were not nearly in the working stage or whose cost made them prohibitive. It was not that Kirstein and Balanchine wanted to fool the people with exaggerated promises. After all, they were under no obligation to produce certain definite works. It was just that they were overenthusiastic and thought that they could perform miracles on every program—something they obviously could not do. These announcements from time to time led many people to reflect that Ballet Society was still run in a tentative, haphazard way. In this particular case it would have been sufficient for the *Bulletin* to say that *Beauty and the Beast* had had to be postponed for reasons of "serious production difficulties" or for any other reason. But why commit Ballet Society to another specific date for the opening of the ballet?

As we know now, *Beauty and the Beast* was not only not produced in time for the opening of the 1948–9 season, but has not yet been produced at all.

It was approximately at the same time that Balanchine and Kirstein woke up from another beautiful but highly improbable and impractical dream.

When Marquis Georges de Cuevas, balletomane and patron of the arts, organized his Ballet International in the summer of 1944, he took over on a long-term lease the Cosmopolitan Theater in Columbus Circle, New York. Originally built by the late William Randolph Hearst, the theater eventually became the property of Billy Rose, who leased it to the Marquis. The Marquis reportedly spent more than one hundred thousand dollars to renovate the theater, which was renamed the International. Ballet International opened there on October 30, 1944, and closed December 23, never to play there again. Two years later, the Marquis was still paying rent for the dark International Theater. He had revived his company under the title Grand Ballet de Monte Carlo in an elaborate set-up that need not be explained here. It was dancing in Europe and had no plans to return to New York. During one of his infrequent visits to New York, the Marquis offered Balanchine and Kirstein the use of the theater for ballet or for anything else they might want to produce.

Balanchine and Kirstein set to work on a detailed program of unusual productions, and submitted a plan for a thirty-six-week season of drama, dance, and lyric theater under the joint artistic direction of the Marquis de Cuevas, Balanchine, and Kirstein.

Nothing ever came of it. The Marquis left for Europe and never mentioned it again.

As a matter of fact, nothing could have come of it. To begin with, the Marquis, though married to an American (his wife is a grand-daughter of John D. Rockefeller), and himself an American citizen by naturalization, much preferred the European way of life and could not tie himself to New York. Then, the artistic taste of Balanchine and Kirstein differs so radically from that of the Marquis that they could never have worked together even had the Marquis been the most civic-minded New Yorker of all the city's eight million inhabitants. Another detail to which neither Balanchine and Kirstein nor the Marquis gave much thought was that the International Theater had a seating capacity of only one thousand, one hundred and seventy-three, which at the highest possible prices of admission and with full houses at every performance could not conceivably bring its income anywhere near necessary expenses.

March 22, the date of the fourth performance of the season, rolled along, and the program included a revival of *The Seasons, Capricorn Concerto* by Todd Bolender, and Balanchine's ballet to Bizet's Symphony in C, given under its musical title.

Capricorn Concerto, set to Samuel Barber's music of the same name, in Esteban Francés' set and costumes (originally designed for *Zodiac*), contained some excellent dancing by Tallchief (Earth), Bliss (Sun), Moncion (Moon), and the *corps*, every one of whose dancers depicted a star, but it fell short of being a good ballet. It was plainly derivative, clearly Balanchinesque in style and approach. The ballet's principal defect was its cerebral quality. The entire composition was mathematical rather than artistic: it had body, but no soul.

The thrill of the evening came with Balanchine's *Symphony in C*. This was the ballet Balanchine had mounted the summer before for the Paris Opéra as *Le Palais de Cristal*. For some reason that he never explained, the choreographer was hesitant to stage it for the Ballet Society troupe, but was finally persuaded to do so.

It was easy to understand why Paris had acclaimed the

ballet. *Symphony in C* is symphonic ballet at its purest. It takes its content and form from the music of the symphony. With no story to restrain its kinetic form or to hinder its choreographic development, it builds with ever-mounting force to an exciting climax. The fifty dancers on the stage at the same time not only give exhilaration to the final movement, but make most other ballets seem puny and pale by comparison. And all the strength of the ballet is achieved by dancing alone. For the girls are dressed in the simplest of white tutus and the boys in black shirts and tights and white socks, and they dance before a simple light-blue cyclorama.

The highest point of *Symphony in C* was probably the adagio of LeClercq and Moncion in the second movement. A true adagio in classic style, it is, nevertheless, free of the clichés found in most ballet adagios. LeClercq danced it with the ease, fluidity, and technical brilliance that the audience was growing accustomed to expect from that young dancer. Moncion gave her sure and strong support, not a simple task in this complicated *pas de deux*.

Tallchief in the first movement surpassed her brilliant dancing in *Symphonie Concertante* on an earlier program. Her very first entrance set the style for the entire ballet, and she sustained it throughout the composition. This was probably the most difficult and exacting part danced by Tallchief to that date. Magallanes supported the ballerina in the grand style.

Beatrice Tompkins and Herbert Bliss carried the third, and Elise Reiman the fourth, movement on the high level set by the first two movements.

Symphony in C was a huge success with the audience and critics, with one exception: John Martin of the *Times* did not seem to like it. Said he in his review: "Mr. Balanchine has once again given us that ballet of his, this time for some inscrutable reason to the Bizet Symphony."

Symphony in C survived this scathing remark.

XIII

1948

"Orpheus"; The New York City Ballet

The fourth program of Ballet Society's second season proved to be a turning-point in its short existence. The success of *Symphony in C*, seen only by the membership, created what press agents love to call a clamor for tickets for the next performance, scheduled for April 28. This time the clamor actually existed. Ballet Society received hundreds of letters and telephone calls, all asking for admittance to the performance or, if this were impossible, for separate performances not restricted to the membership.

Ballet Society had had such requests before, but the pressure had never been so great as it was in the spring of 1948. Left to his own devices, Kir-

194

stein would have probably resisted the pressure by the simple expedient of ignoring it. He had organized Ballet Society for the cognoscenti, was quite satisfied with the response toward his company, was taking its successes and failures in his stride, and was fearful that a wider attendance of nonsubscribers might force him to change the policies of Ballet Society. At the same time he knew, of course, that Ballet Society could not long exist on the limited schedule of four or five performances a season. There was no hope that these performances could begin to pay the expenses of presenting them, let alone of commissioning and mounting new works. By this time Kirstein had contributed about one hundred and fifty thousand dollars to Ballet Society, and only a small part of his contribution had returned in the form of membership subscriptions. Moreover, it was becoming increasingly difficult to keep together the performing company. Dedicated as they were to Ballet Society, the dancers had to earn a living, and the salary for the scattered performances could not provide that. Kirstein knew that eventually he would have to face playing longer seasons open to the general public or closing up shop and chalking up another noble experiment. But somehow he did not want to realize that the time for a decision was at hand.

Frances Hawkins knew as well as Kirstein that Ballet Society would have to reach out to broader horizons if it wanted to continue. She felt that staging a few performances for nonmembers might be a fair test of the possibility of longer seasons for Ballet Society. Reluctantly, Kirstein and Balanchine agreed.

The date originally set for the fifth program, April 28, was still kept to subscribers only (Ballet Society was not going to mix the cognoscenti with hoi polloi), but additional performances were announced for the evenings of April 29, 30, and May 1, and the afternoon of May 1, a Saturday.

The Balanchine-Stravinsky *Orpheus* was to be the principal event of the season.

As mentioned before, *Orpheus* was commissioned from Stravinsky in the fall of 1946. Balanchine, Kirstein, and the composer envisaged it as the second ballet in a future trilogy of classic themes, with *Apollo* and a third ballet to be composed at a later date.

Stravinsky sketched in the main musical themes early in the winter of that year. During the Christmas holidays Balanchine went to Los Angeles to work with Stravinsky on the outline of the action, separate dance-scenes, and other details. By that time Balanchine had the complete ballet in his mind.

If there ever has been a closer collaboration between a composer and a choreographer during the process of composing the score of a ballet, it has never been recorded. Marius Petipa's detailed instructions to Tchaikovsky during the creation of *The Sleeping Beauty* and *The Nutcracker* are well known. Their work was a collaboration to a degree, but it was rather mechanical. Petipa had his ballets on paper in great detail long before the composer was assigned to write the music. The choreographer indicated the duration of each set piece, its rhythm, character, and, occasionally, mood, but there was no direct communion between the two giants. Tchaikovsky in fact resented Petipa's specific directions and felt that they were limiting, rather than assisting, him.

The collaboration between Balanchine and Stravinsky, on the other hand, was basic and all-embracing. They discussed the production as a whole and every moment of it separately. Stravinsky demanded from Balanchine every detail the choreographer could give him, and in return asked Balanchine's opinion on every section of the score. Superb craftsmen and meticulous artisans as well as great artists, both men considered no detail small enough or unimportant

enough to be left to chance. They actually worked with stop-
watches on each scene, each movement.

Balanchine delights in telling how Stravinsky asked him:
"George, how long do you think the *pas de deux* of Eurydice
and Orpheus should run?"

"Oh," replied Balanchine, "about two and a half minutes."

"Don't say 'about,' " shouted Stravinsky. "There is no
such thing as 'about.' Is it two minutes, two minutes and
fifteen seconds, two minutes and thirty seconds, or something
in between? Give me the exact time and I'll try to come as
close to it as I can."

When Balanchine returned to Los Angeles in August
1947, the score of *Orpheus* was complete in sketch. He and
Stravinsky went through it for the final touches just before
Stravinsky began orchestrating it.

By mid-October Balanchine had the score in his pos-
session, ready for his own detailed work before rehearsals.

The scenery and costumes for *Orpheus* were commissioned
from Isamu Noguchi, who had done the décor for Merce
Cunningham's *The Seasons* the year before. He accepted the
idea of Balanchine and Stravinsky that it should be treated as
a universal theme rather than a myth belonging to one nationality or one historic period. The scale models of the set
and costumes which Noguchi had ready at the end of March
showed that the sculptor was perfectly attuned to the creative
conception of the other collaborators.

Igor Stravinsky, who had promised to conduct the *première* of *Orpheus,* arrived in New York on April 6, three weeks
before the performance. He visited Noguchi's studio to inspect
and approve the décor, and attended nearly every rehearsal.
He supervised the playing of his score, indicating and cor-
recting tempos and accents, suggested certain changes in

choreography, and worked with Kirstein in co-ordinating the whole ballet. To Balanchine, Kirstein, and those who were permitted to attend at some of the rehearsals, Stravinsky's presence brought back memories of the winter of 1937, when the American Ballet was rehearsing for the Stravinsky Festival at the Metropolitan. His presence again charged the atmosphere with that rare aura of genius at work. Balanchine is unquestionably as great a genius in choreography as Stravinsky is in music, but one was used to being near Balanchine and his work.

The five principals in *Orpheus*—Tallchief (Eurydice), Magallanes (Orpheus), Moncion (Dark Angel), Bliss (Apollo), and LeClercq (Bacchante)—felt Stravinsky's presence as strongly as the others, probably more strongly. One has seldom seen a group of dancers work harder and in a more dedicated way than the cast of *Orpheus*.

A few days before the company was to move into the City Center for two days of stage rehearsals, Frances Hawkins discovered that Ballet Society did not have enough money to buy the last piece of equipment for *Orpheus*. Noguchi's stage set required a front drop made of a light billowy silk to be used to separate the various scenes and also for some stage business, including the disappearance of Eurydice after the *pas de deux*. The material alone came to about one thousand dollars, and for some reason about which no one was very clear, it had to be bought for cash, not on credit.

To Kirstein this seemed like the good old days of the Ballet Caravan: a "disaster" accompanying the opening of a season. Of all the people around Ballet Society no one had or could spare one thousand dollars. Kirstein had exhausted all the money he could contribute to Ballet Society and had obtained some additional from his mother and brother. Now he was unable or too shy to ask for more from anyone.

Balanchine, who was not supposed to be concerned with

the financial side of Ballet Society, was told about the situation. Without saying anything to anyone he absented himself from the School between two rehearsals and came back after two hours with one thousand dollars in cash. There was great jubilation when he handed over the bills to Frances Hawkins. Despite all the pleading, he refused to reveal the source of the money. All he would say was: "I did not steal it."

The silk curtain was purchased, another Kirstein "disaster" circumvented.

The program of April 28 included repeat performances of *Elegie, Renard*, and *Symphonie Concertante*, in addition to the *première* of Orpheus. The new ballet came between *Renard* and *Symphonie Concertante*. The well-behaved public came in time for *Elegie* and watched attentively the excellent performance by LcClercq and Pat McBride. Its interest somewhat diminished during *Renard*. The atmosphere resembled that of a preliminary bout at a championship prizefight; nobody cared very much.

The intermission that followed was supercharged with expectancy. Advance information and gossip (mostly gossip) were being freely circulated by those who professed to know something about *Orpheus*, the less-knowing listening with respectful curiosity. As usually happens at a *première*, the intermission lasted longer than the announced fifteen minutes and everyone was in his seat long before the house lights were dimmed. Even those hardy individuals who spend every intermission in the bar across the street from the City Center returned to their places in good time.

When the slight figure of Stravinsky appeared at the conductor's stand he was given a tumultuous ovation. A few minutes later, obedient to Stravinsky's baton, the now well-known soft, plaintive notes of the short introduction became audible, and *Orpheus* was on.

The plot of the ballet was as simple as the legend of

Orpheus itself: Orpheus, mourning the death of his wife
Eurydice, accepts the suggestion of the Dark Angel to follow
Eurydice to Hades and lead her away, but never to look back
at her. At the last moment Orpheus cannot resist the temptation to look at his beloved Eurydice. Eurydice falls dead and is
swallowed up by the Hadean forces. Orpheus is tortured to
death by the Bacchantes. The ballet ends with a touching
apotheosis during which Apollo sings the praises of Orpheus,
the poet and lover.

On this plot as a canvas, Balanchine wove an intricate
poetic design, pure and right in every detail. There were no
program notes to outline the plot, no pantomime or histrionics
to explain the action. The entire ballet was conceived in movement, and the movement was sparse and economical. Yet it
not only projected the plot, but produced in the spectators a
deep, poetic, almost religious feeling, as if they were present
at some mysterious rite.

Not in years had there been so fine an example of the
true lyric theater that ballet is supposed to be and so seldom
is. Not in years had there been so fine an example of the
practical application of the principle of the ballet dance—
economy of movement, the reduction of human gesture to
bare essentials, heightened and developed into meaningful
patterns.

Stravinsky's music, classic in style and deep in feeling,
was among the greatest the composer had ever written. It was
of a piece with the ballet; it was clearly evident that it had
been composed to be a homogeneous part of the ballet, with
choreography and stage design as the other parts of a great
collaborative effort.

With the simplicity inherent only in great works of art,
Noguchi's décor furnished the frame that held the ballet together in space, gave its plot a direction and a pattern. The
artist never permitted his scenery and costumes to dominate

the ballet. The white silk curtain that the company almost did
not get was a most effective invention.

Orpheus was an ensemble ballet, and Balanchine found a
way to subordinate the individual talents, and idiosyncrasies,
of the dancers to the ballet as a whole. Magallanes was
Orpheus; Tallchief, Eurydice; Moncion, the Dark Angel;
Bliss, Apollo. They gave their best to create a rarely seen
quality in the production. The large *corps* sustained that
quality.

Francisco Moncion had been with Ballet Society since
early in the year and had danced many important parts well.
The Dark Angel, however, was his first dramatic role in which
the demand was not so much on actual dancing as on theatrical characterization. He made a lasting impression.

Born in La Vega, Dominican Republic, Moncion studied
at the School of American Ballet. He made his professional
debut in 1942 in the New Opera Company. In 1944 he joined
Ballet International as soloist and danced the title roles in
Sebastian and *The Mad Tristan,* the Husband in *The Mute
Wife* and leading roles in *Memories* and *Brahms Variations.* He
was guest artist with the Original Ballet Russe (1946) and
appeared as featured dancer in musicals before joining Ballet
Society.

In Broadway parlance *Orpheus* was a smash hit. There
was a seemingly unending ovation for the dancers, for Balanchine, for Stravinsky, for Noguchi. The audience applauded, stamped, shouted. Everyone, dancer and spectator,
was very happy. With *Symphony in C,* the smash hit of the
previous program, it proved to be the most successful ballet,
and had the strongest drawing-power during the four-per-
formance season open to the general public.

These two ballets, along with *Symphonie Concertante,* made
a strong impression on many people, among them Morton
Baum, Chairman of the Executive Committee of the City

Center and, in effect at least, boss of the entire organization.

Morton Baum was graduated from Harvard Law School in 1928 and is practicing law in New York in partnership with his brother Lester, a former New York state senator. They specialize in tax problems, and Morton Baum is Special Tax Counsel to the City of New York. (It was he, incidentally, who devised and introduced the New York City sales tax, a less-than-popular, but very necessary, measure.) He served as Assistant United States Attorney under Thomas Dewey during the present Governor's racket-busting days in 1930–4, and was elected alderman on the Fusion ticket in the first La-Guardia administration.

A trained amateur musician, thoughtful organizer, and efficient administrator, Baum found an expression for his various talents as a member of the Board of the Metropolitan Opera Association and Chairman of the Executive Committee of the City Center.

His acquaintance with ballet, however, was rather sketchy. He knew nothing of Ballet Society, had never met Balanchine or Kirstein, was unfamiliar with their work. He heard of the organization only because Frances Hawkins talked about it when she leased the City Center for its performances.

Orpheus, Symphony in C, and *Symphonie Concertante* won Baum over to ballet and, what was more important, to Ballet Society. One evening, speaking to Ben Ketcham, the wise and experienced business-manager of the City Center, he mentioned how much he liked the company. He thought that perhaps the City Center could do something for Ballet Society. Ben Ketcham, who also liked the company, suggested that he pay a visit to Kirstein at the Ballet Society office, which was located in the City Center building.

Baum went to see Kirstein the next afternoon.

In Baum's own words: "It was the strangest meeting.

Kirstein was belligerent, almost hostile to me, vituperative against the entire ballet field, its policies, managers, repertoire. He seemed not to believe in the sincerity of my call and was suspicious of everything I said. He told me that the funds of Ballet Society were exhausted and that it might have to fold, but that he would carry on his struggle to create an American ballet."

Despite his belligerence, Kirstein made a very favorable impression on Baum. Baum knew that if there was a ballet company that deserved the help of the City Center, Ballet Society was that company. Before taking leave Baum said in his usual quiet, matter-of-fact voice: "Mr. Kirstein, how would you like the idea of Ballet Society becoming the New York City Ballet?"

Kirstein did not know what to expect of Baum's visit, least of all of this question. He stood speechless for a long minute and then said: "If you do that for us I will give you in three years the finest ballet company in America."

On that they shook hands.

Baum returned to his tax problems. Kirstein ran, not walked over to the School to report the momentous conversation to Balanchine. After a joyful relation he added: "But, George, don't be too optimistic. Baum is only one person, he has a board of directors to contend with, and they'll all be against us."

He did not know that the board of directors would be against them. He could not imagine why it should be against them. He just could not believe that it would be for them.

During the following several weeks Baum discussed the financial problems of Ballet Society with Kirstein and Hawkins; met Balanchine and was enchanted by him; worked out a plan of operation, presented it to the Executive Committee, and had it accepted (not without opposition). He then announced to Balanchine, Kirstein, and Hawkins that if Ballet

Society agreed to the outlined conditions he would be glad to incorporate the performing company of Ballet Society into the scheme of the City Center activities as the New York City Ballet.

Ballet Society agreed, and the New York City Ballet was born.

At that time, in the spring of 1948, the City Center included two performing units, the New York City Drama and the New York City Opera. Between seasons of these troupes, the City Center was rented out to commercial theatrical enterprises or motion-picture concerns on a straight rental basis (i.e., at a stipulated amount per week) or on a percentage basis (i.e., at a certain percentage of the gross income after taxes). The City Center contract with the City of New York now required the corporation to pay the city one and one-half per cent of the gross income of the theater or ten thousand dollars a year, whichever was greater. Actually, the city was collecting about twenty thousand dollars a year from the City Center, or double the required minimum.

The New York City Drama had been a revenue-producing enterprise from the beginning. Not only did it require no orchestra and use a smaller cast than the opera, but, generally speaking, its productions were less costly. The New York City Opera, on the other hand, was a deficit operation. This deficit had to be covered from the profits of the drama season and rental of the house to other attractions, which brought in approximately fifty thousand dollars a year, and occasional contributions.

Baum knew before he signed the contract with Ballet Society that the New York City Ballet would also be a deficit operation and that, at least at the beginning, he could not divert even a small part of his limited funds to finance the ballet. He told Kirstein very frankly that at the beginning Ballet Society would have to cover its deficit, but that the deficit would be considerably smaller than before. Kirstein agreed to this.

To bring some money into Ballet Society, Baum offered the following plan: the New York City Ballet would become the opera ballet of the New York City Opera, thus bringing employment to at least some of its dancers. The opera and the ballet seasons would run concurrently, the Ballet appearing Monday and Tuesday, the Opera Thursday through Sunday. Other saving would be affected by hiring musicians, stage-hands, and front-of-the-house personnel by the week instead of by the day, and by pro-rating the cost.

However tentative, insecure, and financially insufficient this plan may sound now, it appeared as a salvation to Ballet Society: the company's loss would at any rate be smaller than before; it would dance at least twenty times a season instead of five or six; it would have a permanent home and there would be other people, in addition to those immediately connected with it, to help carry the ever-growing burden of constant worry over financial problems.

Back in 1936, after the failure of Balanchine's first *Orpheus* at the Metropolitan, when Kirstein was only twenty-three, he told Balanchine: "I cannot explain it to you, but I have a definite feeling, mystic if you want to, that when I am forty we will have a permanent theater for the company."

Kirstein erred by one year: he was now forty-one. But, then, he had spent thirty-two months in the army.

XIV

1948–1949

First Season; New Problems

The summer of 1948 was quiet if not gainful for Ballet Society dancers. Most of them just rested; a few found temporary jobs in open-air light opera seasons.

George Balanchine had agreed in the spring to stage two ballets for the Marquis de Cuevas's Grand Ballet. He left July 4 with Maria Tallchief for Monte Carlo. There he choreographed his *Night Shadow* and *Concerto Barocco*, as contracted for, and threw in a spectacular short number, *"Pas de Trois"* from *Don Quixote*, as a sort of bonus. The Balanchines spent the rest of the summer in France.

Lincoln Kirstein stayed in and around New York. In mid-August he and Frances Hawkins began to prepare for the first season of the New York City Ballet. Both thought that because the performing company had changed its status by becoming the New York City Ballet they would have to abandon the membership plan of Ballet Society. Kirstein felt, for some reason, that the membership would not respond to an appeal to renew its subscriptions. Later he realized that whatever the response might be, the collected membership dues would help to reduce the inevitable deficit. In September a letter was sent out to the members of Ballet Society offering them a subscription to four performances (opening night and three *premières*) and some special events. The letter produced appreciable results: Ballet Society collected seven or eight thousand dollars.

The first season of the New York City Ballet was officially announced in early September. In the announcement George Balanchine was listed as artistic director, Leon Barzin as musical director, Lincoln Kirstein as general director. Principal dancers were Maria Tallchief, Marie Jeanne, Tanaquil Le-Clercq, Beatrice Tompkins, Jocelyn Vollmar (late of the San Francisco Ballet), Nicholas Magallanes, Francisco Moncion, Herbert Bliss, and Todd Bolender.

Performances at the City Center were scheduled for every Monday and Tuesday between October 11 and November 23, fourteen performances in all. Only two new productions were listed for the season: a revival of Balanchine's *Concerto Barocco* in scenery and costumes by Eugene Berman, and Todd Bolender's *Mother Goose Suite* to Ravel's music.

The opening night was a gala occasion. The audience, which included Ballet Society subscribers as well as what some of them, with not too much grace, termed outsiders, realized that it was attending at an important function, the birth of what John Martin called in his review "the first institutionalized ballet company in these parts."

The program included three Balanchine ballets: *Concerto*

Barocco, *Orpheus*, and *Symphony in C*. The novelty of the evening
was Berman's scenery and costumes for *Concerto Barocco*, never
seen before. Berman designed the décor for the ballet when it
was first produced in 1941 for the Latin American tour of the
American Ballet. At that time he was not satisfied with the
technical execution of the scenery and refused to let the company use it. Now he changed his mind, and the ballet was
presented in full décor. The set and costumes were handsome
enough and may have given the ballet a certain atmosphere,
but the people who had seen *Concerto Barocco* performed in
practice clothes against a plain cyclorama were used to them,
and identified them with the ballet. It appeared at this showing that the simpler décor had a distinct advantage over the
painted set and the designed costumes: they made the dancing so much clearer, the lines so much more classic, the whole
conception of the ballet so much purer, that the simple décor
seemed preferable.

Marie Jeanne, Ruth Gilbert, and Francisco Moncion
were the soloists in *Concerto Barocco*.

The *première* of Bolender's *Mother Goose Suite* came on November 1. The ballet was originally created for the short-lived
American Concert Ballet in 1943, and had not been danced
since. The choreographer changed the ballet somewhat and
increased the number of dancers in some of the scenes. As the
title implied, *Mother Goose Suite* was a series of separate dances,
each dealing with a Mother Goose story, as musically envisaged by Maurice Ravel, and the choreographer changed the
order of the musical pieces to suit stage requirements. The separate numbers are connected by the presence of the Spectator
(Beatrice Tompkins) who dreams of her adventures as a young
girl. Marie Jeanne was excellent as the Young Girl who participates in all episodes (as it were, the alter ego of the Spectator). Bolender was Hop o' My Thumb, Francisco Moncion the

Beast (in Beauty and the Beast), and Dick Beard the Prince (in the Enchanted Princess).

Other ballets during the fourteen-performance season included *Serenade*, *Punch and the Child*, *Symphonie Concertante*, *Four Temperaments* (with simplified costuming, much to the advantage of the ballet), *The Triumph of Bacchus and Ariadne*, and *Divertimento*.

Two novelties of questionable importance were the guest appearances, on separate evenings, of André Eglevsky and John Kriza in *Symphony in C*. These appearances annoyed a good part of the public, which felt that the New York City Ballet could and should stand on its own without succumbing to the guest-artist policy of other ballet companies, who have overworked this device to their subsequent detriment. Neither of the dancers added to the choreographic significance of *Symphony in C* or to its enjoyment by the spectators. It must be said, however, that both Eglevsky and Kriza received a very warm welcome.

A happier novelty was Balanchine's unscheduled appearance in the role of orchestra conductor on November 8, when he directed *Symphony in C*. There was no particular reason for this except Balanchine's desire to do it, and who could begrudge him this desire? After all, where is the man or boy who does not want to lead an orchestra? He was loudly cheered by the audience and given a standing ovation by the orchestra.

John Martin wrote in *The New York Times:* "He [Balanchine] had a wonderful time and managed to convey the pleasure to the dancers on stage and the spectators in the auditorium. A few more of his orchestral appearances and his conducting will not be listable any longer as a novelty. . . ."

Artistically the first season of the New York City Ballet was very successful; financially it could have been better.

There were good reasons for the limited draw at the box office.

The season opened the day after the Ballet Russe de Monte Carlo closed its very successful four-week season at the Metropolitan Opera House (September 18 to October 10). The season had been given at popular prices (three dollars top), and had had Alicia Markova, Mia Slavenska, Agnes de Mille, and Anton Dolin as guest artists with the regular cast headed by Alexandra Danilova and Frederic Franklin. This season, moreover, was preceded by a two-week guest season of the Paris Opéra Ballet, September 21 to October 3, at the very City Center where the New York City Ballet was dancing, also at a three-dollar top. These six weeks of ballet drained off a substantial amount of money from the limited ballet public.

In addition to all this, the New York City Ballet was appearing only on Mondays and Tuesdays, the two poorest theater days of the week.

The result was that the New York City Ballet averaged only a little better than fifty per cent of capacity. In the circumstances this could be considered a fair draw, but expenses do not take circumstances into consideration: the season showed a deficit of about forty-seven thousand dollars. Neither the City Center not Ballet Society had enough money to meet this deficit; Kirstein paid the forty-seven thousand dollars out of his own funds.

Speaking about it some three and one-half years later, Morton Baum said: "The interesting part of it, from a business point of view, was that Kirstein had no contractual obligation to make good the deficit. All I had from him was a verbal promise." He spoke almost as if he had expected Kirstein not to keep his promise.

A little earlier Kirstein had been interviewed by Emily Coleman, the dance and music editor of *Newsweek* magazine and a keen observer of the dance scene. In the October 25 issue of her magazine she devoted to the New York City Ballet a page in which she said: "It has always been Lincoln Kirstein's purpose in life to 'do things nobody else would ever do.' 'That,' he explains, 'is the only reason I exist.' . . . Now Kirstein finds himself on the same hot seat occupied by so many others. The New York City Ballet must support itself or leave the boards. This season, appealing to a broader public at popular prices, is Kirstein's final stand. 'This,' he says, 'is the last formula I can think of.' Those who know him best, however, are sure that this mood will not last for too long. Kirstein is only 42, and there will always be something which 'nobody else would ever do.' "

Kirstein was deeply discouraged with the results of the season, not so much with the loss of money as with the limited public response to the New York City Ballet. Balanchine's reasoning was that the public did like the New York City Ballet, but that the company simply had not had a fair chance, what with two preceding ballet seasons and the necessity of playing at the beginning of the week. Baum agreed with Balanchine. His opinion of the company rose despite its limited financial success.

Soon after the season was over, he offered Balanchine and Kirstein tangible evidence of his opinion of and faith in the company. He proposed that the New York City Ballet, which, during its first season had been more or less a subsidiary of the New York City Opera, become an independent unit of the City Center aggregation of theatrical companies, and that it have its own season in January.

The significance of this offer was in the arrangement by which the City Center and not Ballet Society would sponsor the season and assume financial responsibility for its running expenses. Ballet Society would pay the expenses only of whatever new productions would be scheduled for the season.

This proposition obviously delighted Balanchine and Kirstein, and the latter was soon out of the depression brought about by the October-November season.

The new season was announced to run from January 13 to 16 and 20 to 23, ten performances in all, Thursday through Sunday evenings, and matinees on Sundays. Balanchine and Kirstein set about preparing for their first independent season.

The company still had in its repertoire several ballets not yet seen by the general public, so that only one new production and one revival were scheduled for the season. The new production was Jerome Robbins's *The Guests* (called, in its rehearsal stage, *Incident*), to Marc Blitzstein's music; the revival was Antony Tudor's *Time Table* to Aaron Copland's *Music for the Theatre*, in scenery and costumes by James Stewart Morcom. Tudor's *Time Table* had originally been done in 1941 for the Latin American tour of the American Ballet. Chronologically, this was Tudor's first ballet created in the United States, his *Jardin aux Lilas*, *Judgment of Paris*, and *Gala Performance* having been created in London.

The alliance of Tudor and Robbins with the New York City Ballet was of more than casual importance. For one thing, it meant that the people at the top of the dance profession were realizing the position of the New York City Ballet as a significant producing organization unfettered by the demands and limitations of the commercial ballet companies, and thus offering choreographers a means of expression which the other troupes could not afford or did not know how to offer. For another, it gave the New York City Ballet the much-needed opportunity of filling the creative gap between Balanchine, as principal choreographer and acknowledged master, and the young choreographers, most of whom were pupils of Balanchine and still in their apprentice stage, notwithstanding their record of artistically valid productions. Established choreographers like Tudor and Robbins, working in a style totally different from that of Balanchine and his disciples, helped to round out and eventually to diversify the repertoire of the New York City Ballet.

What consequence the collaboration of Tudor and Robbins with the company would ultimately achieve could not be foreseen at the time by even the most perspicacious observers. It is true, however, that Balanchine said on many occasions, even before Tudor and Robbins joined him, that the New York City Ballet was not a closed organization, not a "Balanchine company" or a "Kirstein company," but a troupe that would welcome any talented choreographer to come and experiment and work with it in any style he might want.

"What we want to do at the New York City Ballet," he said once, "is to create great ballets, and I don't care who creates them. All are welcome, and the only two requirements are talent and a sincere endeavor."

It was clear even in December 1948 that Robbins's joining the New York City Ballet was of more importance than Tudor's. Tudor came to the company to revive an old ballet, not to stage a new one, and he was there because Ballet Theatre, of which he was choreographer and artistic administrator, had canceled its fall season and disbanded the company and he was therefore not doing anything in particular. It was known that Tudor was a guest choreographer and would rejoin Ballet Theatre as soon as the dancers were called together, as actually happened in February.

Robbins, on the other hand, came to the New York City Ballet because he hoped to find in it a medium for his creative work. An alumnus of Ballet Theatre (1940–4 and the London season of 1946), Robbins rose in that company from the *corps* to be an important soloist and to create a number of roles, among them the Youth in Agnes de Mille's *Three Virgins and a Devil*, Benvolio in Tudor's *Romeo and Juliet*, and Hermes in Fokine's *Helen of Troy*, as well as several roles in his own ballets.

It was for Ballet Theatre, too, that he created his *Fancy Free* (1944) and *Facsimile* (1946) and revived *Interplay* (1945), all ballets in his individual style which added a new facet to American choreography. Since 1946 Robbins had been choreographing dances and staging ensemble numbers in Broadway musicals, creating, among others, such classics of the musical comedy as *On the Town* (which, incidentally was an amplification of his immensely popular ballet *Fancy Free*), *Billion Dollar Baby*, and *Look, Ma, I'm Dancin'*.

Here he was, doing exceedingly well on Broadway, earning a princely income compared with what a ballet company could afford to pay, and having more offers to work than he could possibly accept. Yet he went to the New York City Ballet on his own volition and with an artistic humility one would find hard to associate with a successful Broadway "celebrity." One could not help feeling a certain admiration toward Robbins for his unprecedented (in the commercial theater) desire to get away, at least for a while, from the glitter of Broadway. As it turned out later, Robbins identified himself with the New York City Ballet very closely indeed.

The opening night of the New York City Ballet season, January 13, was completely sold out—a heartwarming occurrence for all concerned. The program included *Four Temperaments, Time Table*, and *Symphony in C*.

Time Table, the only new work on the program, was received very politely. It was clearly minor Tudor, and its significance was historic rather than absolute: it offered a view of Tudor's growth in stature as an important choreographer. The plot of *Time Table* concerned the events at a little American railroad station at the end of World War I, when a train is about to arrive and depart. There was a Marine sergeant taking leave from his sweetheart, other Marines, their girl friends, high school boys and girls, a woman waiting for the return of her soldier lover, and so on. It was an atmospheric piece, well made and well suited to Copland's music, but it was not great ballet. Marie Jeanne as the Girl and Moncion as the Sergeant gave excellent performances.

Robbins's *The Guests* was premièred on January 20. It was subtitled a "classic ballet," for no apparent reason. It did not fit into the accepted confines of that classification any more than it would into the accepted classification of romantic ballet. The theme of *The Guests* was intolerance. The plot dealt with the conflict between two groups, one bearing caste marks, the other apparently common people. When a high-caste boy is attracted by a low-caste girl (both wear masks so that their foreheads are hidden) and their respective social standing is subsquently revealed, the obvious drama ensues. In the end the boy and the girl are united, but are ostracized by both groups.

Robbins developed the drama in abstract terms: the basic characteristics of the two groups were not stated (beyond the obvious caste marks), the groups themselves were never identified. The choreographer seemed to be much more concerned with the subject matter than with the choreography; as a result, the choreographic exposition suffered, especially in the dances of the ensemble. The focal point of the work was a wonderfully conceived *pas de deux* lucidly danced by Tallchief and Magallanes. It had the same tender quality as the *pas de deux* in Robbins's *Interplay*.

Marc Blitzstein's music, composed for the most part in a jazz idiom, served its purpose well. The music for the *pas de deux* was on more conventional lines and was admirably suited to the choreography.

The Guests, then, was also not great ballet. The spectators, however, liked it very much indeed, and it remained in the repertoire for a long time.

Other ballets performed during the season included *Mother Goose Suite, Divertimento, The Seasons, Symphonie Concertante, Concerto Barocco, Orpheus,* and *Serenade.*

The season was very successful artistically; financially it came as near to success as one could expect. The City Center lost only about ten thousand dollars, an average of one thousand dollars per performance—a paltry sum as ballet losses go. All concerned agreed that the loss would have been much smaller had the company had ballets suitable for matinee audiences, which would enable it to draw a younger attendance, the mainstay of most ballet matinees.

On the whole, Kirstein and Balanchine were quite satisfied with the season. Baum was sincerely delighted with the showing the New York City Ballet made in its first season under the ægis of the City Center and promised, come what might, to finance the company from then on.

Despite this optimistic outlook, the New York City Ballet was entering a crucial period. Baum's decision to have the City Center finance the future seasons of the company was very encouraging. Its actual fulfillment, however, was quite another thing. The point was that the City Center had no time available to run another season of the company until November, and to keep intact a ballet company that was idle for nine months was an unsurmountable problem. But the company had no alternative. Kirstein was certain that the company would lose all its dancers. Even Balanchine thought that when the company was called together again in October quite a number of the key dancers would be missing. Ballet Society was flat broke. Whatever money it had collected from subscribers had gone into the preparation of the fall and winter seasons. Kirstein's personal contribution of forty-seven thousand dollars to cover the deficit of the fall season had made it impossible for him to maintain the company even on a rehearsal-salary basis. As a matter of fact he had to cut

corners, and the magazine *Dance Index* fell victim to the economy drive.

Several of the ranking dancers of the company found
temporary employment in other companies and in Broadway
musicals. Tallchief joined Ballet Theatre as guest ballerina
for its spring season. Magallanes went to Cuba as *premier
danseur* of Ballet Alicia Alonso, replacing Igor Youskevitch,
who returned to Ballet Theatre. Other dancers went into
musicals, the Radio City Music Hall, *etc.* Those who lived in
New York with their families went on tight budgets to weather
the long layoff as best they could.

The disturbing aspect of the nine-month hiatus was the
dangerous possibility that a pattern might be set for future
seasons of the New York City Ballet—that of having the company appear in the City Center twice a year, each time dancing about two weeks. This would give the company four or
five weeks' work per year. With a very generous rehearsal
period of four weeks before each season, the company would
still be occupied only thirteen weeks per year. What about
the other thirty-nine weeks?

Other American ballet companies, specifically the Ballet
Russe de Monte Carlo and Ballet Theatre, did not play in
New York longer than five or six weeks, divided into two
seasons, generally autumn and spring; one or the other company, on occasion, even skipped a New York season entirely.
But to them New York was at best a terminal point of cross-
country tours. In effect, the autumn season was little more
than a review-gathering period designed to supply quotations
for advertising and publicity releases and encourage local
managers to book the company. The spring season, both
companies being domiciled in New York, was a convenient
method of ending the engagement. The most important and
most lucrative part of the whole season was obviously the tour,
which generally averaged twenty-four weeks (the better-

organized tour of Ballet Russe de Monte Carlo lasted twenty-seven weeks in 1949–50). These twenty-four weeks, together with the four weeks in New York and another four weeks, minimum, of rehearsals, gave the dancers a comfortable working year of about thirty-two weeks.

The New York City Ballet had no such tour, could not get it, and, what is more, actually did not want it. Both Balanchine and Kirstein reasoned, and quite properly, that the New York City Ballet could not appear at its best on tour and, unlike Ballet Russe de Monte Carlo, could not earn its keep. The company by then had a roster of fifty dancers and an orchestra of fifty-odd musicians, far too big an organization for a touring troupe. Moreover, tour managers of ballet companies were less than impressed with the New York City Ballet as a commercial enterprise. It had excellent ballets in its repertoire, they admitted, but all of them were *avant-garde*, unfamiliar to the general public and unsuitable for out-of-New York presentation. Also the company was not spectacular enough, had no famous names on its roster, and would probably not accept guest stars having a definite draw at the box office.

During the long layoff, Balanchine, Kirstein, and Baum had more than enough time to discuss every possibility of supplying additional work for the company. They could not find a solution. Longer or more frequent New York seasons were ruled out as quickly as a tour. What with seasons of Ballet Russe de Monte Carlo and Ballet Theatre and visiting foreign companies—such as the Sadler's Wells Ballet, about to be brought over by S. Hurok—and the four weeks of the New York City Ballet, New York already had more ballet than ever before, and, they all agreed that it could not support any more.

Obviously, the New York City Ballet was in a cul-de-sac.

Like nearly all people in ballet, Balanchine, Kirstein, and

Baum used an empirical method to guide the destinies of the company. Baum had less experience than his colleagues, and therefore, perhaps, was more optimistic.

That spring and summer he told them more than once: "Don't worry. I've managed to get out of tougher situations than this. We'll get out of this one, too."

He did not tell them how because he did not know himself. But he proved to be right in the end.

XV

1949-1950

"Firebird"; "Age of Anxiety"; "Illuminations"

As soon as Balanchine and Tallchief returned from their vacation in Hollywood, late in August, the New York City Ballet announced that it would play a three-week season at the City Center beginning November 23, and called the company together for rehearsals on October 17.

The fears that several of the principal dancers would not return to the company proved unfounded. Only one principal dancer left: Marie Jeanne. A few dancers from other companies asked Balanchine to be permitted to join the New York City Ballet, among them Janet Reed, late ballerina of Ballet Theatre, Melissa Hayden, soloist of Ballet Theatre, and Frank Hobi, soloist of Ballet

220

Russe de Monte Carlo. They were made welcome. Jerome Robbins, who did a superior job during the summer staging the dances in the musical *Miss Liberty*, expressed a desire to dance in the company as well as to choreograph for it. There was an obvious trend among dancers to associate with the New York City Ballet despite its short seasons and the lower-than-average salaries it could afford to pay its principals. (The salary of the *corps de ballet* was regulated by the American Guild of Musical Artists, which has jurisdiction over ballet dancers.)

Balanchine came back from Hollywood with a desire to stage *Firebird*. He had been seeing much of Stravinsky during the summer, and it was Stravinsky's idea that the time was ripe for a revival of this ballet.

Firebird was originally staged by Michel Fokine in 1910 for the Diaghilev company, in Paris, with Tamara Karsavina in the title role, Fokine himself as the Prince, Enrico Cecchetti as Kostchei, and Vera Fokina as the Princess. The décor for this first version was by Alexander Golovine. It was revived in 1920 in décor by Nathalie Gontcharova. American audiences saw this version of the ballet when it was presented here by Col. de Basil's Ballet Russe de Monte Carlo, and later by the Original Ballet Russe. In 1945, Ballet Theatre commissioned Adolph Bolm to stage the ballet for its company with Alicia Markova, Anton Dolin, John Taras, and Diana Adams in the principal roles. The décor and costumes for this version were by Marc Chagall.

As can happen only in ballet, the Bolm choreography of the ballet and the musical material belonged to Ballet Theatre, but Chagall's scenery and costumes were the property of S. Hurok. Here is how this happened. When *Firebird* was produced for Ballet Theatre that company was under the management of Hurok. In fact the ballet was staged at his insistence. Ballet Theatre commissioned Nicholas Remisoff to design the sets and costumes. When the designs were delivered they were not what the company expected, and it was decided that new sets and costumes should be commissioned from Marc Chagall. At the same time Ballet Theatre flatly refused to invest in a second set and left it to Hurok to bear the expense. However reluctantly, the impresario agreed, with the stipulation that the décor and costumes remain his property.

A year later Ballet Theatre and Hurok parted company, and the *Firebird* set was placed in storage by Hurok.

The new season of the New York City Ballet was to be fully a City Center undertaking, i.e., the City Center would pay not only the running expenses of the company, as in January, but would also furnish the necessary funds for the new ballets. This was an important achievement for the company because it relieved Ballet Society of the burden of underwriting new productions. At the same time, however, it placed a limitation on the number of new productions the company would be permitted to do, at least for this season.

The new ballets scheduled, in addition to *Firebird*, were Balanchine's *Bourrée Fantasque* to Emmanuel Chabrier's music, a revival of Lew Christensen's *Jinx*, and William Dollar's *Ondine* to an Antonio Vivaldi score. There was no problem with the décors for *Jinx* and *Ondine*, but *Bourrée Fantasque* and *Firebird* would be expensive productions, and Morton Baum could not see his way clear to financing both of them in one season.

Something had to be done. Balanchine liked the Chagall décor and wanted very much to use it if he could get it from Hurok for a reasonable figure. It was known in ballet circles that the impresario had paid nearly twenty-five thousand dollars for it.

Hurok returned from Europe on September 5 with his left arm in a sling, the result of a nasty fall in Milan. After long preliminary discussions with friends and associates and much speculation whether Hurok would be in a good mood or a bad one because of his injury, Balanchine went to see the impresario. The interview turned out to be much simpler and easier than Balanchine had anticipated. Hurok asked the choreographer how much the company could afford to pay, and when Balanchine could not give a definite answer suggested that Baum call him up and straighten out the matter. Baum telephoned Hurok the next day and said that they could pay about four thousand dollars. Hurok mentioned forty-five hundred, whereupon Baum offered to split the difference, and Hurok agreed. The company had acquired *Firebird*.

Hurok's attitude toward the company was significant in itself, but it was also symptomatic of the general feeling in the dance world toward the New York City Ballet—general, that is, with the exception of other ballet companies, which began to look upon the City Center company as a serious competitor in New York.

Another important person who assumed a helpful attitude toward the company was Barbara Karinska, the famous costume designer and *couturière*. She knew very well that the company could not afford to have its costumes made in her shop, that her fees were far too high. But she also knew that she alone could make ballet costumes look chic and elegant, and that the company needed her work now, at its difficult time, more than it would ever need it. A friend of long standing and an admirer of Balanchine and Kirstein, she told them one afternoon that for the time being she would do their costumes at the actual cost of material and labor. This unexpected offer amounted to a saving of at least fifty per cent on the costumes; some people who know Mme Karinska's fees even said seventy-five per cent. Fifty or seventy-five, the saving was great and the costumes elegant. Balanchine and Kirstein were sincerely grateful.

The autumn of 1949 was a very lively one for ballet.

Ballet Russe de Monte Carlo had a successful two-week season at the Metropolitan Opera House, September 16 to October 2. A week later, on October 9, the Sadler's Wells Ballet, brought over from London by Hurok, broke all attendance records with a four-week season at the same theater. The British company amassed volumes of publicity on its performances as well as on the various receptions, parties, teas, and so forth, that were staged in its honor. The result was that ballet was being talked about, written about, broadcast about, as never before. It became the fashionable thing and the attendant glitter cast its reflection on the modest New York City Ballet at the City Center.

The November season was ambitious. Not only was it a week longer than the previous two seasons, but the weeks themselves were longer now: the company played from Wednesday through Sunday, with matinees on Sundays. The roster of the company included sixty names. The following were listed as principals: Maria Tallchief, Janet Reed, Tanaquil LeClercq, Melissa Hayden, Lois Ellyn, Beatrice Tompkins, Nicholas Magallanes, Frank Moncion, Herbert Bliss, Todd Bolender, and Frank Hobi. Jerome Robbins acquired a new title: Associate Artistic Director.

The season opened November 27 with *Mother Goose Suite*, *Orpheus*, and *Symphony in C*. *Mother Goose* served as a vehicle for the debuts of Janet Reed (the Young Girl) and Jerome Robbins (Hop o' My Thumb).

Janet Reed came to the New York City Ballet after a successful season as the dance lead in the musical *Look, Ma, I'm Dancin'*. Born in Tolo, Oregon, she received her dance education in Portland and San Francisco. In 1937–41 she was ballerina of the San Francisco Ballet under the direction of Willam Christensen. In 1941 she came East to become ballerina of Dance Players, with which company she remained until its dissolution. She then joined Ballet Theatre, also as ballerina, and created a number of roles in such ballets as *Fancy Free*, *Tally-Ho*, *On Stage!*, *Undertow*, *Dim Lustre*, and *Waltz Academy;* she also danced in *Pillar of Fire*, *Gala Performance*, *Graduation Ball*, *Mademoiselle Angot*, *Bluebeard*, *Pas de Quatre*, *Three Virgins and a Devil*, *Judgment of Paris*, and *Princess Aurora*. She left Ballet Theatre in 1946.

In her New York City Ballet debut she brought a young and wistful quality to the role of the Young Girl, which gave a feeling of magic and dreams. Robbins, as Hop o' My Thumb, did unexpectedly well. Unexpectedly, because it was felt that this rather small part would not interest the dancer.

The first *première* of the season came on the second night, November 24. It was Lew Christensen's *Jinx*, to music by Benjamin Britten. The ballet was originally created in 1942 for Dance Players, the short-lived organization sponsored by Mrs. Winthrop Palmer and directed by Eugene Loring. The plot of *Jinx* revolved around the fears and superstitions of circus performers, and its locale was the arena of a small traveling circus.

Christensen succeeded in creating an atmosphere of mystery and suspense, but failed to tell his story in terms understandable to the spectators. Basically, *Jinx* had an excellent idea and there was enough material in it for a good ballet. In fact, during the following season, after Christensen had time to do some additional work on it, it emerged as a very successful ballet. Moncion in the title role, Reed as a Wirewalker, and Bliss as an Equestrian gave excellent performances.

On November 25 Robbins danced his second role in the company: the Host in his ballet, *The Guests*, which had been created by Moncion. He gave the role an interpretation of his own, and the ballet was much applauded.

The great hit of the season came on November 27: Balanchine's version of *Firebird*.

Conceived in simpler terms than the original production of Michel Fokine (and to a shorter, newly arranged score by Stravinsky), the ballet was imaginatively choreographed and superbly danced. The *pas de deux* of the Firebird (Tallchief) and Prince Ivan (Moncion) surpassed any other *pas de deux* staged by Balanchine, and that was saying a great deal, for after Petipa and Ivanov no other choreographer has ever reached such lofty heights in staging *pas de deux*. Kept within the strict limits of the classic adagio, it taxed to the utmost the skill of both dancers. The result was as exciting a choreographic poem as had been seen in quite a while. It was naturally tailormade for Tallchief, and she had never danced better. Moncion was sure and strong and elegantly self-effacing. He projected a true type of a Mongolian prince (which incidentally was ethnically correct) and danced very well.

The Dance of the Maidens emerged as a delightful quasi-folk dance. Pat McBride was a charming Princess. The dance of the Monsters was conceived less as a frightening exhibition than as a fairy-tale bacchanal, more amusing than scary. The final scene, the wedding of the Princess and the Prince, was the weakest. It wanted more invention, more pomp, and more people on the stage.

Chagall's décor, which had been designed for the stage of the Metropolitan, crowded the smaller stage of the City Center, but was wonderful nevertheless. Because of the imaginative and skillful lighting by Jean Rosenthal it somehow made a stronger impression than at the Metropolitan. There it had been on display, here it became part of the ballet.

Firebird received a long and clamorous ovation. Balanchine, Tallchief, and Moncion had to come back again and again. The audience sat and stood clapping and shouting long after the house lights were turned on, a sure sign of sincere acclaim. The press next morning, and for weeks to come, could not praise it enough. Baum, sensing what *Firebird* could do for the box office, was quick to add several performances of the ballet, substituting it for some of the older works, and they were all just as quickly sold out.

To a long article about *Firebird* in the Sunday *Times* (December 5) John Martin added this paragraph:

"There is to be an added performance of it this afternoon, and two others on Wednesday and Thursday evenings. If you cannot get tickets for any of them, do not be surprised; just take warning and get your order in early for the spring season."

The other new ballet by Balanchine, *Bourrée Fantasque*, was premièred on December 1. It was staged to a selection of three unrelated pieces by Emmanuel Chabrier (*Bourrée Fantasque*, *Prelude*, and *Fête Polonaise*) with a fourth serving as an introduction. The set consisted of white gauze draperies against a blue cyclorama. The costumes, by Barbara Karinska, were black, touched with saffron or turquoise, silver or cerise; the girls also wore flowered head-dresses and gloves or carried fans. It was very elegant and very dressy and the audience loved it the minute the curtain was raised.

The choreography of the first part was a parody of Balanchine's own work. It was one of those things in which the dancers start out on a perfectly straight-face dance and suddenly contort it into an awkward pose or group of steps that brings laughter from the spectators. Funny it may have been; good ballet it was not, in my opinion. Tanaquil Le-Clercq and Jerome Robbins had a merry time having a merry time.

The second part was an inventive *pas de deux* for Tallchief and Magallanes, assisted by Edwina Fontaine, Yvonne Mounsey, and an ensemble. It was well arranged, had a romantic mood about it, but suffered from its juxtaposition to the first part. No one, not even Balanchine, could stage a parody on a *pas de deux* and follow it immediately with a straight *pas de deux* and expect the latter to make an impression.

The third section, headed by Janet Reed and Herbert Bliss, belonged to the category of "organized chaos," of which Balanchine used to be very fond at one stage of his career. It was very lively, very gay and very repetitive. Coming after the final sections of *Symphonie Concertante*, *Theme and Variations*, and *Symphony in C*, it looked like early Balanchine.

In fairness to the choreographer it must be recorded that the spectators enjoyed *Bourrée Fantasque* very much indeed and that the daily press gave it a rousing welcome. It obviously was another hit.

On December 9 the company presented the last new ballet of the season, William Dollar's *Ondine*, to a score by Antonio Vivaldi, in a set and costumes by Horace Armistead. The set was not designed specifically for the ballet. It had been done originally for the opera *Far Harbour*, which Ballet Society had presented in January 1948, and was now being used, in the name of economy, as a background for *Ondine*. Despite the expedient nature of the set, it was by no means makeshift. There was a distinctly romantic feeling about it and it suited the ballet very well—better, in fact, than did any of the other ingredients.

Ondine was more or less a re-creation of the ballet of the same title which Jules Perrot staged in 1843 for Fanny Cerito, two years after *Giselle* and his unhappy separation from Carlotta Grisi. A romantic ballet very much in the style of *Giselle*, *Ondine* was never a great masterpiece. It had not improved at the hands of Dollar. The story of *Ondine* is that of a naiad who falls in love with a fisherman and tries to take him away from his human bride-to-be.

Dollar was handicapped before he started by the choice of the music. Instead of the original music by César Pugni, the choreographer decided, or was asked, to use a group of violin concertos by Vivaldi. The superimposition of a tender, emotional, fairly complicated romantic story upon the typical concert-hall music produced an incongruous clash that Dollar could not prevent or remedy. The unsuitable music never let the characters of the ballet come to life, never gave the dancers a chance to dance and act as romantic ballet demands. Dollar's choreography indicated that, given half a chance, he could create an interesting if not perhaps a great composition.

Rightly or wrongly, the romantic ballet has a form defined by the music more than by anything else. The lack of form in *Ondine* made the ballet drag, made it appear spotty and repetitive. Vivaldi was a much more talented composer then Pugni, but he did not write *Ondine;* Pugni did.

Tanaquil LeClercq, Melissa Hayden, Yvonne Mounsey, and Francisco Moncion had the principal roles in *Ondine.* They did what they could, but they could not fight Vivaldi.

Ondine was a failure, and more's the pity, because the company needed a story ballet to offset the ever-growing number of plotless ballets in its repertoire.

The season ended December 11 and the City Center management reported that the engagement had been the most successful so far. The attendance had been better than seventy-five per cent. The company did not make a profit or break even, but the deficit was smaller than ever before.

Another event marked that season, an event the importance of which was not so immediately apparent as the increased attendance and diminished deficit. Ninette de Valois, director of the Sadler's Wells Ballet, which was on its first American tour at the time, spent a few weeks in New York and attended many of the New York City Ballet performances. Asked for her opinion of the company, she said that she was very much impressed with the work the company was doing, with its repertoire, style of dancing, and discipline. It reminded her in many ways, she said, of the beginning of the Sadler's Wells Ballet, and she felt that the company was the most significant manifestation of ballet in America.

At her side often sat David L. Webster, general administrator of the Royal Opera House, Covent Garden, the London home of the Sadler's Wells Ballet, one of the greatest opera houses in Europe. Gratified by Miss de Valois's opinion of the company, I asked Mr. Webster whether there could be a possibility of his inviting the company to dance at Covent Garden. Mr. Webster answered rather diplomatically, as he usually does, that he had not thought about it, but that such a possibility was not excluded. He also thought that the company did not have enough "dressed" ballets; i.e., ballets with scenery and costumes. Without these, he felt, London would find it difficult to accept the company.

At the time there were no actual negotiations or even direct conversations about a London visit of the company among the principals involved, but there was a great deal of persistent talk and rumor: Ninette de Valois said this . . . Webster hinted that . . . Hurok thought that if . . . Balanchine would like to . . .

There was one tangible result of Miss de Valois's liking both the company and Balanchine's choreography. Before she left for London she invited Balanchine to stage a ballet for the Sadler's Wells company. Balanchine suggested his *Ballet Imperial,* and Miss de Valois agreed. They arranged that the choreographer would go to London by the middle of March and *Ballet Imperial* be presented early in April.

To celebrate the success of the season, the Board of Directors of the City Center gave a cocktail party in honor of the company on December 12 at the Gotham Hotel, the first such party the company was ever given. Everyone was very happy.

Despite the success of the company and its growing prestige, some members of the Board of Directors of the City

Center were against the City Center's sponsoring the New York City Ballet. Most outspoken of these was Gerald F. Warburg, a brother, paradoxically, of Edward M. M. Warburg, Lincoln Kirstein's associate in founding the School of American Ballet and the first American Ballet company. More than once he told Baum: "Remember, Morton, the ballet company will drive the City Center to bankruptcy."

As soon as the engagement ended, the New York City Ballet announced a new season: four weeks, February 21 to March 19, 1950, playing a full six days each week. It was to be (and actually was) the most ambitious season ever undertaken by the company up to that time. There were five new ballets and a *pas de deux* on the schedule, an unprecedented number for any company.

Preparations for the season had begun in early fall. When Frederick Ashton, principal choreographer of the Sadler's Wells Ballet, had been in New York with his company, Balanchine and Kirstein had asked him to choreograph a work for the New York City Ballet. Ashton readily agreed. It seemed that he had long wanted to do a ballet based on the life and some of the poems of the French symbolist poet Arthur Rimbaud. He had even selected the music for it, Benjamin Britten's composition on the same subject, for tenor and strings, written in 1939. Kirstein thought that it would be a good idea to make the ballet an all-British affair, and commissioned Cecil Beaton to design the scenery and costumes. The ballet was entitled *Illuminations*, after the name of a group of Rimbaud's poems. Ashton went back to London with the Sadler's Wells Ballet in mid-December, but promised to return early in February to begin rehearsals.

Balanchine, fulfilling a long-standing desire, decided to revive his *Prodigal Son* (to Prokofiev's music), which he had first staged for Diaghilev in 1929, in the last season of the company's existence. The ballet had been seen in the United

States in the original settings by Georges Rouault, but with choreography by David Lichine, in the repertoire of the Original Ballet Russe. Balanchine's choreography had been seen only in Paris and London shortly before Diaghilev died. With many other people, Balanchine thought that the New York City Ballet had too many plotless ballets in its repertoire and that a ballet with a familiar story like that of the Prodigal Son would help to balance the program.

For some reasons that were never explained, Balanchine also wanted to stage a romantic *pas de deux* to Carl Maria von Weber's Clarinet Concertino. The company at that time was presenting three ballets an evening, not four, as later, and there was actually no need for a *pas de deux*. But Balanchine wanted to do it.

Jerome Robbins was contributing his first big ballet to this company, possibly the most important work he has done up to this writing. It was *Age of Anxiety*, a symbolic ballet on a contemporary theme. The choreographer received his inspiration for this ballet from Leonard Bernstein's Symphony No. 2 and the W. H. Auden poem, on which the music was based. Oliver Smith was commissioned to design the scenery, Irene Sharaff the costumes.

William Dollar was to stage *The Duel*, a ballet suggested by two cantos of Torquato Tasso's poem *Jerusalem Delivered*, to music by Raffaello de Banfield, in costumes by Robert Stevenson. A year or so earlier, Dollar had choreographed this ballet, in a slightly different version, under the title *Le Combat*, for Roland Petit's Ballets de Paris.

And finally, Balanchine and Robbins would combine forces to stage *Jones Beach*, a gay ballet to the young Dutch composer Jurriaan Andriessen's *Berkshire Symphonies*, danced in bathing suits contributed (appropriately enough) by the Jantzen Knitting Mills, Inc.

Rehearsals began the second week in January, and a

busier group of people than the New York City Ballet would have been difficult to find. Balanchine and Robbins rehearsed separately the *Prodigal Son* and *Age of Anxiety,* and together *Jones Beach;* Robbins, who was to dance the title role in the *Prodigal,* also rehearsed under Balanchine; Dollar rehearsed *The Duel;* when any of the dancers were free, attempts, not very successful, were made to rehearse the old ballets. To an outside eye it all looked baffling, nay chaotic, but somehow it worked: the new ballets were beginning to take shape.

The idea of taking the company to London was still alive. In retrospect, the company had little reason to believe that it would be invited to appear at Covent Garden. No one promised anything; nothing definite was ever said by anyone who had the power to say it. Yet the hope persisted—in everyone, that is, except Kirstein. "No one will ever invite us to London," he said. "Why should they?"

But even if he had no hope of it, he still wished it. Since the company had begun as Ballet Society, it had danced only in New York; first to a very limited audience, now to a bigger one. But it was still New York. No one outside New York had ever seen the company or knew anything about it, and it was time that other audiences had a look at it and that it got the feel of dancing for other than its faithful New York public. Moreover, and no one tried to deny it, there was a prestige inherent in being invited to dance at Covent Garden, in being accepted by the London audience. It was worth hoping for, wishing for.

Then there was the economic aspect. Everybody in the company, including the dancers, knew that it would be very difficult to keep the troupe together unless more work could be provided for it. Artistic success was a most stimulating motive for joining the company and staying with it, but dancers have to eat. Playing time in New York was, of necessity, limited to eight or possibly ten weeks per year; another eight or ten weeks could be given over to rehearsals. Thus at best the company could be employed some twenty weeks a year. An English engagement of six or eight weeks, with some two or three rehearsal weeks prior to leaving for London, would bring the season up to about thirty-one weeks, a comfortable period, only one week shorter than the average season of the touring ballet-companies.

Yes, it was definitely worth hoping for, wishing for, doing something about.

Although he never said so, Balanchine was probably more eager to get the company to London than was anyone else in the organization. He was going to London in March to stage his *Ballet Imperial* for Sadler's Wells, and he wanted London, which knew his work in the Diaghilev company and Les Ballets 1933, to see his ballets performed by an American company that he was heading. This was an understandable ambition.

In the midst of rehearsals, during the third week of January, Balanchine, Kirstein, and Baum learned that Hurok was flying to London on January 29 to complete arrangements for the second American season of the Sadler's Wells Ballet. It had been known before that Hurok would fly to London early in the new year, but on New Year's eve the impresario had undergone an emergency appendectomy and everyone had thought that the trip would be postponed. When it became known that Hurok had improved sufficiently to fly on the 29th, Balanchine held a hurried conference with Kirstein and Baum. It was decided that Balanchine should go to see Hurok and ask him to take up the matter of a London season for the New York City Ballet.

Hurok, still convalescing, received Balanchine at his home. It did not take long for Balanchine to persuade Hurok to discuss the problem with David Webster, the director of Covent Garden. Hurok promised to do what he could.

Apparently he could do a great deal, for on February 9 he telephoned from London that Webster agreed in principle to inviting the New York City Ballet for a season at Covent Garden, to begin early in July, and that a draft of a contract would be on the way shortly.

The good news added to the excitement of the rehearsal period; to many, July seemed only a few weeks away. Kirstein, Baum, and Frances Hawkins took a very realistic attitude toward the London trip.

"That's all very well," Kirstein said. "But they haven't signed the contract yet, and who knows what conditions they will offer. Mr. Baum says that the City Center cannot afford to lose money on the London season, and that if Covent Garden cannot cover all our expenses we can't go."

Another event happened that winter. It was of much smaller significance than the London invitation, but important nevertheless in the scheme of ballet life in New York. Ballet Associates in America decided to sponsor a dinner dance on April 20 at the Waldorf Astoria in honor of, and for the benefit of, the New York City Ballet on the occasion of the company's first European engagement.

Ballet Associates in America is a nonprofit corporation organized "to foster, encourage and promote the work of choreographers, composers and designers in the field of ballet and to cultivate the appreciation of ballet in America." The organization, formed in 1941, contributed to and sponsored the productions of Antony Tudor's *Pillar of Fire* and *Romeo and Juliet* and Agnes de Mille's *Tally-Ho*, and produced on its own accord Michael Kidd's *On Stage!* and John Taras's *Camille*—all for Ballet Theatre. John Alden Talbot, its current president, founded the organization and is still its moving spirit. Until 1947, Ballet Associates was closely allied with Ballet Theatre; at least, it did not sponsor productions for other companies. Between 1947 and 1950, owing to a chain of circumstances, it did not engage in producing activities. Now it was resuming its work, and its first activity was a dinner dance for the New York City Ballet.

For the company this meant an additional few thousand dollars, which it needed very much, and a certain recognition by social circles that had thus far neglected the company. For New York social-minded balletomanes the New York City Ballet had not been glamorous enough to warrant attention. It was composed of American dancers with little, if any, exciting background. It performed at the unfashionable City Center, not the Metropolitan, and, what was probably most discouraging to the social-minded, it never cultivated an entourage to which it would have been fun to belong. This is not to say, of course, that individual members of New York society did not help support the New York City Ballet or the organizations that preceded it. Mrs. W. K. Vanderbilt, Nelson A. Rockefeller, Mrs. David Pleydell-Bouverie, Mrs. Vincent Astor, and several others contributed to the School of American Ballet, Ballet Caravan, Ballet Society, and the New York City Ballet. But society as a group was as aloof from the company as the company was from it. The announcement that Ballet Associates in America would sponsor a dinner dance in honor of the New York City Ballet was, in a way, a recognition *de facto* of the company.

Frederick Ashton, true to his promise, returned to New York in the beginning of February and immediately commenced rehearsals of *Illuminations*.

Meanwhile it became known that Igor Stravinsky would come to New York from California to conduct his *Firebird* on the opening night of the season and *Orpheus* the following night. About the same time the United States National Commission of UNESCO (The United Nations Educational, Scientific and Cultural Organization) invited the New York City Ballet to participate in the International Theater Month, which it was sponsoring in March, and selected the program of March 2, which included the *première* of *Illuminations*, to inaugurate the proceedings.

Things were popping around the New York City Ballet, and the box office, always quick to reflect additional publicity, was showing an unprecedented advance sale.

Performances began on February 21, and Stravinsky, who conducted the opening night's *Firebird*, set the tone for the entire season. Tallchief in the title role, McBride as the Bride, and Moncion as Prince Ivan had never danced the ballet better, and the company gave them excellent support. Somehow, the whole production acquired a new strength and a new warmth through the presence of Stravinsky. *The Guests*, somewhat rearranged, and a sparkling *Symphony in C*, with Melissa Hayden in Tallchief's part and Janet Reed in the part created by Marie Jeanne, completed the program. Stravinsky's conducting of *Orpheus* the following night added a new depth to the ballet and produced a performance long to be remembered.

The first new ballet of the season, Balanchine's *Prodigal Son*, was premièred on February 23.

Wrote John Martin in *The New York Times* the following day:

"The Balanchine of the classic idiom and the musical visualization is nowhere in evidence. He has here told the familiar Bible story in a style of complete originality, which reflects the lusty music of Prokofieff and adds rich flavors of its own. It is gauche and cruel, funny and naive, lascivious and tender, and its physical and mental energy, though not skill and artistry, could scarcely belong to anyone but a young choreographer of 25. It moves with direct and sweeping force, through fantastically perceptive and daring episodes, to a conclusion of irresistible emotional conviction."

The choreography for Jerome Robbins in the title role

was the finest in the ballet. His variation in the first scene was imaginatively conceived, and Robbins did what was probably the best dancing in his repertoire. The *pas de deux* with the Siren in the second scene and the return home in the third scene were touched with sincere passion and humility, respectively, and left a strong impression.

Maria Tallchief was not quite at home as the Siren. She was magnificent in the complicated *pas de deux* with the Prodigal, but the dramatic undertones of the role escaped her. Much more the ballerina than the enchantress, she remained too cool and detached to be dramatically convincing.

Frank Hobi and Herbert Bliss danced well the roles of the Servants. Michael Arshansky was the patriarchal and rather static Father.

The company could not afford to order new scenery for the *Prodigal Son*, and the old Rouault set belonged to Col. de Basil. The long table, which also serves as a fence and a boat, as it was originally intended by the designer, was properly constructed; the tent of the Father was ingeniously put together with lengths of cloth; but the ballet also needed a backdrop for the first and the last scenes. Rummaging through the property room for something suitable, Balanchine discovered Chagall's floor-cloth for the *Firebird*, which the company was not using. It was painted in more or less the same color scheme as Rouault's backdrop, and Balanchine decided to use it in place of the original until such time as the proper Rouault backdrop could be painted. It was makeshift, of course, but it was better than an ordinary cyclorama. The mother of invention had done her duty.

Dollar's *The Duel* was premièred on February 24. Suggested by Cantos III and IV of Tasso's poem *Jerusalem Delivered*, the ballet told the story of the first encounter of Clorinda, the Saracen girl, and Tancred, the Christian warrior, and of their final meeting—a duel in which Tancred mortally wounds Clorinda and then discovers that she is the girl he loves.

The Duel, in effect a long *pas de deux*, was very well composed. Although all five people engaged in the ballet (there were three Crusaders in addition to the two principals) were depicted on horseback most of the time, Dollar succeeded in avoiding the limitation in movement which such a situation seems bound to impose. He found a way to sustain the impression of mounted people yet have them actually dance. Melissa Hayden and the choreographer danced the principal roles admirably; Val Buttignol, Walter Georgov, and Shaun O'Brien were the Crusaders.

A revised version of Lew Christensen's *Jinx*, on the same program, proved far superior to the original. The ballet had now acquired a lucidity that had been missing from the earlier presentations.

February 26 brought the *première* of Jerome Robbins's *Age of Anxiety*.

Age of Anxiety, at this writing Robbins's most important work, marked the beginning of a new period in his creative life, a period not yet ended. Most of Robbins's ballets created before *Age of Anxiety*—such as *Fancy Free, Interplay*, and *Facsimile*—dealt very much with small themes: three sailors on leave in the big town; youngsters having a good time dancing and showing off; the complex but personal experience of the protagonists in a libidinous triangle.

In *Age of Anxiety* Robbins evoked the basic emotions of a whole generation, a generation that has not yet outlived the horrors of a world war, insecure under the conditions of an uneasy peace and the radical changes in a civilization that had heretofore appeared safe and enduring, a generation that does not quite know where to look for something or someone offering a modicum of assurance that all is not going to be destroyed morally and physically.

It was a theme of monumental proportions, a philosophical, political, and sociological problem that still awaits its solution. Obviously Robbins could not solve the problem; nor did he attempt to do so. The best he could offer was hope and faith, and one felt grateful that the choreographer did not give in to despair.

In his dramatic and choreographic treatment of this overwhelming theme Robbins emerged as an imaginative artist and a superb craftsman. He was still, perhaps, lacking the ultrafine sensitivity needed to steer a completely clear course between the obvious and the abstract, but he succeeded in creating a work of great depth and perception, of beauty and imagination.

Following the outline of Auden's poem, Robbins divided his ballet into six sections: The Prologue, where four strangers meet and become acquainted; The Seven Ages, where they discuss the life of man from cradle to grave; The Seven Stages, where they embark on a poetic journey to find happiness; The Dirge, where they meet the figure of the all-powerful someone who would protect them from all dangers, but turns out to be but an idol easily falling in the face of adversity; The Masque, where they attempt to forget their anxieties in insincere gaiety and reluctant revelry; and, finally, The Epilogue, the return to reality with the problems unsolved by memories, intellectual search, and analysis of dependence on a superman, superstate, or supercondition, but with a hope and faith in the ultimate triumph of good over evil, in this generation or another.

As can be imagined, *Age of Anxiety* was not a simple ballet to watch, or an easy one to understand and appreciate. It was not a work for those whose interest in ballet was limited to the classics, the gay concoctions of Leonide Massine or the perennial folksiness of Agnes de Mille. It is no secret that *Age of Anxiety* alienated a number of conservative balleto-

center—*Francisco Moncion, Melissa Hayden*

THE DUEL

center—*Francisco Moncion, Melissa Hayden*

AGE OF ANXIETY: *Roy Tobias, Todd Bolender, Tanaquil LeClercq, Jerome Robbins*

ILLUMINATIONS: *Tanaquil LeClercq, Nicholas Magallanes, Melissa Hayden*

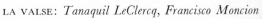

LA VALSE: *Tanaquil LeClercq, Francisco Moncion*

LA VALSE: *Tanaquil LeClercq*

CAKEWALK:
Patricia Wilde,
Frank Hobi

Nicholas Magallanes, Nora Kaye

Nora Kaye, Michael Maule

THE CAGE

Yvonne Mounsey

THE MIRACULOUS MANDARIN: *above—Melissa Hayden, Hugh Laing*
below—Melissa Hayden, Edward Bigelow, Todd Bolender (The Mandarin)

À LA FRANCAIX: *Janet Reed, André Eglevsky, Maria Tallchief*

Jerome Robbins

TYL ULENSPIEGEL

Jerome Robbins,
Frank Hobi,
Beatrice Tompkins

Part of the corps

SWAN LAKE

Maria Tallchief, André Eglevsky, part of the corps

LILAC GARDEN: *Hugh Laing, Tanaquil LeClercq, Antony Tudor, Nora Kaye*

BAYOU: *center—Francisco Moncion; left couples, reading from front to back—Melissa Hayden & Herbert Bliss, Una Kai & Shaun O'Brien, Marilyn Poudrier & Brooks Jackson; right couples, reading from front to back—Diana Adams & Hugh Laing, Irene Larsson & Stanley Zompakos, Barbara Walczak & Walter Georgov*

CARACOLE: *front row—Jerome Robbins, Diana Adams, André Eglevsky, Tanaquil LeClercq, Nicholas Magallanes; second row, center—Patricia Wilde*

LA GLOIRE: *Hugh Laing, Diana Adams, Nora Kaye*

PICNIC AT TINTAGEL: *Jacques d'Amboise, Diana Adams, Robert Barnett,*
Francisco Moncion, Edwina Fontaine, Brooks Jackson, Stanley Zompak

PICNIC AT TINTAGEL: *Diana Adams, Yvonne Mounsey, Jacques d'Amboise*

A THOUSAND TIMES NEIGH!: *Serge Temoff, Betty Gilmore, Marie Jeanne, John Paul Dunphy*

Lincoln Kirstein

George Balanchine

*George Balanchine (right center) rehearsing a group from the School of
American Ballet at Woodland, White Plains, New York, in June 1934
—the first picture taken of Balanchine rehearsing American dancers*

Publicity picture taken in connection with the première *of* CARD PARTY *on April 27, 1937
at the Metropolitan Opera House. Seated at card table, reading clockwise from left—
William Dollar, Edward M. M. Warburg, Igor Stravinsky, George Balanchine; standing, left to right—Hortense Kahrklin, Leyda Anchutina, Helen Leitch, Annabelle Lyon*

Vida Brown and George Balanchine, a news picture in costumes for the "Mazurka" from A LIFE FOR THE TSAR

George Balanchine and Igor Stravinsky conducting a rehearsal of ORPHEUS, *1948*

Some of the choreographers and principal dancers of the New York City Ballet, February 1952: seated on bench—Maria Tallchief, George Balanchine, Tanaquil LeClercq; around the piano, clockwise from left—Melissa Hayden, Frederick Ashton, Diana Adams, Janet Reed, Jerome Robbins, Antony Tudor, Nora Kaye

manes, some of whom have yet to make peace with the company. But its profound and provocative artistry attracted elements who had theretofore considered ballet a light and fluffy sort of entertainment unworthy of serious consideration.

Structurally, *Age of Anxiety* was an ensemble piece. In no other ballet were the dancers more convincing yet more self-effacing than in *Age of Anxiety*. The first cast included Tanaquil LeClercq, Francisco Moncion, Todd Bolender, Jerome Robbins, Yvonne Mounsey, Pat McBride, Beatrice Tompkins, Melissa Hayden, Herbert Bliss, Dick Beard, Shaun O'Brien, Edward Bigelow, and nearly the whole *corps*.

Oliver Smith designed several inventive backdrops, some of them almost photographic in their representational qualities, others poetic and evocative. Irene Sharaff's costumes were functional rather than imaginative, but well in style with the work. Bernstein's music, not great intrinsically, served the purpose admirably.

On March 2 the company presented Ashton's *Illuminations*. This was the program that opened the International Theater Month, sponsored by UNESCO. There were speeches by Lincoln Kirstein and Rosamond Gilder, representing the American National Theater and Academy (ANTA). The evening was dedicated to Great Britain, and the British Ambassador, Sir Oliver Franks, attended with his staff and representatives of the United Nations and of the City of New York. The orchestra played *The Star-Spangled Banner* and *God Save the King*. It was a gala occasion, the first such occasion the New York City Ballet had known.

Illuminations emerged as a series of danced episodes connected by the thread of the poet's biography and by the moral that could be drawn from it: that a genius is only human and cannot take the place of God. Like *Age of Anxiety*, *Illuminations* dealt with a lofty theme, not the simple tale of individuals. It identified and gave substance, as it were, to the ideas and

aspirations Kirstein had always held about the lyric theater—
a mirror of humanity as a whole, not of little people as individuals. Many people felt at the time that *Age of Anxiety* and
Illuminations justified the existence of the New York City
Ballet.

As a ballet *Illuminations* was sheer poetry, beautiful and
exciting, at times brutal, but always poetry. Totally different
from anything else that Ashton had done—and, for that matter, from anything this company had ever danced—*Illuminations* was a magnificent ballet. Its nine scenes were nine little
masterpieces saturated with a wealth of intricate details that
offered new discoveries at every seeing.

Nicholas Magallanes as the Poet, Tanaquil LeClercq as
Sacred Love, and Melissa Hayden as Profane Love were
superb. Magallanes was not perhaps the personification of
Rimbaud, as Ashton might have wanted him to be, but he
created a strong and exciting role that has since grown in
depth and stature and seems right in the ballet. The large
ensemble upheld the illusion created by the choreographer.

Cecil Beaton's décor, as often happens, was overornate
and in many instances superficial and on the sweet side. In
the case of a choreographer of lesser stature than Ashton, it
would have overwhelmed the ballet. Britten's music was a
suitable background for the ballet.

George Balanchine's *Pas de Deux Romantique* for Janet Reed
and Herbert Bliss, premièred the following evening, was a disappointment. It was slight, boring, wrong: one of those things
that should not happen, but does. Balanchine said at the time
that the *pas de deux* should not be construed as a parody on
romantic ballet. It was, he thought, a stylization of a romantic
pas de deux. If he was sincere and this was supposed to be a
straight work, it failed. As soon as Janet Reed in her garish
costume began to stylize the romantic ballet, the audience
began to titter, and as the *pas de deux* progressed the laughs

became louder and more general. If, on the other hand, Balanchine was pulling everybody's leg (as he may have been) and the *pas de deux* was meant to be a parody, it was not amusing enough. For the first time since Balanchine began to create in America he was out of style, out of taste: he was plain bad.

Jones Beach, the last new ballet of the season, was presented on March 9. The *première* served to introduce Netherlands Week of the International Theater Month. The performance was attended by Mr. Willem Cnoop Koopman, Consul General of the Netherlands, with his staff, representatives of the United Nations, New York City's Commissioner of Parks, Mr. Robert Moses (who built the beach after which the ballet was named), and other dignitaries. Lincoln Kirstein, wearing, probably for the first time, the Netherlands decoration he had received during the war, made a speech. The national anthems of the United States and the Netherlands were played, Jurriaan Andriessen, composer of the music for *Jones Beach*, conducting the anthem of his homeland. It was again a gala occasion.

Jones Beach was a gay romp, a whimsical bit of what used to be called in Diaghilev's times *"ballet sportif,"* but with much less pretense than, for example, *Le Train Bleu*. The titles of its four movements: Sunday, Rescue (from drowning), War with Mosquitoes, and Hot Dogs, amply describe the contents.

The first movement was a very amusing ensemble scene, with good-looking girls and strong boys in bathing suits. Melissa Hayden, Beatrice Tompkins, Yvonne Mounsey, Herbert Bliss, and Frank Hobi were the soloists. Tompkins was very funny as the girl chasing a boy. The second movement, which began with Nicholas Magallanes carrying Tanaquil LeClercq, whom he had apparently rescued from the brine, and culminated in an engaging acrobatic *pas de deux*, was the high spot of the ballet. Maria Tallchief was not very convincing in a jazzy *pas de deux* with Jerome Robbins in the fourth movement.

On the whole, this ballet was too long for its slight theme; a well-worked-out over-all plot would have probably helped it. Andriessen's delightful score was tuneful and rhythmic and a lot of fun. The New York City Ballet had long needed a light closing ballet—i.e., a ballet to be given last on a program—and this was it.

More than during any previous season Leon Barzin's talented direction of the excellent orchestra came to the fore. The scope of the music used by the company embraced many shades and styles of composition, from Mozart to Bernstein, from Tchaikovsky to Stravinsky, from Bach to Britten to Blitzstein. Barzin and his orchestra succeeded in being at the top of their musical form. In equally fine form was Jean Rosenthal, the technical director of the company, whose lighting brought to life the designs of such varied artists as Chagall and Noguchi, Beaton and Smith. More than that, working with lights alone, she managed to give form, direction, and space to the many ballets in the repertoire which had no décor at all. It was quite an achievement.

The season closed on March 19. It was the most exciting and successful season the company had had up to that time.

Thanks to the contribution of Mrs. David Pleydell-Bouverie toward the production of *Illuminations* and another sizable contribution by Kirstein, Morton Baum was able to report, gleefully, that the New York City Ballet had the smallest deficit on record.

Speaking of deficits of the company, it should be made clear that according to the accounting system adopted by the City Center all new productions staged during a given season are charged fully to that season; i.e., the cost of production is deducted as an expense from the receipts of the same season. If the receipts are not big enough to cover the whole of the productions, the remaining balance is considered a deficit, to be covered from other sources. Other ballet companies do not follow this procedure. They amortize the production of a new ballet over a period of time, generally the useful life of the scenery, which can be considered to be about ten years. For this reason, the break-even point of a New York City Ballet season is, comparatively, much higher than that of other ballet companies.

XVI

1950

A Season in London

George Balanchine sailed for London on March 11, while the New York season of his company was still on. He could not wait for the end of the season because the *première* of *Ballet Imperial* at Covent Garden was scheduled for April 5. As it was, this gave him less than three weeks to set and rehearse the work for a company that was completely unfamiliar to him, and one that, moreover, had been used to an entirely different style of ballet. But the Sadler's Wells Ballet was well disciplined and enjoyed working with him; the rehearsal time proved sufficient.

Lincoln Kirstein left for London on March 23. His trip had a twofold objective: to conclude ne-

gotiations with David Webster about the company's season at
Covent Garden and to be present at the *première* of *Ballet Imperial*. Kirstein knew as well as anyone else in the New York
City Ballet that he was not the man to negotiate a contract
with Webster, the director of one of the greatest opera houses
in Europe, a seasoned and hardheaded impresario and shrewd
bargainer. It was hoped, however, that Webster might accept
without too much fuss the changes the company wanted to
make in the conditions, and that the signing of the contract
would be a mere formality. But no contract involving a ballet
company of some sixty dancers, tons of scenery, a two-way
transatlantic flight, is simple. In addition problems involving
the basic difference between the British and American ways
of running a theater, local labor conditions, and a hundred
other details had to be straightened out. Kirstein quickly
realized that he was not up to the task, and so reported to
Morton Baum.

Baum could not go to London himself, and sent Frances
Hawkins, business manager of the company, to represent the
New York City Ballet. She took the first available plane and
arrived in London on Thursday morning, March 30, ready
for a session with Webster, only to find that the impresario
had left the evening before for a long weekend in the country.
One could not blame Webster for taking the weekend off: it
was clear, springlike, and mild. Neither could one blame
Frances Hawkins for being as furious as she was: no Webster,
no conference, a waste of time until Monday.

When Webster finally returned from the weekend, rested,
refreshed, with a tinge of the sun on his generally ruddy face,
he was more than a match for the angry and worn Frances
Hawkins. The more she fumed, the cooler Webster became.
He told her that he had offered the company certain conditions and they would have to be accepted. The talks were at an
impasse. Kirstein, to whom Frances Hawkins complained

about Webster's take-it-or-leave-it attitude, was all for forgetting the whole thing. "Webster very obviously doesn't want us," he told her. "We cannot force ourselves on him."

They decided between them that there was nothing to do but return to New York. But as this conversation took place on April 3, two days before the *première* of *Ballet Imperial*, Kirstein thought that Frances Hawkins might as well stay for the gala occasion. She talked again with Webster on the 4th, and again he would not budge.

Then came the first performance of *Ballet Imperial*.

It was an immediate success. There were long ovations for Margot Fonteyn, Beryl Grey, and Michael Somes, who danced the principal parts; Balanchine received seventeen curtain calls; Ninette de Valois, director of the company, honored Balanchine by taking a call with him; the company presented him, on the stage, with a wreath.

The success was obviously a trail-blazer for the New York City Ballet's visit, and everybody so understood it. After the performance Balanchine gave a party for the company and guests in Covent Garden's famed Crush Bar. A good part of literary, artistic, and social London attended, and there was no end to the congratulations for Balanchine and the dancers.

During the party Frances Hawkins walked over to Webster and said: "Mr. Webster, I am flying to New York tomorrow evening, and I want to say good-bye to you."

"This is no place to say good-bye," said Webster. "Besides, we haven't signed the contract yet. Come to see me about eleven and we'll straighten the thing out."

Frances Hawkins was at Webster's office on the dot of eleven. Webster was all smiles, good will, and agreement. He accepted nearly all the conditions she had asked for and brushed aside, as unimportant, details on which he had first insisted. Within an hour the new contract was typed and signed. The New York City Ballet was to appear at Covent

Garden for five weeks beginning July 10 and then have a three-week tour of the English provinces. It would be paid £2,000 per week while at Covent Garden, and Covent Garden would also pay half of its transatlantic transportation costs.

When he handed the signed contract to Frances Hawkins, Webster said: "Miss Hawkins, we shall be very glad to have the New York City Ballet at the Royal Opera House. But I also want you to know that London will make the company."

Balanchine, Kirstein, and Frances Hawkins returned together from London in high spirits.

On April 20, Ballet Associates in America held its dinner dance for the benefit of the New York City Ballet. Douglas Fairbanks was master of ceremonies. He made an excellent speech about the cultural growth of America and the importance of the London visit of the company for demonstrating to Europeans that America can export not only grain and steel and ammunition, but also art. Members of the company danced a divertissement from their repertoire, everyone had a very good time, and, what was perhaps most important, the company netted a few thousand dollars toward new costumes for the London visit.

Rehearsals for the London season began on June 12. The company that assembled for rehearsals included (in alphabetical order): Robert Barnett, Dick Beard, Edward Bigelow, Herbert Bliss, Barbara Bocher, Todd Bolender, Doris Breckenridge, Arlouine Case, Jacques d'Amboise, Ninette d'Amboise, Dorothy Dushok, Edwina Fontaine, Walter Georgov, Melissa Hayden, Frank Hobi, Brooks Jackson, Jillana, Una Kai, Peggy Karlson, Helen Kramer, Harold Lang (guest artist for London), Tanaquil LeClercq, Nicholas Magallanes, Barbara Milberg, Francisco Moncion, Yvonne Mounsey, Shaun O'Brien, Janet Reed, Jerome Robbins, Kaye Sargent, Ruth Sobotka, Harriet Talbot, Maria Tallchief, Roy Tobias, Beatrice Tompkins, Gloria Vauges, Barbara Walczak, Margaret Walker, Patricia Wilde, Jacqueline Williams, Tomi Wortham. Vida Brown, at the time guest artist with the Malmö (Sweden) Opera Ballet, was to join the dancers in London.

Musical director Leon Barzin had a previously signed contract and could not go. In his stead went Emanuel Balaban, who had conducted the American Ballet in Latin America in 1941. Lew Christensen went as ballet master, Nicholas Kopeikine as pianist. The administrative and technical staff included Frances Hawkins, business manager (Miss Hawkins stayed only the first two weeks and then returned to the United States); Betty Cage, general manager; Jean Rosenthal, technical director; Nananne Porcher, stage manager; Eudokia Mironowa, wardrobe mistress. Mrs. Helen Wortham (mother of Tomi Wortham, and a registered nurse by profession) went as nurse and as chaperone for the very young dancers, of whom there were several.

Balanchine and Mr. and Mrs. Kirstein flew to London on June 25 because they had been invited by Ambassador Lewis W. Douglas to attend the Independence Day celebration at the American Embassy. The company left July 3 in a British Overseas Aircraft Corporation chartered Stratocruiser. Morton Baum flew with the company.

The paraphernalia for the eighteen ballets that the company was to perform in England had been shipped by freighter earlier. The ballets were: *Age of Anxiety, Bourrée Fantasque, Concerto Barocco, Divertimento, The Duel, Firebird, Four Temperaments, The Guests, Illuminations, Jinx, Jones Beach, Mother Goose, Orpheus, Pas de deux romantique, Prodigal Son, Serenade, Symphonie Concertante,* and *Symphony in C.*

The visit of the New York City Ballet to London was under the auspices of the Arts Council of Great Britain, with which the Royal Opera House is affiliated, and was considered a quasi-official exchange visit for the Sadler's Wells

Ballet season in the United States in 1949. Information in New
York was that the London Embassy and social circles, as well
as balletomanes, were making preparations for the proper
welcome and entertainment of the company.

I sailed late in June to cover the company's London
season for *Dance News* and, as a special assignment, for the
New York Herald Tribune and *Newsweek*. I arrived in time to
attend the closing performance of the Sadler's Wells season at
Covent Garden on July 8. After the last ballet Ninette de
Valois, the company's director, came on stage with Frederick
Ashton to take the season's last curtain. She made a short
speech, at the end of which she called the audience's attention
to George Balanchine, sitting in a box. After the ovation for
the choreographer, Miss de Valois said: "The greatest reception the Sadler's Wells Ballet ever had was during our season
in New York last October. We shall never forget it. I know
that you will want to repay the New York City Ballet a
thousandfold for the reception New York gave us."

These remarks brought on a new ovation; they also set
the official attitude toward the New York company: Miss de
Valois, now Dame Ninette de Valois, does make ballet
weather in London.

The *première* of the New York City Ballet on July 10 was
an occasion. London's ballet world attended in force; the
literary, music, and art worlds were well represented; with
Ambassador Douglas away from London, the American Embassy sent its ranking personnel; all the London and Paris
newspapers and magazines sent their first-string critics; Scandinavian newspapers sent their correspondents; all wire services were there as well as all photographic services. Americans
who were in London and had been foresighted enough to get
tickets in advance came to the *première;* nearly the entire
Sadler's Wells company stayed over the weekend in London to
attend. S. Hurok flew in for the *première* from Paris, as did

Barbara Karinska and Anton Dolin. The perspicacious Paris
impresario, Leonid Leonidoff, came and stayed a week.
American dance critics in Europe at the time, among them
John Martin and Edwin Denby, were on hand.

The program, which included *Serenade*, *Age of Anxiety*, and
Symphony in C, scored an immediate hit with the audience.
There were loud applause, cheers, shouts, stamping. The
company took fourteen curtain calls after *Symphony in C;*
flowers were heaped high on the stage.

The performance was not without a mishap. Maria Tallchief went over on her right toes on a slippery spot on the
floor and strained her ankle during *Serenade*. Although in pain,
she managed to finish the ballet without a sign of the injury.
In the intermission Dr. Eric Scowen, who usually attends the
dancers of the Sadler's Wells Ballet, examined the ankle and
advised her not to go on in *Symphony in C*. Tallchief, however,
thought that she might be able to dance the ballet. She
danced the first movement, but then realized that she could
not do the fourth. Melissa Hayden, who had danced Tallchief's part in New York, hastily donned her costume and,
with no time left to put on make-up, finished the ballet for
her. Tallchief was out one week.

After the performance the company gave a party in the
Crush Bar attended by some two hundred people. These included the upper stratum of the London ballet world, the two
companies, Embassy officials, and many of the people generally and vaguely called celebrities. Asked about his impression of the New York company, David L. Webster told me:
"The New York City Ballet has achieved tonight the greatest
artistic success of any foreign ballet company which has
played at Covent Garden."

This was quite a statement coming from the diplomatic
and restrained Mr. Webster, for Covent Garden has played

host at one time or another to the Diaghilev company, the various Ballets Russes that followed it, the Anna Pavlova company, Ballet Theatre, the Marquis de Cuevas's Grand Ballet, and others.

Mr. M. Ruddock, the First Secretary of our London Embassy, told me that the opening was the best publicity the United States had had in a long time.

On July 13, after the *première* of the second program—*Serenade*, *Jinx*, and *Bourrée Fantasque*—David Webster responded with a party for the company, also in the Crush Bar. It was again a gala occasion attended by most of the people who were at the first party, with the exception of most of the Sadler's Wells Ballet dancers, who had left on vacation. Again there was enthusiastic comment about the company, its repertoire, style, and technique.

The press, on the whole, was favorable to the company though not enthusiastic. Here are several excerpts that indicate the general trend of the criticism:

The *Times's* first review said: "The American style may be said to be gracefully athletic rather than gracefully poetic. Mr. Robbins' ballet 'Age of Anxiety' . . . will give us enough to talk about for the remainder of the season. Usually these psychological or metaphysical ballets suffer from pretentiousness. This does not, though Heaven knows it is unintelligible enough."

Phyllis Jackson in the *Daily Telegraph* took a deeper view: "This young company imposes a standard of its own. Though respect for the classical tradition is implicit in its work it has followed its own natural bent for improvisation. . . . Age of Anxiety is a highly charged dramatic sequence depicting the struggles of ordinary folk to free themselves from besetting worries."

The *Graphic* did not so much criticize as report: "The

company were facing a British audience for the first time but after the first curtain they knew from their reception they had won the admiration of the 'gods' and the stalls alike."

Paul Holt in the *Daily Herald* went to great length (considering that the average London newspaper is only from eight to ten pages long because of the continuing newsprint shortage) in his first report about the company. Here is what he said: "A much pleasanter return match than usual was played by the New York ballet dancers in answer to the triumphal visit of Sadler's Wells to America last year. Nervous and diffident of their reception they danced with such vigour and athletic enthusiasm that they had the audience in this hallowed theatre whistling its enthusiasm long before the end came—and the whistling came from the stalls as well as the gallery.

"These fresh young Americans bring no mystery or sentiment to their dancing. They are rugged, tough and gay. The men attack feats of grace as a sport and the girls make almost a miracle of their execution of the classical routine. That is the strangest thing about their visit. They are not so much interested in the folksy style. They are pure classicists absorbed by the perfection of the old Imperial Russian Ballet."

Paul Holt's remark that the strangest thing about the company was that it was "not so much interested in the folksy style" was a clue to the attitude of most London critics to the New York City Ballet.

When the Philadelphia Ballet under the late Catherine Littlefield visited London in 1937, the only ballets accepted by the London critics were *Barn Dance* and *Terminal*, two light and insignificant pieces of rather corny "Americana" which the choreographer herself considered very minor works. They were overpraised even by writers who should know better, such as Arnold L. Haskell, and cited as examples of what American companies can and should do as opposed to classic ballets, which they had best leave alone. Ballet Theatre, which played in London in 1946, drew similar comments. Critically, the most successful ballet in its repertoire was Jerome Robbins's *Fancy Free*, and the classic ballets were again considered outside the scope of American dancers.

But here was an American company that practically specialized in classic ballets: it did not have a single ballet in "folksy" style, and if it did deal with American subject matter (*Age of Anxiety, Jones Beach*), it treated this in a style that was not recognizably American, but just plain contemporary. It was indeed "the strangest thing."

In fairness to the London critics and audience, it must be said that the repertoire of the company was anything but balanced. Nine of the eighteen ballets the company took over were so-called abstract ballets by Balanchine; i.e., ballets without any plot. Four of them were danced without scenery and in the simplest of costumes. New Yorkers who had seen these ballets added to the repertoire one by one accepted them one by one, as they were being staged. London, whose ballet companies offer a preponderance of story ballets, received Balanchine's plotless compositions in one batch. The city did not have an easy time trying to find a new criterion of judgment, to revalue its conception of what classic ballet actually was.

No wonder the venerable Cyril W. Beaumont wrote in the *Sunday Times:* "In his fertile invention of beautiful kaleidoscopic patterns and his ability to contrive new steps, new enchaînements and new and exciting lifts, Balanchine is a master without a peer. . . . Dancers and choreographers will find Balanchine's ballets an inexhaustible subject for study and analysis but their cold impersonal quality will appeal less to the general public."

The most controversial ballet of the season was not Ashton's *Illuminations* (though it did have what is called a mixed reception), or Robbins's *Age of Anxiety*, or Balanchine's *Orpheus*, but—of all ballets—*Firebird*.

Said James Monahan in the *Manchester Guardian:* "Anyone not blinded by distaste must admit that Mr. Ashton has done his job adroitly [in Illuminations]. His choreographic touch is light and quick—not least when he is at his naughtiest. Indeed it is rueful to reflect that this, his most unusual work since Symphonic Variations, was done not for his own Sadler's Wells but for an American company. . . .

"The other novelty last night was Balanchine's cut and altered version of the famous Stravinsky-Fokine Firebird. This version was undertaken on the approval of Stravinsky; nevertheless it was inexcusable. The only partly justifiable effect has been to emphasize the Firebird's dances; Maria Tallchief's interpretation deserved all possible emphasis . . . the fairy-tale magic has been torn brutally away."

The critic of *The Times* (criticisms in *The Times* are not signed) was still more outspoken: " 'Firebird' for which London had waited long, was also in last night's bill but alas! this is a poor emaciated creature. Mr. Balanchine's choreography is not Fokine's—where are the golden apples of yester year? Miss Maria Tallchief caught some of the glitter of the bird but none of her aloof, supernatural magic. The whole ballet was danced without the slightest trace of the atmosphere of Stravinsky's music against a decor [Chagall] containing motifs of smartness quite alien to a Russian fairyland. Perhaps this company is too immature for imaginative and romantic ballets." He also disliked Ashton's *Illuminations*.

This was too much for Lincoln Kirstein, and he wrote a letter to the editor of *The Times* which was duly printed without comment a week after the appearance of the review. Here is the letter:

"Sir,

"Your critic's unfavourable opinion of Mr. Frederick

Ashton's ballet 'Les Illuminations' in your issue of July 21
was, so far as I could judge, not shared by the audience, for
the reception was enthusiastic. Your critic is presumably
aware of the mixed beauty and grossness in Rimbaud's life
and work and it is regrettable that he could only recognize
grossness on the stage. As for his condemnation of 'The Firebird' I would ask leave to correct him on a point of fact. He
states that 'The whole ballet was danced without the slightest
trace of the atmosphere of Stravinsky's music.' He seems unaware that the choreography was revived with the composer's
desire and approval and that he conducted the work in the
February 1950 season in New York.

Yours faithfully,
LINCOLN KIRSTEIN,
Director, New York City Ballet"

Actually there was little reason for Kirstein to write this
letter. The company was doing very well at Covent Garden;
the spectators seemed to enjoy most of the ballets; Tallchief
had received a thunderous ovation at the *première* of *Firebird*.
Nearly all the critics had some reservation about *Firebird*, so
why single out *The Times?*

The only critic who accepted *Firebird* without any quali-
fication was Richard Buckle, the *enfant terrible* of the fraternity,
in *The Observer*. Said he: "One thing that is clear about Balanchine's 'Firebird,' which some of my matronly colleagues have
been deploring, is that it is a great deal better than Fokine's.
Fokine's had atmosphere agreed, but so has Victoria Station.
Balanchine's 'Firebird' is an exciting ballet with dancing in
it."

Of all the London critics only one did not like the company or Balanchine. It was Audrey Williamson, writing in the
weekly *Tribune*. Said she: "The legend that Balanchine is the
greatest modern choreographer remains . . . unproved. He
is a diamond with only one facet, the geometric glitter of ab-

stract ballet. Emotionally he can only touch the surface of a
mood, and this is shown especially when he attempts a narrative ballet. 'Orpheus' in his rendering becomes a surrealist
symbol without heart, and the loveliest and most moving of
classical romantic legends remains cold and undramatic. . . .
[*Firebird*] is a bare and curiously untender new version of the
ballet to which Fokine gave such enchantment. The dance
with the golden apples has vanished."

Audrey Williamson, in fact, had taken a dislike to the
company and particularly to Balanchine from the very beginning. On July 16 the London Ballet Circle presented a
lecture by Balanchine and Kirstein on the work of the New
York City Ballet, and Miss Williamson let loose with a long,
vituperative diatribe against Balanchine, accusing him, of all
things, of ruining the classic ballet as an art form. By the time
of the lecture she had seen two performances—six ballets—
but spoke as if she had been following Balanchine's work for
years.

The next day Kirstein said to me: "What has Audrey
Williamson got against us? She shouted as if George had
ruined her life, not only the classic ballet, and accused him of
every artistic crime in history. If what she said represents
what the London critics really think about us, we'd better
pack up and go."

He was very serious about it and it took a while to assure him that Miss Williamson was speaking for herself and
for no one else.

A few days after this incident Sir Osbert Sitwell officiated
at the opening of an exhibition of American Symbolic Realist
painters at the Institute of Contemporary Arts, arranged by
Kirstein and timed to coincide with the New York City
Ballet season at Covent Garden. The collection included
paintings by Paul Cadmus, Jared French, Henry Koerner,
Andrew Wyeth, George Tooker, Ben Shahn, Bernard Perlin,

and several others. Kirstein had assembled the paintings from various museums and private collections, including his own, had paid for their transportation and insurance, and had hung the exhibition—all on his own. He wanted to show London what Americans were doing in painting as well as ballet. London had not seen a similar show of modern art in quite a while.

It created a great deal of interest and a lively controversy. As in the case of the ballet company, the public liked it much more than did the critics. It added to the prestige of American art, but also to the irritation of Kirstein.

He could not understand the attitude of the London critics toward the ballet company or the exhibition. He was not alone in his bewilderment. Wrote Richard Buckle in his magazine, *Ballet*, in February 1952, nearly a year and a half later:

"Could [Cyril W.] Beaumont really not appreciate any ballet without a story? [James] Monahan was supposed to be musical; could he not write more warmly in support of the most musical of choreographers? . . .

"The impercipience of our critics was quite remarkable that summer; I often think about their blindness to what was being born in front of them and chuckle with evil glee. Of course there were a lot of pure dancing ballets in the programmes of New York City Ballet, and too many without scenery; but in the early days of Sadler's Wells there were too many dramatic ballets over-charged with decoration. It takes years to build a balanced repertory. Of course Balanchine had overweighted the programme with so-called 'abstract' ballets, partly in reaction to the sensational ballets of the last decade, partly because he wanted to see his new school of dancers dance, and because, anyway, he had a peculiar bent for that most ancient and noble kind of ballet born from the music's rib and ignorant of rival concubines. Balanchine had one fault: he was not interested in inventing dances for men. But to accuse him of barrenness, soullessness and lack of range in the face of such varied masterpieces as Serenade, Symphonie Concertante, The Prodigal Son, Orpheus, and Bourrée Fantasque smacked of blindness, folly or chauvinistic jealousy."

Having seen most of the company's London performances and read all the reviews, I tend to agree with Buckle about "the impercipience" of the London critics. One cannot, however, accept without proof his hint at "folly or chauvinistic jealousy." The reason for the critics' impercipience was simpler than that: they were not prepared for what the company showed them. As mentioned before, Paul Holt had said in the *Daily Herald:* "They are not so much interested in the folksy style. They are pure classicists absorbed by the perfection of old Imperial Russian ballet." Holt considered this "the strangest thing about their visit," and said so; most of the other critics were equally perplexed, but were not quite frank enough to say it. Scott Goddard's lines in the *News Chronicle* were not so much a review of *Jones Beach* as an unconscious manifestation of wishful thinking. Said he: "Jones Beach went down well at Covent Garden last night. It is one of their most successful ventures."

To put it bluntly the London critics did not quite expect an American company to be able to dance ballet, real ballet, and when it came and did dance ballet, they did not quite know how to take it. Hence the laments about the "golden apples of yester year," the "cold impersonal quality," the "geometrical glitter of abstract ballet."

I had occasion to discuss Balanchine's choreography with several London critics, among them the erudite Cyril W. Beaumont. Speaking about *Symphony in C*, Mr. Beaumont said that Balanchine repeated whole sections of the ballet apparently to conform with the repetitions in the music, and that was bad. When asked why this was bad Mr. Beaumont said: "When a composer repeats a section of his music he does it because that is how his composition develops, but when a choreographer repeats a section of his composition there is always a suspicion that he could not invent something new to go with the music."

The London audience paid little heed to the critics' coolness towards the New York City Ballet. As a matter of fact the controversy over the company's ballets served as excellent publicity. Controversial ballets like *Illuminations, Age of Anxiety, Orpheus,* and *Firebird* attracted wide attention. Technically difficult ballets, the so-called abstracts, never failed to bring out cheers. The *Prodigal Son* (with the real Rouault backdrop, which the company had had freshly painted for the London season) was probably the favorite of all. Yvonne Mounsey took over the role of the Siren from Tallchief and was magnificent in it. Francisco Moncion was superb as the Prodigal.

During the second week, Webster, delighted with the audience response, suggested an extra, sixth, week at Covent Garden, which the company accepted. That it should not have done so became evident later.

London, like any great metropolitan city, has its day when a mass of people leaves for summer vacation. In New York it is the weekend of the Fourth of July, in London the last weekend in July. The first Monday in August is known as Bank Holiday, and during the weekend before, literally millions of people leave London. Crowds at railroad stations and steamship piers queue up Friday evening to get a place in a train or a boat on Saturday, and by Saturday noon the city is half empty. The obvious result is that attendance at theaters drops to the year's low. Baum, Kirstein, and Balanchine were apparently unaware of this, but Webster should have known it.

It takes a hardy balletomane to remain in London during

the first weeks of August, and there were not enough of these
to fill Covent Garden. The company began to play to slim
attendance on July 29, and continued that way through August 19. The day before the company closed its season it presented a new ballet by the young British choreographer, John
Cranko, to Ravel's Piano Concerto, which the company had
commissioned from him in early July. The ballet was called
The Witch. It told the story of a Fair Girl and Her Lover; the
girl has supernatural power which, unknown to her, casts on
the lover an evil spell of such strength that he is corrupted
and killed.

Writing about *The Witch* in her magazine *Ballet Today*,
P. W. Manchester said: "It would be pleasant to be able to
record a triumph for The Witch. . . . Unfortunately this
would not be true, for while the ballet has flashes of great
beauty they are only moments in a somewhat turgid and much
too long work which is handicapped by being arranged to
Ravel's two-handed Piano Concerto which, particularly in the
last movement has a strong 1920 jazz idiom quite out of keeping with the lush Romanticism of the theme. The ballet is
greatly helped by the fine performances of Melissa Hayden
as the girl who, all unknowingly, is a witch, and Francisco
Moncion as the lover she kills in her witch-manifestation."

The Witch was never performed in New York because
Ravel's family, which holds the copyrights, refused permission for use of the music.

Kirstein, with Mrs. Kirstein, left for New York on August
13, a week before the end of the London season.

On closing night, August 19, the company had a full
house despite the heat, and an enthusiastic and demonstrative
audience. It was a very cordial parting. After the performance every girl in the company received a small but beautiful,
obviously homemade bouquet of red and white carnations
with a little card attached that read: "In gratitude and with

admiration for your wonderful dancing throughout the season, from your friends in the Gallery and Amphitheatre at Covent Garden. Please come back."

After a week's rest the company set out on its three-week tour to Croydon, Manchester, and Liverpool. It had only a fair success artistically and a rather poor one financially. Had Baum known then what he knows now about running ballet seasons, the company would not have undertaken this tour.

While the company was resting, Balanchine staged a ballet for the Sadler's Wells Theatre Ballet, *Haydn's Trumpet Concerto*. This was by way of reciprocation for Cranko's *The Witch*. Like *The Witch*, it was not a major work.

Despite the coolness of the critics, the New York City Ballet made a lasting impression on London. It played to an average of seventy-five per cent of capacity and won a large amount of space devoted to articles, criticisms, and pictures in the daily press, as well as in the weekly and monthly magazines and reviews and in the specialized dance press. Kirstein's exhibition of the Symbolic Realist painters, Balanchine's addresses at the London Ballet Circle and the International Faculty of Arts, and his active interest in such dance teacher organizations as the Royal Academy of Dancing and the Imperial Society of Teachers of Dancing, radio broadcasts—all this focused attention on the company. In fact, art and dance publications kept on writing about the visit of the company until the spring of 1952, almost two years after the season. Another tangible sign of the company's success was David Webster's offer of a return engagement in the summer of 1952, made just before the company left for the United States.

Summing up the visit of the New York City Ballet, Arnold L. Haskell, the best-known of all present-day writers on dance, wrote this in the 1951 edition of *Ballet Annual*, which he edits: "Very welcome visitors have been the New York City Ballet, in many respects the [Sadler's] Wells opposite number in America. . . . If I have criticised many of the productions of the new company, and serious work merits serious criticism, let there be no misunderstanding as to its high importance and its complete integrity. Here is an Englishman indulging in the national pastime of seeking dollars, but for an American company this time. If any wealthy American happens to read this, and I believe that men of wealth still exist in America, I would like to assure him that the New York City Ballet has done more for the artistic prestige of his country than a carload of crooners, ten years' run of musicals, a high powered comedian and a million reels of Hollywood celluloid all added together.''

The dancers of the company had a wonderful time in London. Audiences were appreciative and unstinting in their expressions of approval; there were large groups of people nightly at the stage door seeking autographs and pictures; there were many large and small parties (too many, it seemed at times); there were excursions and Sundays spent in the country; there were many new friends; there was, finally, an accumulation of events, people, and episodes which would last as a topic of conversation for months and months.

The company returned to New York without incident on September 21.

When Morton Baum had time to sit down and figure out the net financial result of the English season he discovered that the company had lost much more money than he had expected it to lose: the loss came to about forty thousand dollars instead of the anticipated twenty-five thousand. He was very gloomy over the loss, but not for long. A New York season was scheduled for November, and there was not much time to be spent on being gloomy over past losses.

XVII

1950–1951

"La Valse"; Visit to Chicago; "The Cage"

When David Webster told Frances Hawkins in April that the London season would make the New York City Ballet, he was not bragging about the importance of the Royal Opera House as a center of ballet, or the prestige inherent in the acceptance of a ballet company by the London public. A wise and experienced showman, he realized that the company's successful visit to London would emphasize its artistic significance for the American public, sharpen its appreciation by New Yorkers, bolstering their civic pride, and thus inevitably deepening and widening interest in the company. That all happened.

Moreover, the London season did much for the

morale of the company and provided it with a new stimulus and a deeper regard for its own work. The fact that the company had worked together for a longer period than ever before added greatly to its homogeneity and hence to its sense of style. It now welded itself into a unit, of which every member was an integral part.

Dancers outside the company who had doubted the wisdom of Jerome Robbins, Janet Reed, and Melissa Hayden in aligning themselves with it began to take a different view. With the possible exception of half a dozen ranking soloists, there was not an outstanding dancer in New York who did not ponder the possibility of, or send out feelers about, joining the company. Two such well-known dancers actually joined the company. They were Hugh Laing and Diana Adams of Ballet Theatre (in private life Mr. and Mrs. Laing, since 1947).

Hugh Laing had been a principal dancer of Ballet Theatre since its establishment in 1940. Born in Barbados, British West Indies, he received his ballet education in London, studying under Margaret Craske and Marie Rambert. He made his debut with the Ballet Club under Marie Rambert in 1932 and created leading roles in such Antony Tudor ballets as *Descent of Hebe*, *Jardin aux Lilas*, *Dark Elegies*, and *Judgment of Paris*. In 1938 he danced in the London Ballet, founded by Tudor. He came to the United States with Tudor in the summer of 1939 at the invitation of Ballet Theatre, which was then being formed and, with the exception of the season of 1945–6, when he was a featured dancer in the musical *The Day Before Spring*, remained with that company until the spring of 1950. As *premier danseur* of Ballet Theatre he created a number of great roles, mainly in Tudor's ballets, among them *Pillar of Fire*, *Romeo and Juliet*, *Dim Lustre*, and *Undertow*, and also danced the roles in *Jardin aux Lilas*, *Dark Elegies*, and

Judgment of Paris which he had created in London, as well as the Young Gypsy in Leonide Massine's *Aleko*, A Young Man in Robbins's *Facsimile*, and others.

The American-born Diana Adams began her career as a soloist in the musical *Oklahoma!* in 1943. The following year she joined Ballet Theatre and there danced such roles as Rosalind in *Romeo and Juliet*, the title role in *Helen of Troy*, Mother and Medusa in *Undertow*, Lover in Experience in *Pillar of Fire*, and the Queen of the Wilis in *Giselle*.

Both dancers knew that they were facing a difficult situation in the New York City Ballet. First, the company had an entirely different repertoire from that of Ballet Theatre, not only in the actual works, but also in the general character of the ballets. It had few dramatic ballets, the kind in which both dancers, and especially Laing, had specialized and excelled. Second, most of the principal dancers had grown up with the company; some of them had started with the Ballet Caravan; nearly all had danced with Ballet Society. In fairness to these dancers, their seniority would have to be respected by the management, and a new dancer, especially of the caliber of Laing, who could not be assigned just any part, would have to wait his turn for an old role or for one in a new ballet which would fit his personality. Nevertheless, he and Diana Adams applied for positions, made no special demands in so far as roles were concerned, and decided to hope for the best.

Another thing happened in the fall of 1950. Soon after the company returned from London, Maria Tallchief and George Balanchine decided to separate. Both gave assurances that the change in their marital status would have no effect upon their work in the company, and up to this writing, the fall of 1952, it has not.

The company had a three-week rest before beginning

rehearsals for its "Welcome Home Season." Frances Hawkins did not return to the company because of ill health, and Betty Cage was given a new title, Executive Manager.

The season had first been announced to begin on November 14, but when it became known that the Marquis de Cuevas's Grand Ballet was to open a four-week season in New York on October 30 the New York City Ballet decided to postpone its opening until November 21 and to play through December 10.

New York had its full share of ballet that autumn. The Sadler's Wells Ballet played its second engagement at the Metropolitan Opera House from September 10 to October 1, tickets for which were sold out nearly four months in advance. On October 9 Roland Petit's Ballets de Paris opened its second season, at the National Theater, presenting the sensational *Carmen*, and later *La Croqueuse de Diamants*, with Renée Jeanmaire. On October 30, as mentioned before, the Grand Ballet came in for four weeks, at the Century Theater.

Baum, Kirstein, and Balanchine were somewhat jittery about the effects these three companies would have on the City Center's box office. They need not have been. Although the company announced only a revival of the Balanchine-Stravinsky *Le Baiser de la Fée*, a *pas de deux* from *Sylvia* for Maria Tallchief and Herbert Bliss, and the Mazurka from Glinka's *A Life for the Tsar*, there was eager interest. Mail orders for tickets began to come in as soon as the program was announced, and when the box office opened there was a steady line at its window.

Headed by Maria Tallchief, Janet Reed, Tanaquil LeClercq, Melissa Hayden, Diana Adams, Beatrice Tompkins, Nicholas Magallanes, Francisco Moncion, Herbert Bliss, Hugh Laing, Todd Bolender, Harold Lang, and Frank Hobi, the company opened its season on November 21 with *Serenade*, *Firebird*, and *Bourrée Fantasque*.

John Martin wrote thus about the opening night performance in *The New York Times* (Nov. 22):

"It was a joyous evening at the City Center last night,
for the New York City Ballet company opened its three-week
season at the top of its form in three of George Balanchine's
best ballets. There is no doubt whatever that the successful
outcome of the young company's daring invasion of London's Covent Garden Opera House last summer has done
wonders for its morale, and it has returned to its home stage
in the finest of spirits and raring to go.

"And what a company it is! Without any stars in the nar-
row sense of the term . . . it has a brilliant set of leading
artists. Since its last appearance here it has strengthened this
department by the addition of Diana Adams, Hugh Laing,
and Harold Lang, all previously of the Ballet Theatre company, and by a half dozen others of perhaps less stellar background but of the same general caliber of talent.

"Here, too, is an ensemble of note; there was not one of
them last night who did not dance as if she were herself a
prima ballerina, yet with a feeling for the unity of the group
and the framework of the composition. What more one can
ask of any company it would be difficult to say. . . .

"Leon Barzin and an excellent orchestra proved that it
is quite feasible to have good music for a ballet company, and
Jean Rosenthal was on hand as usual with her lighting wiz-
ardry.

"At this Thanksgiving season, let us acknowledge with
gratitude that we have a ballet company of our own which is
really a ballet company."

Serenade, the opening ballet, had never been danced so
brilliantly. Balanchine had rearranged the feminine parts so
that there were now five principal dancers: Diana Adams,
making· her auspicious debut with the company, Hayden,
Reed, Wilde, and Mounsey. Magallanes and Hobi were the

male partners. *Firebird* had Tallchief in the title role, Moncion as Prince Ivan and Helen Kramer as the Bride. *Bourrée Fantasque* was danced by LeClercq, Reed, Hayden, Lang, Magallanes, and Bliss.

There were tumultuous ovations after every ballet, and heaps of flowers. The season was off to a good start.

On November 28 the company presented the first new ballet of the season, *Le Baiser de la Fée*, staged by Balanchine to Stravinsky's music, in décor and costumes by Alice Halicka. The ballet itself was not new; its first American performance had been given by the American Ballet on April 27, 1937, at the Metropolitan Opera House, as part of the Stravinsky Festival. Balanchine had subsequently lent the production to Ballet Russe de Monte Carlo, which had danced it for several years.

For the present revival, Balanchine reworked the ballet, tightened it up, changed some of the choreography, and staged a new ending. The first tableau acquired a lucidity that it had lacked before, and the dance of the Snowflakes had new and beautiful patterns. The Village Festival (the second tableau), with its theatricalized folk-dances and charming parody on band music, became more of a whole and strengthened its humorous aspect. The *pas de deux* of the Bride and Bridegroom in the third tableau seemed to be built on softer, more romantic lines. The epilogue was practically new.

Maria Tallchief gave a superb performance of the Fairy, but did not look well in a blonde wig, which suited her not at all. Beatrice Tompkins and Helen Kramer were excellent as, respectively, the Mother and the Shadow. Tanaquil LeClercq gave a tentative characterization of the Bride, but danced the role wonderfully. Patricia Wilde was admirable as the Friend; her variation in the third tableau was exciting. Nicholas Magallanes was not quite at home in the role of the

Bridegroom, but danced and supported the ballerina very well.

Jean Rosenthal did an inspired job of lighting the ballet, an advantage it had never had before.

The production of the Mazurka from Glinka's *A Life for the Tsar* was in the nature of whimsy on the part of Balanchine. There was no great reason for doing it, it was of little importance, and, as was suspected from the very beginning, it failed to remain in the repertoire. But it added a little fillip to the season because Balanchine danced in it himself on the opening night, November 30. His appearance created a lot of publicity for the company. Most newspapers printed his picture in the Polish costume. *Time* devoted a page to him, and the wire services thought enough of the event to send it out to out-of-town newspapers.

The company's press agent sent out a report that this had been the first time that Balanchine had danced since his days in the Diaghilev company (someone even fixed the year as 1929, when he danced in the *Cimarosiana pas de trois* at Monte Carlo). Actually, however, Balanchine's last previous appearance on stage had been in 1935 in Mexico City, where he took a group of dancers for a short summer season. To a newspaper reporter who came to interview him backstage and asked him when he had danced last, Balanchine replied: "Half an hour ago when I rehearsed Maria Tallchief in Firebird."

With his customary modesty, Balanchine chose to dance in the second couple, with Vida Brown as his partner. The other couples were Janet Reed and Yurek Lazowski (guest artist for the occasion), the leading couple; Barbara Walczak and Harold Lang; Dorothy Dushok and Frank Hobi.

The Mazurka was arranged with love and performed with fire and elegance. Balanchine held his own during the actual dancing, but appeared somewhat short of breath in the pauses. The audience appreciated the rare treat, and rewarded him with one of the longest and loudest ovations on record for the company. Everybody had a wonderful time.

On December 1 the company presented the third novelty of the season: a classic *pas de deux* choreographed by Balanchine to Leo Delibes's music from *Sylvia*, for Tallchief and Bliss. However, Bliss strained his back a few days beforehand and could not appear, so Nicholas Magallanes stepped in for him at short notice. The *pas de deux* was a brilliant bravura work that permitted Tallchief to show off her enormous technical skill and beautiful classic style. Her fast, clear beats, her easy unforced aplomb, her swift turns, her light jumps, and all her other balletic faculties found expression in this faultlessly staged homage to Marius Petipa, the originator of the *pas de deux* as a choreographic poem, at once a love duet and an exhibition piece for the ballerina and the *premier danseur*. Although Magallanes was only pinch-hitting, he gave a very good performance. Barbara Karinska designed and executed the elegant, chic costumes.

The audience, ever on the alert for balletic fireworks, gave the *pas de deux* a clamorous ovation. It is still one of the most striking numbers in Tallchief's repertoire.

Hugh Laing made his debut with the company on December 3 as the Poet in *Illuminations*. It was easy to understand that Laing was at a disadvantage in this assignment. The company had rehearsed the ballet under its choreographer from the very beginning, had danced it many times, and was thoroughly familiar with it, while he was making his first try at the principal role.

This is not meant as an apology for Laing. He is a great artist who needs no apology. But his characterization of the Poet was of necessity tentative and searching. He underplayed the role, probably purposely, trying to discover for himself the emotional level at which the rest of the company was performing. As a result, he was not so forceful as he became later, when he found the correct pitch of dramatic intensity which permeates Ashton's thrilling composition.

On December 6 Laing performed for the first time the title role in *The Prodigal Son*. He danced it with a simplicity and youthfulness that it had not possessed before and gave it a quite different dramatic interpretation. His Prodigal was much more an erring boy than a deliberate squanderer, drunkard, and debauchee. In the scene with the Siren he was a gull, taken in by the Siren, rather than a sensually experienced lover who has found his mate. This was a new and vital interpretation and it stood up alongside the differing interpretations of Robbins and Moncion.

The season brought a marked advance in the development of Janet Reed. The ballerina was dancing better than ever before; more than that, she had acclimated herself to Balanchine's choreography and the style of the company's dancing, and had become one with the organization. It is interesting to note here that Diana Adams, then in her first season with the company, found herself almost immediately. Probably because she had had less experience than Reed in other companies, Adams, though brought up in a different manner, assimilated the company's style with great ease.

The engagement ended December 10, after three weeks of enormous artistic success. The financial success, though not overwhelming, was solid enough to prompt Morton Baum to announce a month-long midwinter season, February 13 through March 11.

Rehearsals began almost immediately after the close of the season, but the company had a week's vacation at Christmas time.

New productions put into rehearsal included Balanchine's *La Valse*, to the music of Ravel's *Valses Nobles et Senti-*

mentales and *La Valse*, in costumes by Barbara Karinska; a revival of the Balanchine-Stravinsky *Card Game; Pas de Trois* by Balanchine to Leon Minkus's music from *Don Quixote;* and *Lady of the Camellias*, by Antony Tudor, to a score selected from compositions by Verdi, in décor and costumes by Cecil Beaton. The décor and costumes for the last-named work were not new. They were lent to the company by Ballet Associates in America, which had commissioned them from Beaton in 1946, when John Taras staged his version of *Camille* to Schubert music for Alicia Markova and Anton Dolin, then guest artists with the Original Ballet Russe.

Early in the rehearsal period the company received an offer from the Paris impresario Leonid Leonidoff, who had seen it in London, for a four-month tour of Europe in the spring and summer of 1951. The offering was flattering, but the guarantee that Leonidoff suggested could not cover the company's minimum expenses, and Baum had to refuse the offer, much as he hated to do so.

Rehearsals were at their busiest when two bombshells exploded on the never-too-quiet New York ballet scene: in early February Nora Kaye and André Eglevsky announced that they were joining the New York City Ballet. Eglevsky's announcement did not create quite as much stir as Kaye's, and for good reason.

André Eglevsky, one of the two greatest male dancers of the present generation (the other is Igor Youskevitch, currently with Ballet Theatre), was born in Russia. He was brought to Paris in early childhood, when his parents emigrated from Russia after the Bolshevik revolution. He was educated in a French high school, and studied professionally with Lubov Egorova, Mathilde Kchessinska, and Alexandre Volinine in Paris, Nicholas Legat in London, and, later, at the School of American Ballet in New York. He joined Col. de Basil's Ballet Russe de Monte Carlo at the age of fifteen. Six months later he was dancing leading roles. In 1935 he joined Leon Woicikowski's company as *premier danseur*, and a year later transferred to René Blum's Monte Carlo company in the same position. He came to the United States in 1937, and after appearances at Radio City Music Hall joined the American Ballet. He remained with that company for the season of 1937–8, and later danced with Ballet Russe de Monte Carlo (1939–42); Ballet Theatre (1942–4 and 1945–6); the Marquis de Cuevas's Ballet International (1944); Leonide Massine's Ballet Russe Highlights (summer 1945); and the Original Ballet Russe (1946–7). Since the season of 1947–8 he had been *premier danseur* of the Marquis de Cuevas's Grand Ballet. He danced with that company during its New York season in the fall of 1950, returned with it to Europe, left it early in January 1951 to come back to New York, and then joined the New York City Ballet.

Eglevsky's joining the company contained an element of surprise, but because his peripatetic inclinations were well known in the field his action created no sensation. It was different when Nora Kaye left Ballet Theatre for the New York City Ballet.

Nora Kaye, often referred to as America's first dramatic ballerina, had spent most of her professional career in Ballet Theatre, and was identified with that company more closely than was any other ballerina. Born in New York, Kaye studied at the Metropolitan Opera Ballet School and the School of American Ballet, with Michel Fokine, Anatole Vilzak, Ludmila Shollar, Antony Tudor, and Margaret Craske. Her first professional engagement was with the American Ballet at the Metropolitan Opera. She then danced in the ballet of Radio City Music Hall, and appeared in several musicals. She joined Ballet Theatre at its founding (1939) as a member of the *corps*. She became a ballerina a little more than two years later with her memorable performance of the role of Hagar in

Antony Tudor's *Pillar of Fire* (April 8, 1942). Since then she had been considered a mainstay of Ballet Theatre, and numbered in her repertoire several ballets in which she had no peer. Among these, in addition to *Pillar of Fire*, were Tudor's *Lilac Garden (Jardin aux Lilas), Romeo and Juliet, Dark Elegies*, and *Gala Performance;* Balanchine's *Apollo*, Robbins's *Facsimile*, and Agnes de Mille's *Fall River Legend*. She also danced with distinction such standard ballets as *Swan Lake, Princess Aurora*, and *Giselle*. The Tudor repertoire, largely based on Kaye's gifts as a dramatic dancer, had been the hallmark of Ballet Theatre. It set the company apart from all other ballet organizations, gave it substance, form, and prestige. The resignation of Nora Kaye from Ballet Theatre completed the liquidation of the Tudor wing of that company. Tudor had withdrawn from active participation in 1949, Diana Adams and Hugh Laing in the spring of 1950, and now Nora Kaye wrote finis to a chapter in the history of Ballet Theatre.

Aside from the psychological problem inherent in Nora Kaye's resignation from Ballet Theatre, which, interesting though it was, does not concern us here, her joining the New York City Ballet created very real problems for both the ballerina and the company.

Even more than in the case of Hugh Laing, Nora Kaye came to the New York City Ballet with a well-established reputation and a list of lofty achievements. She was in effect, if not in actual billing, the *prima ballerina* of Ballet Theatre, had her own repertoire in which she knew no competition, enjoyed a large, loyal following all over the United States and in London, Paris, Venice, and several other European cities. Kaye knew when she joined the New York City Ballet that she could not expect either the position or the roles she had had in Ballet Theatre. What was she going to dance in the new company? Who would choreograph ballets for her? How would the ballet audience accept her? It was quite a problem, and it weighed heavily on Nora Kaye.

The company's problem was not much lighter. Here was a famous dancer whom they were glad to have in the organization. But what was she going to dance? The problem was especially acute because Nora Kaye joined the company on February 5, only eight days before the beginning of the season. There were few roles in the repertoire which would suit her, and there was not enough time to create anything new for her. There was no immediate solution to the problem, and the company, like many another organization faced with an insoluble problem, just let it take care of itself.

The company had another, less important problem: how would Kaye and Eglevsky be billed? Their names could not very well be placed ahead of the other ballerinas and *premiers danseurs* of the company: that would be patently unfair to the dancers in the company. At the same time, it would be very difficult to find their proper niches among the other principals. The Solomonic decision was to place the names Nora Kaye and André Eglevsky on a separate line, after the names of the soloists, preceded by a small "and."

The season opened February 13 with *The Duel*, *Age of Anxiety*, the *Sylvia pas de deux*, and *Bourrée Fantasque*. The company was in good form and danced well, but somehow the usual excitement of an opening night was missing. Perhaps it was because the previous season had closed only on December 10, and the opening performance seemed more like a continuation of that season than like the beginning of a new one.

The first novelty of the season came on February 15: a revised version of Balanchine's *Card Party*, to Stravinsky's music, in décor and costumes by Irene Sharaff. The ballet gained from Balanchine's revision. It appeared less dry and cold than in the original version. A few simple pantomimic moments made the action clearer, and the humor was not quite so hidden. It was now a slight and frothy musico-balletic joke, sure to amuse at first sight, but hardly something an audience would rush to see again. Top honors for the performance went to Janet Reed as the Queen of Hearts and to Todd Bolender as the Joker. Doris Breckenridge, Jillana, and Patricia Wilde, as the other Queens, danced excellently, and the large cast gave them fine support in a complicated set of dances. There was no excitement about *Card Party* on the stage, in the pit, or in the auditorium.

On February 16 Nora Kaye made her debut with the company in *Symphony in C,* dancing the part created by Maria Tallchief. It was a very gallant, most nerve-wracking experience for the dancer and the audience, and, to be frank about it, an inauspicious performance. That the dancer was very nervous and unsure of herself was understandable—who would not be under similar circumstances? But it was a sad surprise that the ballerina apparently did not have enough technique to cope with Balanchine's intricate enchaînements, was short of breath halfway through her first entrée, and, in general, lacked the brio and aplomb this taxing part required. One remembered Nora Kaye giving notable performances in *Swan Lake, Princess Aurora,* and *Giselle,* in addition to her superb ones in the Tudor ballets and in de Mille's *Fall River Legend,* and here one looked at her and saw at best a good soloist, but with not quite enough stamina and technique. What had happened?

The answer was simple, of course. One remembered seeing her amid the entourage of Ballet Theatre, in the company's repertoire of dramatic, story-telling ballets, in which the precise, brilliant technique of the classic ballet was little in demand and still less in evidence. Paradoxical as it may sound, even the classic ballets that Kaye had danced with

Ballet Theatre did not make such great demands on technique. When one had discounted the supported adagios in *Swan Lake*, *Princess Aurora*, and *Giselle*, which require a different style and technique, the dancer is left with one variation and one coda in the first two ballets and two variations, one coda, and one *ballabile* in the third ballet, all interspersed with long periods of mime and rest. But in the first and fourth movements of *Symphony in C*, the ballerina actually dances as much as, if not more than, in any of the full-evening classic ballets now being performed, with only one long rest between the movements and two or three very brief ones during them. In addition, Tchaikovsky's and Adam's tempos and rhythms are no match for Bizet's. It was obvious to almost anyone that Kaye was simply not in form to dance a Balanchine "symphonic" ballet.

Nora Kaye is not only an excellent dancer—she also has the humility of a true ballerina who knows that her period of training never ends and that a daily lesson is as necessary at the height of her career as during the preparation for it. It was a rare day that Kaye did not take a ballet lesson.

When the debut was over and the polite and benevolent reviews were in and the proper amount of tears shed and dried, Nora Kaye began working harder than ever. The results soon began to show.

André Eglevsky's debut was a happier occasion. It took place on February 17 in the *Sylvia pas de deux*, with Maria Tallchief, a spectacular number for spectacular dancers. With a ballerina of smaller personality and technical accomplishments, the debutant would probably have walked away with the show, but in Tallchief he found a worthy match (I am almost tempted to say adversary). The result was an exciting exhibition by both dancers of technical virtuosity, élan, and brio not often seen on the ballet stage.

The following evening, Eglevsky made his second appearance, in Balanchine's new *Pas de Trois* to Leon Minkus's music from *Don Quixote*, which the choreographer had originally staged for the Marquis de Cuevas's Grand Ballet and now restaged with new and more complicated enchaînements. Nearly as exciting as *Sylvia*, the *Pas de Trois* was a spectacular *tour de force* that made great demands on the dancers and gave the public double its money's worth. Tallchief and Kaye were excellent in their variations, and Eglevsky created a furore of applause with his very first *cabriole battu*, high in the air, hanging there for seconds. Barbara Karinska designed beautiful costumes for the *Pas de Trois*.

The great event of the season came on February 20, the *première* of Balanchine's *La Valse*, staged to Ravel's *Valses Nobles et Sentimentales* and *La Valse*, in costumes by Karinska and an improvised setting that could not have been designed better to go with the mood of the ballet. *La Valse* was a brilliant example of the choreographer's genius and versatility.

If any choreographer can be credited with creating a new style in classic ballet, it is, of course, Balanchine. And if we must have a label for Balanchine's style, it could with excellent justification be called neo-classic. In *La Valse*, however, Balanchine has chosen a different style. If we still want labels, neo-romantic would suit this ballet nicely. Balanchine's *Cotillon*, to Chabrier's music, was more or less in that style. *La Valse* does not have the definite scenario of *Giselle* or the romantic (i.e., amorous) mood of *Les Sylphides*, but it is permeated with the spirit of the romantic period of thirties of the past century, and still more with the sense of futility that pervaded Europe during the 1920's, when Ravel wrote the music, and which, justifiably or not, makes itself felt at the present time.

"We are dancing on the edge of a volcano," Ravel quoted Comte de Salvandy in his notes to *La Valse*, and this short statement is the underlying motif of both the music and the choreography. In a way, then, *La Valse* can be classed with

Jerome Robbins's *Age of Anxiety* as a comment on our times and on all times of insecurity and change.

Structurally, Balanchine has used seven of the eight *Valses Nobles et Sentimentales* as an approach to his main theme, expressed in *La Valse* proper, and to establish the figures who later take part in the denouements of this theme. The first of the eight *Valses* is employed as an overture.

Choreographically, each of the seven *Valses* is different in mood and style; all of them are integral parts of a mounting feeling of restlessness, at some times hidden, at others apparent, but never obviously justified until they culminate in a grand ball with all the couples "dancing on the edge of a volcano." Death finally enters in the shape of a man dressed in all black (Francisco Moncion), who presents black jewels to a dancer in white (Tanaquil LeClercq), dresses her in black, and dances her to death.

If at some moments in the middle of *La Valse* the ballet seems on the verge of falling to pieces, it is not an accident or a choreographic mistake of Balanchine. It was Ravel himself who wrote about the disintegration of the valse. All Balanchine did was to follow the music and give it a choreographic justification.

La Valse is an ensemble ballet in the best sense of that classification. For excellent individual performances and more wonderful teamwork, credit went to the entire company, and particularly to Vida Brown, Edwina Fontaine, Jillana, Patricia Wilde, Frank Hobi, Yvonne Mounsey, Michael Maule, Diana Adams, Herbert Bliss, Nicholas Magallanes, and, of course, to LeClercq and Moncion.

The augmented orchestra directed by Leon Barzin was at the top of its form. Karinska's costumes were elegant and beautiful.

Antony Tudor's *Lady of the Camellias*, presented on February 28, was also a romantic ballet, but in an entirely dif-

ferent vein. Where Balanchine dealt with people as symbols
of time and events, Tudor took the romantic story of two particular people—Marguérite Gautier and Armand Duval—
created by Alexander Dumas *fils*, and brought it to the ballet
stage to enchant the audience, as Dumas did his readers and
Verdi his listeners. The choreographer had elected to concen-
trate on a few episodes that highlight the well-known tale and
preserve its continuity, yet do not make the plot undance-
able. A careful choreographer who generally works deliberately and slowly, Tudor had had only a few weeks in which
to compose this ballet. Consequently, what he presented to
the spectator at the *première* of *Lady of the Camellias* was a
succession of focal points, which at first sight appeared somewhat skeletal. The story was there, but it still wanted detail
in the connecting passages.

Diana Adams and Hugh Laing were the protagonists of
the ballet, and Tudor had created for them a series of long
sequences, imaginative and effective. As in most Tudor ballets, the dances were not set pieces, but rather flowed from
dance to action and back to dance in a manner that offered
striking choreographic invention and at the same time danced
the story.

In subtlety of style, *Lady of the Camellias* resembled *Jardin
aux Lilas* more than any other Tudor ballet, and Adams and
Laing knew exactly how to project this subtlety without un-
necessary histrionics.

There was a good basis for a successful ballet in *Lady of the
Camellias*, but it still wanted building and decorating. The
music was an excellently chosen collection of little-known
pieces by Verdi, which served the choreographer well. Cecil
Beaton's set was as handsome as ever.

The season also brought a new revision of Balanchine's
Le Baiser de la Fée. The choreographer tightened up the ballet
considerably, eliminating the entr'actes and providing a new

and more effective ending. The audience somehow has never warmed up to this basically excellent ballet.

The engagement closed on March 11 with a record of sorts: for the first time in its three-year history as the New York City Ballet, the company not only broke even but also made a small profit. It took in $147,400 at the box office for four weeks of dancing. Balanchine's *La Valse* was the strongest draw, and the presence of Nora Kaye and André Eglevsky did its share toward increased attendance.

The position of the company was now healthy, and there was optimism all around about its future. But there still remained the problem of providing enough work for the dancers. All three heads of the company, Balanchine, Kirstein, and Baum, realized that the ballet could not have a new four-week season in New York every two months. This would mean the production of new works every two months, a costly procedure that no company could afford, and one that might prove a drain on the spending capacity of the New York public, loyal though it might be toward the company.

It has been estimated as nearly correctly as possible by impresarios and ballet directors that the New York ballet-going public consists of twenty-five thousand people. (This number need not be considered alarmingly small when one realizes that the concert and opera patrons in New York number only fifty thousand, according to the same estimates.) The strength of the ballet-going public in New York, as everywhere else for that matter, lies not so much in the number of people who patronize ballet as in the number of times the same people go to the ballet during a season. Impresarios call it a repeater audience.

The company had by this time played two seasons since its return from England; November 21 to December 10 and February 13 to March 11, and the management did not know whether it could risk another engagement in New York. These thoughts modified the jubilation over the success of the past engagement.

Then, like some *deus ex machina*, Herbert Carlin, manager of the Chicago Civic Opera House, showed up at the office of the New York City Ballet. The management of the company knew that Mr. Carlin had been in New York and had attended several of the performances. It was known in the field that Mr. Carlin was a balletomane, and everyone thought that he came to the performances for his own pleasure. At the office, however, the manager revealed his reason for attendance. Having satisfied himself that the company was good enough, he was now offering it a two-week engagement at the Chicago Civic Opera House, from April 23 to May 6. It goes without saying that the company accepted.

Easter that year fell on March 25, and the company was given a vacation until April 2, when rehearsals for the Chicago season began. The following day the company attended in force the second annual dinner dance of Ballet Associates in America, at the Waldorf Astoria Hotel, which netted a few thousand dollars toward the production of new ballets.

The Chicago season was the first American engagement outside New York, and was therefore watched with great attention by the management. The Chicago reception might indicate the reaction that the company could expect in other cities across the United States.

The reaction in Chicago was mixed. Ann Barzel wrote in *Dance News:* "In the New York City Center the New York City Ballet has in some ways been the pet of a partisan audience. The stormy applause is almost a 'family' affair, the acclaim of a group which has helped the company come into being. It was interesting, then, to see what would happen in a new environment, one in which one could even count on sales resistance.

"For the record, the baby is just as appealing outside the

family circle. Chicago was unanimously enthusiastic. There
were bravos in the theatre, vigorous approval in the foyer,
worshipful crowds at the stage door and flowery adjectives in
the press. . . ."

All this was very true. It was equally true, however, that
not enough Chicagoans showed a sufficiently strong interest
in the New York visitors to come to see them more than once.
The considerable Chicago dance-world was elated to have the
company in its city. There were enough receptions, parties,
flowers and other appurtenances of artistic success and the
city's welcome, but the cash customers stayed away.

Many reasons were advanced for the lagging patronage,
among them lateness of the season, the weather, the visit to
Chicago of, and the parade for, General Douglas MacArthur,
the lack of publicity because of the space given by the newspapers to the General, and a number of other bromides. The
fact remained that Ballet Russe de Monte Carlo and Ballet
Theatre had for years found Chicago one of their most profitable engagements, but the New York City Ballet had at best
elicited a mild response.

Lincoln Kirstein advanced the idea that while London
accepted the company on its merits, the Chicago public considered it a purely local New York manifestation, below par,
as it were, with the "big" touring companies. He may have
been right. For, let us face it, Chicago does have an *a priori*
negative attitude toward New York, the obvious reason for
which need not be discussed here. However that may be, the
New York City Ballet, at least in the spring of 1951, was not
Chicago's dish.

No sooner had the company returned from Chicago than
Morton Baum announced an unprecedented three-week New
York summer season, to begin on June 5. Unlike European
capitals and metropolises where the ballet season generally
runs through July, the dance season in New York usually ends

late in May. The latest a ballet company had ever played in New York was from May 19 to June 5, 1943, when the Ballet Russe de Monte Carlo appeared at the Broadway Theater.

The management reasoned that three months was enough of a respite for the New York public, and that the interest shown in the company during its February-March season had been high enough to warrant the experiment of a June season. The City Center had an effective air-conditioning system, and if the temperature during June was not so high as to drive the people out of town, especially on weekends, the company might play three weeks with only a small deficit. It was definitely what the military call "a calculated risk," but Baum considered it was worth taking.

Todd Bolender, whose *Mother Goose Suite* was in the company's repertoire, was to produce *The Miraculous Mandarin*, to Béla Bartók's score, on which he had been working for some time, with Melissa Hayden and Hugh Laing in the principal roles. Jerome Robbins, recuperating after an appendectomy on April 21, which had prevented his going to Chicago with the company, would choreograph *The Cage* (at rehearsal time referred to as *The Amazons*), to Stravinsky's "Basler" Concerto, for Nora Kaye, the first ballet specifically staged for the ballerina in this company. George Balanchine would whip together a short, gay ballet, *Capriccio Brillant*, to Mendelssohn's music. Ruthanna Boris, formerly with Ballet Russe de Monte Carlo, would stage a character work, *Cakewalk*, to music from American traditional sources.

The program sounded like a well-balanced and useful addition to the repertoire: ballets for Kaye, Laing, and Hayden, who did not have enough to dance in the repertoire, and a frolicsome piece of Americana which might be a much-needed closing ballet. Also, three of the four new works would be story ballets, always welcome in a repertoire topheavy with plotless works.

Rehearsals began early in May. Five new dancers joined the company at rehearsal time—Alan Baker, Constance Baker, Irene Larsson, Marilyn Poudrier, and Patricia Savoia. Two others, Dorothy Dushok and Helen Kramer, left.

Midway in the rehearsal period it developed that the production of Bolender's *The Miraculous Mandarin* would have to be deferred until the fall season. This decision had something to do with the financing of the ballet, in which the estate of the late composer was to participate. The choreographer, in fact, welcomed the deferment because he felt that he needed more time on the ballet than this rehearsal period would allow him. Melissa Hayden and Hugh Laing were not so happy, but they had to accept the situation.

The season opened on June 5 with a brilliant all-Balanchine program, including *Serenade, Pas de Trois, La Valse,* and *Symphony in C,* a program to test the artistry, virtuosity, and stamina of any company, at any time, in any part of the world. The City Center was full, and the performance was received with an enthusiasm usually reserved for *premières* of new ballets.

The first *première* of the season, George Balanchine's *Capriccio Brillant,* came on June 7. Set to Felix Mendelssohn's music of the same title, and exquisitely costumed by Barbara Karinska, the ballet was an intimate work for six dancers, employing some of the most intricate choreography in the classic style yet used by Balanchine. It made high demands not only on the principals, Maria Tallchief and André Eglevsky, but also on the supporting dancers, Barbara Bocher, Constance Garfield, Jillana, and Irene Larsson. The dancers fulfilled these demands with the élan, ease, and simplicity of true artists.

The work was given focus by the pianist, Nicholas Kopeikine, who was on the stage playing his solo, accompanied by the orchestra. The dancers gathered around the instrument listening to the music; after a while they began to dance, returning to the piano at the conclusion of the ballet.

Capriccio Brillant was not an important work; it contained, however, a great deal of choreographic invention, which at times was too subtle and intricate to reach the general spectator. It was a dancer's ballet if there ever was one.

At first acquaintance the ballet seemed rather sprawling, probably because the plain backdrop accentuated the large empty space of the stage. A simple décor, perhaps an archway, would have framed it and given it more unity.

The second *première* of the season was Ruthanna Boris's *Cakewalk*, presented on June 12.

New York-born Ruthanna Boris received her ballet education at the Metropolitan Opera Ballet School. She began dancing in opera ballets, and in 1935 joined the American Ballet. When the contract between the American Ballet and the Metropolitan was not renewed (1938), Boris remained with the Opera, of which she became *première danseuse* in 1939. In 1943 she joined Ballet Russe de Monte Carlo, with which company she remained until 1951. Her first choreographic effort was *Cirque de Deux*, a little ballet that she staged for Ballet Russe de Monte Carlo in 1947 to the Walpurgis Night music from Gounod's *Faust*. In 1948 she staged for the same company *Quelques Fleurs*, to music culled from the operas of Auber. This ballet was sponsored by the perfumery firm Houbigant, Inc., as a promotion for their perfume of the same name, the first commercial sponsorship of a ballet on record, at least in the United States.

Cakewalk was produced to a score arranged by Hershy Kay after the music by Louis Moreau Gottshalk, New Orleans-born nineteenth-century composer, pianist, and conductor, in a set and costumes by Robert Drew. The set was not new. It had been used before by Ballet Society for its short-lived *Blackface*.

Cakewalk is a light, enjoyable ballet, a danced minstrel show that fits well into the repertoire of the company. It is a nice opening or closing ballet, a sort of *Gaité Mississippienne* with a cakewalk taking the place of a can-can.

Frank Hobi as the Interlocutor has here probably his best role in the present repertoire. His Sleight of Feet number is delightful to watch. Beatrice Tompkins and Tanaquil Le-Clercq are the End Men, and very amusing. Janet Reed is excellent in "The Wallflower Waltz." Her *pas de deux* with Herbert Bliss (Hortense, Queen of the Swamp Lilies and Harold, the Young Poet) is danced very well indeed, but seems somewhat out of place. Patricia Wilde as the Wild Pony and as the Leader in the "Freebee" has an excellent opportunity to display her wonderful technique. Yvonne Mounsey is properly beautiful and statuesque as Venus.

Ruthanna Boris has not realized all the possibilities inherent in the subject matter or the music. In addition, some of the numbers drag, others are repetitious, still others could be left out entirely. A ten or twelve-minute cut would do this ballet a lot of good.

As might have been expected, the most important *première* of the season was that of Jerome Robbins's *The Cage*, set to Stravinsky's String Concerto in D (the "Basler") in costumes by Ruth Sobotka, a member of the company. It was given on June 14.

The theme of *The Cage* derives from the fact that in some forms of animal life the female of the species considers the male her prey. The mantis, for example, devours her partner immediately after mating; the female spider kills the male unless he attacks first. Greek mythology tells of the Amazons who had established a life completely apart from men except for procreation.

In the ballet, the Novice (Nora Kaye) is freed from her cocoon by the Queen (Yvonne Mounsey). An Intruder

(Michael Maule) enters the nest of the murderous females. The Novice is given her first test in dealing with the male. True to her nature, she breaks the neck of the Intruder between her legs as soon as his function is fulfilled. A second Intruder (Nicholas Magallanes) enters. For a while the Novice displays emotion toward the second Intruder. But the Queen commands, the moment of weakness is gone, and he is destroyed in the same manner as the first.

The Cage is not a pretty work, and it is not for children. It is outspoken, bitter, and violent. The implications of its comment are wider than the abstract insect kingdom it deals with, and these implications are not pleasant to contemplate.

It is also a tremendously exciting work, beautiful in the savagery of its contents, thrilling in its choreographic development. It is probably the most powerful work Robbins has ever done and choreographically his most mature.

Nora Kaye danced the Novice with the great dramatic power she has always commanded, but now multiplied many times. She resorted to no histrionics, no tragic outbursts. Her force here was in the charged intensity of her movements, in the at times frightening matter-of-factness, in the practically immobile features of her face, in her expression of animalism, which all united to produce a superb performance that will be long remembered.

Nora Kaye here finally came into her own in the New York City Ballet. Here was a ballet that was properly hers, a ballet in which she would never have a peer. Once again she assumed her place as a great dramatic dancer.

Yvonne Mounsey as the Queen and Nicholas Magallanes and Michael Maule as the Intruders were excellent in their roles; so were the twelve girls in the horrifying ensemble of the insects.

Ruth Sobotka, whose gift as a costume-designer was known to only a few people in the company though she had been a member of the costume designers' union for several years, created imaginative costumes that added to the starkness of the work. Jean Rosenthal once again worked wonders with the lighting and the few ropes she used for décor.

The Cage received a tremendous ovation. The public knew that it was a great work and also realized that Nora Kaye had come back to the front rank of a ballet company and assumed her rightful position, and it was giving the ballerina a cordial welcome.

Many people in that audience, and in every audience that ever went to see *The Cage*, hated the ballet, considered it ugly, even repulsive. But there was not a single person who accepted it with insulting equanimity or just ignored it. It quickly became the most controversial work in the repertoire of the company, displacing, as it were, Ashton's *Illuminations*, which had occupied that position for more than a year.

Jerome Robbins, still somewhat weak and not fully recuperated after his appendectomy, left the day after the *première* on a long European vacation. He returned in early November. When told about the controversy *The Cage* had provoked in New York he was rather amused. "I don't see why so many people are so shocked by *The Cage*," he said. "If you observe closely you must realize that *The Cage* is actually not more than the second act of *Giselle* in a contemporary visualization."

He was right, of course.

Thanks mainly to *The Cage*, Morton Baum's "calculated risk" in running a New York summer season paid off. The company nearly broke even. The 1950–1 season ended on June 24. It was the biggest and most successful in the company's history. Between November 21, 1950, and June 24, 1951, it had danced twenty-two weeks and had had an aggregate rehearsal period of sixteen weeks, as good a season as any company has in the United States.

The success of the company's summer season and the public's reaction to its repertoire prompted S. Hurok to offer the New York City Ballet a touring contract. Mr. Hurok had long been interested in the development of the company, and in the spring of 1950 had been instrumental in arranging its London season. His suggestion for an American tour seemed to have interesting possibilities. He planned to have the company dance in cities having symphony orchestras that could play for its performances. In addition, he proposed extended seasons in Chicago, San Francisco and Los Angeles. The company would, of course, have its own seasons at the City Center, as before.

The plan sounded good to all concerned except Lincoln Kirstein. Although the least commercial-minded of anyone in the organization, he felt that the kind of tour proposed by Hurok would not be financially feasible.

It happened that he turned out to be right.

Hurok was leaving on his annual visit to Europe and, as he was to see David Webster in London, he offered to begin to talk to him about the company's second London engagement, for the summer of 1952.

The dancers left on their first real vacation in more than a year and a half. They were not due back until August 13.

XVIII

1951

"The Miraculous Mandarin"; "Tyl Ulenspiegel"; "Swan Lake"; "The Pied Piper"

While the dancers were on vacation George Balanchine, Lincoln Kirstein, and Morton Baum were busy outlining plans for the performing year 1951–2.

The problem of financing the production of Todd Bolender's *The Miraculous Mandarin*, which had held up the scheduled *première* of the ballet the season before, was finally settled. The estate of the late Béla Bartók, to whose score the ballet was to be done, agreed to a loan of about ten thousand dollars toward the expenses of the production. This loan was to be paid off in the form of royalties for every performance of the ballet.

Encouraged by the success of Frederick Ashton's *Illuminations*, Kirstein and Balanchine wanted

293

to commission a new ballet from the English choreographer.
Baum readily agreed, and Ashton was given *carte blanche*. He
chose a ballet on the theme of Tristan and Isolde, set in the
locale of Tintagel castle, the legendary birthplace of King
Arthur. The castle, incidentally, actually exists on the west
coast of Cornwall. The music would be the tone poem *Tintagel*
by Sir Arnold Bax, who holds the fascinating (to the American public) title of Master of the King's (now Queen's)
Musick. Cecil Beaton, who had designed the décor for *Illuminations*, would be commissioned to do the sets and costumes,
making it an all-British affair.

Antony Tudor was asked to revive his *Lilac Garden*, which
he had staged for Ballet Theatre in 1939. Now that Nora
Kaye, Diana Adams, and Hugh Laing were in the company,
Lilac Garden would fit well into the repertoire and provide a
proved vehicle for Kaye and Laing, who still did not have
enough to dance. Kirstein also suggested to Tudor that he
think about another ballet for the company, a work that
would suit the dramatic talent of Nora Kaye. He even mentioned a theme, the on-and-off-stage behavior of a great
dramatic actress at the end of her career.

Jerome Robbins, who was expected back from Europe in
early November, would do a new work, to be decided on his
arrival.

Agnes de Mille accepted Kirstein's invitation to choreograph her first ballet for the company, and selected Igor
Stravinsky's "Dumbarton Oaks" Concerto as the musical
background for it. She could not, however, commit herself to
a definite production schedule.

Balanchine had a number of works up his sleeve. First, he
wanted to revive *Apollo*, which had never been danced by this
company. Ever since the production of *Orpheus* by Ballet
Society (April 28, 1948), Balanchine, Stravinsky, and Kirstein
had considered it the second ballet in a Balanchine-Stravinsky

trilogy on classico-mythological themes. *Apollo* was the first ballet in this trilogy, and Balanchine and Stravinsky were planning to get together on a third ballet to complete the trilogy. Quite naturally, therefore, Balanchine wanted to revive *Apollo*. The roles could be well distributed among André Eglevsky, who had danced Apollo before, Maria Tallchief, Tanaquil LeClercq, and Diana Adams. Balanchine also wanted to freshen up *Concerto Barocco* and present it, as he had done before, in simple practice-tunics without scenery.

Then Balanchine had in mind a ballet to Richard Strauss's *Tyl Eulenspiegel*, using an approach ignored by other choreographers and the composer himself. He wanted to base the ballet on the Flemish legend of Tyl, rather than on the generally used German one, and was guided by the Tyl novel of Charles de Coster. Kirstein was already doing the research for this work, and he felt that Esteban Francés would be the proper man to design the scenery and costumes.

Another ballet Balanchine wanted to do was *Bayou Belle*, to Virgil Thomson's *Acadian Songs and Dances*, from the score of the movie *Louisiana Story*.

But Balanchine's most spectacular and (for this company) unorthodox plan was the production of the second act of *Swan Lake*.

The idea of producing a one-act *Swan Lake* belonged to Baum. *Swan Lake* had been a favorite with American audiences ever since the Ballets Russes de Monte Carlo had first brought it here in 1933. Every big touring company had it in its repertoire, and for several years the present Ballet Russe de Monte Carlo looked upon it, along with *The Nutcracker* and *Scheherazade*, as their most financially successful work. It is a matter of record that whenever box office receipts showed a tendency to fall off, *Swan Lake* and the other two ballets would be substituted for whatever program had been announced and the box office would unfailingly show an appreciable spurt. Baum felt that the New York City Ballet, now that it was largely underwritten by the City Center, should produce a bread-and-butter ballet along with its exciting but untried new works.

When Baum first suggested the idea to Balanchine and Kirstein, they rebelled against it. There were talks of "over my dead body" and "next you'll want us to do Scheherazade" and "this isn't that kind of company."

Balanchine felt that there were so many new things that should be done that he did not want to go back to the old classics, and that, besides, the New York City Ballet public was not the kind of public which would respond to *Swan Lake*.

Kirstein advanced other arguments. "Every ballet company in America and in Europe is doing *Swan Lake*," he told Baum. "The Sadler's Wells Ballet has a full-evening *Swan Lake* that tops them all. If we could produce a full-evening *Swan Lake* that would be better than the Sadler's Wells' I'd be all for it, but we cannot. So why attempt it?"

Time and again Baum kept returning to his suggestion, and time and again Balanchine and Kirstein kept on refusing. Finally, Baum said to the two gentlemen in a rather offhand manner: "I agree with you that we cannot do as good or as big a *Swan Lake* as the Sadler's Wells, but I feel instinctively that George can do a *Swan Lake* that will be different from any *Swan Lake* ever seen here or in Europe."

Whether or not this was a maneuver on Baum's part could not be established. Baum only smiles when asked about it. But it did have an effect on Kirstein. He still advanced some arguments, more *pro forma* than for any other reason, and then one day, after a consultation with Balanchine, he telephoned Baum: "Will you let us commission Cecil Beaton to do the scenery and costumes for *Swan Lake*?"

Baum had not expected this question. Beaton receives a

high fee for his designs, and his scenery and especially costumes are very expensive to make. Baum had hoped to use a
simple backdrop and the standard *Swan Lake* costumes. But
he realized that Kirstein's request was in line with his own
words about a "different" *Swan Lake*, and he agreed.

This, then, was the plan for additions to the repertoire in
1951–2. It was ambitious, even grandiose, and, considering
the low price of the tickets at the City Center and hence the
low possible box-office receipts, entirely too costly. But the
company could see no other way of playing at the City Center.

The problem was purely mathematical, and as such apparently only had one solution. Touring ballet companies
present on the average three or four new ballets each year.
They usually play in New York once, for from two to four
weeks, then go on tour. The new ballets are the novelties that
draw the audience and make possible the season. The New
York City Ballet, however, not being a touring company, had
been having three or four engagements per year in New York.
Each engagement was a new season and needed new ballets
to attract the public. If one two-to-four-week season needed
three or four ballets, four seasons needed twelve or sixteen
ballets. It was as simple as that. Moreover, the New York City
Ballet had a number of works originally done for a much
smaller group, when it was still Ballet Society. With a few
exceptions, the present company had outgrown the Ballet
Society repertoire and needed new productions to replace
those which, one by one, were being retired. In addition, the
New York City Ballet did much more experimenting than a
touring company, and therefore had a greater turnover even
in new ballets.

An institutional, *avant garde* company like the New York
City Ballet cannot avoid the expense, great though it may be,
of a constantly growing, changing repertoire. The alternative,

of course, is touring, with the concomitant expediencies, compromises, and lowering of standards. This the company would not do.

Rehearsals began as scheduled, on August 13. The three new works to be presented during the first season were *The Miraculous Mandarin, Apollo,* and *Concerto Barocco.* A few days before the opening, Tanaquil LeClercq sprained an ankle and was out for the season. As a result, *Apollo* had to be postponed. Never at a loss in an emergency, Balanchine put together in a few days a humorous little ballet to Jean Françaix's Serenade for a Small Orchestra, which he named simply *À la Françaix.*

Last to end the previous New York season, the company also began the new one. It opened on September 4, the day after Labor Day, with *Serenade, The Cage, Pas de Trois,* and *La Valse.*

Despite the warm evening, a full house was on hand to greet the return of the company after its estivation. The dancers and the ballets were in excellent form. P. W. Manchester, the well-known London critic and editor of *Ballet Today,* who had come to New York in late August to write for *Dance News,* had this to say in her first American review:

"This [the opening night] was my first view of the company since their London season in the summer of 1950 and I should like to say at once that, good as they were last year, their showing at this performance was a revelation to me. The extra year or so of working together and their first experience of dancing to audiences other than the regular New York ballet public has been of inestimable benefit. The company as a whole danced brilliantly throughout the evening. . . .

"As a newcomer to City Center I was much struck by the similarity in the atmosphere to that of Sadler's Wells Theatre . . . when the company now at Covent Garden was still making its way towards world recognition. . . . There is the same rapport between stage and audience and the same sometimes undiscriminating enthusiasm which fails to distinguish between the good and not-so-good, as though criticism involved some kind of disloyalty to the ideals in which both the company and the audience so truly believe.

"The standard of accomplishment is a remarkable one and so is the company's roster of feminine stars. The girls altogether are still very much stronger than the men whose partnering is on a much higher level than their work as soloists. . . ."

There were two noteworthy changes in casting: Maria Tallchief substituted for LeClercq in *La Valse*, giving a very good performance but not quite coming up to the characterization created by LeClercq; and Melissa Hayden, taking Nora Kaye's place in the *Pas de Trois*, was brilliant in it.

If the company wanted another controversial ballet, it got it in *The Miraculous Mandarin*, which was given for the first time on September 6. Todd Bolender staged the work to Bartók's score, in scenery and costumes by Alvin Colt. The choreography was based on the libretto by Melchior Lengyel written for the music, not for the ballet.

The plot, in outline, concerns a prostitute who acts as a decoy for a gang of robbers and murderers. The gang attacks the men lured by the prostitute and robs and kills them. One of the men who crosses the prostitute's path is the Mandarin. Unlike the others, he actually loves her. When she is through with him and turns him over to the gang, they discover that, try as they will, they cannot kill him. He comes back to life after every onslaught, survives savage beating, knifing, even hanging, and always returns, or tries to return, to the prostitute. Only when, despite herself, she is moved by his devotion to a semblance of love, does the Mandarin succumb, peacefully, as it were.

It was a grim, ugly, sordid, cruel, and violent work, a real shocker. Melissa Hayden as the prostitute (she was called the

Woman in the program) gave a tense and exciting performance, at times the personification of evil, a Gorgon, at others a
tender, loving woman. Hugh Laing as the Mandarin was the
embodiment of Oriental mysticism and quietude. One felt his
burning passion for the prostitute despite his calm exterior;
he wore the still, impenetrable mask even during the most
violent episodes. Frank Hobi succeeded in making the role of
the Old Man stand out in clear relief. The moment he walked
on stage with his furtive steps one knew that he was headed for
physical destruction. Beatrice Tompkins was wonderful as the
pathetic Blind Girl who nearly walks to her death.

The Miraculous Mandarin could have been a truly great
ballet, but was not. Bolender's fault lay in his approach to the
work rather than in the choreography proper. Instead of
basing his ballet on the underlying theme that love is stronger
than death, the choreographer chose to preoccupy himself
with the superficial manifestations of physical violence and, in
a few instances, with vulgarity. As a result he lost the essential, if you wish, philosophical argument for the ballet and
produced instead a group of atmospheric scenes of assault and
battery with intent to kill which are much better done in the
movies. In addition, he never justified the co-existence of the
naturalistic gangsters, prostitute, and other victims, with
the mystic, symbolic figure of the Mandarin. He had no help
in this instance from Alvin Colt, who designed a wonderful
skeletal structure with stairs, columns, and platforms, eerie
and fascinating, but clothed the people in realistic, if somewhat exaggerated, costumes. Even the Mandarin wore an accepted nineteenth-century Chinese costume.

A few minor points also worked against the ballet. The
season before, New York had seen Jean Babilée and Natalie
Philippart in *Le Jeune Homme et la Mort*, presented by Ballet
Theatre, with its exciting suicide scene, and another hanging
on the stage was anticlimactic. Also, Hayden's character as

the prostitute came too close to her portrayal of Profane Love in *Illuminations*. Finally, the basic idea of a gang of thieves headed by a girl had been used, also the season before, by Roland Petit in his *La Croqueuse de Diamants*, and though that was a very light piece the basis was still similar. There is no intention, of course, of suggesting that Bolender borrowed from other ballets: it was only regrettable that the production of his ballet came at the time it did.

Despite its defects, *The Miraculous Mandarin* was an exciting, disturbing work. Many people hated it, some liked it; only the ultra-squeamish and the sempiternal-classic stayed away from it.

The production of *The Miraculous Mandarin* gave a new stimulus to the never-ending discussion in ballet circles about the apparent laxity of the supervision the directorate of the company exercised over the choice of works by choreographers, their approach to and planning and execution of their creations. These discussions were not necessarily limited to controversial works: they revived each time a new ballet did not appeal to a section of the public. Naturally, controversial works created the most eloquent discussions. Some of the protests against *The Miraculous Mandarin* contained more than just a hint of the advisability of some form of censorship. Two or three people, for instance, who contributed modest sums to the New York City Ballet through the purchase of tickets to the dinner dance of Ballet Associates in America, were all for specifying that the money thus contributed only be used toward productions *a priori* approved by Ballet Associates. The interesting point here was that the same people would have been violently opposed to any form of censorship of literature, drama, or the press. Other people, less direct in their ways, or perhaps more open-minded, thought that the company should find a way of adopting a more selective method for commissioning new works, not only from the point of view of subject matter but also from that of the inherent possibilities of public success.

Quite obviously, any restrictive policy in commissioning and producing new works would have been against the basic reason for the existence of an institutional, pioneering, and frankly experimental company. The whole idea of the company was to make it possible for gifted artists—choreographers, composers, painters—to work in an atmosphere of creative freedom, to try out new approaches and old traditions, to say what they wanted to say the way they wanted to say it, within the limitations of the art form.

This is not to say that the management did not exercise a certain discipline, but the discipline rested on two intangibles: talent and taste. Talent can be judged only by its final manifestations; i.e., the completed work. As to taste, one is reminded of the words of Henry Adams: "Everyone carries his own inch-rule of taste."

The other wish, that the directorate gauge the eventual success of a work before it reaches the production stage was, of course, purely utopian. In the two thousand years, more or less, of the existence of the theater no way has been found to determine the ultimate reaction of any public to a theatrical production, be it drama, opera, or ballet, and the management of the New York City Ballet was not superhuman.

Balanchine's *À la Français*, first performed on September 11, proved to be a delightful trifle about a dashing tennis-player (André Eglevsky) who steals away a young girl (Janet Reed) from two boys (Frank Hobi and Roy Tobias), to be in turn lured away by a supercilious sylphide (Maria Tallchief), appearing, it seemed, from nowhere. Because of the caliber of the dancers who participated in this little piece and the tongue-in-cheek choreography set by Balanchine, *À la Français* gave the public a gay quarter of an hour. Everyone took it as lightly as Balanchine staged it. Jean Françaix's Serenade for Small Orchestra sounded as if it had been composed especially for the ballet.

On September 13, the company revived *Concerto Barocco*, minus the costumes and scenery in which it was given in an earlier revival. The simplification was much to the advantage of the ballet. Maria Tallchief, Diana Adams, and Nicholas Magallanes danced the principal parts. Constance Baker, Barbara Bocher, Arlouine Case, Toby Fine, Edwina Fontaine, Barbara Milberg, Ruth Sobotka, and Tomi Wortham were in the ensemble. A perennial favorite, it was enthusiastically received by the public.

The Miraculous Mandarin, Illuminations, The Cage, Age of Anxiety, and *Firebird* showed enough drawing power not only to make the fall season a successful one, but also to prompt the management to announce a winter season right after the autumn season closed on September 23. The winter season was scheduled for five weeks, November 13 to December 16.

With a lavishness that may have been inconsistent with the delicate financial status of the company, but was in line with the general production plan of the company, the management announced five new productions and two revivals. The new ballets were Balanchine's *Tyl Eulenspiegel* (which was now given its proper Flemish name *Tyl Ulenspiegel*), *Swan Lake*, and *Apollo;* Ashton's *Tintagel;* Tudor's *Lilac Garden. The Four Temperaments* and *Le Baiser de la Fée* were the revivals.

Just as rehearsals began it became known that Ashton would not be able to come over from London in time to choreograph *Tintagel* for the winter season. Jerome Robbins, who had returned meanwhile from Europe and was rehearsing the title role in *Tyl Ulenspiegel*, stepped into the breach and began to work on *The Pied Piper*, a ballet to Aaron Copland's Clarinet Concerto.

Kirstein, for once not too much occupied with the business end of the forthcoming season, was in his element digging up book after book for the guidance of Balanchine and Esteban Francés in the production of *Tyl Ulenspiegel*. He conceived the idea that the décor and costumes for the ballet should be based on the paintings of the great fifteenth-century master Hieronymus Bosch, and was now doing all he could to make it easier for Francés to translate his idea into a visual form. It was Kirstein, too, who persuaded Cecil Beaton to leave for once his sweet and elegant style of stage designing and go back to Albrecht Altdorfer, Nicolaus Manuel Deutsch, and Albrecht Dürer for inspiration for the décor of *Swan Lake*, in essence a Germanic tale. He succeeded manifestly in both cases.

November 13, the opening night of the season, rolled around sooner than anyone in the company had expected. The opening night program included *Cakewalk*, in a somewhat shortened, changed, but not improved version; *The Miraculous Mandarin*, with its choreographer, Todd Bolender, in the title role, still as disturbing as ever; *Pas de Trois*, with Maria Tallchief, Nora Kaye, and André Eglevsky; and *Bourrée Fantasque*, with the usual cast, replacing the previously announced *Symphony in C*. It was a well-balanced program, much liked by the audience.

The first new work of the season was presented the following evening: *Tyl Ulenspiegel*. The ballet showed Tyl as the liberator of Flanders from the Spanish invaders under the cruel Duke of Alba. The well-known tone poem by Richard Strauss had one basic shortcoming so far as the ballet was concerned: it was too short. It had been too short earlier that year when Jean Babilée staged his *Till Eulenspiegel* for Ballet Theatre, and Babilée's ballet was much simpler than Balanchine's. The music is written in such a way that it is not possible to repeat individual sections of it to extend the piece, as is occasionally done with other compositions.

To lengthen the ballet somewhat, Balanchine began the

action to a musical prologue consisting of drum rolls. During these he introduced two of his main characters, Tyl and Philip II of Spain, as children, playing on an elongated chessboard with a loaf of bread and armed sailing ships taking the place of conventional chess figures. The loaf of bread in the hands of Tyl clearly represents the simple peasants of Flanders, the ships in the hands of Philip, the Spanish power. At the end of the prologue the boy Philip forces the loaf of bread off the table and a fist fight ensues.

The ballet proper begins with the first chords of Strauss's music and presents the various pranks, taunts, and teases of Tyl, by which he annoys the Spaniards and rouses the Flemish people to revolt against the invaders until they are finally driven out of Flanders.

No other Balanchine ballet contained so much theatrical (not necessarily choreographic) invention as did Tyl, and no other was so much handicapped by the shortness of the musical composition. In this detailed, complicated pantomime, rather than a ballet in the accepted sense, Tyl just did not have a chance. No sooner had he begun a scene, or a prank if you will, than the music drove him right out of it. There was not even enough time to achieve what stage directors call "establishing" the scenes, let alone for developing them. One doubts whether the spectators that opening night saw more than half of what Balanchine staged for Tyl. Only repeated seeings made it possible to have more than just a cursory impression of what was happening on the stage.

Esteban Francés's décor was a wonderfully effective part of the ballet and, by itself, a lucid re-creation of Hieronymus Bosch's work. Emily Genauer, in her Sunday art column of the *New York Herald Tribune* (December 2nd), wrote:

"The backdrop for the New York City Ballet Company's new production of 'Tyl Ulenspiegel' provides an exciting visual experience for audiences at the City Center and man-

ages remarkably well to capture the forms and flavor of that
Bosch we so rarely encounter in substance.

"Frances's adaptation—perhaps interpretation is a better
word—of the great fifteenth-century Flemish master by whom
there are no more than a handful of works in America, recre-
ates no specific painting by him, but is rather, a composite of
several of his works. It employs the familiar jagged architectural fragments (especially as used in his great Temptation
of St. Anthony), the sinister grottoes and caverns, the inevitable waiting gibbet, the monstrous animals (even the
recurrent symbolic owl), the flame-like underbrush. Only the
people are missing.

"These, of course, are the dancers, who, as they strut and
turn, bend and grimace and fall into grotesque and even
obscene postures before the setting, evoke with startling effectiveness the extravagant imagination, lusty mockery, sly
diablerie and savage fantasy of Bosch. As a matter of fact the
dancers perform not only before but even within the setting
and props as they project onto the stage. When Jerome Robbins as Tyl, for instance, dumps a Spanish nobleman into a
barrel so a rear view of him is seen from the waist down, with
legs kicking wildly, the audience is literally getting one of
Bosch's pet images. In addition, the set succeeds wonderfully
well in projecting his depth of design, fluid line, even the
typical Bosch palette."

Jerome Robbins was perfect as the revolutionary, patriotic, and mischievous Tyl. Changing from guise to guise, here
a poor peasant, there a monk, in another place a swordsman,
he seemed to be in two places at the same time, and on one
occasion actually was: George Balanchine in a long robe and
mask had to substitute for him in one scene because Robbins
did not have enough time to change from one costume to
another. This perhaps indicates the pace of the work.

Brooks Jackson as Philip, Frank Hobi and Beatrice Tompkins as the Duke and Duchess, acted very well.

It would be a pity if the company should decide to drop *Tyl Ulenspiegel* from its repertoire because of the inadequacies of the score's length. It would be worth while for Balanchine to find as soon as possible a longer score and then restage the ballet.

On November 15 the company presented the first performance of *Apollo*, now officially called *Apollo, Leader of the Muses* (an exact translation of its original French title, *Apollon Musagète*). Reviewing the performance in *Dance News*, P. W. Manchester wrote:

"Perhaps this will never be a ballet with a universal appeal but for some it has a beauty so poignant that the weak spots are gladly accepted in the over-all magic. Over and over again a limping invention is followed by a moment of revelation.

"It is the work of a young choreographer (Balanchine was only twenty-five in 1928 and he has made few alterations) who, until that time, had leaned heavily towards the 'modern' which in 1928 meant the grotesque.

"The formal, almost icy classicism of Apollo is relieved by flashes of a boy's humor, as when Polyhymnia, Muse of the sacred lyric, suddenly becomes aware that she may be making too much noise and covers her mouth with her hand: and again where Apollo, in youthful sport, drives the Muses round the stage as though already he anticipates the moment when he will, for the first time, step into his chariot and drive the sun across the heavens.

"Then the playfulness ceases. Apollo hears the summons of Zeus. Until then he has been a boy. Now it is time to put away childish things and accept the responsibilities of a man and a god. With an awed solemnity he leads the Muses in the ascent of Olympus and stands ready for what is to come.

"The Muses are most beautifully danced by a dedicated Maria Tallchief as Terpsichore, Tanaquil LeClercq as Polyhymnia (though she is perhaps a shade too pert) and Diana Adams whose Calliope, Muse of eloquence and heroic poetry, has her own unquenchable warmth and womanliness.

"André Eglevsky's build inevitably makes him a Hercules rather than an Apollo, but his dancing is as superb as ever and within the limitations imposed by his particular physique he does present youth growing to manhood with all its wonders and fears.

"Apollo was created for a nineteen-year-old Serge Lifar in the full glow of his adolescent beauty and until such another can be found the part will never be fully realized."

The ovation that greeted the *première* of *Swan Lake* on November 20 will not easily be forgotten by the company or by many of the audience who filled the City Center that evening. It far exceeded those which followed the *Pas de Trois* and the *Sylvia pas de deux*, the most effective claptraps in the repertoire. It is interesting to note, in this connection, the universal appeal of the technical fireworks of the classic ballet. The City Center public is properly considered a sophisticated, even *avant garde*, audience, yet its reaction to a brilliant variation is as clamorous as that of any audience anywhere in America or in Europe, and is far stronger than its reaction to even the most powerful ballet, in theme and execution, which makes no use of ballet pyrotechnics.

Balanchine has left intact most of the set numbers of *Swan Lake:* the *pas de deux*, coda, and *pas de quatre*. The first entry of the swans is almost the same, except for an acceleration of tempo. He has staged an entirely new variation for the Prince, to music borrowed from another part of the ballet and seldom performed. He added a *pas de trois*, a *pas de neuf,* and a completely new finale to the music of the *entr'acte* of the last act. A listing of these changes in no way indicates that he has also transformed the entire ballet, making it an exciting ensemble work rather than a show piece for the ballerina and, to a lesser extent, *the premier danseur,* as all other versions of Act II of *Swan Lake* are. The usually lowly and stage-dressing *corps de ballet* becomes a protagonist on a par with the principals, occasionally more dominant than they.

A great love for the classic ballet and a disciple's faithfulness to tradition were apparent in Balanchine's approach to *Swan Lake.* But there was also the realization of the master that ballet had advanced since the version of *Swan Lake* which our generation knows was created in 1895 by Marius Petipa and Lev Ivanov.

It is common knowledge that Petipa's and Ivanov's preoccupation with the ballerina to the neglect of the *corps* and the lesser soloists was based not only on the then-accepted formula of creating ballets *ad majorem ballerinæ gloriam,* but also on the simple fact that the *corps* and lesser soloists were not good enough dancers to be entrusted with difficult *enchaînements* or permitted to execute dance movements directly connected with and advancing the development of the plot of the ballet. The nineteenth-century division of scenes into *pas dansants* and *pas d'action* was not arbitrary and certainly not a whimsy of the choreographer or even a part of his artistic credo. It was a necessity. The *corps* could not act and did not possess enough ballet technique to dance with the principals. Hence the set dances for the *corps,* mostly classic waltzes or character numbers, with little or no participation in the dances of the principals (*pas dansants*); or the mimed scenes (*pas d'action*), characterized by slow and laborious conventional ballet pantomime, which included only an occasional adagio for the ballerina with a partner or partners (such as, for example, the so-called "Rose Adagio" in the first act of *The Sleeping Beauty*, danced by Aurora and four Princes, which in the original is called a *pas d'action*).

Balanchine, like everyone who stems from the Russian Imperial Ballet, realized that the American soloist and *corps de ballet* dancer have advanced in technique beyond anything the Imperial Theater could have hoped for, and staged his version of *Swan Lake* accordingly.

The ballerina (Maria Tallchief) and the *premier danseur* (André Eglevsky) were still the principals of the ballet, and their adagio and variation still exciting dances. But the *pas de trois* of Patricia Wilde, Edwina Fontaine, and Jillana was as exciting as (on the opening night indeed more exciting than) anything the principals danced. "Magnificent" is the word for Wilde's dancing of the main part of the *pas de trois*. Only slightly less exciting was the *pas de neuf* headed by Yvonne Mounsey. The *pas de quatre* of the little swans, often a show-stopper, was danced with dazzling precision by Doris Breckenridge, Kaye Sargent, Ruth Sobotka, and Gloria Vauges.

Maria Tallchief, who had danced *Swan Lake* before, as guest artist with Ballet Theatre, gave an excellent performance, but because of the new choreography of the whole piece she did not dominate the stage and, at least on opening night, did not quite achieve the emotional quality this part demands. The variation set for André Eglevsky was the least successful choreographically and musically, one might say the least successful choreographically because it was set to the least successful musical number. As mentioned before, Balanchine borrowed the music from another act. It had never been danced to in any of the versions of *Swan Lake*, and perhaps the choreographers who preceded Balanchine had a good reason for not using the music and Balanchine should have followed their example. The variation had a peculiar quality of being, if one may term it so, preparatory: it always seemed on the verge of starting, and then it was over and nothing had happened.

Balanchine made brilliant use of the excellently trained *corps*. There were twenty-four swans on the stage, more than in any other company except Sadler's Wells, and he devised for them an endless number of intricate patterns that developed great dramatic force entirely by means of movement without any resort to conventional pantomime or literal gestures. This was particularly true in the final, climactic scene, just before the disappearance of the Swan Queen.

Cecil Beaton designed an impressive and beautiful black-and-white set after the style of the late-fifteenth-century German engravers, dressed the girls in white tutus, headdresses and big wings (too big, they seemed on the opening night) made out of feathers, and the men in rich red. Only Eglevsky's costume was not up to the standard; it was subsequently changed. The inimitable Barbara Karinska executed the costumes *con amore*. Jean Rosenthal's inspired lighting completed the effect of what probably is the handsomest production in the repertoire.

Swan Lake, as noted before, is generally the most popular ballet in any company. Since it was first presented some seventy-five years ago, it has been variously called the greatest ballet of all time and an old warhorse. John Martin of *The New York Times* belongs to the "old warhorse" group. He professes to dislike the ballet acutely. To me his oft-repeated profession of dislike seems more in the nature of a self-imposed artistic credo. I have never had any reason to doubt Mr. Martin's sincerity, but I do believe (without proof to be sure) that down deep in his emotions, if not in his brain, he enjoys a good performance of *Swan Lake* with most of us. His review of the opening-night performance of *Swan Lake* is therefore illuminating. Here are parts of it:

"For reasons that are far from clear, the New York City

Ballet last night presented its own version of 'Swan Lake' at the City Center. Of all the projects conceivable in the ballet world, another revival of this old warhorse, which is already in the repertoire of every known company to the apparently full satisfaction of its patrons, would seem to be the least explicable.

"It becomes even more bewildering when it is done by an avant-garde organization such as this, which has never before revived anything older than George Balanchine's own creations for Diaghileff, and which, besides, has a list of most intriguing projects in its own metier fairly clamoring for the time, money and opportunity to be brought to fulfillment.

"Once one has registered astonished disapproval of such a wasteful expenditure of energy and taste, however, there remains nothing but praise for the way the dubious assignment has been executed. Though it is fundamentally the same old one-act excerpt that everybody knows backward and forward, Balanchine has put his hand to it with characteristic magic. He has restudied both the traditional choreography, attributed to Ivanov, and the Tchaikovsky score, and has edited them with the most sensitive discrimination.

"Most of the major foolishnesses and minor irritations that clutter the familiar version have been deleted and many fine and ingenious alterations and additions have been made."

John Martin then goes on to give an excellent analysis of the performance, with high praise for everyone.

On Sunday, December 2, Martin devoted a long article to the ballet, again analyzing the production and trying to find a justification for its presentation. He said in part:

"As to George Balanchine's new version of 'Swan Lake,' one can only say that while one agrees with everything he has done in it, one questions his justification for doing it.

"For sixteen years the sturdy line of avant garde progress

in the ballet has been held against the hostile forces of popu-
larity-at-any-price virtually alone by the New York City
Ballet and its ancestors, Ballet Society, Ballet Caravan and
the American Ballet. Now it makes what might easily be
interpreted as a gesture of capitulation by bowing to the chief
god in the enemy's pantheon, violating for the first time its
precedent of freedom from that incubus of safe accumulated
inertias which constitutes the 'standard' repertoire.

"Such an interpretation would patently be wrong, for
the company has built a substantial and articulate following
which comes to the box office so eagerly that it frequently
enables New York seasons to pay for themselves, an almost
unheard of state of affairs in the ballet world. The paying
public has definitely not been trying to bully it into compromise.

"Why then 'Swan Lake' and conformism? Is it perhaps a
slight attack of nostalgia, which will pass with judicious application of the needle? Or is there by some remote chance a
touch of bravado about it, an attempt to show the enemy up
in his own camp? One snatches at straws to explain away any
possible drift towards catering to popularity instead of standing, as this company has consistently done, one step ahead of
opinion, enticing it to follow.

"Perhaps, after all (if one can pursue the Pollyanna attitude still further against gnawing misgivings), that is exactly
what this production is doing. Certainly it is the most sumptuous, elegant and imaginative 'Swan Lake' on record; perhaps if there is a Santa Claus, it may succeed in winning the
worshipers of the old order to fresh standards of artistry.

"One thing is sure: if it does not do that, it will drive
them muttering into the night, for it is not at all what they are
used to. . . ."

Actually John Martin did not have to go so far to look

for a justification for the production of the ballet. A program note that I wrote at the request of Lincoln Kirstein stated the artistic justification very clearly:

" 'Swan Lake,' Act 2, is the only traditional ballet to be revived by the New York City Ballet in seventeen years of collaboration between George Balanchine and Lincoln Kirstein. The revival manifests the tie which exists between contemporary ballet and the source of all ballet as we know it today—the romantic-classic era which began with 'Giselle' in 1841 and ended with 'Les Sylphides' in 1909—the greatest period the classic ballet has ever known."

On November 22 the company presented a revival of the Balanchine-Hindemith ballet *The Four Temperaments.* The novelty of the revival and its principal attraction lay, strange as it may sound, in the absence of the scenery and costumes originally designed for the work. The company was never really happy with Kurt Seligmann's set and costumes. How much these appurtenances had actually interfered with the projection of the ballet became apparent only at this performance. Dressed in what has almost become a uniform for the dancers of the New York City Ballet—simple black tunics for the girls and black tights and white shirts for the boys— against a blue cyclorama, *The Four Temperaments* suddenly blossomed into a wonderfully lucid composition, imaginative rather than only inventive in its conception, exciting in its execution. One did not have to worry about what Hindemith meant under his labels (melancholic, sanguinic, phlegmatic, and choleric), did not have to think that unless one went back to read up on the four cardinal humors and their proportions one was likely to miss the deeper significance of Tallchief's swift *batterie* or LeClercq's sustained *developpés.* One just sat enjoying the ballet, and let philosophy go hang. Perhaps a victory of matter over mind, but kinesthetically a most rewarding one.

November 30 brought the *première* of Antony Tudor's *Lilac Garden*. This was first produced by Ballet Rambert in London, and since 1940 it has been a mainstay in the repertoire of Ballet Theatre. A love story set in Edwardian England, *Lilac Garden* tells the romantic drama of Caroline, her Lover, the Man She Must Marry, and the Woman in His Past, who keep on meeting and parting and observing the etiquette and the niceties of the upper middle class, to the background of Ernest Chausson's *Poème*.

This, perhaps, is as appropriate a place as any to ask a question. The program note to *Lilac Garden* states that the scene is "The lilac garden of Caroline's house." Yet the ballet ends with Caroline and the Man She Must Marry taking leave of the other people on the stage (ostensibly her guests) and departing while the others remain. Would it not be more logical to consider that the ballet takes place in the lilac garden of the Woman in His Past, who acts as hostess throughout the ballet? It is a very minor matter, of course.

" 'Lilac Garden,' observed P. W. Manchester in *Dance News*, "has been breaking our hearts for fifteen years. It would seem to be one of the very few ballets headed for immortality. With the choreographer himself, Nora Kaye and Hugh Laing in their well beloved roles this revival could hardly fail, but even so one was hardly prepared for the beauty and wonder of this production. Perhaps the revelation of the ballet was Tanaquil LeClercq as the Woman in His Past whose brittle, frantic gaiety hides her anguish."

Horace Armistead constructed a beautifully atmospheric set; Barbara Karinska designed very lovely costumes.

The evening was a triumph for all concerned, and especially, of course, for the three Tudorites in the company: Nora Kaye, Hugh Laing, and the choreographer himself.

The last new ballet of the season was Jerome Robbins's *The Pied Piper*, to Aaron Copland's Concerto for Clarinet and

String Orchestra, presented on December 4. It was in a way a strange composition, similar in vein to the choreographer's earlier *Interplay*, but more theatrical and staged with greater abandon—which, at moments at least, seemed somewhat labored.

Here is how Walter Terry described *The Pied Piper* in a Sunday article in the *New York Herald Tribune* (December 9th):

"The curtain rises upon an empty stage. A ladder or so, a section of a theatrical flat and doors leading to backstage quarters are all we see. Through the dimness, the Piper approaches. He is a man dressed in ordinary street clothes and he carries a clarinet. His amblings lead him eventually to a music stand, stage left and front. He glances at a musical score, adjusts a light so that he can see, tootles tentatively and then bursts into Aaron Copland's Concerto for Clarinet and String Orchestra.

"A little light filters through the dimness as the dancers enter. The music is slow, a trifle sad and two of the young pursuers of sound, Diana Adams and Nicholas Magallanes, commence to dance a fairly gentle, almost formal pas de deux. Jillana and Roy Tobias enter. Doors open, letting in more light, obliterating a few of the shadows but not so many of them but that a pair can dance, backs to audiences, with their silhouettes reflected in giant size against the walls.

"The tempo changes, the lights come up, Janet Reed and Todd Bolender enter and soon the stage is flooded with people ensnared by the now wild, insistent, cajoling, dictating notes of the music. Melissa Hayden, Herbert Bliss, Tanaquil LeClercq and Mr. Robbins himself join the throng in an intricate, unpredictable and throbbing kinetic response to the Piper and his abettors in the pit. They do the Charleston, they lie on the floor in a vast vibrating mass, they freeze into contorted immobilities, they pretend to resist or they yield crazily to the screaming command of the clarinet, to an ir-

resistible rhythmic pattern, to a musical jolt, to the lash of a
cadenza, to the tickle of a single pointed note.

"And yet 'The Pied Piper' is by no means a disorderly,
illogical ballet. It has form in stage design, in movement con-
trasts and parallels, in spatial patterns and it has kinetic logic.
This kinetic element (which is, of course, present in all dance)
is the key to this ballet's purpose and power. The majority of
the movements in the work may be classified as kinetic pantomime. In other words, the movements have meanings but
they are neither literal nor symbolic meanings. They are
kinetic, they make muscle-sense. In this specific instance, the
music is the stimulus, the body reacts or comments upon it
immediately and impulsively and instinctively. It is danced
pantomime in its purest, most primal, most potent form."

The other critics, and certainly the majority if not all of
the spectators on the opening night and thereafter, shared
Walter Terry's appreciation of *The Pied Piper*. P. W. Manchester spoke for the minority when she wrote:

"In spite of public acclamation which demanded additional performances, I cannot feel that it [The Pied Piper]
has any lasting quality. It has its amusing aspects on first
sight but all there is to see is immediately observable and the
work does not grow on further viewing. . . . I wish I felt
that The Pied Piper has the same endearing and enduring
charms as the choreographer's earlier Interplay. There is a
family resemblance but the former is the rich, vulgar relative."

Speaking for myself, I have a long-standing prejudice
against naturalistic ballets given on bare stages with the
dancers in sweaters and everyday dress. Like most idiosyncrasies in the arts (or politics) this one is probably eminently
unfair as a generalization, but also probably not without
foundation.

Despite the artistic success of the season, it closed with a
deficit of about twenty thousand dollars.

Two important offstage events took place during the season; European impresario Leonid Leonidoff arrived in New York on November 21 to make final arrangements for a European tour, and on December 5 Ballet Associates held its third annual dinner dance for the benefit of the company. The dinner dance, for the first time, had acquired commercial sponsors, the jeweler Trifari and the perfumer Lanvin. The sponsors paid most of the expenses of the affair, and Ballet Associates was able to send the New York City Ballet a check for five thousand dollars, which came in very handy.

Mr. Leonidoff's arrival in New York had greater significance. This was the impresario who had offered the company a European tour for the summer of 1951. The company then could not accept the offer because Mr. Leonidoff's fee would not cover the troupe's expenses, especially as he could not pay the company's transatlantic transportation. Now, however, conditions were different.

To begin with, the company had the invitation from Mr. Webster to dance at Covent Garden during July, on more or less the same terms as in the summer of 1950; i.e., a guarantee of £2,000 per week, a percentage of the profits, if any, and one-way transportation across the Atlantic. Then Mr. Leonidoff, who had had time to investigate the company's potentialities on the Continent, found it possible to raise his guarantee to $5,500 per week. To top it all, the company received two other very flattering invitations. One was from the Edinburgh Music Festival, to appear there for a week in August, following the Covent Garden season.

The other came from the Paris Exposition, "Masterpieces of the Twentieth Century," sponsored by The Congress for Cultural Freedom, a worldwide anti-Communist "organization of writers, philosophers, creative artists and scientists dedicated to the assertion and defense of freedom of thought, free enquiry, free expression and to the continuing expansion

of intellectual freedom everywhere." The Exposition was set
to be held in Paris from April 30 to June 1. Among those invited to participate were the Boston Symphony Orchestra;
the Paris Opera House Orchestra under Bruno Walter; the
Vienna State Opera and the Vienna Philharmonic Orchestra
under Karl Boehm; the Royal Opera, Covent Garden, under
Benjamin Britten; the French National Radio Orchestra
under Igor Stravinsky; L'Orchestre de la Suisse Romande
under Ernest Ansermet; and the American National Theatre
and Academy (ANTA).

Nicolas Nabokov, the composer and friend of Balanchine,
Kirstein, and the New York City Ballet, was the director of
the exposition committee, and the invitation obviously origi-
nated with him. An interesting point here was that the
American Chairman of the Exposition was Julius Fleischmann, long a supporter of Ballet Russe de Monte Carlo and
a founder and chairman of Ballet Foundation, which sponsored that company. It must have riled him no little that he
had to agree to inviting the New York City Ballet rather than
Ballet Russe de Monte Carlo.

And there was still another invitation to dance in Paris.
M. Hervé Dugardin, the new director of the Théâtre des
Champs-Élysées, who had spent some time in New York and
had attended some of the company's performances, invited
the ballet to hold its own season at his theater sometime in
June, after the Exposition.

Morton Baum felt that all these invitations together
offered an attractive possibility of giving the company an additional four and one-half months of work, and at the same
time of letting the company be seen in Continental Europe
and play a return engagement in London. He consequently
signed with Mr. Leonidoff and the Paris Exposition and
agreed in principle to the other propositions. There was one
aspect of Mr. Leonidoff's contract which Baum and Kirstein

and Balanchine did not like: the contract called for a three-week season in Barcelona, and they did not relish the idea of the troupe's appearing in Franco Spain. They argued the point with the impresario, but he was adamant. Barcelona, he told them, was the most profitable engagement of the whole tour. It not only would pay for itself, but would also make it possible for him to tour the company. Without Barcelona he could not afford to pay the company's Continental transportation, and would have to cancel the entire season. Reluctantly the management of the company had to agree.

If Baum visualized the European season mainly as a means of furnishing employment for the company and thus keeping it together during the summer, Balanchine and Kirstein were delighted for other reasons.

Balanchine wanted to show the company to Europe, particularly to Paris, where he had begun his career in the Diaghilev ballet. Paris had seen his work quite recently, in 1947, when he was guest choreographer at the Opéra. But he felt that showing two or three ballets staged for the Opéra and showing his own company were quite different things. He wanted, in a way, to show off, and who could blame him?

Kirstein had another reason to be satisfied with the prospect of a European season. More than anyone else in the New York City Ballet, he was averse to a United States tour for the company. He knew that even the best-arranged tour would necessarily include a number of one-night stands and split weeks, and he realized that the company could not be shown to best advantage under these conditions. The only way to avoid touring in America would be to play some fifteen or sixteen weeks, in three or four seasons, in New York and in the spring go to Europe and play there another fifteen or perhaps eighteen weeks. The offers for the spring and summer of 1952 just filled the bill, and he hoped that a similar arrangement could be made for 1953.

By the time Mr. Leonidoff was ready to sail back to France in mid-December the European tour of the company was fully mapped.

The company would open in Barcelona at the Gran Teatro del Liceo on April 15, and would play there through May 8. On May 10 it would dance one performance at the Paris Opéra as part of the Exposition. Then it would continue its performances for the Exposition through May 15 at the Théâtre des Champs-Élysées. From May 18 through 30 it would appear at the Teatro Communale in Florence, as part of the annual Maggio Musicale Festival. This would be followed with performances at the Théâtre Municipal, Lausanne, Switzerland, from June 1 to 4, and in Zurich from June 6 and 7. On June 9 the company would open a season of its own—i.e., not as part of the Exposition, at the Théâtre des Champs-Élysées, Paris—and dance through the 25. The Continental season would end on July 3, with performances in the Netherlands. On July 7 the company would open a seven-week season at Covent Garden, London; it would finish the European engagement with performances at the Edinburgh Music Festival from August 25 to 30.

Quite a tour, one was ready to admit!

XIX

1952 (1)

"Bayou"; "Caracole"; "La Gloire";
"Picnic at Tintagel"

The dancers had only a short vacation after the season. Early in 1952 they were called for rehearsals for another five-week season, set to begin on February 12.

There was some doubt whether George Balanchine would be able to give this season as much time as he had given the other seasons. It was a problem of bread and butter.

Ever since the establishment of the New York City Ballet, and, as a matter of fact, of the companies that preceded it, both Balanchine and Lincoln Kirstein had worked without any financial compensation. Morton Baum similarly headed the Executive Committee of the City Center without

322

pay. It was very well known that had these men been paid salaries commensurate with the work they were doing, the New York City Ballet could not possibly have existed.

Kirstein had an income left him by his father, and therefore did not have to depend for existence on a salary from the New York City Ballet. Baum had a lucrative law-practice that provided an income and left him enough time to conduct the affairs of the City Center. Balanchine, however, had to work for a living. Never a well-to-do, let alone a wealthy, man, he managed modestly but fairly well on the royalties from the musicals for which he had choreographed dances. He had also saved some money from his fees for staging dances in films. But by the middle of 1951 his savings were nearly exhausted and the musical *Where's Charley?*, his latest work on Broadway, closed after a run of about two years. Balanchine needed to make a living.

In January 1951 Samuel Goldwyn, on a short visit to New York, offered Balanchine the assignment of directing the choreography in a film based on the life of Hans Christian Andersen, in which Moira Shearer, ballerina of the Sadler's Wells Ballet, would dance and act the role of the Danish ballerina, Blanchette, and the comedian Danny Kaye would play Andersen. Balanchine readily accepted the contract. Later in 1951 he flew to Hollywood to read the script of the film and discuss the production. He was not happy with the treatment of the story by the studio. He also learned that the picture, originally scheduled for the fall would not go before the cameras until early January 1952, at the time when the New York City Ballet would have to begin rehearsals for the February-March season. When he came back to New York he decided that much as he needed the money he would ask Mr. Goldwyn to release him from the contract. Mr. Goldwyn promised to think it over. It was not until the latter part of November that Hollywood finally agreed to release Balanchine and signed Roland Petit to direct the dances in his stead. As is well known, Moira Shearer subsequently also withdrew from the picture.

Balanchine was thus free to devote his attention to the new season of his company, but he was also nearly without funds. Morton Baum then decided that neither the City Center nor the New York City Ballet had a right to accept Balanchine's services without at least a nominal salary that would just about pay the choreographer's living expenses. Balanchine, reluctantly, agreed.

If Balanchine was short of cash at that time, he was long on honors. He had invitations from opera houses in Europe and South America to stage his ballets, among them houses in Buenos Aires, Milan, and Paris. Because the engagements would conflict with his work for the New York City Ballet, he could not accept the offers from Buenos Aires and Paris, but the Milan season was set for March, between his company's season in New York and the European tour, and he accepted it. In January he received an invitation from the "Masterpieces of the Twentieth Century Exposition" in Paris to stage two new ballets for the New York City Ballet especially for the Exposition. They were *Cordélia* (called earlier *Une Histoire d'Amour*), to a score by Henri Sauguet, and *Coup de Feu*, to music by Georges Auric, commissioned by the Exposition. He had to excuse himself from this honor owing to lack of time, and both ballets were subsequently presented by the Grand Ballet du Marquis de Cuevas, with choreography by John Taras and Aurel Milloss, respectively.

If Balanchine's financial situation did not improve with the increased activities of the company, the principal dancers did receive substantial additional income. The fact that they stayed in New York most of the season rather than traveling made them available for guest television appearances, which paid handsome fees. Maria Tallchief, Tanaquil LeClercq, Nora Kaye, Melissa Hayden, André Eglevsky, Nicholas Magallanes, Herbert Bliss, and others appeared several times during the year on network shows. LeClercq, incidentally, not only danced, but also acted: she played one of the principal roles in the television adaptation of Rumer Godden's novel *A Candle for St. Jude*, presented by CBS-TV on Studio One program.

Hayden and Eglevsky danced for two weeks, between seasons, at the Roxy Theater, New York. The same two dancers also made a quick trip to Hollywood late in December to dance in the Charlie Chaplin picture *Limelight*. Hollywood also claimed, for a short while, Maria Tallchief, who was invited to impersonate Anna Pavlova and dance that ballerina's famous *The Dying Swan* in the Metro-Goldwyn-Mayer film about the life of the swimmer Annette Kellerman, entitled *Million Dollar Mermaid*. Incidentally, when Tallchief reported at the studio and danced for the director *The Dying Swan* that she had prepared in New York with the help of George Balanchine, he stopped her in the middle and said: "Sorry, Miss Tallchief, this won't do. The number is too quiet, not spectacular enough. Please do some fast turns and jumps so that the audience will have something to look at."

Tallchief could do nothing but comply.

The program of new works for the February-March season was laid out as follows: *Bayou* (earlier called *Bayou Belle*), by George Balanchine, to Virgil Thomson's *Acadian Songs and Dances*, in scenery and costumes by Dorothea Tanning; *Caracole*, also by Balanchine, to music by Mozart (Divertimento No. 15 in B-flat Major, K.287), in costumes by Christian Bérard, which the late painter had designed for the 1933 production of *Mozartiana; Ballade*, by Jerome Robbins to music by Claude Debussy (*Six Epigraphes Antiques*), in scenery and costumes by Boris Aronson; *La Gloire*, by Antony Tudor, to the *Egmont, Coriolanus*, and *Leonore* No. 3 overtures by Beethoven, in scenery by Gaston Longchamp and costumes by Robert Fletcher; and *Picnic at Tintagel* (earlier called *Tintagel* and *Iseult at Tintagel*), by Frederick Ashton, to music by Sir Arnold Bax (*The Garden of Fand*, instead of *Tintagel*, which Ashton had found to be too short for the purpose of the ballet), in scenery and costumes by Cecil Beaton.

The last-named ballet had been postponed from an earlier season because Ashton had been unable to come over from England at that time to stage it. Even now there was some doubt about Ashton's rehearsal schedule. When Moira Shearer had to withdraw from the Hans Andersen film because of pregnancy (she was expecting her child in August), Metro-Goldwyn-Mayer offered her a starring role in an episode of the film *Three Love Stories*. The Andersen film would have entailed three months' work for Shearer; her sequence in *Three Love Stories* would only take some three weeks. At the ballerina's suggestion the studio invited Ashton to choreograph her dances. Ashton accepted and flew from London to Hollywood in mid-January to begin work on the film. The New York City Ballet was hoping that he would be able to get to New York in time to stage the ballet in February. He finally did manage to do it, but the company had a few uneasy weeks.

While the company was rehearsing the new ballets, Jean Rosenthal, its technical director and lighting magician, left for Europe at the invitation of impresario Leonid Leonidoff to visit the theaters in which the company was scheduled to dance on its European tour, inspecting the lighting equipment and other facilities, so that proper cue-sheets could be worked out before the company left New York. Mr. Leonidoff apparently understood how much the successful presentation of the company's repertoire depended on proper lighting. Miss

Rosenthal returned to New York in time to begin work on the new ballets of the season.

The first ballet of the new season was presented on February 13. It was Jerome Robbins's *Ballade* to Debussy's *Six Epigraphes Antiques*, in a décor by Boris Aronson.

The music of Claude Debussy has closed without a ripple over the heads of many a choreographer before Robbins, and will probably do so many more times before the lesson is learned that some music absolutely defies choreography.

The *Epigraphes* therefore became something in the nature of epitaphs, written, moreover, in an unknown language. This is a ballet that absolutely demands a program note, for if its theme is clear to the choreographer, the least he can do is give a lead to the audience and let their imagination take it from there.

The curtain rises on a dim stage peopled by half a dozen figures huddled on chairs against a back cloth. Snow is falling heavily, adding to the melancholy of the scene. A balloon-vendor enters, places a balloon in each inert hand and walks away. The balloons endow the puppets with life, and each rises to his or her feet with the pull of the balloon.

This is a striking opening, but after that Robbins seems to be completely at a loss. The characters are all broken-down fugitives from the *commedia dell'arte* or Toulouse-Lautrec, but their functions are never made clear. Three boys dance together, but for no particular reason. Nora Kaye in an unbecoming Harlequin leotard and tights caricatures many of the movements of *The Cage*, but the audience is plainly not intended to laugh. Tanaquil LeClercq, also *en travesti*, is a Pierrot who makes cabalistic signs on the floor and then lets her balloon float away.

When the balloon-seller returns and collects his wares, all but one of the protagonists collapse back into their original positions, presumably dead. Tanaquil LeClercq, having lost her balloon, is left alive, but this does not seem to be a good thing, for she looks very miserable indeed and is staring blankly into the wings as the curtain falls.

If only we knew of what the balloons are symbols, what the dance of the three boys means, or what the Kaye-Harlequin and the LeClercq-Pierrot represent, all the rest might fall into place.

As it was, only one episode came to life. This was the dance in which a terrifyingly silly Columbine is wooed by one of the three boys. He, poor fool, cannot understand that she is not a living creature until she shows him her heart filled only with sawdust. It sounds ridiculously sentimental, but as performed by Janet Reed and Roy Tobias it has a pitiful quality, and the shaking out of the sawdust becomes a horrible moment of realization.

Had Robbins maintained this level and that of the opening and the conclusion, *Ballade* might have proved to be his best ballet to date, except that the music would have remained intractable.

February 19 marked the introduction to the repertoire of *Caracole*, George Balanchine's interpretation of Mozart's Divertimento No. 15, K.287, in terms of white-plumed ballerinas supported by pink-limbed *premiers danseurs* and a *corps de ballet* of eight girls, all in a framework of black velvet and swatches of white silk.

The result is crisp, sparkling, lyrical, gay, wistful, gracious, and altogether brilliant, though rather too long, as ballets to pre-existing music tend to be when they are not too short.

Caracole is not a work that can be taken in at a first viewing; each performance for a long time to come will yield up fresh treasures. Some of the choreography for the *corps de ballet* struck me as a little perfunctory and stiff. Nor is the music effective for male dancing, so that Eglevsky's very difficult solo is not particularly eye-catching to the ordinary observer.

But when this has been said, there remains a world of enchantment, with variations for the ballerinas which are designed to enhance the individual quality of each: the amazing thrust and attack of Patricia Wilde, the clarity of every step taken by Melissa Hayden, the lyrical grace of Diana Adams, the last remaining trace of coltishness in Tanaquil LeClercq which yet has a charm of it own, and the speed and brio of Maria Tallchief.

The Andante in which the three men partner the five girls in varying combinations is perhaps the most beautiful section of all.

Jerome Robbins and Nicholas Magallanes are the other two cavaliers, the former a little ill at ease in this milieu, but both most gallant partners.

If a superb set and charming music were sufficient for success, *Bayou*, which was given for the first time on February 21, would be a knockout. Dorothea Tanning's décor was one of the most beautiful in years, exuding the mist and warmth and damp of the bayou country. Virgil Thomson's folksy score was an ideal accompaniment; having been written as film music, it is incomplete in itself.

But a ballet has to have choreography, and on this occasion Balanchine failed to provide any of even momentary interest. Instead, he became involved in an incredible bit of whimsy in which the spirits of leaves and flowers are paired off with the "starched white people," who seem to be having a wedding celebration.

A very simple story of a bayou boy and girl attracting for a few moments the interest of the sophisticated visitors before they all return to their own lives would be sufficient to bear us along on the charm of the atmosphere and the music. Instead, the plot does not altogether avoid the ludicrous.

Dorothea Tanning's costumes are much less successful

than her set. The boy, who should be a kind of elfin Huck Finn, wears clean and beautifully cut pink satin pants and a nicely arranged lei, while the costumes for the Trees and Flowers are embarrassing.

Francisco Moncion and Doris Breckenridge as the Boy and Girl of the Bayou, Melissa Hayden and Hugh Laing leading the Trees and Flowers, and Diana Adams and Herbert Bliss doing the same for the Starched White People all did their best with their material, but the magic we had hoped for when the curtain rose on the river with the Boy gravely paddling his boat through the mist unhappily never began to work.

Antony Tudor started out with a magnificent idea for *La Gloire*, which was premièred on February 26. The star of a European State Theater (Comédie Française?) is seen in three of her great roles, while at the same time we have glimpses of her offstage, graciously accepting the homage of her colleagues, but living in the shadow of the fear of her approaching decline when a younger actress will take her place.

By choosing as the musical basis for this theme three famous overtures, Tudor threw away all possibility of developing his idea, for Beethoven refuses to accept the second place allotted to him. Furthermore, Tudor has assumed what no choreographer has any right to do—that his audience has the same knowledge as he of the fictional characters he is presenting.

In other words, he entirely failed to establish in action the relationship between Lucretia and the Tarquin, Phædra and Hippolytus, Hamlet and Ophelia: no distinction was made between the agonies of Lucretia and those of Phædra, although the emotions that inspire them are entirely different.

Owing to the lack of time caused by the inexorable pace set by *Egmont*, *Coriolanus* and *Leonore* No. 3, the choreographer was also unable to make clear the offstage tragedy.

Nora Kaye had the embryo of a part that she could play magnificently. As it stood on the opening night, she could only tear a meaningless passion to tatters. Francisco Moncion as Sextus Tarquinius and Claudius, and Hugh Laing as Hippolytus and Laertes were in a similar case. Diana Adams as the mysterious understudy looked ravishing and fully capable of playing any role allotted to her.

La Gloire is shot through with moments of grandeur, and if Tudor were allowed six months to reconsider it, and it was provided with a new score (of twice the length if necessary), it might well prove to be the most important ballet for many years.

Tudor made some changes in *La Gloire* after the opening performance, and continued to rehearse it almost to the end of the season. It did acquire a measure of unity after the changes, but they were still not sufficient to make it a great ballet. He will eventually have to do something about the music or abandon the work.

The performance of February 27 was the kind that confirmed balletomanes would give their eyeteeth to attend. Owing to the absence of Maria Tallchief, who was in Hollywood dancing in the film *Million Dollar Mermaid*, Tanaquil LeClercq appeared for the first time in *Swan Lake*. For the occasional spectator this may have been a very nervous, rather tentative performance; for the seasoned balletomane it was a never-to-be-repeated exciting moment in the development of a very talented dancer; for LeClercq herself it was probably the most important moment in her career.

No matter how modern-minded a ballet company may be, no matter how *avant garde* its principles and policies, no matter how advanced the dancer herself, only a performance of the ballerina role in a classic ballet, especially *Swan Lake*, establishes her as a ballerina. She may have danced all the great roles in the modern repertoire, may have been acknowledged the greatest dancer in the company by public and press alike, yet she does not become a ballerina, accepted without question by everyone, until she has danced the ballerina role in a classic ballet.

This may sound antediluvian and anachronistic to the casual observer, but it is surprising how many people in contemporary ballet in America as well as in Europe accept this tradition and abide by it.

According to this tradition, a ballerina is a being apart from all other people in ballet, whether a particular company is or is not based on the so-called star system. A soloist in a company, just to cite one example, dances a certain role, but a ballerina dances a ballet, whatever her part in the ballet may be. How strong this tradition is, even in America, may be judged from the fact that John Martin of *The New York Times*, an *avant gardiste* if there ever was one, and certainly no great respecter of ballet tradition, announced in his review of February 28 the elevation of Tanaquil LeClercq to ballerinadom.

The new ballerina gave a timid but romantically glowing conception of the role. Once her nervousness is overcome, she should be a wonderful Swan Queen, an exciting addition to the exalted circle of ballerinas.

Frederick Ashton's long-awaited *Picnic at Tintagel*, premièred on February 28 as the last novelty of the season, was exactly the kind of work the company needed, telling a story succinctly without depending on program notes to eke out choreographic vagueness, and giving the dancers one of their rare opportunities to characterize.

It had a handsome set with a fine transformation scene devised by Cecil Beaton, wonderfully colorful medieval costumes and some "amusing" ones for the picnickers before they are transported back a thousand years in time, though if one wanted to quibble they were at least fifteen years earlier than the 1916 quoted in the program. And it had an Ashton *pas de deux* out of his top drawer.

The warm audience response to *Picnic at Tintagel* indicated that the story ballet still has a strong appeal when the story is told with as skillful a mixture of mime and dance as it is here. Ashton's craftsmanship was everywhere in evidence, and in the passage for Iseult and Tristram he also showed us Ashton the fine and sensitive artist.

Diana Adams glowed with tenderness and danced exquisitely as the young wife transformed into Iseult; Jacques d'Amboise, very youthful despite the red beard, had a forthright directness and simplicity as the potential lover turned Tristram; Francisco Moncion glowered finely as the Husband-King Mark.

Robert Barnett played the Caretaker of the castle, who was apparently a reincarnation of the magician Merlin, and once again, as in the previous Ashton ballet, *Illuminations*, was given a chance to prove himself an outstandingly clever dancer-actor.

During a performance of *Serenade* on the program with *Picnic at Tintagel*, Janet Reed tore the soleus muscle in her right calf at the very beginning of the ballet. She walked offstage with a slight limp unnoticed by most of the spectators. Patricia Wilde, another principal dancer in this ballet, took over the moment Reed left and danced Reed's part, as well as her own, so expertly that there was not even a second's break in the performance.

In spite of the disappointment over *Ballade* and *La Gloire*, the season as a whole was an exciting one with the company in its finest form throughout.

The season ended March 16 with a fondly enthusiastic farewell ovation from the full house. The company took in

$198,700 during the five weeks, a very substantial sum, but still short of its expenses. Morton Baum's financial worries were not over.

Balanchine had left on February 28 for Milan to stage his *Ballet Imperial* at the Teatro alla Scala. The ballet was premièred on March 25, with Olga Amati, Gilda Maiocchi, and Guilio Perugini in the main parts. According to reports, *Ballet Imperial* created a sensation and Balanchine was immediately invited to return to La Scala the next season.

The dancers had only three weeks in which to prepare for the adventure of a five-month European tour. They were scheduled to leave on April 7 aboard a chartered BOAC Stratocruiser for Barcelona. The scenery, property, and costumes were shipped ahead late in March.

Right after the season ended, two groups instituted a protest against the company's appearances in Spain. One was the Spanish Refugee Appeal of the Joint Anti-Fascist Refugee Committee, and the other was a group of thirty-five dancers, choreographers, and musicians headed by Anita Alvarez, an American dancer of Spanish descent. The Spanish Refugee Appeal was directed to Newbold Morris, chairman of the board of directors of the City Center, and to City Center audiences; Miss Alvarez and her co-signatories addressed themselves to Vincent R. Impellitteri, Mayor of the City of New York. The Spanish Refugee Appeal protest spoke of Franco's fascism in general and also referred to the recent attacks on Protestants in Spain.

On April 4, two days after Miss Alvarez's protest, Jacob S. Potofsky, a member of the board of directors of the City Center and president of the Amalgamated Clothing Workers of America, announced that he had resigned his position at the City Center because of the scheduled season in Barcelona.

In his letter of resignation to Newbold Morris, the labor leader, one of the original supporters of the Center, wrote that "this latest step makes any further association with the City Center untenable as far as I am concerned."

He said that he had made clear his opposition to the appearance of the ballet in Barcelona in a communication on March 19 to Ben Ketcham, manager of the Center. Declaring then that the Franco regime in Spain had killed outstanding Spanish artists and driven others into exile and had suppressed a free trade labor union movement, Mr. Potofsky remarked that the "financial considerations" of the tour "are of little consequence." The union head emphasized that he was dismayed that "financial advantages outweighed all considerations of a humane, moral and democratic nature."

The New York City Ballet was in a tough spot and could do little about it. It goes without saying that the directors of the company had little sympathy for Franco and his regime, and would much rather not have sent the troupe to Spain. But they had signed a contract with Leonidoff for the entire tour and could not back out of it. No court of law would consider the protest against the Barcelona season or Mr. Potofsky's resignation *force majeure*, unexpected and disruptive though these events may have been. The company left with a heavy heart.

Before the management could write finis to the 1951–2 season it had to settle one more important problem: would the New York City Ballet go on an American tour under the management of S. Hurok?

In the spring of 1951 Hurok had offered the company a tour of the United States, of some ten or twelve weeks. The conversations then revolved around a tour of cities having symphony orchestras with which the company could dance, thus keeping up the musical standard to which it was accustomed in New York. But when Hurok actually began corresponding with local managers about booking the company it developed that a "symphonic" tour was easier to plan than to book. The elements of time, distance, and routing presented so many complications that such a tour could not be arranged, at least not for the 1952–3 season. Not wishing to give up entirely the idea of a tour for the company, the Hurok office began booking the ballet as it was booking any other ballet. By early spring of 1952, Hurok had a fairly well-arranged tour, which, however, included a number of one-night stands, something the management of the company had always objected to. Also, it became apparent that if the company wanted to make ends meet on tour it would have to reduce the number of dancers as well as the number of musicians. This Kirstein and Baum (Balanchine was in Italy at the time) refused to do. They maintained that it would be unfair to audiences outside New York and to the company itself to present its productions on a lower standard than at home.

Hurok, who by now had some definite bookings and others "penciled in"—i.e., tentative—quite naturally did not want to agree with their point of view and volunteered to show them means of economizing without putting the reputation and standard of the company in jeopardy. One suggestion was to take on tour only ballets that required less than the full company and whose accompaniment was limited to the string section of the orchestra. Kirstein and Baum could not accept this or any other compromise.

Another consideration, from a different quarter, worked against this, or for that matter any other, tour during the height of the season. Most of the principal dancers of the company did not want to tour at all. They claimed that they could stay in New York during the layoff periods and, by appearing on television a few times, earn more money than by touring the whole season. Obviously, it was much less expensive to live in New York than to tour and also much less tiring and much more pleasant.

By mid-April Hurok had to accept the inevitable and cancel the projected tour.

The problem of having enough playing time in New York was still very acute. During the season then just past, the company had played in New York thirteen weeks and had had rehearsal periods of ten or twelve weeks. This alone, naturally, would not have been enough to keep the company together, but the five-month European season, for all practical purposes considered part of the 1951–2 season, brought the employment time up to forty-four weeks or more, a much-longer-than-average ballet season.

But would the company be able to go to Europe every spring and summer? And if not, what would take the place of the European season? These questions occupied the minds of Kirstein and Baum most of the summer.

In its issue of May 12, *Life* devoted a photographic spread to the New York City Ballet on the occasion of the company's appearance at the "Masterpieces of the Twentieth Century Exposition" in Paris. The feature was headlined "Tops in the Dance: New York's brilliant ballet becomes ambassador of U. S. culture." The text of the article succinctly crystallized the company's position: "Imported from Russia by way of Europe, ballet has become a bigtime phenomenon of U. S. show business only in the past 20 years. American audiences have taken to it with enthusiasm and so have U. S. dancers and choreographers, who have been busily expanding ballet's bounds and repertory. . . . This season it suddenly became clear that the U. S. has the best-balanced and most theatrically satisfying ballet company now performing. Though only four years old, the New York City Ballet has earned a place with the world's oldest established companies. Even England's Sadler's Wells company, when it temporarily lost its great Margot Fonteyn, lost luster by comparison. And the Russians, unsurpassed in classics, are by their own admission weak in contemporary choreography."

XX

1952 (2)

A Season in Europe

Whatever the success of the New York City Ballet in Europe may have been, and, as the reader will see, it varied from country to country and from critic to critic, one thing remains certain: ballet in Europe will never be the same after its visit. If it did not do anything else, it acted as a catalyst in the hitherto self-sufficient and complacent sphere of ballet on the Continent.

Perhaps without realizing it, ballet in Continental Europe had adopted the formula established by Serge Diaghilev during the last period of the existence of his company: novelty for novelty's sake, a sharp deviation from the tradition and esthetics of the classic dance, and an overemphasis of the decorative aspect of ballet to the neglect of the dance proper.

The little companies that mushroomed in Paris after the war—all those Ballets des Champs-Élysées, Ballets de Paris, Ballets de Janine Charrat, and whatever else they were and still are called—are telling manifestations of this formula. The ballet at the Paris Opéra, which considers itself (and is considered by many in Europe) the stronghold of Continental European ballet esthetics, also subscribes to this formula. Serge Lifar's self-styled neo-classicism is much more neo-Diaghilevism than it is anything else. There are reasons for this phenomenon, but I cannot go into them here. The fact remains that when the New York City Ballet danced in Europe, the public, and, still more, European dancers, choreographers, composers, and stage designers suddenly realized that what the American company had to offer was something entirely different from what they had been seeing and doing all these years. It was a shock for them, and their reaction ranged from fawning to fault-finding, the latter concentrating mainly on the lack of "soul" or "expression" or "warmth" of the American dancers and the prevalence of "technique," the absence of plot and "subservience to music" in Balanchine's choreography, and the dearth of décor in the productions.

The company opened its first season on the Continent on April 15 in the historic Gran Teatro del Lico, Barcelona, with a program made up of *Serenade*, *Lilac Garden*, *Swan Lake*, and *La Valse*. If the company had had no idea what its reception in Barcelona would be, the Barcelonians, as sophisticated an audience as one can find in western Europe, were frankly dubious about an American company's having much to offer in so purely a European art form as ballet. Another doubtful point for the company was its opening date: the Tuesday of Easter Week. The Barcelona elite, who alone can make or break a season at the Liceo, are accustomed to leave the city for the Easter holidays, and usually to return by the end of the week, if not the following Monday. This time they had to return on Tuesday, which upset many a social plan and did not predispose them favorably toward the company. Barcelonian friends wrote to me that the social lions and lionesses returned to the city only because it became known that the diplomatic and consular corps stationed in Barcelona and the high officials of the province, headed by the Governor, would attend the *première* and thus make attendance *de rigueur* for Barcelonian society.

All the skepticism and displeasure toward the company for the interrupted holiday disappeared, however, the minute the curtain came down on *Serenade*. The gala audience of the orchestra and loges and the less glamorous one of the balconies and gallery gave the company as enthusiastic a reception as it had ever had.

The opening night's reviews, like the reviews during the entire three-week season, echoed the acclaim of the first-night audience. The company had conquered its first city on the Continent.

On closing night, May 8, the audience and the Liceo gave the company a farewell that Barcelonians reserve only for those who make a deep impression on them. M. Maurice Rapin, the Paris journalist and critic, whom the famous French newspaper *Figaro* had sent to Barcelona to cover performances of the company, wired to his paper the following description of the farewell demonstration:

"This [*Symphony in C*] is the end of the performance and the beginning of the homage. The last measures of the music end; a rain of roses and laurel leaves begins to fall from the balconies and the upper tier loges, while attendants start to bring in for the dancers, grouped on the stage around their ballet master, baskets of multicolored flowers. The stage is transformed into an immense garden. And, the supreme and

very rare homage that Barcelona pays to artists she admires, a
flight of doves, traverses the auditorium in all directions. The
dancers, motionless on the stage, continue to receive the rain
of flowers. . . . Eight minutes, by my watch, the public applauded the New York City Ballet, who, by now, had stiffened
almost to 'attention,' and George Balanchine, who was visibly
moved. It was a great evening in Barcelona."

Backstage, after the ovation, the direction of the Liceo
presented to every girl in the company a small lace mantilla
and a high decorative comb to go with it.

While the company was having its Barcelona triumph
and the dancers were adjusting themselves to Spanish ways
(including the double standard of the Spanish peseta which
was worth one amount in American money if you were a
tourist, another, much less, if you were earning your living in
Spain), Paris was having a lively polemic in anticipation of
the visit of the company.

The attentive reader may remember that the occasion for
the debut of the company in Paris, on the stage of the sacrosanct Palais Garnier, or Académie Nationale de Musique,
popularly known as the Opéra, was the "Masterpieces of the
XXth Century International Exposition of the Arts," sponsored by the Congress for Cultural Freedom, April 30 to June
1. Nicolas Nabokov, Secretary-General of the Congress for
Cultural Freedom, was President of the Organization Committee and Director of the Festival. Hervé Dugardin, Director of the Théâtre des Champs-Élysées, was General Manager,
and, with Julius Fleischmann, American Chairman of the
Festival, and Madame Denise Tual formed the Artistic Direction. The Boston Symphony Orchestra and the American
National Theatre and Academy (ANTA) were the other
American participants in the Festival.

On April 30, the day the Festival opened with a program
of sacred music at the Church of Saint Roch, Serge Lifar, bal-

let master and choreographer of the Opéra, addressed an open letter to the directorate of the Festival demanding to know why the ballet of the Opéra had not been invited to participate in the Festival. The letter appeared in the newspaper *Combat.*

Lifar wrote, among other things:

"The directorate of the Paris Opéra, prompted by the wish to co-operate in your demonstration of the world vitality of art in the twentieth century, has spontaneously welcomed the New York City Ballet, which is so competently directed by my old friend and colleague of the Diaghilev Ballet, George Balanchine, whose great choreographic talent was shown to Paris in 1947 on the stage of the Palais Garnier. This is very satisfying, and the Opéra is very happy to open its doors to a company of this quality.

"In return, however, is it not a painful surprise to discover that the organizing committee of the Exhibition of XXth Century Art has intentionally and deliberately excluded the ballet of the Paris Opéra from its programs? Is it not a matter for indignation that you appear to have scorned openly this unique ensemble whose achievements during the past twenty-five years, thanks to the ceaseless work of all its members, have attained a perfection that is not only the wonder of foreign tourists visiting Paris, but of audiences in all the capitals where, as a glorious ambassador of French art, it has appeared during the last five years?"

On May 2, *Combat* printed the Festival's reply to Lifar. The Committee stated that in February, Maurice Lehmann, Administrator of the National Lyric Theaters, and Emmanuel Rondeville, Director of the Opéra, had discussed the plans for French participation in the Festival with the Committee and that it was in the spirit of the Festival that the National Theaters were producing works by Honegger, Richard Strauss, and Ravel.

"Finally," the reply said, "on March 12th last the Direction of Masterpieces of XXth Century proposed to M. Lehmann that the Opéra ballet produce two new works by Georges Auric and Henri Sauguet. To his great regret, and in most amicable terms, M. Maurice Lehmann had to refuse the collaboration of the troupe of the Opéra on the grounds of the importance of the schedule of work which had been laid out for the spring season."

Lifar countered with another long letter, printed on May 5, in which he said that the Opéra ballet would have been glad to perform some of its standard works, but that the directorate of the Festival refused this offer.

Although Maurice Lehmann did not say so, I have it on excellent authority that the Festival Committee's suggestion that the Opéra ballet—i.e., Lifar—stage Georges Auric's *Coup de Feu* and Henri Sauguet's *Cordélia* was considered an added insult. The Committee had earlier offered these ballets to Balanchine, who had had to decline the offer owing to lack of time—he was leaving for Milan to stage *Ballet Imperial* for La Scala. Paris, however, thought that he had refused to stage them because he did not find the music worth while. Aurel Milloss subsequently staged *Coup de Feu* and John Taras *Cordélia*, and the ballets were performed by the Grand Ballet du Marquis de Cuevas on May 7 at the Théâtre des Champs-Élysées, as part of the Festival, with rather indifferent results.

Notwithstanding Lifar's faint praise for the New York City Ballet, his euphemistic reference to Balanchine as an old friend and colleague, and his exaggerated opinion of the achievements and artistic value of the Opéra ballet, one cannot help feeling that the exclusion of the Opéra ballet from participation in the Festival was a serious tactical error on the part of the Festival Committee. Whatever the artistic (and technical, if you wish) defects of the Paris Opéra ballet, it is one of the few permanent ballet organizations on the Euro-

pean continent this side of the Iron Curtain; as such, if for
no other reason, it was entitled to a place in the Festival. The
Festival Committee, like us in America, may not have liked
most of the Opéra ballet's works, and may have seriously
disagreed with Lifar's ballet esthetics and his onstage and
offstage behavior, but these were still not reasons for exclud-
ing the Opéra ballet, especially as the Festival was held in
Paris, and still more because the attitude of the French toward
the Opéra ballet, and their intense sensitiveness, are so well
known.

The New York City Ballet had no part in arranging the
program of the Festival performances, or in the decision of
who should and who should not be invited to participate in
it, but the personal friendship between Balanchine and
Nabokov made the company an involuntary party to the
controversy.

Whether the polemic had anything to do with it or not,
the demand for tickets for the debut of the New York City
Ballet at the Opéra on May 10 was unprecedented even for
Paris, where a theatrical *première* can create more excitement
than anywhere else in Europe. The result was a "black
market" that sold seats regularly priced at 1,000 francs for
6,000 francs (roughly $18). The program was made up of
Swan Lake, La Valse, The Cage, and *Bourrée Fantasque.*

A brilliant and enthusiastic audience, which included
Ambassador James C. Dunn and "all Paris," cheered itself
hoarse. There were twenty-nine curtain calls after the performance, and a separate ovation for Balanchine. The United
Press reported that the company was given one of the most
spectacular welcomes ever seen in the Paris Opéra. The greatest success went to *The Cage* and *Bourrée Fantasque.*

After the performance, the Cercle Carpeaux gave a reception for the company in the Foyer de la Danse. This was

followed by a supper given by Julius Fleischmann, American Chairman of the Festival, at his Paris home.

Opening-night reviews were unanimous in their praise, reserving, however, their opinions on the esthetics of the company as a whole and of Balanchine as the company's artistic director and principal choreographer.

André Warnod, for instance, wrote in the influential *Figaro* (May 12): "In the framework of the Masterpieces of the XXth Century the New York City Ballet gave at the Opéra its first of Paris performances. It was a remarkable evening. One loves the deep-rooted rhythm of this young troupe. Everything is clear, without bravura, subjected to a strict discipline. It is a marvelous instrument for the choreographer who searches for purity, for the always greater abstraction, for the precision in whose name George Balanchine seems to be always ready to sacrifice the humanity of the work on the altar of abstraction."

On May 13, after the company had moved (on May 11) to the Théâtre des Champs-Élysées for five more performances, Olivier Merlin wrote a most laudatory review of the company in *Le Monde* and used the opportunity to lash the Opéra ballet. Said he in an introduction to his article:

"In two days the American ballet has established itself in Paris in a glittering manner. You will read below the reflections that have been suggested to us by the first six works presented by the New York City Ballet.

"But one evidence is already certain. The choreographic art that was endeavoring to find itself in New York in the past five years . . . and that we had received without fondness when it came to us under the false nose of 'avant garde' (Ruth Page in 1949), and with sympathy when it appeared with its young muscles (Ballet Theatre in 1950)—this choreographic art has today a right to its place under the sun.

"For several seasons a determined giant, Lincoln Kirstein, and a disciple of Diaghilev, the Americanized Byzantine, George Balanchine, with the contributions of a young, talented choreographer, Jerome Robbins, have not only formed the best dance company of New York, but have created the American style of dance.

"Before the war the *corps de ballet* of the Paris Opéra reigned supreme over all stages of the world. Today . . . a company, where every schoolgirl has the personality of a star, and which has at its commands an immense stage and matchless equipment, an excellent orchestra in its vast pit, the old House [the Opéra], has become, even in the eyes of its faithful, aged and wrinkled. Since the Liberation, as a consequence of competition from troupes better administered, like the Sadler's Wells of London, or more modern or more daring, like the Ballets des Champs-Élysées, or also as a consequence of internal crises of authority the effects of which are still being felt—as a consequence, finally, of the recent 'flops' and a rare poverty of native creations, the Opéra sees its supremacy contested. Yesterday it had to contend with London. Today, here is a New York troupe, singularly more brilliant, more strong and more alive. . . ."

Not all critics agreed, however, with M. Merlin. Roger Dugard (the *nom de plume* of Georges Hirsch, former director of the Opéra) wrote in the weekly *Candide:* "The young company formed by George Balanchine with the students of his classical American school has carried off a success, merited in part. Certainly, taken individually, the artists who comprise the company are far from having the qualities of those of our national ballet. But the team is wonderfully united. Its discipline is perfect. Each dancer gives himself or herself wholeheartedly for the success of the ensemble. . . . However, in the New York City Ballet it is the mechanics which triumph. The soul is absent. On the day when the artists of the *corps de ballet* of the Opéra choose to dissolve their personalities in the collective melting pot, they will definitely prove their superiority."

As one who has seen "the artists of the *corps de ballet* of the Opéra" as recently as July of this year, I can only add that deep in his heart M. Dugard-né-Hirsch could only *wish* that this were true.

No sooner had the New York City Ballet opened at the Théâtre des Champs-Élysées than a new polemic broke out, this one minor in substance and short in duration. Marc Chagall, designer of the décor and costumes for *Firebird*, addressed the following open letter to Balanchine, via *Figaro*, on May 12:

"My dear Balanchine,

"You have just presented Igor Stravinsky's Firebird at the Champs-Élysées Theater in Paris. I created the costumes and the sets for this ballet and they were executed in New York in 1945 under my personal supervision.

"The sets and costumes now shown in Paris by your company as being my creation have only the remotest connection with the ones I created in 1945. As a result, I consider my artistic reputation as seriously damaged and the audience as being regrettably misled.

"I am compelled to publish this letter because you have acknowledged neither my letters nor the previous steps taken. You know that I was very happy to hear that you were again working on the choreography of this ballet, and that I was ready to help you redesign the costumes. To that end, I had proposed to you my closest and most disinterested collaboration. You did not consider my proposals or my misgivings.

"We are faced with this result: the new costumes are an outrageous caricature of the ones I created. As a matter of fact, the original costumes were inspired by the book and the settings: this harmony is now completely broken, not to speak of the sets, which are betrayed by the lighting and by a rhythm for which they were not created.

"Under such conditions I demand that you remove my name (in so far as the costumes of the Firebird are concerned) from your posters, programs and advertisements in France as well as in any other country.

> With regret,
> MARC CHAGALL"

Balanchine's reply was printed the next day. It ran as follows:

"My dear Chagall:

"As soon as I got notice of your open letter about the costumes and sets of the Firebird, I ordered, quite willingly, that your name be removed from my posters and programs. I assure you they will not mention it again in the future.

"As to the substance of your letter, I do not wish to start a controversy, for, as you are well aware, your accusations are not well founded: you did not attend the performance of the Firebird Sunday evening, at the Théâtre des Champs-Élysées, and consequently you have no grounds to make a judgment or reproach me concerning the sets and the costumes of this ballet.

> With regret,
> G. BALANCHINE"

And that was that.

Incidentally, the performance of *Firebird* on May 13, the day of Balanchine's reply, was canceled, but not for any reasons connected with Chagall's protest. It happened that Maria Tallchief was indisposed and could not go on, and *The Cage* was substituted for *Firebird*.

The five-day post-Opéra season at the Théâtre des Champs-Élysées showed that the most popular ballets in Paris were *The Cage* and *The Pied Piper*. The last-named was called in French *Le Joueur de Flûte*, probably, the wags in the Parisian American colony had it, because it was done to a clarinet concerto. Balanchine's ballets, about which most people spoke and wrote, enjoyed much more of a *succès d'estime* than a popular success. His *Orpheus*, so very popular in New York and London, was considered too prolix. The only time *Orpheus* excited any great attention was on May 15, when Stravinsky conducted the ballet at the Théâtre des Champs-Élysées during a gala attended by President Vincent Auriol and Madame Auriol. The composer received a tremendous ovation.

Perhaps Emile Vuillermoz was right when he wrote in *Paris Soir* on May 16:

"The success of this ballet [*The Pied Piper*] was such that Stravinsky's Orpheus, with its discretion, its simplicity, its gravity, its wonderful modesty and, it might as well be said, its a little too monotonous choreography, suffered from this gay proximity. This score, however, contains all the rhythmic elements of a danced drama which are bound to excite the imagination of a choreographer."

Paris amusement editors had a field day describing and hinting at the erotic nuances, real and imaginary, in *The Cage*, and illustrating their text with photographs of the ballet.

The performance of May 15 was the last one under the ægis of the "Masterpieces of the XXth Century." On May 16 the company left for Florence, back under the wing of Leonid Leonidoff, its European impresario, to participate in the Maggio Musicale Festival beginning on May 18.

The *Maggio Musicale Fiorentino*, as it is called in Italian, is one of the most important summer festivals of Europe. In its fifteenth year in 1952, it rates with the Salzburg Festival, and has been an example for perhaps a dozen festivals in Italy, France, and Holland which came into being after the war. If most summer festivals in Europe are organized with a frank eye toward attracting tourists, the Florence festival is one of the few exceptions. It hopes to get an influx of tourists to Florence, yes, but its main purpose is to stimulate new expressions in music and dance. As a matter of fact, it is held too early in the season to be an out-and-out tourist venture. The Teatro Comunale, perhaps one of the most beautiful in Europe, helps in making the festival into a favorite performance-spot for opera and ballet companies and individual artists.

The sophisticated, cosmopolitan and, one might add, well-to-do, public includes a generous representation of the Italian nobility and upper middle class, whose roots go back to the nobles and merchant princes who sponsored the arts during the Renaissance. Ballet may have fallen on skimpy ways in Italy since the beginning of the nineteenth century, but the public at the Maggio Musicale Fiorentino was not depending on Italian ballet to keep up its interest in the art form.

The opening performance of the New York City Ballet in Florence (and, in fact, the entire two-week season) was a triumph for the company. The forty-five-hundred-seat Teatro Comunale was sold out to the last bench in the gallery, and there were as many standees as the fire department would permit.

Trudy Goth, the correspondent of *Dance News* in Italy, joyfully cabled on May 19:

"The New York City Ballet opened last night and had a tremendous success. Each of the four ballets on the program— Serenade, The Pied Piper, the pas de deux from Sylvia and Bourrée Fantasque—received at least seven curtain calls. In the glittering audience were the new American Ambassador to Italy, Ellsworth Bunker, the Italian nobility in force, and all the local dignitaries. The ladies present made the auditorium look like a high class fashion show. The biggest hit of the evening was Jerome Robbins' The Pied Piper.

"The press today called the New York City Ballet the best company seen here. It raved about the American carefree manner and appreciated the jazz forms incorporated into the ballet. It praised the individual personalities of each soloist as well as the uniformity of the perfect style of the troupe as a whole."

In addition to their glowing reviews, such well-known Italian music critics as Gualtiero Frangini, Olga R. Signorelli, and Oriana Fallaci kept on writing newspaper and magazine articles long after the company left Florence, their general approach being succinctly expressed by a headline on the cover of the Milan magazine *Tempo:* ARRIVATI DA NEW YORK I REVOLUZIONARI DELLA DANZA.

Again, as in Paris, *The Cage* and *The Pied Piper* were the most successful ballets. *Lilac Garden*, among others, was considered "old-fashioned."

The success of the company led to speculation by the Florentine city fathers and theater directors on the possibility of offering the Teatro Comunale as a permanent home for the New York City Ballet, a sort of latter-day Monte Carlo. Farfetched as the idea may seem—I can just see a sign on a theatre marquee: NEW YORK CITY BALLET DI CITTÀ DI FIRENZE—a similar possibility had been seriously discussed earlier in the season by the director of the Teatro alla Scala in Milan, after the success of Balanchine's *Ballet Imperial* there in March. What is more, Balanchine saw some merit in it.

Following the Florence season the company gave four performances (June 1 to 5) in the Théâtre Municipal, Lau-

sanne, Switzerland, where it inaugurated the Grandes Fêtes
du Juin. As in Florence, the theater was sold out in advance
for all performances and the welcome was great.

After Lausanne the company danced two days (June 6
and 7) in the Stadtheater at Zurich, as part of the June
Festival (Juni Festwochen). The troupe was accorded one of
the most enthusiastic receptions ever given a theatrical organization there. At the end of the second performance there
were more than fifteen curtain calls, cheers and applause, and
a general wave of enthusiasm rarely observed in Swiss audiences, usually very reserved and difficult to win over. The
greatest success went to *Serenade*, *Swan Lake*, *Pas de Trois*, and
Bourrée Fantasque. *The Cage*, *La Valse*, and *Lilac Garden* were
more moderately received.

The *Zürcher Zeitung*, a newspaper of international reputation, duly analyzed the performances and reported on the
great popular success of the company but made the following
reservation: "If technical precision-work and virtuosity are
the main purpose of contemporary ballet art, then, without a
doubt, we have met the master. . . . One can bring forth
for them an intense interest and an astonished admiration,
but one cannot follow them with a sincere heart."

From Switzerland the company went back to Paris for
a nineteen-performance season (June 9 to 25) of its own; i.e.,
one not sponsored by the "Masterpieces of the XXth Century," which by then had run its course. Leonidoff installed
the company once again at the Théâtre des Champs-Élysées.
After a gala opening the company settled down to moderately
well-attended performances, excellent receptions by the audience, and a continued good press, which, however, soon
began to show signs of wearying of the novelties of *The Cage*
and *The Pied Piper* and of some of Balanchine's plotless ballets.
Whether Leonidoff had figured out the possible length of the
second Paris season to the day, or it was just a coincidence, the

company closed its Paris engagement not a day too soon. Paris, always on the lookout for novelties, has never been able to support a sustained, normal ballet season of any appreciable length, and two weeks were always considered the outside limits of such a season. Even in the halcyon days of the Diaghilev company, a ballet season could not last much longer.

The company left Paris on June 26 for The Hague for six performances in the Holland Festival, from June 27 to July 3.

The usually placid, conservative, and well-mannered Netherlands greeted the New York City Ballet with the loudest and most heated controversy the company had ever experienced in New York or in Europe. The center of the controversy was *The Cage*. Here is how Daniel Schorr, correspondent of *The New York Times*, reported it under a Hague dateline of July 3:

"A capacity audience of 2,100 gave an ovation tonight to the new ballet The Cage, whose performance by the New York City Ballet Company had been the subject of the first morals controversy in the six-year history of the Holland Festival.

"The applause was not only in praise of Jerome Robbins, the choreographer, Nora Kaye, the principal, and the other dancers, but in derision of the Dutch officials who had sought to keep the work off the stage in the Netherlands as 'not fit for the Dutch public.'

"Comment after the performance took the form of bewildered questions as to why the ballet had been considered objectionable. To many in the audience, some of whom had paid a high premium for tickets to the disputed work, it was an anti-climax. A quick canvass of Dutch newspaper critics showed that the consensus was favorable. . . .

"First performed at the New York City Center on June 14th last year, it has since been given in France, Italy and

Switzerland without producing any objections on moral grounds, and will be in the company's repertory for a Covent Garden engagement in London, beginning next week.

"But when it was put down for three performances during the week-long engagement at the Holland Festival, opposition appeared from some Dutch officials on the strength of reports from one or two persons who had seen it in New York.

"Two enterprising critics, hearing that it might be banned, went to Paris and Florence, Italy, to see it and reported that it was 'pornographic' and 'shameless.'

"This had two results. One was that The Hague burgomaster, whose name happens to be Frans Schokkink, led a crusade to get it removed from the festival program. The other result was that the public clamored for tickets.

"Mr. Robbins said that George Balanchine, director of the company, had been approached in Florence and asked to omit The Cage from The Hague engagement.

"Mr. Robbins threatened to withdraw all his works if this was done, saying: 'I will not stand for censorship,' and Miss Kaye said she would not dance at all if the work was omitted.

"Finally, it was agreed as a compromise, to perform The Cage only once instead of the scheduled three times. J. H. Reinink, chairman of the festival board, denied that it was ever intended to ban the ballet, but admitted that the Government was unhappy about it.

"Even after the one-performance compromise had been reached, Burgomaster Schokking appealed to United States Ambassador Selden Chapin to induce the company not to perform it. Mr. Chapin replied that the matter was somewhat outside his competence.

"As rumors of the controversy spread, the perverse Dutch, instead of co-operating in protecting their morals, flocked to the box office. By this afternoon, premiums as high as triple the normal prices—unusual at the Holland Festival—were being offered."

The Associated Press reported, less colorfully, that the New York City Ballet scored a smash success with *The Cage*, a modern ballet Dutch officials had thought too daring for Dutch tastes. The dancing, it said, was greeted by thunderous applause and numerous curtain calls, and leading critics called the work an "interesting experiment" and a "beautiful modern ballet." Some members of the audience, the dispatch concluded, however, complained that they "waited and waited and nothing happened."

The controversy, adding to the financial success of the company (all performances were sold out), did not detract from its artistic success or interfere with the acceptance of the company as a major artistic expression by the Dutch world of arts and letters, Dutch society, and even Dutch officialdom. The Netherlands Minister of Education, Arts, and Sciences, Dr. F. J. Th. Rutten, and the Secretary-General and Manager of the Holland Festival, Mr. Peter Diamand, both attended the luncheon given in honor of the company by the Dutch Ballet Association. A few weeks later Leonidoff received an invitation from the management of the Festival to bring the company again in 1953.

The end of the performances in The Hague also meant the termination of the company's contract with Leonid Leonidoff, for the engagements that followed, six weeks at Covent Garden, London, a week at the Edinburgh Festival, and a week in Berlin, had been booked by the company itself.

Balanchine, Betty Cage (the manager of the New York City Ballet), and the dancers had nothing but praise for Leonidoff's management. Transportation from country to country, hotel accommodations, baggage collections, the hundred and one little things that make the difference between a pleasant trip and an irritating chore had been taken care of by Leonidoff and his associates with an efficiency and attention to detail beyond the requirements of the contract. Similarly, in the more important arrangements, such as theater accommodations, provision for rehearsal time, and program planning, he had showed himself to have at heart the best interests of the company. The parting was a cordial one, both the company and its impresario expressing a desire for future work together, perhaps as soon as the next season.

In The Hague, too, the company parted from André Eglevsky. Eglevsky had let it be known as far back as February that he could not afford to go to Europe for the rather modest salary that the company could afford to pay him. Leonidoff, who was then in New York, stepped into the breach and offered to pay out of his own funds the difference between what Eglevsky wanted and what the company could afford to pay him. Returning now to its own budget, the company could not add Leonidoff's share to Eglevsky's salary, and the dancer took his leave.

The company arrived in England by ship on the Fourth of July and reached London late that evening. The next morning (it was the last day of the Sadler's Wells Ballet season at Covent Garden) the Directors and General Administrator (David L. Webster) of the Royal Opera House, Covent Garden, and the members of Sadler's Wells Ballet and the Sadler's Wells Theatre Ballet gave a welcoming party for the New York City Ballet in the Crush Bar of Covent Garden, attended by Dame Ninette de Valois, Director of Sadler's Wells Ballet; the co-director and principal choreographer of the company, Frederick Ashton; Lord Wakehurst, Governor of Covent Garden; Mr. Webster; dancers of both companies; newspapermen; critics; painters; composers; ballet masters; dance photographers—most of the London ballet world.

I had arrived in London on a busman's holiday in mid-

June, and the party was the first occasion I had had to see the company since it had left New York in April. The dancers looked very well, not a bit tired, sunburned (they had stayed at a seaside hotel in Holland and because they had had few rehearsals had managed to spend several hours a day on the beach, the weather being with them), and were ready to begin the arduous task of eight performances a week for seven weeks at Covent Garden. The only one who looked and felt tired was Balanchine, and no wonder. He had been on the go constantly since the company's arrival in Barcelona on April 11, doing double work as Artistic Director and General Director, a schedule that would tax anyone's stamina.

Even before the company arrived in London it was clear that Lincoln Kirstein should have come to the British capital for the company's season. He had a variety of good reasons for not going to London, chief among them the illness of his mother, who died at the end of July.

George Balanchine had made a bad mistake in setting up the initial program. It included *Serenade*, an excellent opening ballet, much liked in London and almost a hallmark of the New York City Ballet; *The Cage*, a controversial work with elements of danger in it, and certainly not the best choice for an opening night; *Firebird*, which London had thoroughly and generally (rightly or wrongly) disliked in 1950, and whose placing on the opening night's program, consequently, amounted almost to a defiance of the taste and opinion of the Covent Garden audience; and *La Valse*, an unknown quantity that, according to the demands of the estate of Maurice Ravel, was listed in the program as two separate ballets, *Valses Nobles et Sentimentales* and *La Valse*—without any program note whatsoever that would give a new audience a general idea of what this evocative ballet was about.

The opening night, July 7, was a brilliant social affair, with the United States Ambassador Walter S. Gifford and

Mrs. Gifford and guests in the Royal Box, the French Ambassador, a number of titled personages, and an excellent representation of London's artistic and literary worlds.

Serenade was received with great acclaim. It was clear that London was glad to see the company back. *The Cage* did not do so well. London, forewarned by continental publicity and reviews, was waiting to be shocked, but was not. It took the proceedings on the stage with its usual calm. Nora Kaye, however, was given a personal ovation. The dancer has had a large, loyal public in London since the days of Ballet Theatre, and they were happy to see her, though they did not like the ballet. *Firebird* fared even worse than in 1950, but here again the audience was glad to see Maria Tallchief, and gave her an ovation to prove it. *La Valse* came at the end of the program, a wrong place for this delicate work, and the audience, having no program note to guide it and seeing the two musical titles listed as separate ballets, was not entirely able to decipher the work and accepted it with a polite coolness. Moreover, the ballet, which fits so well on the stage of the City Center, lost its form and went sprawling on the huge stage of Covent Garden. It was not an auspicious opening. The company and the audience knew it immediately. The rest of London read about it the next day.

The reviews were well-wishing, polite, and cold. All papers liked *Serenade*, none *Firebird*. The tabloids and the standard size "populars" made a great to-do about *The Cage*. No one especially liked it or disliked it; it was just another quaint "American" ballet. Only two critics, Phyllis Jackson of the *Daily Telegraph* and James H. Monahan of the *Manchester Guardian*, liked *La Valse*. *The Times* disliked it; the others barely mentioned it.

It is strange that an unfortunate arrangement of an opening night's program should cast its reflection on an entire season, but that is how London is. The company was, on the

whole, very successful during its London season. It had good
audiences nearly all seven weeks, and most of its new ballets
were liked very much, yet something was missing during the
entire season. Somehow the group never hit the artistic stride
it had reached in 1950, never created the excitement that
surrounded it on that first visit.

Part of this was no doubt owing to the fact that the company had played London before; part of it could be charged
to the selection of the repertoire; and part to the absence of
Kirstein. It is not that Kirstein could have remedied whatever
was wrong with the season, but that he would have been a
liaison between the company and the public, a sort of top-
level public-relations man. A ballet, especially a visiting company, does not play in a vacuum, and the relation between a
ballet company and the audience is not just across the footlights. More than those of any other city, London's artistic
and literary circles, the social world, balletomanes' groups,
etc., play an important part in creating for the ballet an atmosphere which, however superficial it may appear to the
casual eye, plays an important part in stimulating an artistic
and, parallel with it, a business, interest in the company. As
it was, the Covent Garden Public Relations Officer, Michael
Wood, did his share so far as publicity was concerned. Lord
Wakehurst, president of the English-Speaking Union, a Governor of Covent Garden, and a sincere friend of the company,
went out of his way to arrange events to keep the company in
the public eye, including an official reception of the company
by Sir Leslie Boyce, Lord Mayor of London, the first such
honor given to a ballet company, and a tea for the company
at the House of Lords. But the personality of Kirstein, as a
man in the art world and as General Director of the company,
was absent and missed.

Of the ballets presented in London for the first time by
the company, *Lilac Garden* (which had had its origin there with

Ballet Rambert in 1936) was greeted like an old friend; *Swan Lake* evoked a great deal of discussion, was generally liked very much, and was a strong pull at the box office; *The Pied Piper* was universally liked as a "typical American ballet"; *Caracole* was liked by most people, but considered just another Balanchine "abstraction." Nora Kaye was a great success in *La Gloire*, but the ballet itself got only a mild reception; *À la Françaix* was accepted for what it was, a balletic comic strip; and, finally, *Cakewalk* was the hit of the season, parenthetically, much to the dismay of all those, Americans and Britons alike, who know what the New York City Ballet stands for.

A. V. Coton, the erudite critic of the *Evening Standard* and London correspondent of *Dance News*, gave the following incisive summary of the London season:

"New York City Ballet's second London visit arouses as many strong emotions as did the first; the admirers of Balanchine's neo-classicism found that they could take plenty of it, while those who thought that Concerto Barocco, Four Temperaments, Symphony in C, and Caracole were boring because too much alike, usually found something else in the programmes to please them. It is difficult to recall any season by any company in which such a high level of good dancing was maintained night after night.

"General opinion has been that Nora Kaye was a fine acquisition for the season; that the Robbins' ballets really looked good and obviously have established him as a potential first-rater; that Tudor put some marvelous things into La Gloire but that it fails in its all-over effect. In fact it has been much like a season by any other foreign company; more people disapprove than approve simply because it is strange and novel and unlike what they are used to.

"Those—quite a large section of the ballet following— who find the company's work irritating are not to be dismissed for their blind chauvinism. The trouble is that New

York City Ballet is American, and it is far from easy to extend
the widest sympathy to an alien kind of art—even when it
comes from another part of the same culture. We here may
take a new French ballet company to our hearts but it is
largely because we admire or like French things in general;
we accept easily the newness of dance-style, themes and décor
because they explain, to a large extent, the quality of 'French-
ness' of the ballets. But we cannot give this easy sympathy to
ballets from a country which we do not understand.

"Very few of us here do understand America, or the
American scheme of values about the important things in life;
and in addition we cannot make ourselves understand easily
because the common bonds of language and strong racial connection are not really deep enough to make understanding
easy from both parties. It is a fallacy to believe that Americans and English are closer than, say, English and Germans or
French and Italians.

"Apart from the sensuous splendour of watching so much
exuberant, masterly and revealing dancing—Tallchief,
Adams, Hayden, Mounsey, Wilde and Le Clercq were a constant delight through the season—there has been the quieter,
more secret, personal pleasure of reflecting that Balanchine
is still, almost single-handed, keeping alive and flexible the
practice of ballet in the historic classical style.

"No matter how many disapprove of Caracole and Four
Temperaments and La Valse in 1952, one is absolutely sure
that the dance world of 1982 will give thanks that there was
a Balanchine working through the first half of the twentieth
century."

After all is said and done, then, the company did very
well in London. The impact of its works, successful, unsuc-
cessful, and controversial, will be felt in the London ballet-
world as much as on the Continent. In this connection it is
interesting to report that during the company's stay at Covent

Garden at least a dozen European dancers and choreographers from France, Denmark, Sweden, and Yugoslavia, among other countries, went to London to watch performances night after night.

The London season was followed by a very successful appearance at the Edinburgh Festival, August 25 to 30. As this is written, the New York City Ballet is in Berlin, dancing at the Schiller Theater as part of the second Berlin Cultural Festival under the ægis of the State Department. It was acclaimed by the audience on its opening night, September 3, and had an enthusiastic press the next day. The loudest ovation went to *Swan Lake*.

* * *

This narrative began with an incident, thirty-six years ago, when the conservative parents of a tall and lanky nine-year-old boy refused him permission to attend a Boston performance of the Ballets Russes de Serge Diaghilev. This boy is still tall, but not quite so lanky. His crew-cut hair is beginning to thin, and he wears glasses. He talks fast, walks with long strides, affects a pea-jacket instead of an overcoat, seldom laughs, gets easily excited, and is forever pessimistic; he has brilliant ideas, superb taste, great knowledge. He could have been a professor of philosophy, a great writer, a merchant prince, a captain of industry. Instead he elected to become associated with ballet, perhaps as a retribution for his parents' refusal to take him to see the Diaghilev ballet.

In 1933 he teamed up with another young man, only three years his senior, a Russian Georgian with an almost unpronounceable name, who became a great choreographer against his earlier wish, because his aunt made him attend the St. Petersburg Imperial Ballet School instead of pursuing the

military career that most of the men in his family had followed.

Together these two men, Lincoln Kirstein and George
Balanchine forged and wrought and hammered out what is
now the New York City Ballet, an American institution to be
proud of, a credit to the art form and to the city whose name
it carries. They had help from many quarters and hindrances
from more. The organization they formed is far from complete and not nearly ideal. They have made many mistakes
and will make still more (and worse ones) than before, but
they have created something alive and growing, something
that adds to the sum total of our culture, something that will
go down in history as a significant and unselfish achievement.

For this, then, a blessing on Kirstein's parents and Balanchine's unnamed aunt. If they had acted differently we
might not have had the New York City Ballet.

Appendix

Chronological Check List of Ballets

*produced by the American Ballet, Ballet Caravan,
Ballet Society and the New York City Ballet
from 1935 through the autumn of 1952.*

1. *The American Ballet*

SERENADE

Choreography by GEORGE BALANCHINE
Music by TCHAIKOVSKY (*Serenade for Strings in C major*)
Décor by GASTON LONGCHAMP
Costumes by JEAN LURÇAT
Première, March 1, 1935, Adelphi Theater, New York. (Prior to the official *première*, *Serenade* was presented by the Producing Company of the School of American Ballet, December 6, 1934, in Hartford, Connecticut.) PRINCIPAL DANCERS: *Leyda Anchutina, Ruthanna Boris, Gisella Caccialanza, Kathryn Mullowny, William Dollar, Charles Laskey.*

ALMA MATER

Choreography by GEORGE BALANCHINE
Music by KAY SWIFT, *arranged by Morton Gould*

365

Décor by EUGENE DUNKEL
Costumes by JOHN HELD JR.
Book by EDWARD M. M. WARBURG
Première, March 1, 1935, Adelphi Theater, New York. (Prior to the official *première*, *Alma Mater* was presented by the Producing Company of the School of American Ballet, December 6, 1934, in Hartford, Connecticut.) PRINCIPAL DANCERS: *Leyda Anchutina, Ruthanna Boris, Gisella Caccialanza, Kathryn Mullowny, Heidi Vosseler, William Dollar, Charles Laskey, Eugene Loring.*

ERRANTE

Choreography by GEORGE BALANCHINE
Music by FRANZ SCHUBERT (Wanderer Fantasy *for piano*), *orchestrated by* CHARLES KOECHLIN
Costumes, lighting, and dramatic effects by PAVEL TCHELITCHEW
Première, March 1, 1935, Adelphi Theater, New York. (Revival from the repertoire of Les Ballets 1933.) PRINCIPAL DANCERS: *Tamara Geva, Charles Laskey, William Dollar.*

REMINISCENCE

Choreography by GEORGE BALANCHINE
Music by BENJAMIN GODARD, *orchestrated by* HENRY BRANT
Costumes and décor by SERGEI SOUDEIKINE
Première, March 1, 1935, Adelphi Theater, New York. PRINCIPAL DANCERS: *Leyda Anchutina, Ruthanna Boris, Gisella Caccialanza, Elena de Rivas, Holly Howard, Annabelle Lyon, Elise Reiman, William Dollar, Paul Haakon, Joseph Levinoff.*

MOZARTIANA

Choreography by GEORGE BALANCHINE
Music by TCHAIKOVSKY (*Suite No. 4,* MOZARTIANA)
Costumes and décor by CHRISTIAN BÉRARD
Première, March 5, 1935, Adelphi Theater, New York. (Revival from Les Ballets 1933. Prior to the official *première*, *Mozartiana* was presented by the Producing Company of the School of American Ballet, December 6, 1934, in Hartford, Connecticut.) PRINCIPAL DANCERS: *Rabana Hasburgh, Holly Howard, Helen Leitch, Daphne Vane, Heidi Vosseler, Charles Laskey.*

TRANSCENDENCE

Choreography by GEORGE BALANCHINE
Music by FRANZ LISZT, *orchestrated by* GEORGE ANTHEIL

Décor by GASTON LONGCHAMP
Costumes by FRANKLIN WATKINS
Book by LINCOLN KIRSTEIN

Première, March 5, 1935, Adelphi Theater, New York. (Prior to the official *Première*, *Transcendence* was presented by the Producing Company of the School of American Ballet, December 6, 1934, in Hartford, Connecticut.) PRINCIPAL DANCERS: *Elise Reiman, William Dollar.*

DREAMS

Choreography by GEORGE BALANCHINE
Music by GEORGE ANTHEIL
Book, costumes, and décor by ANDRÉ DÉRAIN

Première, March 5, 1935, Adelphi Theater, New York. (Revival from Les Ballets 1933.) PRINCIPAL DANCERS: *Leyda Anchutina, Ruthanna Boris, Paul Haakon.*

THE BAT

Choreography by GEORGE BALANCHINE
Music by JOHANN STRAUSS (*Overture to* Die Fledermaus)
Costumes by KEITH MARTIN
Book by LINCOLN KIRSTEIN

Première, season 1935–6, Metropolitan Opera House, New York. PRINCIPAL DANCERS: *Leyda Anchutina, Rabana Hasburgh, Annabelle Lyon, Lew Christensen, Charles Laskey.*

ORPHEUS AND EURYDICE

Choreography by GEORGE BALANCHINE
Music by GLUCK
Costumes and décor by PAVEL TCHELITCHEW

Première, May 22, 1936, Metropolitan Opera House, New York. PRINCIPAL ROLES: *Orpheus*, LEW CHRISTENSEN; *Eurydice*, DAPHNE VANE; *Angel*, WILLIAM DOLLAR.

APOLLON MUSAGÈTE

(later called *Apollo*, and *Apollo, Leader of the Muses*)

Choreography by GEORGE BALANCHINE
Music by IGOR STRAVINSKY
Costumes and décor by STEWART CHANEY

Première, April 27, 1937, Metropolitan Opera House, New York. (Revival from the Diaghilev Ballets Russes.) DANCERS: *Lew Christensen, Daphne Vane, Holly Howard, Elise Reiman, Kyra Blank, Rabana Hasburgh, Jane Burkhalter.*

THE CARD PARTY
(later called *Card Game*)

Choreography by GEORGE BALANCHINE
Music by IGOR STRAVINSKY
Costumes and décor by IRENE SHARAFF
Book by IGOR STRAVINSKY *in collaboration with* M. MALAIEFF

Première, April 27, 1937, Metropolitan Opera House, New York. PRINCIPAL ROLES: *The Joker*, WILLIAM DOLLAR; *Aces*, ANN CAMPBELL, JANE BURKHALTER, LILLIAN MOORE, VERA VOLKENAU; *Kings*, LEW CHRISTENSEN, JOSEPH LANE, DOUGLAS COUDY, ERICK HAWKINS; *Queens*, ANNABELLE LYON, LEYDA ANCHUTINA, ARIEL LANG, HORTENSE KAHRKLIN; *Jacks*, CHARLES LASKEY, JOSEPH LEVINOFF, EUGENE LORING, SERGE TEMOFF.

LE BAISER DE LA FÉE
(later called *The Fairy's Kiss*)

Choreography by GEORGE BALANCHINE
Music by IGOR STRAVINSKY
Costumes and décor by ALICE HALICKA
Book by IGOR STRAVINSKY, *based on a story by* HANS CHRISTIAN ANDERSEN

Première, April 27, 1937, Metropolitan Opera House, New York. PRINCIPAL ROLES: *The Fairy*, KATHRYN MULLOWNY; *Shadow*, RABANA HASBURGH; *Bride*, GISELLA CACCIALANZA; *Friend*, LEYDA ANCHUTINA; *Bridegroom*, WILLIAM DOLLAR; *Mother*, ANNABELLE LYON.

JUKE BOX

Choreography by WILLIAM DOLLAR
Music by ALEC WILDER
Costumes and décor by TOM LEE
Book by LINCOLN KIRSTEIN

Première, May 28, 1941, Hunter College Playhouse, New York. PRINCIPAL DANCERS: *Yvonne Patterson, Rabana Hasburgh, Lew Christensen, William Dollar.*

PASTORELA

Choreography by LEW CHRISTENSEN *and* JOSÉ FERNÁNDEZ
Music by PAUL BOWLES
Costumes and décor by ALVIN COLT
Book by JOSÉ MARTÍNEZ

Première, May 28, 1941, Hunter College Playhouse, New York. PRINCIPAL DANCERS: *Gisella Caccialanza, Beatrice Tompkins, Lew Christensen, José Fernández Todd Bolender, Nicholas Magallanes, Charles Dickson, José Martínez.*

CONCERTO BAROCCO

Choreography by GEORGE BALANCHINE
Music by JOHANN SEBASTIAN BACH (*Double Violin Concerto in D minor*)
Costumes and décor by EUGENE BERMAN
Première, May 28, 1941, Hunter College Playhouse, New York. PRINCIPAL DANCERS: *Marie Jeanne, Mary Jane Shea, William Dollar.*

BALLET IMPERIAL

Choreography by GEORGE BALANCHINE
Music by TCHAIKOVSKY (*Piano Concerto in G major*)
Costumes and décor by MSTISLAV DOBOUJINSKY
Première, May 29, 1941, Hunter College Playhouse, New York. PRINCIPAL DANCERS: *Marie Jeanne, Gisella Caccialanza, William Dollar, Nicholas Magallanes, Fred Danieli.*

2. *The Ballet Caravan*

TIME TABLE

Choreography by ANTONY TUDOR
Music by AARON COPLAND (*Music for the Theater*)
Costumes and décor by JAMES MORCOM
Première, May 29, 1941, Hunter College Playhouse, New York. PRINCIPAL DANCERS: *Marie Jeanne, Gisella Caccialanza, Mary Jane Shea, Beatrice Tompkins, Lew Christensen, John Kriza.*

ENCOUNTER

Choreography by LEW CHRISTENSEN
Music by MOZART (*"Haffner" Serenade*)
Costumes by FORREST THAYR, JR.
Première, July 17, 1936, Bennington, Vermont. PRINCIPAL DANCERS: *Annabelle Lyon, Ruby Asquith, Charles Laskey, Lew Christensen, Harold Christensen.*

HARLEQUIN FOR PRESIDENT

(later called *Harlequin*)

Choreography by EUGENE LORING
Music by DOMENICO SCARLATTI, *orchestrated by* ARIADNA MIKESHINA
Costumes by KEITH MARTIN

Book *by* LINCOLN KIRSTEIN
Première, July 17, 1936, Bennington, Vermont. PRINCIPAL DANCERS: *Annabelle Lyon, Eugene Loring, Charles Laskey, Harold Christensen, Fred Danieli.*

FOLK DANCE

Choreography by DOUGLAS COUDY
Music by EMMANUEL CHABRIER
Costumes by CHARLES RAIN
Première, July, 1936, Burlington, Vermont. PRINCIPAL DANCERS: *Ruthanna Boris, Lew Christensen.*

PROMENADE

Choreography by WILLIAM DOLLAR
Music by MAURICE RAVEL (*Valses Nobles et Sentimentales*)
Costumes after HORACE VERNET
Première, July 17, 1936, Bennington, Vermont. PRINCIPAL DANCERS: *Annabelle Lyon, Ruthanna Boris, Charles Laskey, Erick Hawkins.*

POCAHONTAS

Choreography by LEW CHRISTENSEN
Music by ELLIOTT CARTER, JR.
Costumes by KARL FREE
Book *by* LINCOLN KIRSTEIN
Première, August 17, 1936, Colonial Theater, Keene, New Hampshire. PRINCIPAL DANCERS: *Ruthanna Boris, Lew Christensen, Charles Laskey, Harold Christensen, Erick Hawkins.*

YANKEE CLIPPER

Choreography by EUGENE LORING
Music by PAUL BOWLES
Costumes by CHARLES RAIN
Book *by* LINCOLN KIRSTEIN
Première, July 12, 1937, Town Hall, Saybrook, Connecticut. DANCERS: *Eugene Loring and company.*

SHOW PIECE

Choreography by ERICK HAWKINS
Music by ROBERT MCBRIDE
Costumes by KEITH MARTIN

Première, August 1937, Bar Harbor, Maine. PRINCIPAL DANCERS: *Marie Jeanne, Annabelle Lyon, Eugene Loring, Fred Danieli, Erick Hawkins.*

FILLING STATION

Choreography by LEW CHRISTENSEN
Music by VIRGIL THOMSON
Costumes and décor by PAUL CADMUS
Book by LINCOLN KIRSTEIN

Première, January 6, 1938, Avery Memorial Theater, Hartford, Connecticut. PRINCIPAL DANCERS: *Jane Deering, Marie Jeanne, Marjorie Moore, Todd Bolender, Harold Christensen, Lew Christensen, Douglas Coudy, Fred Danieli, Erick Hawkins, Eugene Loring.*

BILLY THE KID

Choreography by EUGENE LORING
Music by AARON COPLAND
Costumes by JARED FRENCH
Book by LINCOLN KIRSTEIN

Première, October 16, 1938, Chicago Opera House. PRINCIPAL ROLES: *Billy,* EUGENE LORING; *Mother and Sweetheart,* MARIE JEANNE; *Pat Garrett,* LEW CHRISTENSEN; *Alias,* TODD BOLENDER.

AIR AND VARIATIONS

Choreography by WILLIAM DOLLAR
Music by JOHANN SEBASTIAN BACH *("Goldberg" Variations, arranged for two pianos by* TRUDE RITTMANN*)*
Costumes by WALTER GIFFORD

Première, November 1938, Athens, Georgia. DANCERS: *The entire company.*

CHARADE, or THE DEBUTANTE

Choreography by LEW CHRISTENSEN
American melodies, arranged by TRUDE RITTMANN
Costumes by ALVIN COLT
Book by LINCOLN KIRSTEIN

Première, December 26, 1939, St. James Theater, New York. PRINCIPAL DANCERS: *Gisella Caccialanza, Lew Christensen, Harold Christensen.*

CITY PORTRAIT

Choreography by EUGENE LORING
Music by HENRY BRANT

Décor by JAMES MORCOM
Costumes by FELIPE FIOCCA
Book by LINCOLN KIRSTEIN

Première, December 28, 1939, St. James Theater, New York. DANCERS: *Eugene Loring and entire company.*

3. *Ballet Society*

THE SPELLBOUND CHILD

Choreography by GEORGE BALANCHINE
Music by MAURICE RAVEL (*L'Enfant et les sortilèges*)
Costumes and décor by ALINE BERNSTEIN
Poem by COLETTE

Première, November 20, 1946, Central High School of Needle Trades, New York. PRINCIPAL DANCERS: *Gisella Caccialanza, Ruth Gilbert, Georgia Hiden, Tanaquil LeClercq, Elise Reiman, Beatrice Tompkins, Paul d'Amboise, William Dollar.*

THE FOUR TEMPERAMENTS

Choreography by GEORGE BALANCHINE
Music by PAUL HINDEMITH
Costumes and décor by KURT SELIGMANN

Première, November 20, 1946, Central High School of Needle Trades, New York. PRINCIPAL DANCERS; *Gisella Caccialanza, Georgia Hiden, Rita Karlin, Tanaquil LeClercq, Mary Ellen Moylan, Elise Reiman, Beatrice Tompkins, Todd Bolender, Lew Christensen, Fred Danieli, William Dollar, José Martínez, Francisco Moncion.*

RENARD (THE FOX)

Choreography by GEORGE BALANCHINE
Music by IGOR STRAVINSKY
Costumes and décor by ESTEBAN FRANCÉS
Book by IGOR STRAVINSKY, *English text by* HARVEY OFFICER

Première, January 13, 1947, Hunter College Playhouse, New York. PRINCIPAL ROLES: *The Fox*, TODD BOLENDER; *The Rooster*, LEW CHRISTENSEN; *The Cat*, FRED DANIELI; *The Ram*, JOHN TARAS.

DIVERTIMENTO

Choreography by GEORGE BALANCHINE
Music by ALEXEI HAIEFF

Première, January 13, 1947, Hunter College Playhouse, New York. DANCERS: *Gisella Caccialanza, Tanaquil LeClercq, Mary Ellen Moylan, Elise Reiman, Beatrice Tompkins, Todd Bolender, Lew Christensen, Fred Danieli, Francisco Moncion, John Taras.*

THE MINOTAUR

Choreography by JOHN TARAS
Music by ELLIOTT CARTER
Costumes and décor by JOAN JUNYER
Book by LINCOLN KIRSTEIN *and* JOAN JUNYER

Première, March 26, 1947, Central High School of Needle Trades, New York. PRINCIPAL ROLES: *Pasiphaë, Queen of Crete*, ELISE REIMAN; *Minos, King of Crete*, EDWARD BIGELOW; *Ariadne*, TANAQUIL LECLERCQ; *Theseus*, JOHN TARAS; *Bulls*, FRED DANIELI *and* PAUL D'AMBOISE.

ZODIAC

Choreography by TODD BOLENDER
Music by RUDI REVIL
Costumes and décor by ESTEBAN FRANCÉS

Première, March 26, 1947, Central High School of Needle Trades, New York. PRINCIPAL DANCERS: *Virginia Barnes, William Dollar, Todd Bolender, Job Sanders, Pat McBride, Janice Roman, Ruth Sobotka, Jean Reeves, Irma Sandré, Joan Djorup, Marc Beaudet, John Scancarella, Betty Nichols, Gisella Caccialanza, Edward Bigelow, Gerard Leavitt.*

HIGHLAND FLING

Choreography by WILLIAM DOLLAR
Music by STANLEY BATE
Costumes and décor by DAVID FFOLKES

Première, March 26, 1947, Central High School of Needle Trades, New York. PRINCIPAL ROLES: *Bride*, GISELLA CACCIALANZA; *Groom*, TODD BOLENDER, *Sylphide*, ELISE REIMAN; *Bridesmaids*, TANAQUIL LECLERCQ AND BEATRICE TOMPKINS; *Minister*, JOSÉ MARTÍNEZ.

THE SEASONS

Choreography by MERCE CUNNINGHAM
Music by JOHN CAGE
Costumes and décor by ISAMU NOGUCHI

Première, May 18, 1947, Ziegfeld Theater, New York. PRINCIPAL DANCERS: *Gisella Caccialanza, Tanaquil LeClercq, Beatrice Tompkins, Merce Cunningham.*

BLACKFACE

Choreography by LEW CHRISTENSEN
Music by CARTER HARMAN
Costumes and décor by ROBERT DREW

Première, May 18, 1947, Ziegfeld Theater, New York. PRINCIPAL DANCERS: *Betty Nichols, Beatrice Tompkins, Talley Beatty, Marc Beaudet, Fred Danieli, Paul Godkin.*

PUNCH AND THE CHILD

Choreography by FRED DANIELI
Music by RICHARD ARNELL
Costumes and décor by HORACE ARMISTEAD

Première, November 12, 1947, City Center of Music and Drama, New York. PRINCIPAL ROLES: *Father and Punch*, HERBERT BLISS; *Mother and Judy*, BEATRICE TOMPKINS; *the Child*, JUDITH KURSCH; *Fishwife and Polly*, GISELLA CACCIALANZA; *Peg Leg and Constable*, CHARLES LASKEY; *Puppeteer and Devil*, LEW CHRISTENSEN; *Musician and Doctor*, EDWARD BIGELOW; *Street Cleaner and Hangman*, VICTOR DUNTIERE; *Professor*, LUIS LÓPEZ.

SYMPHONIE CONCERTANTE

Choreography by GEORGE BALANCHINE
Music by MOZART (*Symphonie Concertante in E flat, K.364*)
Costumes and décor by JAMES STEWART MORCOM

Première, November 12, 1947, City Center of Music and Drama, New York. (Prior to *première, Symphonie Concertante* was presented November 5, 1945, at Carnegie Hall, New York, on a program *Adventure in Ballet* by pupils of the School of American Ballet.) PRINCIPAL DANCERS: *Maria Tallchief, Tanaquil LeClercq, Dorothy Dushok, Ruth Gilbert, Georgia Hiden, Rita Karlin, Pat McBride, Irma Sandré, Todd Bolender.*

THE TRIUMPH OF BACCHUS AND ARIADNE
(Ballet-Cantata)

Choreography by GEORGE BALANCHINE
Music by VITTORIO RIETI
Costumes and décor by CORRADO CAGLI

Première, February 9, 1948, City Center of Music and Drama, New York. PRINCIPAL ROLES: *Major-domo*, LEW CHRISTENSEN; *Bacchus*, NICHOLAS MAGAL-LANES; *Ariadne*, TANAQUIL LECLERCQ; *First Satyr*, HERBERT BLISS; *First Nymph*, MARIE JEANNE; *Silenus*, CHARLES LASKEY; *Midas*, FRANCISCO MONCION; *the Little Girl*, CLAUDIA HALL; *the Young Girl*, PAT MCBRIDE.

CAPRICORN CONCERTO

Choreography by TODD BOLENDER
Music by SAMUEL BARBER
Costumes and décor by ESTEBAN FRANCÉS

Première, March 22, 1948, City Center of Music and Drama, New York. PRINCIPAL DANCERS: *Maria Tallchief, Herbert Bliss, Francisco Moncion.*

SYMPHONY IN C

Choreography by GEORGE BALANCHINE
Music by GEORGES BIZET

Première, March 22, 1948, City Center of Music and Drama, New York. (First produced for the Paris *Opéra* under the title *Palais de Cristal,* July 28, 1947.) PRINCIPAL DANCERS: *First Movement, Maria Tallchief, Nicholas Magallanes; Second Movement, Tanaquil LeClercq, Francisco Moncion; Third Movement, Beatrice Tompkins, Herbert Bliss; Fourth Movement, Elise Reiman, Lew Christensen.*

ELEGIE

Choreography by GEORGE BALANCHINE
Music by IGOR STRAVINSKY

Première, April 28, 1948, City Center of Music and Drama, New York. (Prior to *première, Elegie* was presented November 5, 1945, at Carnegie Hall, New York, on a program *Adventure in Ballet* by pupils of the School of American Ballet.) *Danced by* TANAQUIL LECLERCQ *and* PAT MCBRIDE.

ORPHEUS

Choreography by GEORGE BALANCHINE
Music by IGOR STRAVINSKY
Costumes and décor by ISAMU NOGUCHI

Première, April 28, 1948, City Center of Music and Drama, New York. PRINCIPAL ROLES: *Orpheus,* NICHOLAS MAGALLANES; *Dark Angel,* FRANCISCO MONCION; *Eurydice,* MARIA TALLCHIEF; *Apollo,* HERBERT BLISS; *Pluto,* EDWARD BIGELOW; *Satyr,* JOB SANDERS; *Leader of the Bacchantes,* TANAQUIL LECLERCQ; *Leader of the Furies,* BEATRICE TOMPKINS.

4. *New York City Ballet*

MOTHER GOOSE SUITE

Choreography by TODD BOLENDER
Music by MAURICE RAVEL

Première, November 1, 1948, City Center of Music and Drama, New York. (Revival from the American Concert Ballet, 1941.) PRINCIPAL ROLES: *Spectator*, BEATRICE TOMPKINS; *Young Girl*, MARIE JEANNE; *Hop o' My Thumb*, TODD BOLENDER; *Bird*, UNA KAI; *Prince*, DICK BEARD; *Beast*, FRANCISCO MONCION.

THE GUESTS

Choreography by JEROME ROBBINS
Music by MARC BLITZSTEIN

Première, January 20, 1949, City Center of Music and Drama, New York. PRINCIPAL DANCERS: *Maria Tallchief, Francisco Moncion, Nicholas Magallanes.*

JINX

Choreography by LEW CHRISTENSEN
Music by BENJAMIN BRITTEN (*Variations on a theme by Frank Bridge*)
Costumes and décor by GEORGE BOCKMAN
Story by LEW CHRISTENSEN

Première, November 24, 1949, City Center of Music and Drama, New York. (Revival from Dance Players, 1942.) CAST: *Jinx, a Clown*, FRANCISCO MONCION; *Wirewalkers*, JANET REED, RUTH SOBOTKA, FRANK HOBI; *Equestrians*, HERBERT BLISS, BARBARA MILBERG, BARBARA WALCZAK; *Bearded Lady*, BEATRICE TOMPKINS; *Strong Lady*, GEORGIA HIDEN; *Tattooed Lady*, DOROTHY DUSHOK; *Ringmaster*, VAL BUTTIGNOL.

FIREBIRD

Choreography by GEORGE BALANCHINE
Music by IGOR STRAVINSKY
Costumes and décor by MARC CHAGALL

Première, November 27, 1949, City Center of Music and Drama, New York. PRINCIPAL ROLES: *Firebird*, MARIA TALLCHIEF; *Prince Ivan*, FRANCISCO MONCION; *Prince's Bride*, PAT MCBRIDE; *Kastchei*, EDWARD BIGELOW.

BOURRÉE FANTASQUE

Choreography by GEORGE BALANCHINE
Music by EMMANUEL CHABRIER
Costumes by KARINSKA

Première, December 1, 1949, City Center of Music and Drama, New York. PRINCIPAL DANCERS: *Bourrée Fantasque*—TANAQUIL LECLERCQ, JEROME ROBBINS; *Prelude*—MARIA TALLCHIEF, NICHOLAS MAGALLANES, EDWINA FONTAINE, YVONNE MOUNSEY; *Fête Polonaise*—JANET REED, HERBERT BLISS.

ONDINE

Choreography by WILLIAM DOLLAR
Music by ANTONIO VIVALDI (*Violin concertos*)
Costumes and décor by HORACE ARMISTEAD
Première, December 9, 1949, City Center of Music and Drama, New York.
PRINCIPAL ROLES: *Ondine*, TANAQUIL LECLERCQ; *Matteo*, FRANCISCO MONCION; *Giannina*, MELISSA HAYDEN; *Hydrola*, YVONNE MOUNSEY.

THE PRODIGAL SON

Choreography by GEORGE BALANCHINE
Music by SERGE PROKOVIEV
Costumes and décor by GEORGES ROUAULT
Première, February 23, 1950, City Center of Music and Drama, New York. (Revival from the Diaghilev Ballet, 1929.) PRINCIPAL ROLES: *The Prodigal Son*, JEROME ROBBINS; *The Siren*, MARIA TALLCHIEF; *The Father*, MICHAEL ARSHANSKY; *Servants to the Prodigal Son*, FRANK HOBI, HERBERT BLISS; *the Two Sisters*, JILLANA, FRANCESCA MOSARRA.

THE DUEL

Choreography by WILLIAM DOLLAR
Music by RAFFAELLO DE BANFIELD
Costumes by ROBERT STEVENSON
Première, February 24, 1950, City Center of Music and Drama, New York. DANCERS: *Melissa Hayden, William Dollar, Val Buttignol, Walter Georgov, Shaun O'Brien.*

AGE OF ANXIETY

Choreography by JEROME ROBBINS
Music by LEONARD BERNSTEIN (*Symphony No. 2*)
Décor by OLIVER SMITH
Costumes by IRENE SHARAFF
Based on the poem of the same name by W. H. AUDEN
Première, February 26, 1950, City Center of Music and Drama, New York. PRINCIPAL DANCERS: *Tanaquil LeClercq, Todd Bolender, Francisco Moncion, Jerome Robbins, Melissa Hayden, Pat McBride, Yvonne Mounsey, Beatrice Tompkins, Edward Bigelow, Herbert Bliss.*

ILLUMINATIONS

Choreography by FREDERICK ASHTON
Music by BENJAMIN BRITTEN (*Les Illuminations*, for tenor and strings)

Costumes and décor by CECIL BEATON
Based on poems by ARTHUR RIMBAUD
Première, March 2, 1950, City Center of Music and Drama, New York.
PRINCIPAL ROLES: *Poet*, NICHOLAS MAGALLANES; *Sacred Love*, TANAQUIL
LECLERCQ; *Profane Love*, MELISSA HAYDEN.

PAS DE DEUX ROMANTIQUE

Choreography by GEORGE BALANCHINE
Music by CARL MARIA VON WEBER (*Concertino for Clarinet*)
Costumes by ROBERT STEVENSON
Première, March 3, 1950, City Center of Music and Drama, New York.
DANCERS: *Janet Reed and Herbert Bliss.*

JONES BEACH

Choreography by GEORGE BALANCHINE *and* JEROME ROBBINS
Music by JURIAAN ANDRIESSEN (*Berkshire Symphonies*)
Première, March 9, 1950, City Center of Music and Drama, New York.
PRINCIPAL DANCERS: *Melissa Hayden, Tanaquil LeClercq, Yvonne Mounsey,
Maria Tallchief, Beatrice Tompkins, Herbert Bliss, Todd Bolender, William
Dollar, Frank Hobi, Nicholas Magallanes, Jerome Robbins, Roy Tobias.*

THE WITCH

Choreography by JOHN CRANKO
Music by MAURICE RAVEL (*Piano Concerto*)
Costumes and décor by DOROTHEA TANNING
Première, August 18, 1950, Royal Opera House, Covent Garden, London.
PRINCIPAL DANCERS: *Melissa Hayden, Francisco Moncion.*

MAZURKA from A LIFE FOR THE TSAR

Choreography by GEORGE BALANCHINE
Music by MIKHAIL GLINKA
Première, November 30, 1950, City Center of Music and Drama, New York.
DANCERS: *Janet Reed and Yurek Lazowski; Vida Brown and George Balanchine;
Barbara Walczak and Harold Lang; Dorothy Dushok and Frank Hobi.*

SYLVIA: PAS DE DEUX

Choreography by GEORGE BALANCHINE
Music by LÉO DELIBES
Costumes by KARINSKA

Première, December 1, 1950, City Center of Music and Drama, New York. DANCERS: *Maria Tallchief and Nicholas Magallanes.*

PAS DE TROIS

Choreography by GEORGE BALANCHINE
Music by LEON MINKUS (From *Don Quixote*)
Costumes by KARINSKA
Première, February 18, 1951, City Center of Music and Drama, New York.
(Revival from Grand Ballet du Marquis de Cuevas, 1948.) DANCERS: *Maria Tallchief, Nora Kaye, André Eglevsky.*

LA VALSE

Choreography by GEORGE BALANCHINE
Music by MAURICE RAVEL (*Valses Nobles et Sentimentales,* and
   La Valse)
Costumes by KARINSKA
Première, February 20, 1951, City Center of Music and Drama, New York.
PRINCIPAL DANCERS: *Diana Adams, Tanaquil LeClercq, Yvonne Mounsey, Patricia Wilde, Herbert Bliss, Frank Hobi, Nicholas Magallanes, Francisco Moncion.*

LADY OF THE CAMELLIAS

Choreography by ANTONY TUDOR
Music by GIUSEPPE VERDI (*selection*)
Costumes and décor by CECIL BEATON
Story after the novel by ALEXANDRE DUMAS *fils*
Première, February 28, 1951, City Center of Music and Drama, New York.
PRINCIPAL ROLES: *Prudence,* VIDA BROWN; *Marguerite Gautier,* DIANA ADAMS;
M. le Comte de N., BROOKS JACKSON; *Armand Duval,* HUGH LAING; *Armand's Father,* JOHN EARLE (Antony Tudor).

CAPRICCIO BRILLANT

Choreography by GEORGE BALANCHINE
Music by FELIX MENDELSSOHN
Costumes by KARINSKA
Première, June 7, 1951, City Center of Music and Drama, New York.
DANCERS: *Maria Tallchief and André Eglevsky; Barbara Bocher, Constance Garfield, Jillana, Irene Larsson.*

CAKEWALK

Choreography by RUTHANNA BORIS
Music by LOUIS MOREAU GOTTSCHALK, *arranged and orchestrated by*
   HERSHY KAY

Costumes and décor by ROBERT DREW
Première, June 12, 1951, City Center of Music and Drama, New York.
PRINCIPAL DANCERS: *Tanaquil LeClercq, Yvonne Mounsey, Janet Reed, Beatrice Tompkins, Patricia Wilde, Herbert Bliss, Frank Hobi.*

THE CAGE

Choreography by JEROME ROBBINS
Music by IGOR STRAVINSKY (*String Concerto in D*)
Costumes by RUTH SOBOTKA
Première, June 14, 1951, City Center of Music and Drama, New York.
PRINCIPAL ROLES: *The Novice,* NORA KAYE; *The Queen,* YVONNE MOUNSEY;
The Intruders, NICHOLAS MAGALLANES, MICHAEL MAULE.

THE MIRACULOUS MANDARIN

Choreography by TODD BOLENDER
Music by BÉLA BARTÓK
Costumes and décor by ALVIN COLT
Libretto after MELCHIOR LANGYEL
Première, September 6, 1951, City Center of Music and Drama, New York.
CAST: *The Men,* ROBERT BARNETT, EDWARD BIGELOW, JACQUES D'AMBOISE,
WALTER GEORGOV, MICHAEL MAULE; *The Woman,* MELISSA HAYDEN; *An Old Man,* FRANK HOBI; *A Young Man,* ROY TOBIAS; *A Blind Girl,* BEATRICE TOMPKINS; *The Mandarin,* HUGH LAING.

A LA FRANÇAIX

Choreography by GEORGE BALANCHINE
Music by JEAN FRANÇAIX (*Serenade for Small Orchestra*)
Première, September 11, 1951, City Center of Music and Drama, New York.
DANCERS: *Janet Reed, Maria Tallchief, André Eglevsky, Frank Hobi, Roy Tobias.*

TYL ULENSPIEGEL

Choreography by GEORGE BALANCHINE
Music by RICHARD STRAUSS
Costumes and décor by ESTEBAN FRANCÉS
Première, November 14, 1951, City Center of Music and Drama, New York.
PRINCIPAL ROLES: *Tyl Ulenspiegel as a child,* ALBERT GRANT; *Philip II as a child,* SUSAN KOVNAT; *Tyl Ulenspiegel,* JEROME ROBBINS; *Nell, his wife,* RUTH SOBOTKA; *Philip II, King of Spain,* BROOKS JACKSON; *Duke and Duchess,* FRANK HOBI and BEATRICE TOMPKINS; *Woman,* TOMI WORTHAM.

SWAN LAKE

Choreography by GEORGE BALANCHINE (*after Lev Ivanov*)
Music by TCHAIKOVSKY
Costumes and décor by CECIL BEATON
Première, November 20, 1951, City Center of Music and Drama, New York.
PRINCIPAL ROLES: *Odette*, MARIA TALLCHIEF; *Prince Siegfried*, ANDRÉ EGLEVSKY; *Benno*, FRANK HOBI; *Leading Swans*, PATRICIA WILDE *and* YVONNE MOUNSEY; *Cygnets*, DORIS BRECKENRIDGE, KAYE SARGENT, RUTH SOBOTKA, GLORIA VAUGES; *Von Rothbart, a Sorcerer*, EDWARD BIGELOW.

LILAC GARDEN

Choreography by ANTONY TUDOR
Music by ERNEST CHAUSSON (*Poème*)
Décor by HORACE ARMISTEAD
Costumes by KARINSKA
Première, November 30, 1951, City Center of Music and Drama, New York. (Revival from Ballet Rambert, 1936, when it was given under the title *Jardin aux Lilas*.) PRINCIPAL ROLES: *Caroline*, NORA KAYE; *Her Lover*, HUGH LAING; *The Man She Must Marry*, ANTONY TUDOR; *The Woman in His Past*, TANAQUIL LECLERCQ.

THE PIED PIPER

Choreography by JEROME ROBBINS
Music by AARON COPLAND (*Concerto for Clarinet and String Orchestra*)
Première, December 4, 1951, City Center of Music and Drama, New York.
PRINCIPAL DANCERS: *Diana Adams, Melissa Hayden, Jillana, Tanaquil LeClercq, Janet Reed, Barbara Bocher, Herbert Bliss, Todd Bolender, Nicholas Magallanes, Jerome Robbins, Roy Tobias.*

BALLADE

Choreography by JEROME ROBBINS
Music by CLAUDE DEBUSSY (*Six Epigraphes Antiques*)
Costumes and décor by BORIS ARONSON
Première, February 14, 1952, City Center of Music and Drama, New York.
DANCERS: *Nora Kaye, Tanaquil LeClercq, Janet Reed, Robert Barnett, Brooks Jackson, Louis Johnson, John Mandia, Roy Tobias.*

CARACOLE

Choreography by GEORGE BALANCHINE
Music by MOZART (*Divertimento No. 15 in B flat major, K.287*)

Costumes by CHRISTIAN BÉRARD
Première, February 19, 1952, City Center of Music and Drama, New York.
PRINCIPAL DANCERS: *Diana Adams, Melissa Hayden, Tanaquil LeClercq, Maria Tallchief, Patricia Wilde, André Eglevsky, Nicholas Magallanes, Jerome Robbins.*

BAYOU

Choreography by GEORGE BALANCHINE
Music by VIRGIL THOMSON (*Acadian Songs and Dances*)
Costumes and décor by DOROTHEA TANNING
Première, February 21, 1952, City Center of Music and Drama, New York.
PRINCIPAL ROLES: *Boy of the Bayou*, FRANCISCO MONCION; *Girl of the Bayou*, DORIS BRECKENRIDGE; *Leaves and Flowers*, MELISSA HAYDEN, HUGH LAING, IRENE LARSSON, BARBARA WALCZAK, WALTER GEORGOV, STANLEY ZOMPAKOS; *Starched White People*, DIANA ADAMS, HERBERT BLISS, UNA KAI, MARILYN POUDRIER, BROOKS JACKSON, SHAUN O'BRIEN.

LA GLOIRE

Choreography by ANTONY TUDOR
Music by BEETHOVEN (*Egmont, Coriolanus, Leonora III* overtures)
Décor by GASTON LONGCHAMP
Costumes by ROBERT FLETCHER
Première, February 26, 1952, City Center of Music and Drama, New York.
PRINCIPAL ROLES: *La Gloire*, NORA KAYE; *Sextus Tarquinius and Hamlet's Step-father*, FRANCISCO MONCION; *Hippolytus and Laertes*, HUGH LAING; *Ophelia*, DORIS BRECKENRIDGE; *Hamlet's Mother*, BEATRICE TOMPKINS; *the Dancer in Gray*, DIANA ADAMS.

PICNIC AT TINTAGEL

Choreography by FREDERICK ASHTON
Music by SIR ARNOLD BAX (*The Garden of Fand*)
Costumes and décor by CECIL BEATON
Première, February 28, 1952, City Center of Music and Drama, New York.
CAST: *The Husband (King Mark)*, FRANCISCO MONCION; *The Wife (Iseult)*, DIANA ADAMS; *Her Maid (Brangaene)*, YVONNE MOUNSEY; *Her Lover (Tristram)*, JACQUES D'AMBOISE; *His Rivals (the False Knights)*, STANLEY ZOMPAKOS, BROOKS JACKSON; *Her Chauffeur and Footman (Heralds)*, ALAN BAKER, JOHN MANDIA; *The Caretaker (Merlin)*, ROBERT BARNETT.

Index

Acadian Songs and Dances, 295, 325

Adam, Adolphe, 279

Adams, Diana, 221, 266–267, 268, 269, 273, 276, 281, 282, 284, 295, 303, 308, 316, 329, 330, 331, 333, 361

Adams, Henry, 302

Adventures in Ballet, 151, 182

Age of Anxiety, 232, 233, 239–241, 242, 250, 252, 253, 255, 256, 261, 277, 281, 303, 377

Aïda, 64, 65

Air and Variations, 117, 371

À la Française, 298, 302, 360, 380

Albertieri, Luigi, 34

Aleko, 267

Alma Mater, 31, 32, 33, 38, 40, 41, 43, 44, 48, 51, 365–366

Altdorfer, Albrecht, 304

Alvarez, Anita, 334

Amahl and the Night Visitors, 165

Amati, Olga, 334

Amazons, The (see *The Cage*)

Amelia Goes to the Ball, 165

American Ballet, The, *ubique*

American Ballet, The (book), 49

American Concert Ballet, 149–150

American Guild of Musical Artists (AGMA), 158, 221

American National Theatre and Academy (ANTA), 241

Anchutina, Leda (also, Leyda), 38, 44, 63, 82, 86, 91, 98, 122

Andrews, E. O., 146

Andriessen, Jurriaan, 232, 243, 244

Anna Pavlova (book), 158

Antheil, George, 30, 31, 38

Apollo (see also *Apollon Musagète*), 276, 294, 295, 298, 303, 307–308

Apollo, Leader of the Muses (see *Apollo* and *Apollon Musagète*)

Apollon Musagète (see also *Apollo*), 14, 85–86, 134, 175, 181, 196, 307, 367

Apparitions, 45

i

Archibald, William, 185–186
Archives Internationales de la Danse, 141
Armistead, Horace, 165–166, 183, 185, 228, 315
Armstrong, Robert, 123
Arnell, Richard, 183
Aronson, Boris, 326, 327
Arshansky, Michael, 238
Arts Council of Great Britain, 250
Ashton, Frederick, 45, 85, 92, 231, 236, 242, 251, 255, 256, 257, 291, 293, 294, 303, 326, 332, 333, 356
Association of Dance Critics (Paris), 175
Asquith, Ruby, 78, 82, 94, 108
Astor, Mrs. Vincent, 236
A Thousand Times Neigh!, 122
Auber, Daniel François, 288
Auden, W. H., 232, 240
"Augusta Maywood" (article), 146
Auric, Georges, 14, 15, 185, 324, 343
Auriol, Vincent, 349
Auriol, Mme Vincent, 349
Aurora's Wedding, 112
Austin, A. Everett, 24
Avray, Robert, 135

Babes in Arms, 88
Babilée, Jean, 300, 304
Bach, Johann Sebastian, 92, 117, 134, 148, 244
Baiser de la Fée, Le, 85, 96, 175, 181, 268, 270, 282, 303, 368
Baker, Alan, 287
Baker, Constance, 287, 303
Bakst, Leon, 8
Bal, Le, 14
Balaban, Emanuel, 135, 164, 250
Balanchine, George, *ubique*
Balantchivadze, Gheorghi Melitono-vitch, 7, 8, 9, 10, 11, 12, 13
Balantchivadze, Meliton, 7
Ballade, 325, 327, 328, 333, 381
Ballet (publication), 259–260
Ballet Alicia Alonso, 217
Ballet Alphabet (book), 141
Ballet Annual (publication), 263–264
Ballet Associates in America, 235–236, 249, 274, 284, 301, 318
Ballet Caravan, *ubique*
Ballet Club (London), 266

"Ballet d'Action Before Noverre, The" (article), 146
Ballet Imperial, 134, 148, 151, 230, 234, 246, 247, 248, 334, 343, 351, 369
Ballet International, 165, 169, 187, 191, 201, 275
Ballet Rambert, 315, 360
"Ballet: Record and Augury" (article), 127–129
Ballet Russe de Monte Carlo, 78, 81, 90–91, 102, 103, 111, 137, 150, 151, 169, 175, 180, 181, 182, 187, 188, 189, 210, 217, 218, 220, 221, 224, 270, 274, 275, 285, 286, 288, 295, 319
Ballet Russe Highlights, 275
Ballet Society, *ubique*
Ballet Society Bulletin, 157–158, 190
Ballet Society Year Book, 157–158, 172
Ballet Theatre, 119, 120, 121, 123, 131, 135, 150, 151, 168, 177, 180, 183, 213, 214, 217, 218, 220, 221, 222, 224, 225, 235, 253, 255, 266, 267, 269, 274, 275, 276, 278, 279, 285, 294, 300, 304, 310, 315, 345, 358
Ballet Today (publication), 262, 298
Ballets de Janine Charrat, 339
Ballets de Paris, 232, 268, 339
Ballets des Champs-Elysées, 339, 346
Ballets 1933, Les, 15, 16, 18, 19, 20, 30, 70, 102, 234
Ballets Russes de Monte Carlo, 15, 16, 17, 37, 50, 295
Ballets Russes de Serge Diaghilev, 3–5, 13, 14, 35, 51, 85, 126, 164, 221, 234, 253, 271, 342, 353, 362
Barabau, 14
Barber, Samuel, 192
Barn Dance, 254
Barnes, Virginia, 158
Barnett, Robert, 249, 333
Baronova, Irina, 14, 137
Bartók, Béla, 280, 293, 299
Barzel, Ann, 95, 115, 146, 173, 284
Barzin, Jane, 160
Barzin, Leon, 152, 156, 159, 189, 207, 244, 250, 269, 281
Bat, The, 65, 82, 134, 367
Bate, Stanley, 168
Baum, Lester, 202

Baum, Morton, 178–179, 180, 201–
205, 210, 211, 216, 218, 219, 222,
223, 227, 234, 235, 244, 247, 250,
261, 264, 268, 273, 274, 282, 285,
286, 291, 293, 294, 295, 296, 297,
319, 320, 322, 323, 324, 334, 336,
337
Bax, Sir Arnold, 295, 326
Bayou (see also *Bayou Belle*), 325,
329, 382
Bayou Belle (see also *Bayou*), 295, 325
Beard, Dick, 189, 209, 241, 249
Beaton, Cecil, 168, 231, 242, 244, 274,
282, 294, 296, 304, 311, 326, 332
Beau Danube, Le, 112, 138
Beaumont, Cyril W., 255, 259, 260–
261
Beauty and the Beast, 190–191
Becque, Don Oscar, 83
Beethoven, Ludwig van, 326, 330
Belcher, Ernest, 180
Belle et la Bête, La, 185
Bellini, Vincenzo, 151
Bennett, Tom, 122
Benois, Alexandre, 8, 151
Bérard, Christian, 15, 38, 185, 325
Bergerson, Baldwin, 185
Berkshire Symphonies, 232
Berlin Cultural Festival 1952, 362
Berman, Eugene, 134, 146, 150, 151,
207–208
Berners, Lord, 14
Bernstein, Aline, 160
Bernstein, Leonard, 232, 241, 244
Bibliography of Dancing, A (book),
141–142
Bien-Aimée, La, 45
Bigelow, Edward, 149, 158, 183, 241,
249
Billion Dollar Baby, 214
Billy the Kid, 114, 115, 116, 117, 118,
134, 138, 155, 173, 371
"Birth of the Waltz, The" (article),
146
Bizet, Georges, 175, 192, 193, 279
Blackface, 171, 172, 288, 347
Bland, Hubert, 158
Blank, Kyra, 82, 98, 102, 124
Blast at Ballet (book), 16, 64, 71, 88,
89, 93, 109–113, 120, 141
Bliss, Herbert, 180, 181–182, 183, 185,
189, 192, 193, 198, 201, 207, 224,
225, 228, 238, 241, 242, 243, 249,

Bliss (*continued*)
268, 270, 272, 281, 289, 316, 325,
330
Blitzstein, Marc, 212, 215, 244
Block, May, 98
Blok, Alexander, 9
Bluebeard, 225
Blue Bell, or the Favorite, 171
Blum, René, 15, 34, 102, 275
Bobitcheff, Vera, 122
Bocher, Barbara, 249, 287, 303
Bolender, Todd, 108, 123, 135, 149,
152, 158, 161, 164, 168, 169, 183,
184, 192, 207, 208, 224, 241, 249,
268, 278, 286, 293, 299, 300, 301,
304, 316
Bolger, Ray, 66, 67
Bolm, Adolph, 35, 85, 120, 221
Boris, Ruthanna, 38, 78, 82, 94, 286,
288, 289
Bosch, Hieronymus, 304, 305, 306
Bourgeois-Gentilhomme, Le, 15, 150
Bourman, Anatole, 35
Bourrée Fantasque, 222, 227–228, 250,
253, 260, 268, 270, 277, 304, 344,
350, 352, 376
Bowles, Paul, 93, 134, 161
Bowman, Patricia, 36
Boyce, Sir Leslie, 359
Brahms Variations, 201
Brand, Henry, 38, 92, 118
Brecht, Berthold, 15
Breckenridge, Dorothy, 249, 278, 310,
330
Breyman, Annia, 38, 63
Britten, Benjamin, 225, 231, 242, 244
Brown, Vida, 250, 271, 281
Bruce, Betty, 106
Buckle, Richard, 257, 259–26
Bunker, Ellsworth, 351
Burkhalter, Jane, 82
Buttignol, Val, 239

Caccialanza, Gisella, 38, 63, 78, 82,
86, 91, 98, 108, 135, 158, 161, 164,
183
Cadmus, Fidelma (see also, Kirstein,
Mrs. Lincoln), 135
Cadmus, Paul, 94, 141, 258
Cafarelli, Angelo, 149
Cage, Betty, 250, 268, 355
Cage, John, 171

Cage, The, 286, 289–291, 298, 303, 327, 344, 348, 349, 351, 352, 353, 354, 355, 357, 358, 380
Cagli, Corrado, 154, 188, 189
Cakewalk, 286, 288–289, 304, 360, 379–380
Call Me Mister, 183
Camille, 168, 235, 274
Campbell, Ann, 82, 108
Candide (Paris weekly), 346
Candle for St. Jude, A, 325
Cantilena for Oboe and String Orchestra, 184–185
Caponsacchi, 82
Capriccio Brillant, 286, 287–288, 379
Capricorn Concerto, 192, 375
Caracole, 325, 328, 360, 361, 381–382
Card Game (see also *Card Party*), 274
Card Party (see also *Card Game*), 85–88, 277–278, 289, 368
Carlin, Herbert, 284
Carmen (ballet), 268
Carmen (opera), 64, 65, 82
Carnegie Hall, 152, 182
Carousel, 105
Carrefour (Paris newspaper), 176
Carter, Elliott, Jr., 79, 167
Cartier-Bresson, Henri, 163
Case, Arlouine, 249, 303
Cavalleria Rusticana, 70
Cave of Sleep, The, 160
Cecchetti, Enrico, 29, 34, 38, 221
Central High School of Needle Trades, 159, 162, 168, 170
Cercle Carpeaux (Paris), 344
Cerito, Fanny, 228
Chabrier, Emmanuel, 15, 79, 94, 222, 227, 280
Chaffee, George, 146
Chagall, Marc, 221, 222, 226, 228, 244, 256, 347, 348
Chaliapin, Feodor, 38
Chaney, Stewart, 86
Chapin, Selden, 354
Charade or The Debutante, 118, 134, 371
Chase, Lucia, 119
Chaplin, Charles, 325
Chatte, La, 14
Chausson, Ernest, 315
Chicago Civic Opera House, 284
Chopin Concerto, 58, 65, 79
Christensen, Harold, 78, 82, 94, 95, 118

Christensen, Lew, 69, 78, 79, 82, 86, 94, 95, 96, 97, 108, 114, 117, 118, 124, 134, 135, 156, 158, 161, 163, 164, 171, 172, 183, 222, 225, 239, 250
Christensen, Willam, 224
Chujoy, Anatole, 146
Cimarosa, Domenico, 83
Cimarosiana, 271
Circus Polka, 152
Cirque de Deux, 288
City Center (see New York City Center of Music and Drama)
City Portrait, 118, 371–372
Classic Ballet, The (book), 141
Cleopatra, 35
Cocteau, Jean, 185
Colbath, Mary, 122, 135
Coleman, Emily, 210
Coleman, Leo, 166
Colette, 160
Collins, Janet, 126
Colman, John, 171
Colt, Alvin, 118, 134, 151, 163, 164, 168, 299, 300
Combat (Paris newspaper), 342
Combat, Le, 232
Comedia Balletica, 169
Concerto Barocco, 92, 134, 149–150, 151, 206, 207–208, 216, 250, 295, 298, 303, 260, 269
Concurrence, La, 15
Congress for Cultural Freedom, The, 318
Connoly, Joseph, 160
Constantia, 169
Coolidge, Mrs. Elizabeth Sprague, 85
Copland, Aaron, 92, 114, 115, 134, 212, 215, 303, 315, 316
Coppélia, 34, 35
Coq d'Or, Le (ballet), 35, 111
Coq d'Or, Le (opera), 83
Cordélia, 324, 343
Coriolanus (overture), 326, 330
Cosmopolitan Theater, 191
Cotillon, 15, 20, 280
Coton, A. V., 360
Coudy, Douglas, 39, 78, 79, 82, 86, 94, 95, 108, 123, 135
Coup de Feu, 324, 343
Coutsoudis, Iolas, 82
Covent Garden (see Royal Opera House, Covent Garden)

Cowles, Chandler, 167
Cranko, John, 262, 263
Craske, Margaret, 266, 275
Croqueuse de Diamants, La, 268, 301
Cunningham, Merce, 171, 190, 197

Daily Herald (London), 254, 260
Daily Telegraph (London), 253, 358
Dali, Salvador, 16
D'Amboise, Jacques, 158, 249, 333
D'Amboise, Ninette, 249
Dance (book), 59, 141
Dance Archives, 121, 133, 141, 142
"Dance in Bali" (article), 146, 163
Dance Index (publication), 143–148,
    157, 163, 173, 217
"Dance in Shaker Ritual, The"
    (article), 146
Dance International, 95–96
Dance Magazine, 95, 96, 115, 118, 136,
    137
Dance News, 161, 176, 251, 284, 298,
    307, 315, 360
Dance Players, 224, 225
Dance Project (WPA), 83–84
Danieli, Fred, 95, 108, 123, 135, 158,
    161, 164, 182, 183
Danilova, Alexandra, 11, 13, 85, 137,
    150, 151, 210
Danses Concertantes, 152
D'Arcy, Peggy, 122
Dark Elegies, 266, 276
Davidson, Jean, 122
Day Before Spring, The, 266
De Banfield, Raffaello, 232
De Basil, Col. W., 15, 16, 36, 102, 103,
    130, 221, 238
De Beaumont, Comte Étienne, 184
Debussy, Claude, 325, 327
De Coster, Charles, 295
De Cuevas, Marquis Georges, 165,
    189, 191–192
De Kova, Margit, 123, 135
Delarue, Allison, 146
Del Bondio, J. H., 105
Delibes, Léo, 34, 272
De Maré, Rolf, 141
De' Medici, Lorenzo, 188
DeMille, Agnes, 120, 155, 210, 213,
    235, 240, 276, 278, 294
Denby, Edwin, 161, 252
"Denishawn Era, The" (article), 146
Derain, André, 15, 38

De Rivas, Elena, 38
De Salvandy, Comte, 280
Descent of Hebe, 266
Deutsch, Nicolaus Manuel, 304
De Valois, Dame Ninette, 229, 230,
    248, 251, 356
Devil and Daniel Webster, The, 117
Dewey, Thomas, 202
Diaghilev Ballet (see Ballets Russes de
    Serge Diaghilev)
Diaghilev, Serge, 3–7, 8, 13, 14, 15,
    16, 17, 18, 19, 37, 40, 68, 70, 109,
    184, 185, 231, 232, 243, 312, 320,
    338, 346
Diamand, Peter, 355
Dickson, Charles, 135
Dimitriew, Vladimir, 3, 9, 11, 12, 13,
    15, 20, 21, 22, 23, 27, 28, 29, 39, 55,
    63, 85, 99–103, 104, 105, 106, 125
Dim Lustre, 225, 266
Ditson, Alice M., 152
Ditson (Alice M.) Fund of Columbia
    University, The, 165
Divertimento, 164, 189, 209, 216, 250,
    372–373
Djurop, Joan, 158
Dobujinsky, Mstislav, 134
Doering, Jane, 94, 112
Dohnányi, Ernst von, 149
Dokoudovsky, Vladimir, 123
Dolin, Anton, 120, 168, 210, 221, 252,
    274
Dollar, William, 39, 40, 44, 45, 58, 63,
    65, 78, 79, 82, 86, 87, 91, 99, 108,
    117, 122, 123, 125, 134, 135, 149,
    158, 161, 168, 169, 171, 182, 189,
    222, 228–229, 232, 233, 238–239
Don Quixote (Pas de Trois), 206, 274,
    280, 287
Douglas, Lewis W., 250, 251
Downes, Olin, 70–71
Doyle, James, 135
Draper, Paul, 92, 106
Dreams, 30, 38, 44, 47, 367
Drew, Robert, 171, 172, 288
Duane, John, 123
Dubrovska, Felia, 85, 126
Duel, The, 232, 233, 238–239, 250, 277,
    377
Dugard, Roger, 346, 347
Dugardin, Hervé, 319, 341
Duke, Vernon, 105
Dumas *fils*, Alexandre, 282

Dumbarton Oaks Concerto, 294
Duncan, Isadora, 28, 64, 84, 146
Dunham, Katherine, 166
Dunn, James C., 344
Dunphy, John Paul, 123, 135
Dürer, Albrecht, 304
Dushok, Dorothy, 158, 249, 271, 287
Dyer, Carlus, 141, 185
Dying Swan, The, 325

Eames, Marian, 148
Edinburgh Music Festival, 318, 321, 355, 362
Efimoff, Nicholas, 11, 13
Eglevsky, André, 99, 137, 209, 274–275, 277, 279, 280, 282, 287, 295, 302, 304, 308, 310, 311, 325, 328, 356
Egmont (overture), 326, 330
Egorova, Lubov, 274
Elegie, 152, 199, 375
"Elie Nadelman: Sculptor of the Dance" (article), 146
Ellyn, Lois, 224
Encounter, 79, 369
Enfant et les sortilèges, L' (see also *Spellbound Child*), 159, 160
Errante, 16, 19, 38, 40, 43, 44, 47, 50, 70, 134, 366
Ethel Barrymore Theater, 167
"European Dance Teachers in the United States" (article), 146
Evening Standard (London), 360
Evenings of the Young Ballet, 9

Facsimile, 214, 239, 267, 276
Fairbanks, Douglas, 249
Fallaci, Oriana, 351
Fall River Legend, 276, 278
Fancy Free, 155, 214, 225, 239, 255
Far Harbour, 185–186, 228
Fastes, Les, 16
Faust, 65
Fernandez, José, 120, 125, 134
Ffolkes, David, 168
Figaro (newspaper), 340, 345, 347
Filling Station, 94, 96, 97, 113, 114, 116, 117, 134, 138, 371
Fine, Toby, 303
Firebird, 221, 222, 223, 225–227, 236, 237, 238, 250, 256, 257, 261, 268, 270, 303, 347, 348, 357, 358, 376
Five Boons of Life, 149

Flanagan, Hallie, 83
Fledermaus, Die, 65, 148
Fleischmann, Julius, 319, 341, 345
Fletcher, Robert, 326
Fokina, Vera, 221
Fokine, Michel, 8, 9, 18, 35, 39, 62, 111, 120, 213, 221, 226, 256, 257, 275
Folk Dance (a ballet) 79, 94, 370
Fontaine, Edwina, 227, 249, 281, 303, 310
Fonteyn, Margot, 248, 337
Ford Motor Company, 121, 122
Forest, Milton (see also Kidd, Michael) 114
Four Temperaments, The, 160, 162, 189, 209, 214, 250, 303, 314, 360, 361, 372
Françaix, Jean, 298, 302
Francés, Esteban, 164, 168, 190, 192, 295, 304, 305, 306
Francesca, Piero della, 69
Frangini, Cualtiero, 351
Franklin, Frederic, 137, 150, 210
Franks, Sir Oliver, 241
Frederix, Arthur, 39, 99
Free, Karl, 79
French, Jared, 114, 115, 259
Fundamentals of the Classic Dance (book), 141

Gaîté Parisienne, 138
Gala Performance, 212, 225, 276
Galakhoff, Basil, 99
Galli, Rosina, 35
Gambarelli, Maria, 36
Garden of Fand, The, 326
Garfield, Constance (see Baker, Constance)
Garrett, Pat, 114
Garrett, William, 123, 135
Gatti-Casazza, Giulio, 35
Genauer, Emily, 305
Genée, Adeline, 35
"George Washington Smith" (article), 146
Georgov, Walter, 239, 249
Geva, Tamara, 11, 39, 40, 43, 66, 67
Gevergeieva, Tamara (see also Geva, Tamara), 11, 13, 39
Ghost Town, 134
Gifford, Mrs. Walter S., 358
Gifford, Walter S., 357

Gilbert, Ruth, 158, 208
Gilder, Rosamond, 241
Gilmore, Betty, 122, 135
Gioconda, La, 83
Girard, Aaron, 149
Giselle, 228, 267, 276, 278, 279, 280, 281, 314
Giselle, Sylvia (see Caccialanza, Gisella)
Giuri, Maria, 34
Glazunov, Alexander, 151
Gloire, La, 326, 330, 331, 333, 360, 382
Gluck, Christoph Willibald von, 68, 69, 71
Gluck-Sandor, 84
Godard, Benjamin, 38, 44
Goddard, Scott, 260
Godden, Rumer, 325
Godkin, Paul, 99, 158
Gods Go a-Begging, The, 14
Golden Bough, The, 45
Goldwyn Follies, 90
Goldwyn, Samuel, 90, 99, 323
Goleizovsky, Kassian, 8, 9
Golovine, Alexander, 221
Gontcharova, Nathalie, 221
Goth, Trudy, 350
Gottshalk, Louis Moreau, 288
Gould, Morton, 38
Gounod, Charles, 288
Graduation Ball, 225
Graham, June, 135
Graham, Martha, 78, 92, 118, 128, 171
Gran Teatro del Liceo (Barcelona), 321, 339, 340, 341
Grand Ballet de Monte Carlo, 191
Grand Ballet du Marquis de Cuevas, 189, 206, 253, 268, 275, 280, 324, 343
Graphic, The (London), 263
Graziana, 168, 169
Grey, Beryl, 248
Grieg, Edvard, 150
Grisi, Carlotta, 228
Guerard, Audrey, 38
Gustav, King of Sweden, 175
Guests, The, 212, 215, 225, 237, 250, 376

Haakon, Paul, 39, 40, 44, 106
Hageman, Richard, 83
Haieff, Alexei, 164, 189, 190
Halicka, Alice, 86, 270

Handel, George Frideric, 14
Hans Christian Andersen Story, The, (motion picture), 323, 326
Hänsel and Gretel, 63, 82
Harlequin for President, 79, 81, 113, 369–370
Harman, Carter, 171, 172
Harmati, Sandor, 39, 41
Hasburgh, Rabana, 39, 63, 82, 87, 94, 98
Haskell, Arnold L., 254, 263–264
Hastings, Baird, 143, 146, 147, 148
Hawkins, Erick, 51, 78, 82, 86, 94, 95, 96, 108, 265
Hawkins, Frances, 78, 79, 80, 91, 107, 114, 118, 177, 178, 180, 182, 195, 198, 199, 202, 203, 206, 235, 247–249, 250, 268
Hawkinson, Hermione, 98
Hayden, Melissa, 132, 220, 224, 229, 237, 239, 241, 242, 243, 249, 252, 266, 268, 269, 270, 286, 287, 299, 300, 316, 325, 329, 330, 361
Heater, Mary, 94, 108
Heath, Babs, 122, 135
Heckscher Theater, 165
Held, John, Jr., 31, 38, 41
Helen of Troy, 213, 267
Helmy, Cecil, 92
Hiden, Georgia, 135, 149, 158, 161
Highland Fling, 168, 169, 182, 183, 185, 373
Hindemith, Paul, 160, 189, 314
Hirsch, Georges, 346
Histoire d'un Soldat, L', 92
History of American Dance, The (pageant), 84
Hitler, Adolf, 41, 50
Hobi, Frank, 220, 224, 238, 243, 249, 268, 269, 271, 281, 289, 300, 302, 307
Hoctor, Harriet, 36
Hoffman, Gertrude, 35
Holland Festival, 353–355
Holt, Paul, 254, 260
Honegger, Arthur, 149, 342
Horowitz, Vladimir, 38
Horst, Louis, 92
Horwitz, Michael Rainer, 135
Hound and Horn (magazine), 16, 17, 24
Housman, A. E., 93
Howard, Andrée, 120
Howard, Holly, 39, 63, 82, 86, 91, 98

Humphrey, Doris, 84
Hunter College Playhouse, 162, 186
Hurok, S., 36, 103, 218, 221, 222–223, 224, 230, 234–235, 251, 292, 335–336

Illuminations, 231, 236, 237, 241–242, 244, 250, 255, 256, 257, 261, 272, 291, 293, 298, 301, 303, 333, 377–378
Impellitteri, Vincent R., 334
Imperial Society of Teachers of Dancing, 263
Incident, 212
Institute of Contemporary Arts (London), 258
International Faculty of Arts (London), 263
International Theater, 191–192
International Theater Month, 236, 241, 243
Interplay, 214, 215, 239, 316, 317
Isaacs, Jeanne, 123
Isadora Duncan (book), 157
"Isadora Duncan and Basic Dance" (article), 143, 146
Island of God, The, 165
Ivanov, Lev, 226, 309, 312

Jack in the Box, 14
Jackson, Brooks, 158, 249, 307
Jackson, Phyllis, 253, 358
James, Edward, 15
Jantzen Knitting Mills, Inc., 232
Jardin aux Lilas (see also Lilac Garden), 212, 266, 282
Jasinsky, Roman, 19
Jeanmaire, Renée, 268
Jerusalem Delivered, 232, 238
Jeu de Cartes (see Card Party)
Jeune Homme et la Mort, Le, 300
Jillana, 249, 278, 281, 287, 310, 316
Jinx, 222, 225, 239, 250, 253, 376
Johnson, Edward, 52, 60, 63, 68, 104, 105
Jones Beach, 232, 233, 243–244, 250, 255, 260, 378
Jones, Jeanne, 149
"Juba and American Minstrelsy" (article), 146
Joueur de Flûte, Le, 349
Judgment of Paris, 212, 225, 266, 267
Judson, Arthur, 38, 86

Juke Box, 134, 138, 368
"Jules Perrot" (article), 146
Junyer, Joan, 167, 170

Kahrklin (also called Karklin), Hortense, 39, 82, 86, 91, 98, 135
Kai, Una, 249
Kalin, Lillian, 98
Karinska, Barbara, 223, 227, 252, 272, 274, 280, 281, 287, 311, 315
Karlin, Rita, 161
Karlson, Peggy, 249
Karnakoski, Kari, 123
Karsavina, Tamara, 221
Kavan, Albia, 39, 78, 82, 94, 108
Kay, Hershy, 288
Kaye, Danny, 323
Kaye, Nora, 274–279, 280, 282, 286, 289, 290, 291, 294, 299, 304, 315, 325, 327, 328, 331, 353, 354, 358, 360
Kchessinska, Mathilde, 274
Keller, Evelyn, 166
Kellerman, Annette, 325
Ketcham, Ben, 202, 335
Kidd, Michael, 114, 235
Ki He Kah Stah Tsa (see also Maria Tallchief), 180
Kirstein, Lincoln, ubique
Kirstein, Mrs. Lincoln, 135, 250, 262
Kitzinger, Fritz, 117
Kochno, Boris, 15
Koechlin, Charles, 15, 38
Koerner, Henry, 258
Knapman, Willen Cnoop, 243
Kopeikine, Nicholas, 30, 161, 250, 287
Kosloff, Alexis, 123
Kramer, Helen, 135, 249, 270, 287
Kreutzberg, Harald, 78, 92
Krimsky, John, 105
Kriza, John, 135, 209
Kursch, Judith, 183

Lac des Cygnes (see also Swan Lake), 128
Lady of the Camellias, 274, 281–282, 379
La Guardia, Fiorello H., 178–180, 202
Laing, Hugh, 120, 266–267, 268, 269, 272–273, 276, 282, 286, 287, 294, 300, 315, 330, 331
Lakmé, 64, 82
Lamballe, Lucille, 28
Lane, Joseph, 82, 91, 99
Lanese, Lillian, 149

Lang, Ariel (see also Leitch, Helen),
    86, 91,
Lang, Harold, 249, 268, 269, 270, 271
"Language of the Classic Ballet, The"
    (lecture), 182
Larsson, Irene, 287
Laskey, Charles, 39, 43, 63, 78, 82, 86,
    91, 99, 183, 188
*Latin-American Collection at the Museum
    of Modern Art* (book), 147
Lazarewitch, Anne, 98
Lazowski, Yurek, 126, 271
Leavitt, Gerald, 158
LeClercq, Tanaquil, 126, 158, 164,
    170, 173, 180, 181, 184, 185, 188,
    193, 198, 199, 201, 207, 224, 227,
    229, 241, 242, 243, 249, 268, 270,
    281, 289, 295, 298, 299, 308,
    314, 315, 316, 325, 327, 328, 329,
    331, 332, 361
Lederman, Minna, 146
Ledoux, Claude-Nicholas, 184
Lee, Mary Ann, 146
Lee, Tom, 134
Legat, Nicholas, 274
Léhar, Franz, 149
Lehmann, Maurice, 342, 343
Leitch, Helen, 39, 86, 91
Lengyel, Melchior, 299
Lenin, Nicolai, 8, 10
Leonidoff, Leonid, 252, 274, 318, 319,
    321, 326, 335, 349, 352, 355–356
Leonore No. 3. (overture), 326, 330
Leporsky, Zoya, 149
Lesand, John, 184
Lester, Edwin, 150
Levine, Doris R., 135
Levinoff, Joseph, 39, 82, 86, 91, 99
Leweck, Madeline, 82, 91, 98
Lichine, David, 180, 232
Lidji, Jacques, 102–103, 106
Lifar, Serge, 28, 85, 174, 175, 308, 339,
    341, 342, 343, 344
Life (magazine), 337
Life for the Tsar, A, 63, 268, 271, 278
Lilac Garden (see also *Jardin aux Lilas*),
    276, 294, 303, 315, 339, 351, 352,
    359, 381
Limelight, 325
Liszt, Franz, 31, 38, 44
Littlefield, Catherine, 254
Littlefield, Dorothie, 28
London Ballet, 266

London Ballet Circle, 258, 263
London, Lorna, 95, 108, 135
Longchamp, Gaston, 38, 326
Look, Ma, I'm Dancin', 214, 224
Loring, Eugene, 39, 78, 79, 81, 82, 86,
    93, 94, 95, 108, 114, 115, 116, 118,
    120, 134, 155, 225
Losch, Tilly, 15
Louisiana Story, 295
Luján, James Graham-, 135
Lunacharsky, Anatole, 8
Lurçat, Jean, 38, 41
Lutyens, Edith, 167
Lyon, Annabelle, 39, 63, 78, 82, 86,
    87, 91, 98, 106

MacArthur, General Douglas, 285
McBride, Pat, 158, 199, 226, 237, 241
McBride, Robert, 94
McPhee, Colin, 146, 163
McVoy, Robert, 123
Mabley, Edward, 122
Mabry, Iris, 162–163, 171
Mademoiselle Angot, 225
Mad Tristan, The, 201
Magallanes, Nicholas, 123, 135, 151,
    187–188, 189, 193, 198, 201, 207,
    215, 217, 224, 227, 242, 243, 249,
    268, 269, 270, 272, 281, 290, 303,
    316, 325, 329
Maggio Musicale Fiorentino (festival,
    Florence), 321, 349–350
Magriel, Paul David, 121, 141–142,
    143, 147, 148, 156, 157
Mahler, Fritz, 137
Mahoney, Arthur, 84
Maiocchi, Gilda, 334
Malmö Opera Ballet, 250
Manchester Guardian, 256, 358
Manchester, Miss P. W., 262, 298,
    307, 315, 317
Mann, Frances, 39
Marie Jeanne (see also Pelus, Marie
    Jeanne), 106, 108, 123, 135, 187,
    188, 207, 208, 215, 220, 237
"Marius Petipa" (article), 146
Markova, Alicia, 137, 168, 210, 221,
    274
Martin, John, 24, 25, 29, 42–50, 52,
    55–57, 77, 110–111, 143, 146, 147,
    193, 207, 209, 227, 237, 252, 269,
    311–313, 332
Martin, Keith, 79, 94

Martinez, José (Jay), 123, 135, 158, 161, 163
"Mary Ann Lee, First American Giselle" (article), 146
Masaccio, 69
Massine, Leonide, 8, 16, 35, 45, 102, 137, 150, 240, 267
Masterpieces of the Twentieth Century Exposition, 318, 319, 321, 324, 337, 341, 342, 343, 345, 349, 352
Matlin, Marjorie, 82, 91
Maule, Michael, 281, 290
Maywood, Augusta, 146
Mazurka from "A Life for the Tsar," 63, 268, 271, 278
Mecca Temple, 178–179
Medium, The 165–167, 185
Memories, 201
Mendelssohn, Felix, 286, 287
Menotti, Gian-Carlo, 165–166
Mercury Theater, 166
Merlin, Olivier, 345–346
Merovitch, Alexander, 37, 38, 51, 52, 58
Merry Widow, The, 149
Merveilleuses et Incroyables, 79
Metropolitan Opera Association, 202
Metropolitan Opera Ballet, 135, 275, 288
Metropolitan Opera Company, 52, 60, 63, 68, 165, 205
Metropolitan Opera House, 180, 198, 210, 224, 226, 236
Midiel, Artur, 146
Mikeshina, Ariadna, 30, 79
Milberg, Barbara, 249, 303
Milhaud, Darius, 15, 30, 92
Million Dollar Mermaid, 325, 331
Milloss, Aurel, 324, 343
Milstein, Nathan, 38
Minkus, Leon, 274, 280
Minotaur, The, 167, 169, 170, 172, 373
Minute Operas, 92
Miraculous Mandarin, The, 286, 287, 293, 298, 299–301, 303, 304, 380
Mironowa, Eudokia, 135, 250
Miss Liberty, 221
Miss O'Grady, 92
Mohini, Ratna, 162–163
Monahan, James, 256, 259, 358
Moncion, Francisco, 149, 158, 161, 164, 188, 192, 193, 198, 201, 207, 208, 215, 224, 225, 226, 229, 237,

Moncion (*continued*)
    241, 249, 261, 268, 270, 273, 281, 330, 331, 333
Monde, Le (newspaper), 345–346
Monteverdi, Claudio, 73
Montez, Monna, 82
Moon, Jane, 99
Moore, Douglas, 117
Moore, Hannah, 39, 78, 82, 91, 99
Moore, Lillian, 82, 91, 99, 146
Moore, Marjorie, 108, 135
Morcom, James Stewart, 134, 184, 212
Mordkin Ballet, 119
Mordkin, Mikhail, 35, 119, 120
Morris, Newbold, 178–179, 334
Moses, Robert, 243
Mother Goose Suite, 149–150, 207, 208, 216, 224, 250, 286, 375–376
Mounsey, Yvonne, 227, 229, 241, 243, 249, 261, 269, 281, 289, 290, 310, 361
Moylan, Mary Ellen, 151, 158, 161, 164, 189
Mozart, Wolfgang Amadeus, 152, 168, 182, 244, 325, 328
Mozartiana, 16, 30, 31, 32, 33, 38, 151, 325, 366
Mullowny, Kathryn, 39, 63, 82, 86, 91, 98, 108
Munson, Marie, 95
Museum of Modern Art, 121, 133, 141, 142, 147, 161, 163, 173, 177, 185
Music for the Theatre, 212
Mute Wife, The, 201

Nabokov, Nicolas, 319, 341, 344
Nadelman, Elie, 146
National Broadcasting Company, 165
National Music League, 160
National Orchestral Association, 151–152, 159
National Theatre Conference, 182
Neher, Caspar, 15
Nettl, Paul, 146
New Amsterdam Theater, 165
New Opera Company, 148, 149, 201
New York City Ballet, *ubique*
New York City Center of Music and Drama, 178–180, 183, 188, 199, 201–205, 207, 210, 211, 216, 217, 222, 223, 224, 226, 229, 230, 231,

New York City Center of Music and Drama (*continued*)
235, 236, 244, 268, 284, 286, 287, 292, 297, 298, 305, 308, 312, 322, 323, 324, 334, 335, 353, 358
New York City Drama, 204
New York City Opera, 165, 204, 205, 211
New York Herald Tribune, 136, 251, 305, 316
New York Sun, The, 41
New York Times, The, 42–44, 52, 57, 70, 110, 147, 193, 209, 227, 237, 269, 311–313, 332, 353
New York World's Fair, 121, 122, 123, 124, 125, 133, 135, 187
News Chronicle (London), 260
Newsweek, 210, 251
Nichols, Betty, 158
Nightingale, The, 14
Night Shadow, 151, 206
Nijinska, Bronislava, 13, 14, 45, 85, 120, 164, 180
Nijinska, Romola, 17, 19
Nijinsky, Vaslav, 28, 53
Nikitina, Alice, 85
Nillo, David, 135
Noguchi, Isamu, 74, 171, 197, 198, 200, 201, 244
Noonan, Peggy, 123, 135
"Notes on Choreography" (article), 146
Noverre, Jean-Georges, 146
Nutcracker, The, 196, 295

Oboukhoff, Anatole, 148
O'Brien, Shaun, 239, 241, 249
Observer, The (London), 257
Officer, Harvey, 164
Oklahoma!, 267
Old Maid and the Thief, The, 165
Olmstead, Rem, 123
Ondine, 222, 228–229, 377
On Stage!, 225
On the Town, 214
On Your Toes, 66, 67, 90
Opéra, 167, 174, 175, 176, 210, 320, 339, 341, 342, 343, 344, 345, 346, 347, 349
Opéra (publication), 175
Original Ballet Russe, 168, 187, 201, 221, 232, 274, 275

Orpheus (Stravinsky), 74, 177, 196–202, 208, 216, 224, 236, 237, 250, 256, 258, 260, 261, 294, 349, 375
Orpheus and Eurydice, 68–74, 75–76, 85, 88, 90, 160, 205, 367
Ouroussow, Eugenie, 28, 125

Paganini, Nicolò, 45
Palais de Cristal, Le (see also *Symphony in C*), 175, 176, 192
Palmer, Mrs. Winthrop, 225
Parade, 92
Paris-Soir (newspaper), 349
Pas de Deux Romantique, 242–243, 250, 378
Pas de Quatre, 225
Pas de Trois (see also *Don Quixote*), 206, 280, 298, 299, 304, 308, 352, 379
Pastorale, La, 14
Pastorela, 134, 138, 163–164, 368
Pastores, Los, 163
Patterson, Yvonne, 39, 82, 91, 99, 135, 149
Pattison, Lee, 117
Pavlova, Anna, 35, 51, 53, 253, 325
Pelus, Marie Jeanne (see also Marie Jeanne), 94, 95, 187
Perlin, Bernard, 258
Perlman, Felicia, 82
Perrot, Jules, 228
Perugini, Giulio, 334
Petipa, Marius, 9, 64, 146, 196, 225, 272, 309
Petit, Roland, 232, 301, 324
Petolas, Micheline, 82, 91, 99
Petrouchka, 35
Piatigorsky, Gregor, 38
Philadelphia Ballet, 135, 168, 254
Philippart, Natalie, 300
Photographs of Henri Cartier-Bresson, The (book), 163
Picnic at Tintagel (see also *Tintagel*), 326, 332, 333, 382
Pied Piper, The, 303, 315–316, 349, 350, 351, 352, 360, 381
Pillar of Fire, 225, 235, 266, 267, 276
Pleasant, Richard, 119
Pleydell-Bouverie, Mrs. David, 236, 244
Pocahontas, 79, 117, 370
Poème, 315
Porcher, Nananne, 250
Potofsky, Jacob S., 334–335

Potteiger, Jack, 39, 91
Poudrier, Marilyn, 287
Powers, Marie, 166
Preobrajenska, Olga, 14
Présages, Les, 43
Prince Igor, 62
Princess Aurora, 225, 276, 278, 279
Prodigal Son, The, 14, 231, 233, 237–
238, 250, 260, 261, 273, 377
Producing Company of the School of
American Ballet, 31, 32, 37
Prokofiev, Sergei, 14, 231, 237
Promenade, 79, 370
Pugni, César, 228–229
Punch and the Child, 182, 183, 185, 209,
374

Quarequio, Maria, 123, 135
Quelques Fleurs, 288
Quinn, Jack, 39, 91

Radio City Music Hall, 217, 275
Rain, Charles, 93, 94
Rambert, Marie, 266
Ramey, Carlyle, 149
Rapin, Maurice, 340
Ravel, Maurice, 79, 149, 159, 207,
208, 273, 280, 281, 342, 357
Raymonda, 151
Reed, Janet, 132, 220, 224–225, 228,
237, 242, 249, 266, 268, 269, 270,
271, 273, 278, 289, 302, 316, 328,
333
Reeves, Jean, 158
Reiman, Elise, 39, 63, 82, 86, 91, 98,
126, 158, 161, 164, 183, 193
Reminiscence, 38, 40, 44, 47, 51, 63, 366
Remisoff, Nicholas, 221
Reinink, J. H., 354
Renard (The Fox), 163–164, 186, 199,
372
Revil, Rudi, 168
Rice, Newcomb, 123, 135
Rieti, Vittorio, 141, 151, 168, 188
Rilley, Lillian, 99
Rimbaud, Arthur, 231, 242, 257
Rittmann, Trude, 118, 135
Robbins, Jerome, 155, 212–214, 215,
221, 224, 225, 227, 232, 233, 237–
238, 239–241, 244, 249, 253, 255,
256, 266, 273, 276, 281, 286, 289,
290, 291, 294, 303, 306, 315, 316,
325, 327, 328, 329, 346, 351, 353,
354, 360

Rockefeller, John D., 191
Rockefeller, Nelson A., 133, 136, 139,
236
Rodeo, 155
Rogers, John William, 116
Rogge, Florence, 36
"Romantic Ballet in London, The"
(article), 146
Romeo and Juliet, 91, 213, 235, 267, 276
Rondeville, Emmanuel, 342
Roosevelt, Franklin Delano, 133
Rosalinda, 148, 182
Rose Adagio, 310
Rose, Billy, 191
Rosenheimer, Arthur, Jr., 173
Rosenthal, Jean, 156, 160, 164, 166,
226, 244, 250, 269, 270, 290, 311,
326, 327
Rouault, Georges, 232, 238, 261
Roxy Theater, 325
Royal Academy of Dancing, 263
Royal Opera House, Covent Garden,
230, 233, 234, 235, 246, 248–249,
250, 251, 257, 258, 260, 261, 262,
263, 265, 269, 318, 321, 355, 356,
357, 358, 359, 361
Rubinstein, Ida, 85
Rutten, Dr. F. J. Th., 355
Ruddock, M., 253
Ruiz, Maclovia, 82, 91

Sadler's Wells Ballet, 218, 224, 229,
230, 231, 234, 246, 250, 251, 252,
253, 254, 256, 259, 263, 268, 296,
311, 337, 346, 356
Sadler's Wells Theatre Ballet, 263, 356
Sadoff, Simon, 135, 149
Sailor Bar 1943, 149
St. Matthew Passion, 148–149
Sai, Shoki, 118
Samson and Delilah, 64, 83
Sanders, Job, 158
Sandré, Irma, 158
San Francisco Ballet, 224
Saratoga, 134
Sargent, Kaye, 249, 310
Satie, Eric, 14, 92
Sauguet, Henri, 14, 15, 324, 343
Savoia, Patricia, 287
Saylor, Oliver M., 38, 39
Scarlatti, Domenico, 79
Scheherazade, 35, 67, 138, 295, 296
Schenkman, Edgar, 97

Schindehette, John, 123
Schokkink, Frans, 354
School of American Ballet, *ubique*
Schorr, Daniel, 353
Schubert, Franz, 168, 274
Schwarz, Pearl, 123
Scowen, Dr. Eric, 252
Seasons, The, 171, 172, 190, 192, 197, 216, 373
Sebastian, 165, 201
Second Hurricane, The, 92
Seligmann, Kurt, 161, 162, 189, 314
Sept Péchés Capitaux, Les, 16
Serenade, 30, 31, 33, 38, 40, 43, 44, 47, 51, 134, 175, 209, 216, 250, 252, 253, 260, 268, 269, 287, 298, 333, 339, 340, 350, 352, 357, 358, 365
Shahn, Ben, 258
Sharaff, Irene, 86, 87, 232, 241, 277
Shawn, Ted, 49, 77
Shea, Mary Jane, 123, 135, 149
Shearer, Moira, 323, 324, 326
Shollar, Ludmila, 125, 275
Show Piece, 94, 96, 97, 370–371
Signorelli, Olga R., 351
Sitwell, Sir Osbert, 258
Six Epigraphes Antiques, 325, 327
Slaughter on Tenth Avenue, 67
Slavenska, Mia, 137, 210
Sleeping Beauty, The, 96, 190, 196, 310
Slonimsky, Yury, 146
Smith, George Washington, 146
Smith, Oliver, 151, 232, 241, 244
Sobotka, Ruth, 158, 249, 289, 290–291, 303, 310
Soby, James, 24
Solov, Zachary, 135
Somes, Michael, 248
Songes, 16, 30
Song of Norway, 150–151, 182
Soudeikine, Sergei, 38, 41
Soul Kiss, The, 35
Soviet State Dancers, 11, 13
Spectateur (publication), 176
Spectre de la Rose, Le, 128
Spellbound Child, The, 159–160, 186, 372
Stadtheater (Zurich), 352
"Stage and Ballet Designs of Eugene Berman, The" (article), 146
Stalin, Joseph, 10
Stane, Walter, 158
Stepkowska, Eugenia, 99

Stevenson, Robert, 232
Stoes, Paul H., 114
Stokowski, Leopold, 149
Strauss, Johann, 65
Strauss, Richard, 15, 151, 295, 304, 305, 342
Stravinsky, Igor, 14, 38, 74, 84–89, 90, 92, 100, 104, 108, 150, 152, 163, 164, 177, 196–197, 198, 199, 200, 201, 221, 226, 236, 237, 244, 256, 257, 268, 270, 274, 277, 286, 294, 295, 347, 349
"Strawinsky in the Theatre" (article), 146
Stuart, Barbara, 123
Stuart, Helen, 95
Stuart, Muriel, 51, 125, 141
Suarez, Olga, 135
Sumner, Charlotte, 123
Sun, The (New York), 41
Sunday Times (London), 255
"Sur un Panegyrique de M. Balanchine et Mme Toumanova" (article), 176
Swan Lake, 96, 112, 138, 276, 278, 279, 295, 297, 303, 304, 308–314, 331, 339, 344, 352, 360, 362, 381
Swift, Kay, 31, 38
Sylphides, Les, 35, 128, 280, 314
Sylvia (pas de deux), 268, 272, 277, 279, 280, 308, 350, 378–379
Symphonic Variations, 256
Symphonie Concertante, 152, 182, 184, 193, 199, 201, 202, 209, 216, 228, 250, 260, 374
Symphonie Fantastique, 45
Symphony in C (see also *Palais de Cristal*), 175, 192–193, 194, 201, 202, 208, 209, 214, 224, 228, 237, 250, 252, 260–261, 278, 279, 287, 304, 340, 360, 375

Talbot, Harriet, 249
Talbot, J. Alden, 235
Tallchief, Maria, 151, 175, 176, 177, 180–181, 184, 189, 192, 193, 198, 201, 206, 207, 215, 217, 220, 224, 226, 227, 237, 238, 243, 249, 252, 256, 257, 261, 267, 268, 270, 271, 272, 278, 279, 280, 287, 295, 299, 302, 303, 304, 308, 310, 314, 325, 329, 331, 348, 358, 361
Tally-Ho, 225, 235
Tamiris, Helen, 83–84

Tannhäuser, 64
Tanning, Dorothea, 151, 171, 325, 329
Taras, John, 135, 158, 164, 168–169,
221, 235, 274, 324, 343
Tasso, Torquato, 232, 238
Tchaikovsky, Peter, 30, 38, 43, 134,
177, 196, 244, 279, 312
Tchelitchew, Pavel, 15, 38, 39, 41, 43,
69–70, 72, 75–76, 108, 161
Tchernitcheva, Lubov, 85
Teague, Walter Dorwin, 122
Teatro alla Scala (Milan), 334, 343,
351
Teatro Comunale (Florence), 321,
350, 351
Telephone, The, 165–167, 186
Temoff, Serge, 82, 86, 91, 99, 123
Tempo (Italian magazine), 351
Tennyson, Alfred, Lord, 93
Terminal, 254
Terry, Emilio, 15
Terry, Walter, 136, 316–317
Tertulia de Swing, see *Juke Box*
Thayr, Forrest, Jr., 79, 118
Theatre Arts (magazine), 127
Théâtre des Champs-Elysées, 319,
321, 343, 345, 347, 348, 349, 352
Théâtre Municipal (Lausanne), 321,
352
Theme and Variations, 177, 228
This Is the Army, 183
Thomas, Theodore, 43
Thomson, Virgil, 19, 94, 295, 325,
329
Three Love Stories (motion picture), 326
Three Virgins and a Devil, 213, 225
Till Eulenspiegel (see also *Tyl Eulen-
spiegel* and *Tyl Ulenspiegel*), 304
Time (magazine), 271
Time Table, 134, 212, 214, 369
Times, The (London), 253, 256, 257,
358
Tintagel (see also *Picnic at Tintagel*),
294, 303
Tobias, Roy, 249, 302, 316, 328
Tompkins, Beatrice, 114, 135, 158,
161, 164, 183, 193, 207, 208, 224,
241, 243, 249, 268, 270, 289, 300,
307
Tooker, George, 258
Toumanova, Tamara, 14, 15, 112,
174, 176
Train Bleu, Le, 343

Transcendence, 31, 32, 38, 44, 45, 47, 50,
336–367
Tribune, The (London), 257–258
Triumph of Bacchus and Ariadne, 188–
189, 209, 374
Triumph of Neptune, The, 14
Trumpet Concerto, 263
Tual, Mme Denise, 341
Tucker, Dorothy, 95
Tudor, Antony, 120, 134, 212–213,
214, 235, 266, 274, 275, 276, 278,
281, 282, 294, 303, 315, 326, 330,
331, 360
Tyl Eulenspiegel (see also *Tyl Ulen-
spiegel*), 295, 303
Tyl Ulenspiegel (see also *Tyl Eulen-
spiegel*), 303, 304–307, 380
Twain, Mark, 149

Undertow, 225, 266, 267
Union Pacific, 134
United Nations, 243
United Nations Educational, Scientific
and Cultural Organizations
(UNESCO), 236, 241
United States Office for Coordination
of Commercial and Cultural Re-
lations between the American Re-
publics, 133, 147

Vaganova, Agrippina, 141
Vaillat, Léandre, 176
Vallon, Jean, 114
Valse, La, 273, 280, 281, 283, 287, 298,
299, 339, 344, 352, 357, 358, 361,
379
Valses, Les, 16
Valses Nobles et Sentimentales, 79, 273–
274, 280, 281, 357
Vanderbilt, Mrs. W. K., 236
Vane, Daphne, 39, 82, 86, 91
Varicchio, Adelaide, 99, 135, 149, 158
Vasilieff, Nicholas, 123
Vaslav Nijinsky (book), 157
Vauges, Gloria, 249, 310
Verdi, Giuseppe, 274, 282
Vernet, Horace, 79
Villan, Demetrius, 67
Vilzak, Anatole, 51, 63, 82, 125, 275
Vitak, Albertina, 36
Vivaldi, Antonio, 222, 228–229
Vladimiroff, Pierre, 28, 125, 126
Volinine, Alexander, 274

Volkenau, Vera, 82, 99
Vollmar, Jocelyn, 207
Volodine, George, 82, 91, 99
Vosseler, Heidi, 39, 82, 91, 98
Vuillermoz, Emile, 349

Wagner, Hilda, 82, 91, 99, 123, 135
Wagner, Richard, 64
Wakehurst, Lord, 356, 359
Walczak, Barbara, 158, 249, 271
Walker, Margaret, 249–250
Waltz Academy, 151, 225
Warburg, Edward M. M., 3, 18, 21,
    23, 24, 25, 26, 29, 32, 33, 37, 39, 40,
    55, 56, 57, 59, 63, 68, 75–76, 85, 86,
    89, 91, 99–101, 106, 231
Warburg, Felix, 30, 99
Warburg, Gerald F., 231
Ward, Jane, 149
Warnod, Andre, 345
Watkins, Franklin, 38, 44
Weber, Carl Maria von, 232
Webster, David L., 230, 234, 235,
    247–249, 253, 261, 263, 265, 292,
    318, 356
Weidman, Charles, 84
Weill, Kurt, 15
Well-Beloved (Bien-Aimée), 45
Welles, Orson, 166
Where's Charley?, 323
White, Audrey, 95
White, John, 79
White, Patricia (see Wilde, Patricia)
Wiener, Anne, 123
Wilcox, Virginia, 123

Wilde, Patricia, 149, 250, 269, 270,
    278, 281, 289, 310, 329, 333, 361
Wilder, Alex, 134
Williams, Jacqueline, 250
Williams, Ray, 123
Williamson, Audrey, 257–258
Wiman, Anna Deere, 123
Wiman, Dwight Deere, 60, 67, 88, 105
Windham, Donald, 147, 148
Winter, Marian Hannah, 146
Witch, The, 262, 263, 378
Woicikowski, Leon, 275
Wolff, Robert, 123
Wood, Michael, 359
Workman, Jenny, 158
Wortham, Mrs. Helen, 250
Wortham, Tomi, 250, 303
Wyeth, Andrew, 258
Wynn, Billie, 123, 135

Yankee Clipper, 93, 94, 96, 97, 113, 114,
    115, 370
Yeats, W. B., 93
Young Men's Hebrew Association, 81,
    149
Youskevitch, Igor, 137, 217, 274

Ziegfeld Theater, 170
Ziegler, Edward, 64
Zimbalist, Efrem, Jr., 167
Zodiac, 168, 169, 192, 373
Zompakos, Stanley, 149
Zorina, Vera, 90, 91, 106, 175
Zoritch, George, 137
Zürcher Zeitung (newspaper), 352

A Note on the Type in Which This Book is Set

This book is set in Monotype BASKERVILLE, a facsimile cutting from type cast from the original matrices of a face designed by John Baskerville. The original face was the forerunner of the "modern" group of type faces.

John Baskerville (1706–75), of Birmingham, England, a writing-master, with a special renown for cutting inscriptions in stone, began experimenting about 1750 with punch-cutting and making typographical material. It was not until 1757 that he published his first work, a Virgil in royal quarto, with great-primer letters. This was followed by his famous editions of Milton, the Bible, the Book of Common Prayer, and several Latin classic authors. His types, at first criticized as unnecessarily slender, delicate, and feminine, in time were recognized as both distinct and elegant, and his types as well as his printing were greatly admired. Four years after his death Baskerville's widow sold all his punches and matrices to the Société Littéraire-typographique, which used some of the types for the sumptuous Kehl edition of Voltaire's works in seventy volumes.

Composed, printed, and bound by KINGSPORT PRESS, INC., Kingsport, Tennessee. Designed by HARRY FORD.